W9-BXV-764

# THE MACMILLAN ILLUSTRATED ENCYCLOPEDIA OF

# BIRDS
## A VISUAL WHO'S WHO IN THE WORLD OF BIRDS

# THE MACMILLAN ILLUSTRATED ENCYCLOPEDIA OF
# B I R D S
## A VISUAL WHO'S WHO IN THE WORLD OF BIRDS

EDITED BY DR. PHILIP WHITFIELD
AMERICAN CONSULTANT: PROFESSOR EDWARD S. AYENSU

Collier Books
Macmillan Publishing Company
New York

F3764–Birds Ency—Prelims——

Consultant Editor: **Dr. Philip Whitfield,**
Zoology Department, King's College, University of London

American Consultant: **Professor Edward S. Ayensu,**
Office of Biological Conservation, Smithsonian Institution, Washington D.C.

Consultant: **I. C. J. Galbraith,**
Ornithology Department, British Museum (Natural History), Tring, Hertfordshire

Artists:

**Michael Woods**

**Malcolm Ellis** (pp. 117, 139, 141, 171, 175, 177, 193, 213, 215)

**Keith Brewer** (pp. 87, 89, 173)

Conceived, edited and designed by
Marshall Editions Ltd, 170 Piccadilly, London W1V 9DD

· Editor: **Jinny Johnson**
Text Editor: **Gwen Rigby**
Art Director: **John Bigg**          Production: **Barry Baker**
Researcher: **Pip Morgan**                    **Janice Storr**

Copyright © 1984, 1988 by Macmillan Publishing Company,
a division of Macmillan, Inc.
All rights reserved. No part of this book may be reproduced or
transmitted in any form or by any means, electronic or mechanical,
including photocopying, recording, or by any information storage
and retrieval system, without permission in writing from the Publisher.

Collier Books
Macmillan Publishing Company
866 Third Avenue, New York, NY 10022
Collier Macmillan Canada, Inc.

Library of Congress Cataloging-in-Publication Data
Macmillan illustrated encyclopedia of birds.
   Includes index.
   1. Birds. I. Whitfield, Philip. II. Ayensu,
Edward S.
QL673.M34     1988     598     88-16141
ISBN 0–02–044462–1

Macmillan Books are available at special discounts for bulk purchases
for sales promotions, premiums, fund-raising, or educational use.
For details contact:
                Special Sales Director
             Macmillan Publishing Company
                  866 Third Avenue
                  New York, NY 10022

First Collier Books Edition 1988

10  9  8  7  6  5  4  3  2  1

Printed in Singapore

# Contents

# Introduction

The *Macmillan Illustrated Encyclopedia of Birds* sets out to provide a comprehensive catalog of the staggering range of birds. It is clearly impossible to be comprehensive at the species level, so we have looked at a higher level in the classification hierarchy and organized the book at family level, at which it is possible to be comprehensive.

The classification of birds into groups often seems a mystifying or intimidating exercise, as does the scientific naming of birds that goes with it. But both are merely an attempt to organize the creatures into recognizable groups which show their relationships. The Latin- or Greek-based names are enormously useful because of their stability: the scientific name of a creature remains the same all over the world, but it may have dozens of common names. A bird species is a group of birds that can, at least potentially, successfully breed with one another. This is a natural grouping based on the intrinsic attributes and activities of the birds themselves. Each species is given a unique, two-part name in which the second component is specific to that species. The kestrel, for example, is called *Falco tinnunculus*. *Falco* is its generic name — the genus *Falco* contains 5 different species of falcon — while *tinnunculus* is its specific name, which refers only to the kestrel. The generic and specific names are always printed in italics.

The species names are only the first two levels of a taxonomical hierarchy. Many more levels are required in order to encompass the patterns of similarity which exist. In ascending order, the most commonly used levels are species, genus, family, order, class, and phylum.

To return to the kestrel, this bird and all other falcons belong to the falcon family, Falconidae, and all have certain physical and behavioral characteristics in common. This family is grouped with other families of related birds, such as eagles, vultures and hawks, in the order Falconiformes, birds of prey, and this and all other orders of birds belong to the class Aves. It is at the vital, family level that this book is comprehensive. A discussion of the major characteristics of each family is accompanied by a number of representative examples of the family; thus, if a given species is not shown, a close relative of it will be. Each order is also mentioned. Some of the larger families, such as Songbirds, Muscicapidae, are split up into many subfamilies, since this facilitates the description of the various groups and avoids the gross generalization that would otherwise result in these cases.

In something so complex as taxonomy, there is bound to be argument. Where there is a particular controversy over the placing of a particular species, the problem is mentioned in the text.

The kestrel is a species of falcon, and everyone knows — or thinks they know — what a kestrel looks like. However, species do not consist of identical individuals. Enormous genetic diversity exists within a species, as a cursory examination of our own species, *Homo sapiens*, reveals. In many bird species it is possible to identify groupings, known as subspecies or races. These often represent geographically distinct forms of a species that show characteristic differences from one another. This accounts, for example, for the sometimes quite striking differences in plumage between individuals of the same species. The peregrine falcon has 17 subspecies. Subspecies of a species can still interbreed. All subspecies, however, are human-defined and they are essentially arbitrary, unlike the species themselves, which correspond more or less precisely to actual interbreeding groups of animals.

This book is a catalog and, as with any catalog, part of its organization emphasizes similarities. Similar birds are grouped into their family assemblages and this format enables the shared habits and structures of related birds to be easily grasped. Ultimately, though, there is another way of responding to the patterns of bird organization delineated here. Instead of emphasizing the shared characteristics, one can marvel at the almost infinite range of life-styles and physical structure of birds that is a joy in itself. There is space and opportunity enough in this book to savor the amazing diversity of birds and to find fascination in the contrasts, even between members of the same family.

*Philip Whitfield*

## Conservation Status

Many of the world's bird species are in danger of extinction or are becoming rare, often as a direct result of human activity. All birds, particularly threatened species, are monitored by the International Union for Conservation of Nature and Natural Resources (IUCN) and listed in the Red Data books that are produced by this organization.

The status of threatened species is indicated in this book by symbols, the meaning of which is given below. This information is printed with the kind assistance of the IUCN Conservation Monitoring Centre, Cambridge, England.

### ENDANGERED  Ⓔ

Species in grave danger of extinction which can survive only if effective conservation measures are adopted and the causes of their difficulties cease.

### VULNERABLE  Ⓥ

Species which may become endangered if their numbers continue to diminish at the present rate.

### RARE  Ⓡ

Species which are at risk because their population is already small; e.g., those with restricted distribution.

### INDETERMINATE  Ⓘ

Species which are suspected of being endangered, vulnerable or rare, but about which there is insufficient information to permit classification.

### NAMES

Common and scientific names are given for each species. Common names tend to vary greatly, but the most generally accepted version is used. In some instances, where there are two names of equal importance, both are given thus: Little Grebe/Dabchick. Where there is an alternative name that is subordinate to the main choice but still interesting, this is given in brackets: (European) Bee-eater.

### RANGE AND HABITAT

The normal range of a species is explained as fully as possible, given the limitations of space. The bird's particular habitat helps to clarify its precise occurrence within a large range. The book notes instances where a species has been introduced outside its native range by human agency.

### SIZE

Sizes are given as approximate total lengths unless otherwise stated; this is the length from bill tip to tail tip. Exceptions are made where individual circumstances demand: for example, where a bird has an exceptionally long tail, this measurement may be given separately. The vast range of sizes of the birds has meant that the drawings cannot be to a single scale.

# Birds – feathered conquerors of the air

Distributed over the surface of the earth and inhabiting almost every possible area other than the deep ocean are about 8,600 species of bird. Ranging in size from tiny hummingbirds weighing only a few grams to the ostriches that stand taller than the average human being, birds have a special place in human consciousness. Birds are often boldly marked or colored, have complex family and group behavior, are easily observed and, above all, have the power of flight. Consequently they have always stimulated much interest, pleasure, wonderment, even envy, in human beings.

Birds are warm-blooded, air-breathing vertebrates with four limbs, the front pair of which are modified to form muscle-powered wings that, in the vast majority of living birds, give the potential for active flight. Birds can be unambiguously identified as such by their feathers — a feature which all birds possess and which no other animal shares.

Much of the unique nature of a bird's body structure is linked to its need for a low takeoff weight and a good power-to-weight ratio. Like mammals, birds are descended from reptilian ancestors. In the course of evolving, they have taken the heavy-boned, scaly, elongate body of a reptile and turned it into a light, compact flying machine with a feather-covered outer surface. The bones have become slim, thin-walled and filled with air sacs deriving from the walls of the lungs. All skeletal structures are pared down to produce maximum strength with minimum weight, and the heavy reptilian skull has changed to a light, almost spherical cranium, terminating in a toothless beak covered with horny plates. The number of bones is reduced, and some have been fused for greater rigidity.

Like reptilian scales and mammalian hairs, feathers are constructed largely from the tough protein keratin. They exist in a vast range of shapes, sizes and colors and have a variety of functions. First, they provide a light, flexible, thermally insulating protective layer over the bird's surface, crucial for maintaining the bird's high constant body temperature, which can reach 42°C (107.6°F). Second, the colors and patterns of feathers are the prime means of visual communication between birds. Third, and perhaps most importantly, the large, airfoil-shaped feathers of the wings and those of the tail provide the bird's flight surfaces. The wing feathers are attached to the highly modified bones of the forelimbs and provide the main lift and thrust for flight, while the tail feathers help the bird steer during flight. The tail feathers are attached to a stumpy remnant of a tail, quite unlike that of the birds' reptilian ancestors.

The earliest fossil bird, *Archaeopteryx*, dating from the Upper Jurassic period 140 million years ago, demonstrates an intriguing intermediate stage in the progressive loss of reptilian characteristics as birds evolved. *Archaeopteryx* had feathers and wings, but it also had teeth in its jaws and a typically reptilian set of tail vertebrae — it was essentially a feathered, winged reptile.

Although air offers relatively little resistance to motion, takeoff and active flight require a massive output of power from the bird. The relatively huge breast muscles of a bird, attached to a deep keel on the breastbone, deliver this power to the basal bone of the wing, the humerus. For these muscles to operate at the necessary high power output requires good blood circulation and an exceptionally efficient respiratory system, to supply oxygen at the required rate. Birds have four-chambered hearts, similar to those of mammals but independently evolved, which can operate extremely rapidly: a sparrow's heart beats 500 times a minute, a hummingbird's up to 1,000 times a minute in flight.

A bird's respiratory system seems to take the air-breathing lung to the limits of its capability. The lungs are paired and operate in conjunction with an extensive system that includes numerous air sacs as well as thin tubes that efficiently pass oxygen into the bloodstream.

The ability to extract oxygen from the air much more rapidly and efficiently than a mammal is able to do helps to explain the astoundingly fast wing-beats of a hummingbird, the lightning flight of some swifts and the capacity of some birds to fly at altitudes where the atmosphere contains little oxygen.


In some bird families it is usual for males and females to have similar plumage; in others, the sexes differ in appearance. Although there are some interesting exceptions (for example, the females of many species of birds of prey are larger than the males), when the sexes differ, the male bird is normally the larger and more colorfully feathered, and the female has duller plumage, which may help to conceal her on the nest. For most, but not all, birds, there is a single breeding season in any year. Typically, in this period cock birds find and protect nesting territories and may sing or display to intimidate rival males and attract mates. Fertilization is internal, but apart from a few species, the male bird does not possess a penis but only a small erectile protuberance at the base of his cloaca (the reproductive opening) through which sperm passes into the female's cloaca.

Birds lay eggs containing large yolks, the food reserves for the developing embryo, surrounded by a tough, mineralized shell. The egg is formed as the ovum passes from the ovary down the oviduct to the outside world, successive layers of white inner and outer shell membranes being added on the way. Most birds lay their eggs in some form of nest, where they are incubated by one or both parents while the embryo develops. The young of some birds, such as ducks and pheasants, hatch covered with downy feathers and are able to walk immediately, while the young of others, such as blackbirds and most other songbirds, are born naked and helpless and need a period of feeding and care.


Among the 27 orders of living birds, a remarkable variety of modifications has taken place to the basic avian body, with the most crucial adaptations being to feet, legs, beaks and wings. There are large, long-legged walking birds, such as ostriches, rheas, emus and cassowaries, that have completely lost the power of flight. There are other flightless birds, such as the penguins, that have wings adapted as underwater paddles. At the opposite extreme are the insectivorous swifts, birds so aerial that it is possible that their only contact with the ground throughout life may be at the nest. There are highly specialized predators of the night (owls, nightjars) and of the daylight hours (eagles, hawks, falcons), with strong beaks and killing talons. Almost any type of small animal or vegetable food is the diet of some bird species — a shrike pouncing on a grasshopper, a hummingbird extracting nectar and a parrot feeding on jungle fruit, all testify to the breathtaking diversity of the world of birds.

# Ratites, Tinamous

## STRUTHIONIDAE: Ostrich Family

Ostriches are the largest living birds. There is now only a single species, living in Africa, but formerly the family's range extended from southern Europe to Mongolia as well as throughout Africa.

NAME: **Ostrich**, *Struthio camelus*
RANGE: **Africa**
HABITAT: **grassland, arid land**
SIZE: **1.75–2.75 m (6–9 ft) tall**

The ostrich is too big to fly but has become so perfectly adapted to high-speed running that it is the fastest creature on two legs. At speeds of up to 70 km/h (44 mph), it can easily outstrip most enemies. Powerful legs, flexible knees and supple, two-toed feet are its adaptations for speed. The ostrich has lost its strong wing feathers, but the male has soft, curling plumes, once much in demand for fashionable hats and boas. Female birds are slightly smaller than males and have brownish plumage and off-white wings and tails. Juveniles are grayish-brown.

Ostriches eat mostly plant matter but occasionally feed on small reptiles. They are nomadic, wandering in small groups in search of food. At breeding time, the male collects a harem of 2 to 5 females. One female scrapes a shallow pit in the ground in which to lay her eggs, and the rest of the harem probably uses the same nest. The eggs are the biggest laid by any bird — the equivalent in volume of about 40 hen's eggs. The male bird takes over the incubation of the eggs at night and shares in the care of the young.

## DROMAIIDAE: Emu Family

The one surviving species in the emu family is the second-largest living bird. It is closely related to the cassowaries, although they are externally dissimilar.

NAME: **Emu**, *Dromaius novaehollandiae*
RANGE: **Australia**
HABITAT: **arid plains, woodland, desert**
SIZE: **2 m (6½ ft) tall**

Emus have remained common in Australia despite having been destroyed as serious pests on farmland. They can run at speeds of 48 km/h (30 mph) and swim well. Fruit, berries and insects make up the bulk of their diet. The female lays 7 to 10 dark-green eggs, with a characteristic pimply texture, in a hollow in the ground. The male incubates the eggs for about 60 days.

## RATITES

"Ratites" is the informal name given to a mixed group of running birds with some dramatic morphological differences from all other birds. Apart from the fowl-sized kiwis of New Zealand, ratites are all extremely large, ground-living birds, with massive, muscular legs for powerful running. Their wings are much reduced in size and are not functional. The ratite breastbone is flat and small and has no central keel — in other birds this keel serves for the attachment of the flight muscles. The word "ratite" means "raftlike," as opposed to carinate, applicable to all other birds and meaning "keeled."

The living ratite families (ostrich, rheas, kiwis, emu and cassowaries) are grouped in 4 orders; cassowaries and the emu share the same order.

## CASUARIIDAE: Cassowary Family

There are 3 species of cassowary, all in Australasia, but because of the isolating effects of island habitats, many races have evolved with minor differences. All are large powerful birds and are well adapted to forest life.

NAME: **Common Cassowary**, *Casuarius casuarius*
RANGE: **N. Australia, New Guinea, E. Indonesia**
HABITAT: **rain forest**
SIZE: **1.5 m (5 ft) tall**

The common cassowary is an impressive bird with long, hairlike quills which protect it from the forest undergrowth. Its wings are vestigial, but its legs are extremely powerful and armed with sharp-toed feet, capable of inflicting severe wounds. The bald but brightly colored head and neck bear brilliant wattles and a horny casque. As the cassowary moves through the dense forest in search of seeds, fruits and berries, it holds this prominent casque well forward to help break a path. Male and female look alike, but the female is larger. The female lays 3 to 6 green eggs in a shallow, leaf-lined nest on the ground.

## RHEIDAE: Rhea Family

Rheas are the South American equivalents of the ostrich and the heaviest of the New World birds. Although they have larger wings than other ratites, they are still unable to fly, but they are good swimmers and fast runners.

NAME: **Greater Rhea**, *Rhea americana*
RANGE: **South America, east of the Andes**
HABITAT: **open country**
SIZE: **1.5 m (5 ft) tall**

Greater rheas live in flocks of 20 to 30 birds. Male and female look much alike. They feed on plants, seeds, insects and small animals. At breeding time, the male displays and gathers a harem of females. He leads his mated females to a shallow nest which he has prepared, and they all lay their eggs in this one nest, making a clutch of up to 18 eggs, which the male incubates.

## APTERYGIDAE: Kiwi Family

Kiwis are flightless forest birds. There are 3 species, all living in New Zealand.

NAME: **Brown Kiwi**, *Apteryx australis*
RANGE: **New Zealand**
HABITAT: **forest**
SIZE: **50 cm (19¾ in)**

The brown kiwi, emblem of New Zealand, is a rarely seen, nocturnal creature. It has rudimentary wings concealed under coarse, hairlike body feathers. Its legs are short and stout, with powerful claws for scratching around the forest floor in search of insects, worms and berries. The nostrils are at the tip of the bird's pointed bill, and it seems to have a good sense of smell — rare among birds. Females are larger than males, but the sexes otherwise look similar. The female lays 1 or 2 eggs in a burrow, where they are incubated by the male. Each egg weighs about 450 g (1 lb) and is exceptionally large in proportion to the bird's body weight.

## TINAMIDAE: Tinamou Family

Tinamous are fowl-like ground birds, found in a variety of habitats from Mexico to Argentina. They can fly but are weak and clumsy, and although built for running, their best defense is to remain still, relying on their protective coloring. They feed on seeds, berries and insects. There are 47 species of tinamou.

NAME: **Great Tinamou**, *Tinamus major*
RANGE: **S. Mexico, Bolivia, Brazil**
HABITAT: **rain forest, cloud forest**
SIZE: **46 cm (18 in)**

The great tinamou, like all members of its family, is polygamous, and females lay up to 12 eggs, often in different nests. With their vivid, clear colors — blue, green and pink — and highly glazed surface, these eggs are among the most beautiful of all birds' eggs.

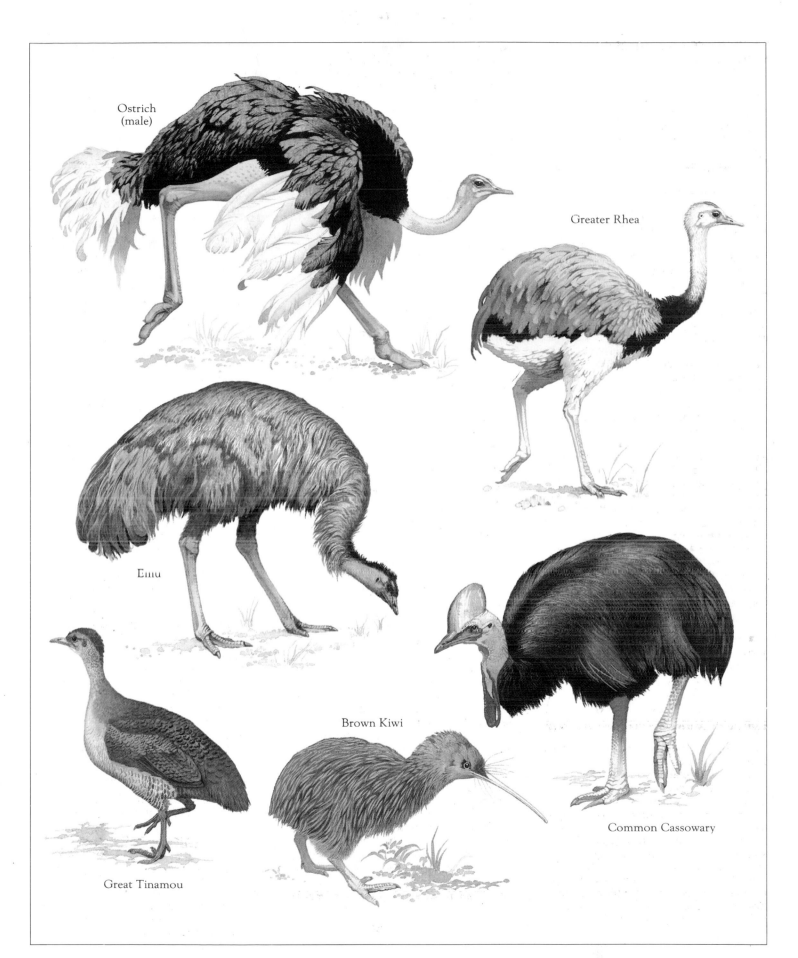

Ostrich
(male)

Greater Rhea

Emu

Brown Kiwi

Common Cassowary

Great Tinamou

# Penguins, Grebes, Loons

## ORDER SPHENISCIFORMES
## SPHENISCIDAE: Penguin Family

Penguins are a primitive and highly specialized group of marine birds. All 18 species are flightless and exquisitely adapted for marine existence. Their wings have been modified into flat, unfoldable paddles which are used propulsively for rapid underwater swimming in pursuit of fish and squid. Feathers are short and glossy and form a dense, furlike mat which is waterproof, streamlined and a superb thermal insulating layer. Their short legs, with webbed feet, are set far back to act as swimming rudders, but this position means that the birds must stand upright on land or slide along on their bellies.

Penguins usually come ashore only to breed and molt; the rest of the year is spent entirely at sea. All forms, except the Galápagos penguin, breed on the Antarctic continent, subantarctic islands or the southern coasts of South America, southern Africa and Australia, often in extremely harsh conditions.

NAME: **Little Blue/Fairy Penguin,** *Eudyptula minor*
RANGE: **New Zealand: South Island; Tasmania, S. Australia**
HABITAT: **coastal waters**
SIZE: **40 cm (15¾ in) tall**

The smallest penguin, the little blue penguin lives around coasts and islands in its range, seeking food in shallow waters. Breeding birds tend to return each year to the same nesting sites and to the same mates. A brief courtship reestablishes the pair bond. The little blue nests in crevices or in a burrow, which it digs or takes over from other birds. The females lays 2 eggs, and both male and female incubate for 33 to 40 days.

NAME: **Galápagos Penguin,** *Spheniscus mendiculus*
RANGE: **Galápagos Islands**
HABITAT: **coastal waters**
SIZE: **51 cm (20 in) tall**

The rarest of penguins and the only species to venture near the equator, the Galápagos penguin owes its presence there to the exceptional situation of its native islands. Although so close to the equator, the Galápagos are bathed by the cool waters of the Humboldt Current, which makes the area habitable for a cold-loving penguin. The current is also rich in nutrients, supplying plenty of food right up the food chain. The penguins breed from May to July and make a nest of stones in a cave or crevice on the coast. Two eggs are laid.

NAME: **Emperor Penguin,** *Aptenodytes forsteri*
RANGE: **southern oceans**
HABITAT: **ocean and pack ice**
SIZE: **1.2 m (4 ft) tall**

Emperor penguins, largest of the penguin family, endure the worst breeding conditions of any bird. These penguins never actually come to land but gather in huge colonies on the pack ice of the antarctic seas. After pairing, the female lays her 1 egg at the beginning of winter and at once returns to the sea. Her partner incubates the egg on his feet, where it is protected by a flap of skin and feathers. All the males in the colony huddle together for warmth and protection during their vigil in the bitterly cold, totally dark antarctic winter. As the male cannot leave the egg, he fasts during the 64-day incubation period. When the chick is born, he feeds it from secretions in his crop, and the chick remains protected on his feet. By this time the ice is breaking up, and the female returns to take over while the male recovers and feeds. Both parents then care for their chick.

## ORDER PODICIPEDIFORMES
## PODICIPEDIDAE: Grebe Family

Nineteen species of these satin-plumaged water birds are found scattered around the world; some species are widespread. They all breed in fresh water, usually making a nest of floating, decaying vegetation. Like penguins, grebes are fast swimmers, with legs set well back on the body. The large grebes are highly streamlined birds which chase and catch fish underwater with their long pointed beaks. Other species feed on bottom-feeding mollusks and are smaller and more compact, with stubby thick bills. Males and females look similar, while juveniles have striped heads and necks.

NAME: **Little Grebe/Dabchick,** *Tachybaptus ruficollis*
RANGE: **Europe, Africa and Madagascar, Asia, Indonesia, New Guinea**
HABITAT: **lakes, ponds, rivers**
SIZE: **27 cm (10½ in)**

The little grebe is one of the smaller grebes and is rotund and ducklike in shape. It feeds on insects, crustaceans and mollusks. In winter its plumage is gray-brown and white, but in the breeding season it has a reddish throat and foreneck. The female lays 2 to 10 eggs in a floating clump of vegetation in shallow water or among aquatic plants. Both parents incubate the clutch for a total of 23 to 25 days.

NAME: **Great Crested Grebe,** *Podiceps cristatus*
RANGE: **Europe, Asia, Africa, south of the Sahara; Australia, New Zealand**
HABITAT: **lakes, ponds, rivers, coastal waters**
SIZE: **51 cm (20 in)**

Easily recognized on water by its long slender neck and daggerlike bill, the great crested grebe is rarely seen on land, where it moves awkwardly, or in flight. It feeds mainly on fish, which it catches by diving from the surface of the water. The great crested is one of the largest grebes; adults are particularly striking in their breeding plumage, when they sport a double-horned crest on the head and frills on the neck. In winter this crest is much reduced, the frills lost and the head largely white. The sexes look alike, but males generally have longer bills and larger crests and frills. Before mating, these grebes perform an elegant mutual courtship dance to establish the pair bond. Both partners perform head-wagging and reed-holding displays and other ritualized movements. They mate on a reed platform near the nest, which is among the reeds. The female lays 2 to 7 eggs, which are incubated by both parents for 27 to 29 days.

## ORDER GAVIIFORMES
## GAVIIDAE: Loon Family

Loons are foot-propelled diving birds. All 4 or 5 species live in the high latitudes of the northern hemisphere and are the ecological counterparts of grebes in those areas. The birds feed primarily on fish, which they chase and seize under water. Males and females look alike.

NAME: **Red-throated Loon,** *Gavia stellata*
RANGE: **circumpolar: N. America, N. Europe, N. Asia**
HABITAT: **lakes, ponds, seas**
SIZE: **53–69 cm (21–27 in)**

The red-throated loon has a thin grebe-like bill and a reddish throat patch at breeding time; in winter its back is spotted with white, and its head is gray and white. Like the others in the family, the red-throated loon flies strongly and, because it is smaller than other species, takes off from the water more easily. After a courtship display of bill-dipping and diving, the female lays 1 to 3 eggs in a heap of moss or other vegetation or in a shallow dip in the ground. Both parents share the 24- to 29-day incubation of the clutch and feed the young.

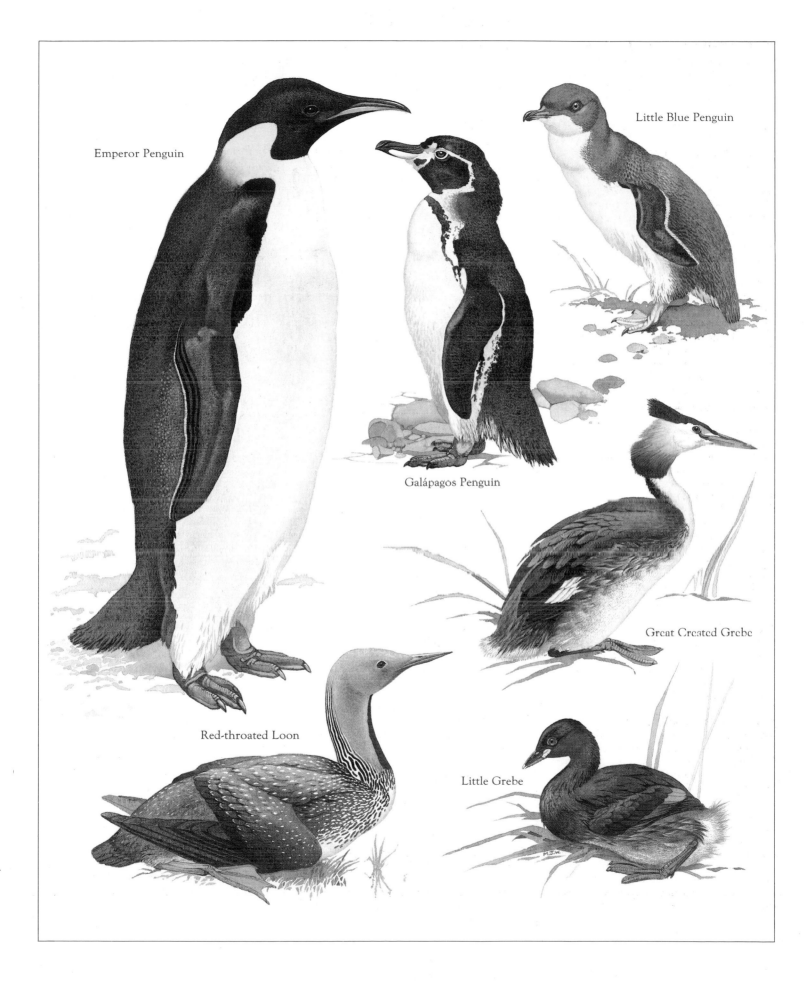

Emperor Penguin

Little Blue Penguin

Galápagos Penguin

Great Crested Grebe

Red-throated Loon

Little Grebe

# Albatrosses, Petrels

## ORDER PROCELLARIIFORMES

This order of birds contains 4 families, namely, the albatrosses, petrels, storm-petrels and diving-petrels. All are totally marine birds with webbed feet and hooked beaks surmounted by elongated tubular nostrils. Between 80 and 100 species (according to different classifications) of these "tubenoses" are distributed around the oceans of the world. Most species store stomach oil as a long-distance food reserve; this oil can also be discharged from mouth or nostrils as a foul-smelling chemical defense. Typical species in this order have low reproductive rates, long periods of immaturity and long life-spans.

## DIOMEDEIDAE: Albatross Family

The 13 species of albatross are all large pelagic birds, noted for their spectacular gliding flight over vast ocean distances. Most occur in the southern hemisphere, but a few do live in the North Pacific. The birds have an unmistakable body form with extremely long narrow wings. The albatross bill is large and hooked. Male and female look alike in all species except the wandering albatross. Albatrosses feed on fish, squid and other marine animals which they catch at the surface of the water or just below it. Most species are migratory.

NAME: **Wandering Albatross,** *Diomedea exulans*
RANGE: **southern oceans, approximately 60° S to 25° S**
HABITAT: **oceanic**
SIZE: **110–135 cm (43–53 in)**
  **wingspan: 290–324 cm (114–127½ in)**
The wandering albatross is the largest species in its family and the longest-winged of all birds. Using the strong winds of the oceans of the southern hemisphere, it glides and soars for long periods. As well as feeding on fish and squid, these albatrosses follow ships and gather to scavenge when refuse is dumped. Female birds have brown flecks on the crown; juveniles have brown bodies and underwings, which gradually become mottled, then white.

The wandering albatross comes to land on subantarctic islands in the South Pacific, Indian and South Atlantic oceans only to breed. Courtship displays and greeting ceremonies are elaborate: the birds rattle their bills, touch bill tips and spread their huge wings. The female lays 1 egg, which is incubated for about 80 days by both parents. Since both parents feed the chick intermittently for about a year, the birds can breed only every other year.

NAME: **Light-mantled Sooty Albatross,** *Phoebetria palpebrata*
RANGE: **southern oceans to about 33° S**
HABITAT: **oceanic**
SIZE: **72 cm (28 in)**
A small graceful albatross, the light-mantled sooty is far better able to maneuver in the air than the large seabirds. It breeds on antarctic and subantarctic islands and makes a neat cup-shaped nest of plant material. The female lays 1 egg, and both parents care for the chick for a few months. Eventually the parents desert the chick, which soon follows them out to sea.

## PROCELLARIIDAE: Petrel Family

This family, with about 66 species, is the largest group of tubenoses and contains birds such as petrels, shearwaters, fulmars and prions. Most species have long slender wings and short tails. Males and females look alike. Representatives of the family occur in all oceans; most species are migratory. Except when breeding, these birds rarely come to land and spend most of their lives flying over the ocean. They are expert at flying through the most severe weather.

Within the family, species have become adapted to different feeding methods. Fulmars feed on plankton and scavenge around fishing fleets; prions filter planktonic animals from the water; the gadfly petrels (such as *Pterodroma* sp.) catch squid and octopus at night, and shearwaters are surface predators of fish.

Most species nest in burrows or rock crevices, although a few nest on cliff ledges or open ground. The female usually lays a single egg, which both parents incubate in shifts of 2 to 12 days. Petrels usually nest in colonies.

NAME: **Broad-billed Prion/Whale Bird,** *Pachyptila vittata*
RANGE: **southern oceans**
HABITAT: **oceanic**
SIZE: **31 cm (12¼ in)**
The 6 species of prion, all in the genus *Pachyptila*, are similar in appearance and size and virtually indistinguishable at sea. The broad-billed prion is slightly larger than the others and can be identified by its markedly broader bill. It feeds on small planktonic animals, which it filters from the water through the hairlike fringes of lamellae at the sides of the bill. The birds often form huge feeding flocks in areas of plankton-rich water. Colonies of broad-billed prions breed in summer on islands in the South Atlantic and southern Indian oceans and off New Zealand.

NAME: **Manx Shearwater,** *Puffinus puffinus*
RANGE: **Atlantic and Pacific Oceans, Mediterranean Sea**
HABITAT: **oceanic and coastal**
SIZE: **30–38 cm (11¾–15 in)**
There are several geographically distinct races of the Manx shearwater with slight plumage differences. Shearwaters feed by day, seizing fish, squid, crustaceans and debris at the water surface or diving in pursuit of prey. They have complex migration routes between feeding grounds and travel long distances. A shearwater removed from its burrow in Britain and taken to the USA returned home, a distance of about 4,500 km (2,800 mi) in 13 days. The birds nest in huge colonies on offshore islands. The female lays her egg in a burrow, and both parents care for the chick.

NAME: **Northern Fulmar,** *Fulmarus glacialis*
RANGE: **N. Atlantic, N. Pacific Oceans**
HABITAT: **oceanic**
SIZE: **45–50 cm (17¾–19¾ in)**
Fulmars exploit the waste from commercial fishing, and with the spread of this industry, these large, robust petrels have dramatically increased their numbers. They swim but seldom dive, catching most of their food at the water surface. Male and female birds look alike, but the males have bigger bills. They nest on cliff ledges on coasts or islands; the female lays 1 egg, incubated by both parents. The adults feed the chick and defend it by spitting stomach oil at predators.

NAME: **Scaled Petrel,** *Pterodroma inexpectata*
RANGE: **S. and N. Pacific Oceans to 55° N**
HABITAT: **oceanic**
SIZE: **36 cm (14¼ in)**
The scaled petrel is a fairly small species with long narrow wings. Its flight is fast, and it swoops and dives with great ease. Primarily a nocturnal bird, it feeds largely on squid and octopus. It breeds on Stewart and Snares islands near New Zealand and migrates north in winter to the western North Pacific. Like most petrels, it lays only 1 egg.

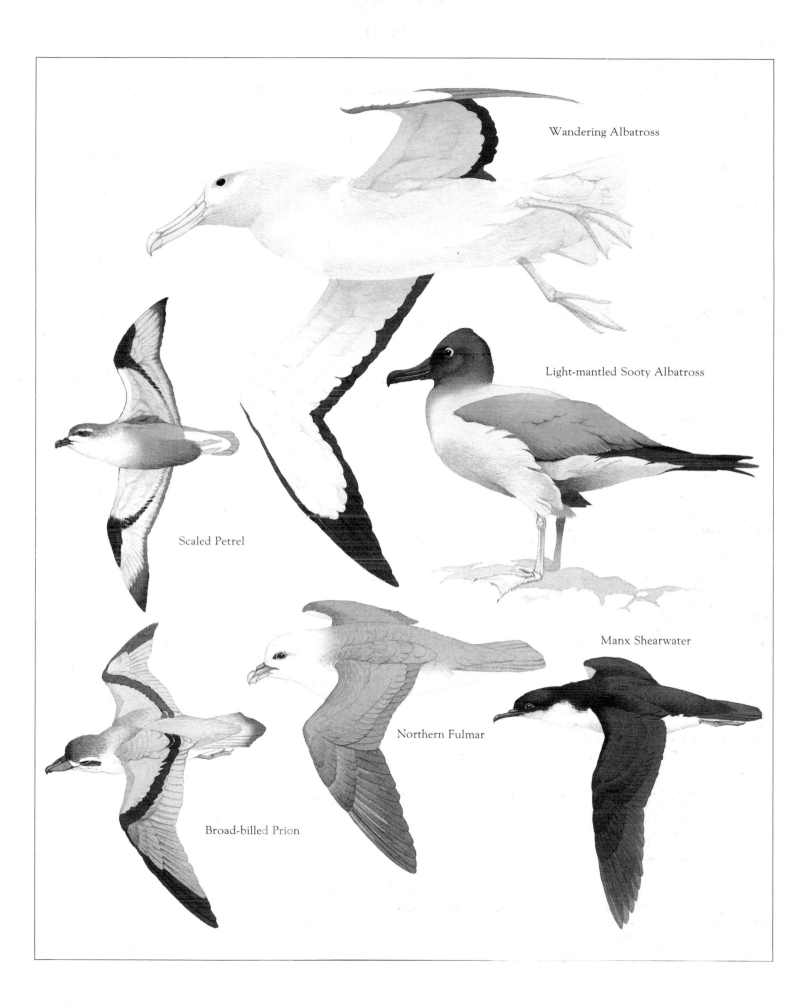

Wandering Albatross

Light-mantled Sooty Albatross

Scaled Petrel

Manx Shearwater

Northern Fulmar

Broad-billed Prion

# Storm-petrels, Diving-petrels

## HYDROBATIDAE:
### Storm-petrel Family

These small seabirds occur in most oceans, mainly south of the Arctic Circle. There are about 21 species, which are divided into 2 distinct groups, each one characteristic of the northern or southern hemisphere; their ranges overlap in the tropics. The northern birds have short legs, long pointed wings and forked tails; they feed by swooping and skimming low over the water. The southern birds have long slender legs, short rounded wings and square tails; they are adapted for a particular method of feeding: "stepping" over the surface of the water with wings spread to seize items of food.

All storm-petrels are small birds, reaching a maximum length of about 25 cm (10 in). All have black, or black and brown, plumage with white rump feathers. Males and females look alike, and all have a distinctive musky smell. Juveniles are similar to adults. Most storm-petrels are deepwater birds and come to land and inshore waters only to breed. Some species are not known to settle on the sea and they seldom dive. Many storm-petrels follow ships and take refuse and animals disturbed by the wake.

Storm-petrels breed in colonies, usually on remote offshore islands. Long-term pair bonds are the rule, but this may be due largely to the birds' habit of returning to the same nest sites year after year. They often come to land at night to breed; consequently vocal displays are more important than visual. They nest in crevices and burrows. Most migrate after breeding.

NAME: **Black Storm-petrel,**
  *Oceanodroma melania*
RANGE: **eastern N. Pacific Ocean:**
  **California to Peru**
HABITAT: **coastal and offshore waters**
SIZE: **21–23 cm (8–9 in)**

With its deeply forked tail, the black storm-petrel is characteristic of the northern group of storm-petrels and is one of several species inhabiting the nutrient-rich waters of the Pacific. This storm-petrel feeds on plankton and on the larvae of the spiny lobster.

The black storm-petrel breeds on islands off the coast of Baja California. The female lays 1 egg in a nest in a burrow or rock crevice.

NAME: **Storm-petrel,** *Hydrobates*
  *pelagicus*
RANGE: **N.E. Atlantic Ocean,**
  **W. Mediterranean Sea**
HABITAT: **oceanic**
SIZE: **14–18 cm (5½–7 in)**

The storm-petrel is the smallest European seabird and one of the 3 Atlantic species of storm-petrel. It is more aerial than aquatic but will land and swim briefly on the sea in all weather. It feeds on fish, squid and crustaceans and often follows ships to feed on waste thrown into the water. The only time it comes to land is in the breeding season, to nest on remote islands and promontories. The nest is a burrow, dug by both partners, or a hole or cavity in the cliff face. The female lays 1 egg, and both parents share the incubation duties and the care of the chick. In the winter the birds migrate south of their breeding range to the Red Sea and the west coast of Africa.

NAME: **Wilson's Petrel,** *Oceanites*
  *oceanicus*
RANGE: **Antarctic, Atlantic and Indian**
  **Oceans**
HABITAT: **oceanic**
SIZE: **15–19 cm (6–7½ in)**

Wilson's petrel is typical of the southern group of storm-petrels. Its legs are long and toes short, and it is ideally suited for hopping and paddling over the water surface to pick up prey. On occasion it also hovers over the surface. This species feeds mostly on plankton and the oil and fat debris from whaling stations.

Breeding pairs nest in burrows or in crevices under rocks. In experiments, banded individuals were found to return to the same nest sites year after year, usually on islands off the tip of South America. The female lays 1 egg, which her mate helps to incubate. Both feed the chick. In winter the birds migrate north to the tropics or even north of the equator, and they can sometimes be seen off the Atlantic coast of North America. Some ornithologists believe Wilson's petrel to be the most abundant bird species in the world.

NAME: **Ringed Storm-petrel,**
  *Oceanodroma hornbyi*
RANGE: **Pacific coast of South America**
HABITAT: **oceanic**
SIZE: **20–22 cm (7¾–8½ in)**

The ringed storm-petrel has a distinctive plumage pattern, with a white collar around the neck and a dark band across the chest. Although a seabird, this species flies inland to breed in the Chilean Andes.

NAME: **White-faced Storm-petrel,**
  *Pelagodroma marina*
RANGE: **Atlantic, Indian and S. Pacific**
  **Oceans**
HABITAT: **oceanic**
SIZE: **20.5 cm (8 in)**

This species has distinctive black and white plumage. Like all southern storm-petrels, it lowers its long legs and splashes down on the sea to feed at the water surface. It takes plankton and also catches small squid. Colonies breed on many islands in the Atlantic and around the coasts of Australia and New Zealand. The female lays 1 egg in a burrow dug in soft ground. The white-faced storm-petrel's choice of ground nest sites, combined with its awkwardness on land, makes it vulnerable to severe predation by cats and by other birds during its breeding season.

## PELECANOIDIDAE:
### Diving-petrel Family

Diving-petrels are a highly distinctive group of 5 tubenose birds, all classified in a single genus: *Pelecanoides*. All species have a compact body form, with short neck, wings, legs and tail, and their overall appearance is similar to that of the auks (Alcidae). The similarities are linked to their shared basic feeding method: they dive from the air into the sea and use their short wings to swim underwater in search of prey. Their food includes crustaceans and small schooling fish such as anchovies. Diving-petrels fly with rapid wing beats. All species are found in the southern oceans and along the west coast of South America as far north as Peru.

NAME: **Subantarctic Diving-petrel,**
  *Pelecanoides urinatrix*
RANGE: **S. Atlantic and Indian Oceans**
HABITAT: **coastal waters**
SIZE: **18–21 cm (7–8¼ in)**

This diving-petrel, like its fellows, is a coastal rather than an oceanic seabird. It breeds, sometimes colonially, on South Atlantic islands, from the Falklands east to Australia and New Zealand. Breeding birds dig a burrow nest several feet long. The parents take turns incubating their 1 egg for a total of about 8 weeks, and they share the feeding of the chick. The chick leaves the nest when it is about 7 or 8 weeks old.

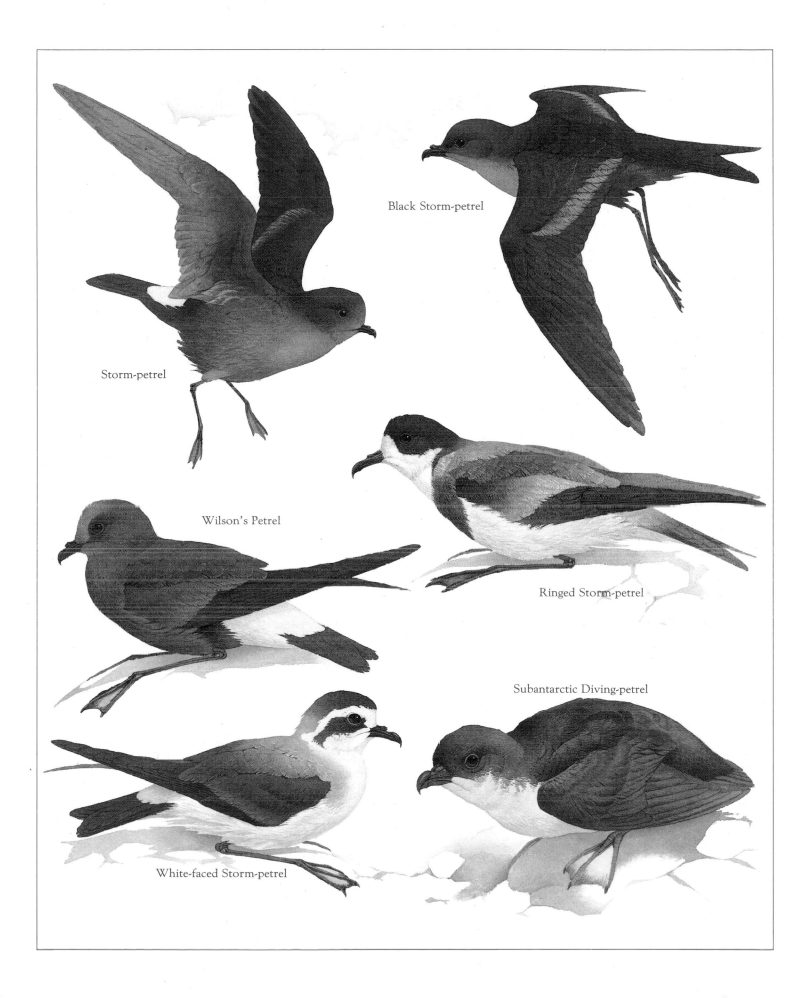

Black Storm-petrel

Storm-petrel

Wilson's Petrel

Ringed Storm-petrel

Subantarctic Diving-petrel

White-faced Storm-petrel

# Tropicbirds, Gannets and Boobies, Pelicans

## ORDER PELECANIFORMES

This order contains 60 species of birds grouped into 6 families: pelicans, gannets and boobies, tropicbirds, cormorants, darters and frigatebirds. All are medium to very large aquatic birds with webbed feet and are found in both marine and freshwater habitats.

## PHAETHONTIDAE:
### Tropicbird Family

Tropicbirds are elegant white seabirds, easily distinguished by their two elongated central tail feathers. The 3 species in the family all occur in tropical oceans, where they fly far out to sea and breed on islands. They are poor swimmers and tend to catch food by hovering above the water, then plunging down to seize the prey. Fish, squid and crustaceans are their main food. Male and female look alike.

**NAME: Red-tailed Tropicbird, *Phaethon rubricauda***
**RANGE: Indian and Pacific Oceans**
**HABITAT: oceanic**
**SIZE: 41 cm (16 in)**
**tail: 51 cm (20 in)**

The red-tailed tropicbird, with its dark-red tail feathers, is a particularly striking species; in the breeding season, the bird's white plumage takes on a rosy tinge. Tropicbirds move awkwardly on land, so they tend to nest on ledges or cliffs where they are in a position for easy takeoff. Although usually solitary at sea, they are numerous at breeding grounds and fight over nest sites and partners. No actual nest is made; the single egg is laid on the ground. Both parents incubate the egg for about 42 days and feed the downy chick until it leaves the nest at 12 to 15 weeks.

## SULIDAE:
### Gannet and Booby Family

The 9 birds in this family fall into two distinct groups: the 6 species of booby and the 3 species of gannet. They occur in all the oceans of the world: the boobies in tropical and subtropical areas, and the gannets generally in temperate zones. All are impressive marine birds that feed by plunge-diving for prey. Most have stout bodies, long pointed wings and short legs. Male and female generally look alike, occasionally differing in bill and foot color. Juveniles have brownish feathers at first and develop the adult plumage over a few years.

**NAME: Brown Booby, *Sula leucogaster***
**RANGE: tropical Atlantic and Pacific Oceans**
**HABITAT: mostly coastal**
**SIZE: 64–74 cm (25–29 in)**

Boobies were apparently given their common name because of their folly in allowing sailors to approach and kill them for food. Like gannets, boobies plunge-dive for fish and squid but specialize in feeding in shallow water and in the catching of flyingfish. The brown booby stays nearer the coast than the gannet and breeds on cliffs and rocks or even on beaches and coral reefs. The female lays 1 or 2 eggs in a hollow on the ground or among rocks, and both parents share the incubation and feeding duties.

**NAME: Northern Gannet, *Sula (= Morus) bassana***
**RANGE: N. Atlantic Ocean**
**HABITAT: coastal waters**
**SIZE: 87–100 cm (34–39¼ in)**

Gannets are streamlined, heavily built seabirds with thick necks, strong legs and webbed feet. Offshore rather than oceanic birds, they are magnificent in the air and fly or soar over the water searching for fish and squid. Once prey is sighted, the gannet will plummet 30 m (100 ft) or more down to the sea, grasp the catch and bring it to the surface. The bird's stout bill and specially adapted skull, with resilient, air-filled spaces, take much of the initial impact of these expert dives. Other adaptations perfect gannets for marine life. First, there are no external nostrils. The nostril openings are covered by bony flaps so that water cannot be forced into them when the bird dives. The rear edge of the upper bill bows outward so that the gannet can breathe. Second, salt glands above the eye orbits produce a concentrated salt solution which enters the mouth by the internal nostrils and drips away from the beak, and this enables the gannet to feed on salty fish and to drink seawater without having to excrete vast quantities of urine to eliminate the salt.

Gannets are extremely gregarious birds, breeding in colonies of thousands of birds on rocks and islands. Attempts to breed gannets in small groups have failed, and it could be that the social stimulation of the colony is a crucial factor for breeding success. The birds display to establish and maintain pair bonds, and each pair occupies and defends a breeding territory. Nests are so closely packed that incubating birds can reach out and touch one another. The female lays 1 egg, which both parents incubate for 43 to 45 days.

## PELECANIDAE: Pelican Family

The pelicans, which give this order its name, comprise 8 species found in large lakes and on seacoasts. They are gregarious, strong-flying birds which feed on fish, caught while the birds are swimming in shallow water or, in one case, by diving from the air. The most dramatic anatomical feature is the huge gular pouch beneath the long broad bill. Males and females look alike.

**NAME: Great White/Rosy Pelican, *Pelecanus onocrotalus***
**RANGE: S.E. Europe, Asia, Africa**
**HABITAT: inland lakes, marshes**
**SIZE: 140–175 cm (55–69 in)**

A large white bird with the characteristic pouched bill, the great white pelican is well adapted for aquatic life. The short strong legs and webbed feet propel it in water and aid the rather awkward takeoff from the water surface. Once aloft, the long-winged pelicans are powerful fliers, however, and often travel in spectacular V-formation groups. The pelican's pouch is simply a scoop. As the pelican pushes its bill underwater, the lower bill bows out, creating a large pouch which fills with water and fish. As the bird lifts its head, the pouch contracts, forcing out the water but retaining the fish. A group of 6 to 8 great white pelicans will gather in a horseshoe formation in the water to feed together. They dip their bills in unison, creating a circle of open pouches, ready to trap every fish in the area.

Large numbers of these pelicans breed together in colonies. The female lays 2 to 4 eggs in a nest of sticks in a tree or on the grass. The young are cared for by both parents.

**NAME: Brown Pelican, *Pelecanus occidentalis***
**RANGE: USA, Caribbean, South America, Galápagos Islands**
**HABITAT: coasts**
**SIZE: 127 cm (50 in)**

The brown pelican is the smallest pelican and is rather different from the rest of its family. It is a seabird and catches fish by diving into the water from as high as 15 m (50 ft). When it dives, it holds the wings back and the neck curved into an S-shape so that the front of the body, which is provided with cushioning air sacs, takes some of the impact of the plunge into the water. The successful bird generally returns to the surface to eat its catch.

The female brown pelican lays her 2 or 3 eggs in a nest which is built in a tree or sometimes on the ground.

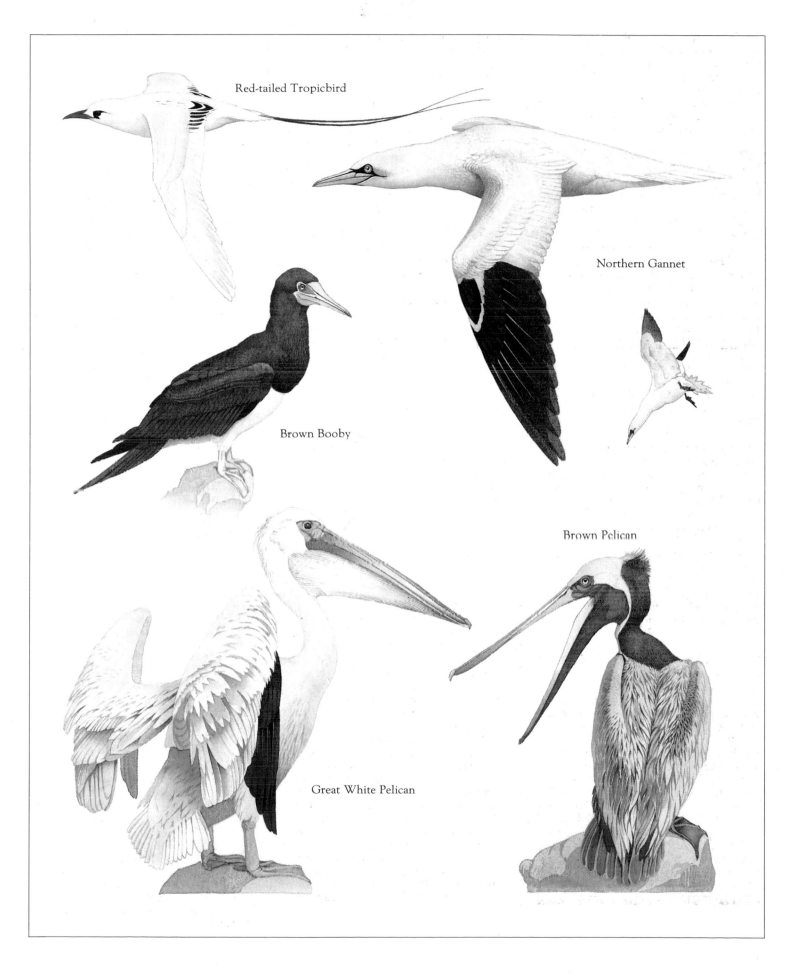

Red-tailed Tropicbird

Northern Gannet

Brown Booby

Brown Pelican

Great White Pelican

## ANHINGIDAE: Darter Family

These superb underwater fish-hunters look much like streamlined cormorants but have longer, slender necks and sharply pointed bills. Also known as anhingas, the 4 species of darter are found in a variety of freshwater habitats throughout the tropics. There are some differences in the plumage of males and females, and males have light plumes on head and neck in the breeding season.

NAME: **Anhinga/Snakebird, *Anhinga anhinga***
RANGE: **S. USA to Argentina**
HABITAT: **lakes, rivers**
SIZE: **90 cm (35 in)**

Like cormorants, anhingas dive deep in pursuit of fish, keeping their wings in at their sides and paddling with their feet. While underwater, the anhinga keeps its long neck folded in, ready to dart out and impale prey with the sharp beak. The edges of the beak are serrated, providing a firm grip on the fish once it has been transferred from the impaled position. At the water surface, the anhinga often swims with all but its head and sinuous neck submerged — hence its other common name, "snakebird." Crustaceans, amphibians and insects also form part of the anhinga's diet.

Anhingas are colonial breeders, often nesting near other large water birds. They build nests in a tree near or overhanging water. The female lays 3 to 6 eggs, which both partners incubate.

## PHALACROCORACIDAE: Cormorant Family

There are about 30 species of these mainly black, medium-sized water birds. Typically, cormorants have long necks and bodies, wings of moderate length, short legs and large webbed feet. Male and female resemble each other, with small plumage differences in the breeding season. All cormorants are specialist fish-eaters and are found in marine and freshwater habitats. They are coastal birds, rarely seen over open sea. They swim well and dive from the surface to catch prey. In flight, their necks are fully extended, and they often fly in lines or V-formations.

Cormorants are gregarious birds; they nest colonially and defend small nest territories. After feeding excursions they rest on rocks, trees or cliffs, often with their wings, which quickly become waterlogged, spread out to dry.

NAME: **Great Cormorant, *Phalacrocorax carbo***
RANGE: **N. America, Europe, Africa, Asia, Australia**
HABITAT: **coasts, marshes, lakes**
SIZE: **80–100 cm (31–39¼ in)**

Also sometimes known as the black cormorant, this bird is the largest species in its family and also the most widely distributed. Habitats and nesting sites vary greatly over its enormous range. Male and female birds look alike, but the breeding male acquires some white feathers on the head and neck and a white patch on each flank. Immature birds have brownish plumage with pale underparts.

Cormorants feed primarily on fish, but they will also eat crustaceans and amphibians. Prey is caught underwater during dives lasting 20 or 30 seconds. The bird swims by using its webbed feet for propulsion and its long tail as a rudder. Most prey is brought back to the surface and shaken before being swallowed.

Breeding pairs make their nests in trees or on the ground, inland or on the coast, depending on the situation in their particular range. The usual clutch is 3 or 4 eggs. Both parents incubate the eggs and feed the chicks. The chicks make their first flight about 50 days after hatching but are not completely independent for another 12 to 13 weeks.

NAME: **Reed Cormorant/Long-tailed Shag, *Halietor africanus***
RANGE: **Africa, Madagascar**
HABITAT: **rivers, lagoons**
SIZE: **58 cm (23 in)**

One of four small, long-tailed, shorter-necked cormorants, the reed cormorant is primarily an inland water bird but is also found on the west coast of southern Africa. Male and female generally look alike, but in the breeding season the male's plumage darkens and he also develops a tuft of feathers on the forehead and white plumes on face and neck. Young birds are brown and yellowish-white.

Reed cormorants feed on fish and some crustaceans, which they catch underwater by diving from the surface. Like other cormorants, they return to the surface to swallow their prey. In the breeding season, reed cormorants make their nests on the ground or in trees, and the female lays 2 to 4 eggs.

NAME: **Flightless Cormorant, *Nannopterum harrisi***
RANGE: **Galápagos Islands**
HABITAT: **coastal waters**
SIZE: **91–99 cm (36–39 in)**

This large bird, clumsy on land but superb in the water, has lost all power of flight. Its wings are tiny, with only a few flight feathers remaining. The flightless cormorant is able to catch all the food it needs in the nutrient-rich waters around the island coasts, and there are no mammalian predators in the Galápagos. Thus, unlike its fellow cormorants, this species has no need to fly great distances in search of food or to escape from danger. However, the population of these birds is small and they are now rare.

## FREGATIDAE: Frigatebird Family

Frigatebirds are the most aerial of all water birds and are graceful and spectacular in flight. They are masters of the air above the sea and soar over huge oceanic distances. They are large birds with extremely long, pointed wings and long forked tails. All 5 species inhabit tropical and subtropical areas. Females are generally larger than males and have white breasts and sides. Males have bright-red throat pouches, which they inflate to enormous size in their courtship displays.

NAME: **Magnificent Frigatebird, *Fregata magnificens***
RANGE: **Central America; South America; Galápagos Islands**
HABITAT: **coastal waters, islands, bays, estuaries**
SIZE: **95–110 cm (37–43 in)**
   **wingspan: 215–245 cm (85–96 in)**

The male magnificent frigatebird has a particularly large and splendid throat pouch, and the species has the greatest wing area, relative to body size, of any bird. It feeds chiefly on fish, squid, crustaceans and jellyfish, which it catches by swooping down to the water surface. It rarely alights on the sea. Frigatebirds supplement their diet by stealing fish from other birds. Having spotted a booby or other seabird returning to land, the frigate gives chase and forces its quarry to regurgitate its catch, which it then grabs in midair.

The nest of the magnificent frigatebird is a flimsy construction of sticks. The female lays a single egg, which both parents incubate. Both feed and care for the chick for a total of about 7 weeks. Both parents bring the chick food until it is able to fly at 4 or 5 months old and continue feeding it intermittently for some weeks more.

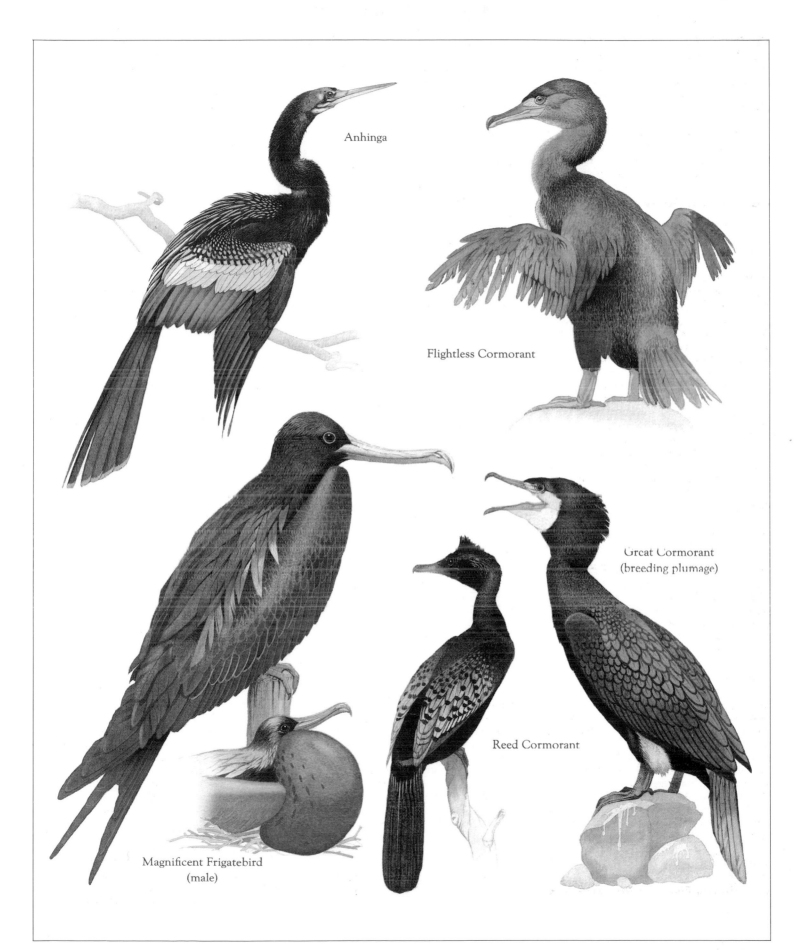

Anhinga

Flightless Cormorant

Great Cormorant
(breeding plumage)

Magnificent Frigatebird
(male)

Reed Cormorant

# Herons and Bitterns

NAME: **American Bittern,** *Botaurus lentiginosus*
RANGE: **N. America; winters in South America**
HABITAT: **marshland**
SIZE: **66 cm (26 in)**

The American bittern has a distinctive cry, rather different from the characteristic boom of other bitterns. This strange, three-syllable cry has inspired one of the bird's common names: "thunder pumper." This bittern feeds alone, moving slowly and deliberately with bill always at the ready to jab quickly at fish, crabs, snakes, frogs, insects or small mammals. It is a migratory species; although birds in milder areas do not actually migrate, they do disperse after breeding. The clutch of 4 to 6 eggs is laid in a nest platform on land or in water, and the female bird seems to perform most of the parental duties.

NAME: **Black-crowned Night Heron,** *Nycticorax nycticorax*
RANGE: **Europe, Asia, Africa, N. and South America**
HABITAT: **varied, usually near marshes**
SIZE: **61 cm (24 in)**

Probably the most numerous of all herons, the black-crowned night heron is an attractive, stocky bird with white, ribbonlike plumes extending from the back of its head; these are erected in courtship display. As its name suggests, this bird feeds mainly at night and at dusk; it preys on fish, reptiles, frogs and insects and also raids the nests of other birds.

At the beginning of the breeding season, the male finds a nest site, usually among reeds or in a bush or a tree, which he then uses as a base for his displays. His mate finishes the building of the nest and lays 3 to 5 eggs. Both parents feed and care for the chicks.

NAME: **Gray Heron,** *Ardea cinerea*
RANGE: **Europe, Asia, Africa**
HABITAT: **varied, near shallow water**
SIZE: **92 cm (36 in)**

A large, long-legged, long-billed bird, the gray heron is familiar throughout most of the Old World except Australia. Its New World equivalent, the great blue heron, A. *herodias*, is similar but slightly larger, with reddish coloring on neck and thighs. The heron feeds on fish, eels, young birds, eggs, snakes and plants. To obtain its food, the heron fishes from the land, with its head stretched forward into the water, or wades in to forage. Once prey is spotted, the bird grasps it with a swift, lethal thrust of the bill.

Gray herons breed in colonies; the female lays 3 to 5 eggs, and both parents feed the young.

## ORDER CICONIIFORMES

This order of wading birds contains 6 families. Four of these, the herons, storks, ibises and flamingos, are widespread groups with a variety of adaptations. The remaining 2 families are monotypic, represented by the shoebill and the hammerkop — both specialized African forms.

## ARDEIDAE:
### Heron and Bittern Family

The 60 or more species of heron, bittern and egret in this family are all moderate to large birds with slim bodies, long necks and legs, and large broad wings. Male and female look alike in most species. All herons have patches of powder-down feathers on the breast and rump — a feature probably associated with their mucus-laden diet of fish and amphibians. The powder produced by these specialized feathers is utilized in preening to remove slime from the plumage.

Herons hunt in water of varying depth, either while standing motionless or while wading. Prey is grasped (not impaled) with the powerful, dagger-shaped beak. Herons usually breed in colonies. During the breeding season, many species undergo changes of plumage color and develop long plumes on the head or back.

NAME: **Cattle Egret,** *Ardeola ibis*
RANGE: **Iberia, Africa, Asia, Indonesia, N. and South America, Australia**
HABITAT: **open land, drier than the habitat of most herons**
SIZE: **50 cm (19¾ in)**

The cattle egret is an extremely successful species and has expanded its range all over the world. Its success is partly due to its association with herbivorous animals. The birds follow large grazing animals, wild or domesticated, and catch the insects, particularly grasshoppers, disturbed by them. Cattle egrets feeding in this way gain about 50 percent more food for less effort than birds feeding by other methods. The cattle do not really benefit from the association, since cattle egrets do not remove parasites; the cattle may, however, be warned of approaching danger by the birds. Cattle egrets have now learned that the same results can be achieved by following farm machinery. In water the egrets feed on frogs and fish in the main.

The male gathers material for the nest, and the female builds it, usually in a small tree. The pair copulate on the nest, and the female lays 2 to 5 eggs.

NAME: **Black Heron,** *Egretta ardesiaca*
RANGE: **Africa, south of the Sahara**
HABITAT: **swamps, mangroves, mud flats**
SIZE: **48–50 cm (18¾–19¾ in)**

Physically, the black heron is much like a black-plumaged version of an egret, but it is well known for its odd feeding method. The heron stands in shallow waters, bill pointing downward, and spreads its wings in a circle, forming a canopy over its head. Specialized broad flight feathers aid the effectiveness of the canopy. The exact purpose of this habit is not known, but it has been suggested that fish are attracted to the seeming shelter of the patch of shade that is formed, thus becoming easy prey for the heron. Fish must also be more easily visible in the canopy's shade. When young birds first start to fish, they make one-winged canopies. The canopy posture is also used in the courtship display. Black herons build a nest of twigs above the water in a tree or bush. The clutch usually contains 3 or 4 eggs.

NAME: **Great Egret,** *Egretta alba*
RANGE: **almost worldwide; absent from much of Europe**
HABITAT: **shallow water**
SIZE: **90–120 cm (35–47 in)**

This egret, also sometimes known as the American egret, is one of the most widespread of its family. Nonbreeding and immature birds have yellow bills, but as the breeding season approaches, the adult's bill becomes mostly black. It finds its food — fish, mollusks, insects, small mammals, birds and plants — either by standing and waiting in the water or by slowly stalking its prey. The nest is made in a tree or reedbed, and the female lays 2 to 5 eggs. Both parents incubate the clutch in shifts for a total of 25 or 26 days.

NAME: **Boat-billed Heron/Boatbill,** *Cochlearius cochlearius*
RANGE: **Mexico to Peru and Brazil**
HABITAT: **swamps and wetlands**
SIZE: **45–50 cm (17¾–19¾ in)**

The classification of this species has been the subject of some dispute, and it is sometimes placed in a family on its own. Its only important distinction from other herons is the broad, scoop-like bill. Boat-billed herons generally feed at night on fish and shrimps. The bill seems to be extremely sensitive and opens at the merest touch, drawing in water and prey; it is also used with a scooping action. These birds perform bill-clattering and preening displays, accompanied by vocal signals, at mating time. They nest alone or in groups in trees and bushes. The female lays 2 to 4 eggs which both parents incubate.

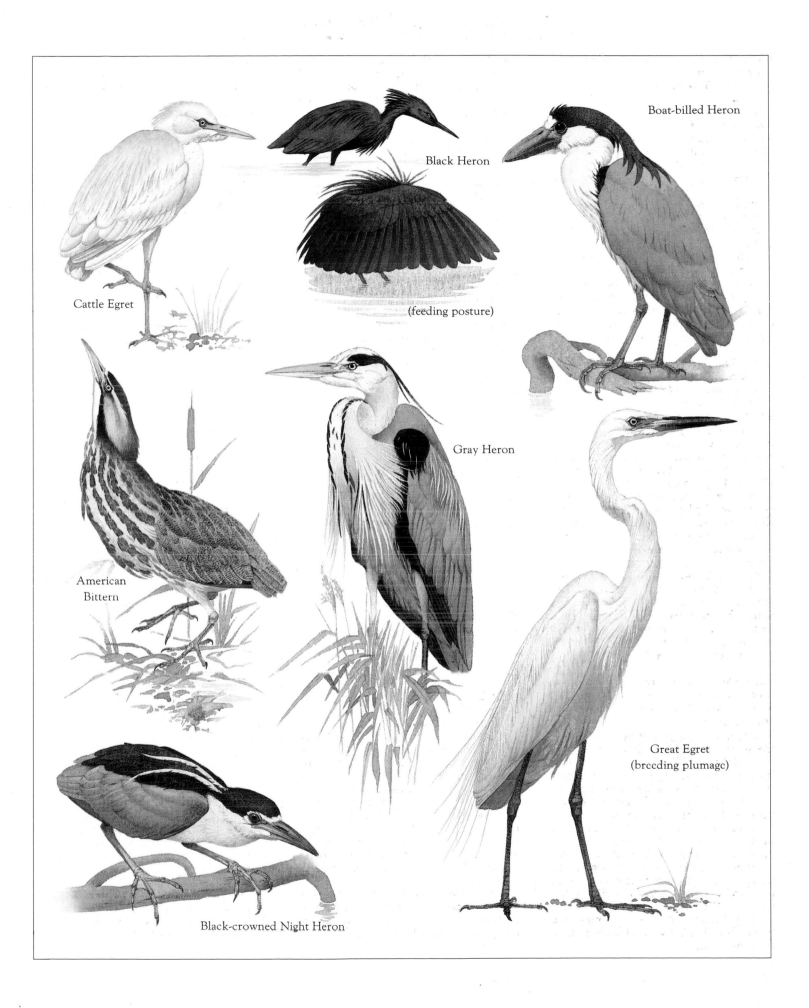

Cattle Egret

Black Heron

(feeding posture)

Boat-billed Heron

American
Bittern

Gray Heron

Great Egret
(breeding plumage)

Black-crowned Night Heron

# Storks, Flamingos, Ibises, Hammerkop, Shoebill

## CICONIIDAE: Stork Family

Storks are large, long-legged birds with elongated necks and long broad wings. Although their feet are webbed at the base, denoting aquatic habits, storks tend to feed in drier areas than most other members of their order. They are strong fliers and are particularly striking in flight, with neck and legs stretched out, the legs trailing down slightly. Males and females look alike. There are 17 species, all but 3 in the Old World. Northern populations are migratory.

**NAME: White Stork, *Ciconia ciconia***
**RANGE: E. Europe, W. Asia; winters in Africa**
**HABITAT: forest and near human habitation**
**SIZE: 102 cm (40 in)**
**1.2 m (4 ft) tall**

Legend has it that the white stork brings babies, and for this reason these birds have always been popular and protected to some degree. They are gregarious birds and tolerant of human habitation. They feed mostly on frogs, reptiles, insects and mollusks. The nest is a huge structure of sticks, which the stork builds up in a tree or on a building. The female lays 1 to 7 eggs, which both parents incubate. Although not vocal birds, white storks perform a greeting ceremony, making bill-clattering sounds as they change shifts at the nest. In doing so, they turn their heads around over their backs thus turning away their bills — or weapons. This action, in direct contrast to their bill-forward threat display, appeases any aggression between the partners. In winter white storks migrate south; most go to Africa by way of Gibraltar or Istanbul, so avoiding long journeys over open sea, for which their type of soaring flight is not suited.

**NAME: Openbill, *Anastomus oscitans***
**RANGE: India to S.E. Asia**
**HABITAT: inland waters**
**SIZE: 81 cm (32 in)**
**61 cm (24 in) tall**

The openbill, as its name suggests, has a remarkable bill: there is a gap between the mandibles, which meet only at the tips. This feature, which develops gradually and is not present in juvenile birds, seems to be an adaptation for holding the large, slippery water snails on which the birds feed. Openbills are more aquatic than most storks but still make their nests in trees. The female lays 3 to 6 eggs, which are incubated by both parents. The African openbill, *A. lamelligerus*, has the same bill shape.

## PHOENICOPTERIDAE: Flamingo Family

There are 5 species of flamingo. All are tall, pinkish-white birds with long necks, large wings and short tails. Their toes are short and webbed. All swim and fly well; the neck and legs are extended in flight. Males and females look alike. Huge numbers of flamingos live and breed in colonies; in Africa, a colony of lesser flamingos, *Phoeniconaias minor*, may number a million or more individuals. They are irregular breeders and may only breed successfully every two or three years.

Flamingos feed in the water, filtering out minute food particles with their highly specialized bills.

**NAME: American Flamingo, *Phoenicopterus ruber***
**RANGE: Caribbean, Galápagos Islands**
**HABITAT: lagoons, lakes**
**SIZE: 114 cm (45 in)**

The American flamingo has an air of frivolous fantasy, but, in fact, it is perfectly adapted for its way of life: the long legs enable it to stand in shallow water while it filter-feeds with the strangely shaped bill. The flamingo holds its bill so that it lies horizontally beneath the water, the upper half below the lower. Water flows into the bill and, by movements of the large, fleshy tongue, is pushed through hairlike lamellae which sieve out food particles before the water is expelled at the sides of the bill. Flamingos feed on mollusks, crustaceans, insects, fish and minute aquatic plants.

The nest is a mound of mud which the female scrapes together with her bill. She lays 1 or 2 eggs in a shallow depression at the top of the mound. The young birds are dependent on their parents for food until their filtering mechanism develops and they are able to fly — about 65 to 70 days.

## THRESKIORNITHIDAE: Ibis Family

Ibises and spoonbills are medium-sized wading birds. The typical family member has a moderately long neck, long wings, short tail and toes webbed at the base. Male and female look more or less alike. In some species the face or even the whole head and neck is unfeathered. All ibises fly well, with neck extended. There are about 25 species of ibis, all with long curved bills, and 6 species of spoonbill, with broad spatulate bills. Most are gregarious birds. Northern species are migratory.

**NAME: Glossy Ibis, *Plegadis falcinellus***
**RANGE: temperate and tropical Eurasia, Indonesia, Australia, Africa, West Indies, Caribbean**
**HABITAT: marshes, lakes**
**SIZE: 55–65 cm (21½–25½ in)**

The glossy ibis is the most widespread member of the family. It feeds on insects and small aquatic life. The female lays 3 or 4 eggs in a nest in a tree or reedbed. Both parents incubate the eggs and care for the young. The range and numbers of this species have been reduced by the drainage of large areas of marshland.

## SCOPIDAE: Hammerkop Family

The sole member of this family has been the subject of much dispute as to its classification.

**NAME: Hammerkop, *Scopus umbretta***
**RANGE: Africa, Madagascar, Middle East**
**HABITAT: tree-lined streams**
**SIZE: 50 cm (19¾ in)**

The hammerkop gets its common name from the resemblance of its head in profile — with its long, heavy, slightly hooked bill and backward-pointing crest — to a hammer. In flight the hammerkop holds its neck slightly curved back. Male and female birds look alike. Hammerkops are generally active at dusk and feed on amphibians, fish, insects and crustaceans. They live in pairs and build remarkable nests — elaborate roofed structures of sticks and mud, measuring up to 1.8 m (6 ft) across, placed in the branches of trees. The female lays 3 to 6 eggs, and both parents care for the downy young.

## BALAENICIPIDAE: Shoebill Family

The single species in this family is a little-known, nocturnal bird which, like the hammerkop, has links and similarities to several groups.

**NAME: Shoebill, *Balaeniceps rex***
**RANGE: E. central Africa**
**HABITAT: marshes**
**SIZE: 117 cm (46 in)**

The shoebill is a large bird, its most obvious feature being a monstrous shovel-like bill with a hooked tip. The bird seems to use this bill for searching out food — fish, frogs, snakes, mollusks and carrion — in the mud of its marshland home.

A solitary bird, the shoebill can fly well and even soar, holding its neck drawn in, pelican-fashion. It lays 2 eggs on the ground in a nest made of rushes and grass.

White Stork

Openbill

Hammerkop

American Flamingo

Shoebill

Glossy Ibis

# Screamers, Ducks

**ORDER ANSERIFORMES:**
A highly successful and diverse group of birds, this order contains 2 families: the Anatidae (ducks, geese and swans), and the Anhimidae (screamers).

## ANHIMIDAE: Screamer Family
The 3 species of screamer are similar to geese in body size but have longer legs and large feet with only partial webbing. The toes are long, enabling the birds to walk on floating vegetation. All live in South America.

NAME: **Black-necked/Northern Screamer,** *Chauna chavaria*
RANGE: **N. Colombia, Venezuela**
HABITAT: **marshes, wet grassland**
SIZE: **71–91 cm (28–36 in)**
Like all screamers, the black-necked has a noisy trumpeting call (the origin of its common name) which it uses as an alarm signal. It feeds mostly on water plants. The female lays 4 to 6 eggs in a nest of aquatic vegetation, and both parents incubate the eggs.

## ANATIDAE: Duck Family
This family contains an assemblage of water birds, found in all areas of the world except continental Antarctica and a few islands. There are about 140 species, grouped into 3 subfamilies: first, the Anseranatinae, with a single species, the magpie goose; second, the Anserinae, which contains the whistling-ducks, swans, true geese and the freckled duck; third, the Anatinae, with all the true ducks.

All members of the family are aquatic to some degree and feed on plant and animal life from the surface of the water or beneath it by up-ending or diving. The majority are broad-bodied birds with shortish legs, and feet with front toes connected by webs. Beaks vary according to feeding methods but are usually broad, flattened and blunt-tipped, with small terminal hooks. In many species males have brightly colored plumage and females plain, brownish feathers. Generally in such sexually dimorphic species, the female performs all parental duties.

Most ducks molt all their flight feathers simultaneously after the breeding season and undergo a flightless period of 3 or 4 weeks. During this period, males of some species adopt "eclipse" plumage, similar to the female's muted plumage. After breeding, many species migrate to winter feeding grounds.

NAME: **Magpie Goose,** *Anseranas semipalmata*
RANGE: **Australia, Tasmania, S. New Guinea**
HABITAT: **swamps, flood plains**
SIZE: **76–86 cm (30–34 in)**
An interesting, apparently primitive species, the magpie goose is the only true waterfowl to have only partially webbed feet. Its bill is long and straight, and the head is featherless back to the eyes. Females resemble males but are smaller. Plant material is its major food source, and the magpie goose forages by grazing and digging and by bending down tall grasses with its feet to reach the seeds. Magpie geese are gregarious birds and move in flocks of several thousand. Mates are usually kept for life, but a male may mate with two females. The female lays about 8 eggs in a nest of trampled vegetation; both partners incubate the clutch for a total of 35 days and feed the chicks.

NAME: **White-faced Whistling-duck,** *Dendrocygna viduata*
RANGE: **tropical South America, Africa, Madagascar**
HABITAT: **lakes, swamps, marshes**
SIZE: **43–48 cm (17–19 in)**
The 8 species of whistling-duck all live in the tropics. The white-faced whistling-duck feeds on aquatic insects, mollusks, crustaceans and plant matter such as seeds and rice; it will often dive for food. Much of the foraging activity takes place at night; during the day the birds roost near the water, often in flocks of several hundred, and preen themselves and others. Mutual preening plays an important part in the formation of pairs and maintenance of bonds. Between 6 and 12 eggs are laid in a nest made in a hole in a tree. Both partners incubate the eggs for 28 to 30 days.

NAME: **Tundra Swan (Bewick's/Whistling Swan),** *Cygnus columbianus*
RANGE: **Holarctic**
HABITAT: **tundra, swamps and marshes**
SIZE: **114–140 cm (45–55 in)**
Bewick's swan and the whistling swan are sometimes treated as 2 separate species, but are so alike that they are now generally regarded as conspecific. Both breed in the far north of their range and migrate enormous distances to winter in Europe, China, Japan and the USA. Males and females look alike — the female is sometimes slightly smaller — and juveniles have mottled grayish plumage. The swans feed in shallow water on aquatic vegetation. The bonds between mates are strong and permanent and are formed and maintained by mutual displays. The female lays her clutch of 3 to 5 eggs in a nest of sedge and moss lined with down, usually near water. She incubates them for 35 to 40 days. The cygnets must make the long migration south when only 80 to 90 days old.

NAME: **Graylag Goose,** *Anser anser*
RANGE: **Europe, Asia**
HABITAT: **flood plains, estuaries**
SIZE: **76–89 cm (30–35 in)**
The graylag is the most numerous and widespread goose in Eurasia. Males of this sturdy, large-headed species are bigger than females, but otherwise the sexes look alike. The geese feed on plant materials, such as roots, leaves, flowers and fruit, both on the ground and in water. A nest of vegetation and twigs is made on the ground near a tree or bush or among reedbeds, and the female incubates the 4 to 6 eggs for 28 days. The male helps to defend the goslings.

NAME: **Canada Goose,** *Branta canadensis*
RANGE: **N. America; introduced in Europe and New Zealand**
HABITAT: **varied**
SIZE: **56–110 cm (22–43 in)**
Habitats of the 12 geographically distinct races of Canada goose vary from semidesert to temperate rain forest and arctic tundra. The races also vary greatly in size. Canada geese feed by day on grassland vegetation and aquatic plants. It is a migratory species and uses the same routes from generation to generation. There is a tendency, particularly in females, for Canada geese to return to their own birthplace to breed, thus quickly producing local races and variations. Pair and family bonds are strong and are maintained by displays. The female goose lays about 5 eggs in a shallow scrape on the ground, lined with down and plant material. While her mate stays nearby to defend her, she incubates the clutch for 25 to 30 days.

NAME: **Shelduck,** *Tadorna tadorna*
RANGE: **Europe, central Asia**
HABITAT: **coasts and estuaries**
SIZE: **61 cm (24 in)**
Shelducks are a group of large, goose-like ducks. The shelduck feeds on mollusks, particularly on the estuarine snail *Hydrobia*, as well as on fish, fish eggs, insects and their larvae, and algae. Females are smaller than males and have white feathers between eyes and bill. Pair bonds are strong and thought to be permanent, and at breeding grounds the pairs take up territories. The female lays about 9 eggs in a burrow or cavity nest or in the open. While she incubates the clutch for 28 to 30 days, the male defends her.

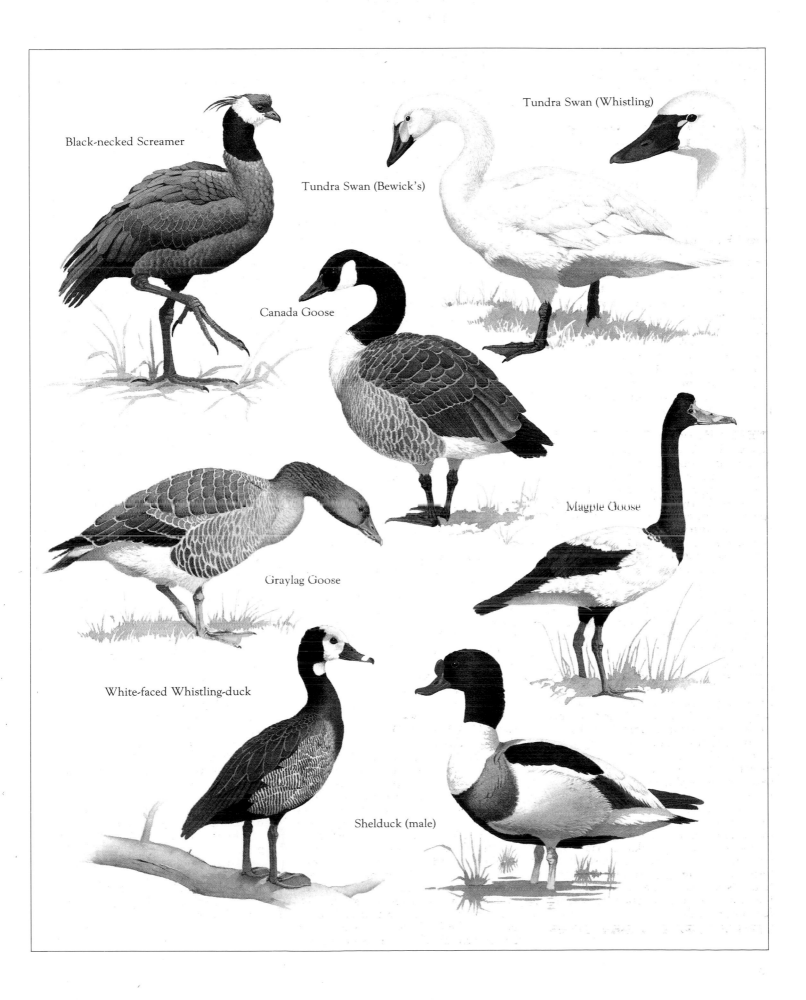

Black-necked Screamer

Tundra Swan (Bewick's)

Tundra Swan (Whistling)

Canada Goose

Graylag Goose

Magpie Goose

White-faced Whistling-duck

Shelduck (male)

# Ducks

**NAME: Falklands Steamer Duck,**
    *Tachyeres brachypterus*
**RANGE: Falkland Islands**
**HABITAT: coasts**
**SIZE: 61–74 cm (24–29 in)**

Steamer ducks are heavily built marine diving ducks; 2 of the 3 species are flightless. The female is smaller than the male and has a yellow-green bill and dark brown head with white rings around the eyes. These coastline foragers feed primarily on mollusks, bivalves, crabs and shrimps — there is a record of one bird found to have 450 mussel shells in its stomach and crop. The Falklands steamer duck makes a nest on grass or dry seaweed, or even in an abandoned penguin burrow, and lines it with down. The female lays 5 to 8 eggs; the male guards her attentively while she incubates.

**NAME: Mallard,** *Anas platyrhynchos*
**RANGE: throughout northern hemisphere**
**HABITAT: almost anywhere near water**
**SIZE: 41–66 cm (16–26 in)**

The mallard is a typical dabbling duck, often feeding tail-up in shallow water. Female mallards have plain brownish plumage, with distinctive blue feathers on the wings. Pair bonds are renewed each year with a prolonged period of intricate social displays, including the ritualized preening of the bright wing patches. The female lays her 8 to 10 eggs in a nest on the ground. Her mate deserts her early in the incubation period and flies off to undergo his annual molt with the other males. The mallard is the ancestor of all domestic ducks except muscovies.

**NAME: Northern Shoveler,** *Anas clypeata*
**RANGE: Europe, Asia, N. America**
**HABITAT: inland marshes, coastal waters**
**SIZE: 43–56 cm (17–22 in)**

The shoveler's distinctive spatulate bill is an adaptation for feeding on plankton. As the bird swims, it sucks water into the bill; the water is strained out through hairlike lamellae lining the bill which retain the tiny planktonic creatures. Female birds have much duller plumage than males; they are mostly brown but have blue and green feathers on the wings. Northern shovelers usually move in small groups or pairs for most of the year. The female makes a nest in a reedbed and lays 7 to 14 eggs, which she incubates for 23 to 25 days. The ducklings are born with normal bills; the spatulate shape develops as they mature.

**NAME: Common Eider,** *Somateria mollissima*
**RANGE: circumpolar (north)**
**HABITAT: coasts, inland rivers and lakes**
**SIZE: 56–71 cm (22–28 in)**

Like most ducks, the female eider lines her nest with down plucked from her breast. The down of the eider is particularly soft and warm and has long been collected and used by man. The female duck has barred, brownish plumage, and both male and female have Y-shaped bill extensions of membrane reaching almost up to the eyes. During the breeding season, eiders frequent coasts and feed on mollusks, crustaceans and other small creatures. They nest in colonies but fight over nest sites, and each pair holds its own territory. The female incubates the clutch of about 5 eggs alone for 27 to 28 days, while her mate goes off with the other males to undergo his annual molt.

**NAME: Greater Scaup,** *Aythya marila*
**RANGE: circumpolar (north)**
**HABITAT: coastal and inland waters**
**SIZE: 41–51 cm (16–20 in)**

One of the group of ducks known as pochards, the scaup breeds in tundra regions and winters to the south. It feeds on small invertebrates such as mollusks and crustaceans. Like other pochards, such as the canvasback, A. *valisineria*, and the tufted duck, A. *fuligula*, it is an excellent diver and frequently dives as deep as 8 m (26 ft) in search of food. Scaups gather in huge flocks, and at breeding grounds pairs overlap their ranges. The female lays 8 to 10 eggs, which she incubates for 23 to 27 days.

**NAME: Mandarin Duck,** *Aix galericulata*
**RANGE: E. Asia, Korea, China, Japan;**
    **introduced in Britain and N. Europe**
**HABITAT: inland swamps, lakes and pools**
**SIZE: 43–51 cm (17–20 in)**

The exquisite mandarin duck has been celebrated in Japanese and Chinese art for centuries. In China, mandarins were symbols of fidelity and were given as wedding gifts.

Mandarins are most active at dawn and dusk; they feed on vegetable matter, such as seeds, acorns and rice, and on insects, snails and small fish. They are social ducks, and the pair bond continues from year to year when possible. Their courtship displays are particularly elaborate, including ritualized preening of the enlarged sail-like feathers on the flanks and display drinking. The female lays 9 to 12 eggs, often in a tree-hole nest, and incubates them. The closely related wood duck, A. *sponsa*, of North America is also brilliantly marked.

**NAME: Red-breasted Merganser,** *Mergus serrator*
**RANGE: Holarctic**
**HABITAT: coastal and inland waters**
**SIZE: 48–66 cm (19–26 in)**

Mergansers are fish-eating, diving ducks with long, thin, serrated bills, well adapted for catching fish underwater. They also feed on crustaceans. Courtship rituals are complex. The male stretches his neck and sprints over the water; before copulating he performs a series of drinking, preening and wing-flapping movements. The female lays her 9 or 10 eggs in a hole or cavity. The male deserts his mate early in the incubation period. Once the young have hatched, several females collect their young together into one brood, which they tend together.

**NAME: Muscovy Duck,** *Cairina moschata*
**RANGE: Central America, tropical**
    **South America**
**HABITAT: rivers and marshes in forest**
**SIZE: 66–84 cm (26–33 in)**

These birds, familiar in their domestic form, are rare in their pure form outside the native range. The male has warty skin around the eyes and an enlarged bill base; the female's head is entirely feathered, and there is no bill enlargement. The wild form is attractive, but some of the domestic muscovies have evolved with grotesque warts and bill caruncles. Muscovies feed on plants, seeds, small fish and insects and are also fond of termites, which are plentiful in their forest habitat. As they are tropical birds, muscovies have no real migratory pattern but may move to coasts in dry seasons. They do not form large flocks, and pair and family bonds are weak. Courtship displays are simple and brief. The female lays 8 to 15 eggs in a hollow or among rushes and incubates them alone. The male plays no part in the care of the young.

**NAME: Ruddy Duck,** *Oxyura jamaicensis*
**RANGE: USA, Central America, Andes;**
    **introduced in Britain**
**HABITAT: inland lakes and rivers;**
    **estuaries**
**SIZE: 35–48 cm (14–19 in)**

The ruddy duck is one of a group of ducks known as stifftails. All are small, stocky, freshwater diving ducks with the distinctive habit of holding the tail up at an angle while swimming. Ruddy ducks are usually active at night and feed on aquatic plants, insects and small invertebrates. They are not highly developed socially and do not hold nesting territories. Females lay about 8 eggs in a ground nest but will sometimes lay more eggs in other nests.

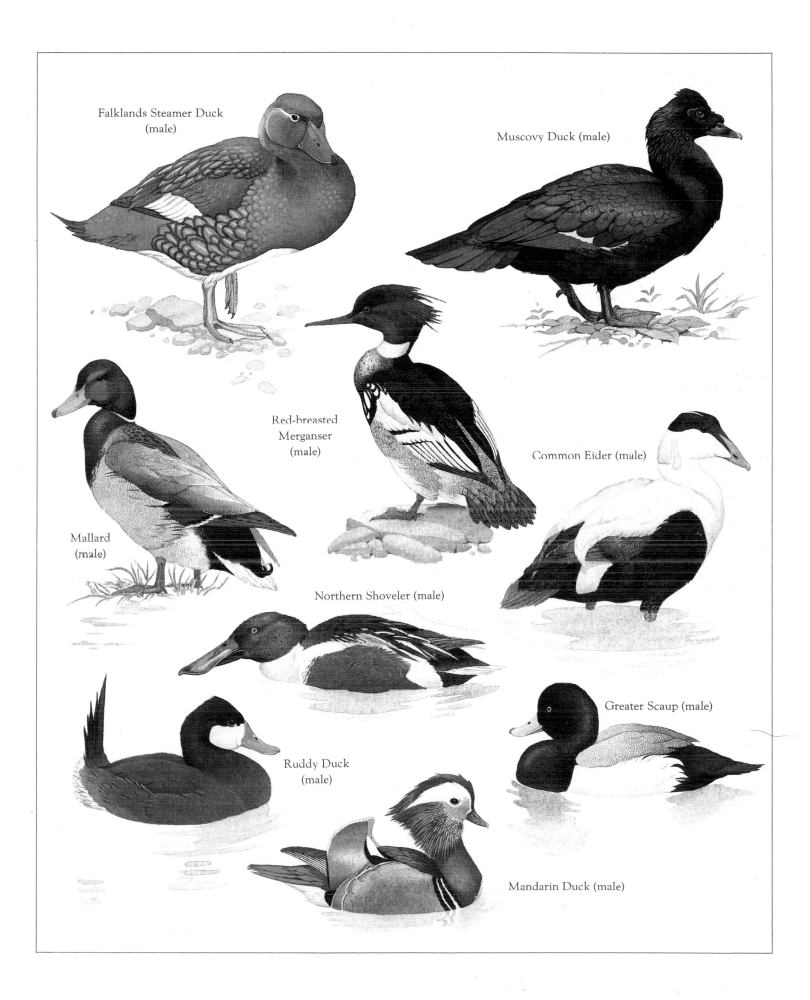

Falklands Steamer Duck
(male)

Muscovy Duck (male)

Red-breasted
Merganser
(male)

Common Eider (male)

Mallard
(male)

Northern Shoveler (male)

Greater Scaup (male)

Ruddy Duck
(male)

Mandarin Duck (male)

## ORDER FALCONIFORMES

Birds of prey are birds that hunt and kill other animals (particularly the higher vertebrates) for food. They include the specialist nocturnal predators — the owls — and the daytime hunters. The latter group makes up the order Falconiformes. The order contains almost 300 species spread around the world, with general names such as eagle, hawk, falcon and vulture. It contains 2 large and diverse families — the Accipitridae and the Falconidae — and 3 smaller and more specialized families, the Cathartidae (New World vultures), the Pandionidae and the Sagittariidae.

## CATHARTIDAE: New World Vulture Family

There are 7 species of New World vultures and condors, with a geographical range from Tierra del Fuego and the Falkland Islands to as far north as southern Canada. The cathartid vultures are superficially similar to Old World vultures but are, in fact, a quite distinct family, as internal anatomical features show. Nonetheless, like their African cousins, these birds feed on carrion, and their unfeathered heads and necks enable them to plunge into messy carcasses without soiling plumage. The feet, with long toes and weakly hooked claws, are adapted for perching rather than grasping. Vultures and condors are solitary birds, although some do roost in colonies. Nests are usually made in hollow trees. Males and females look alike.

NAME: **King Vulture, *Sarcoramphus papa***
RANGE: **Mexico to Argentina**
HABITAT: **tropical forest, savanna**
SIZE: **79 cm (31 in)**

The king is a medium-sized vulture with broad wings and tail. The featherless skin on its head is marked with extraordinary, garish patterns. It is reputed to kill live animals but feeds mainly on carrion. As its name suggests, this big-billed bird takes precedence over other vultures at carcasses. Carrion can be hard to spot in the dense tropical forest, so the king vulture is one of the few birds that relies heavily on its sense of smell to detect food. Stranded fish on riverbanks are an important food item.

The breeding habits of this vulture are poorly known, but in one observation an egg was laid in a hollow tree stump and incubated by both parents. Young king vultures in their first full plumage have black feathers. The brilliant facial markings and creamy plumage develop over the first 2 years.

NAME: California Condor, *Gymnogyps californianus*
RANGE: USA: California
HABITAT: **mountains**
SIZE: 114–140 cm (45–55 in)            Ⓔ

One of the largest birds in the world, this immense vulture is also one of the heaviest flying birds at over 11 kg (25 lb). The range of this bird was once much larger, but the population has declined drastically because of the destruction of its habitat and the onslaught of hunters, and the species is now probably on the verge of extinction. The condor is fully protected under the United States Endangered Species Act and by California law. There are plans to breed the condors in captivity as a last attempt to save the species.

A spectacular bird in flight, with its extremely long, broad wings, the California condor soars at great heights and can glide as far as 16 km (10 mi) without wing movements. It must have the right air conditions for soaring and may stay at its roost in bad weather or on calm days. The California condor spends at least 15 hours a day at the roosting area; outside of the breeding season, roosting and foraging are its main activities. It feeds on carrion, mostly large animals, and is not known to attack living creatures.

At the start of the breeding season, the male displays to his prospective mate. The female lays her egg on the ground in a cave or hole in a cliff. Both parents incubate in shifts. The young bird is fed and tended by the parents for over a year; thus California condors can breed only every other year.

NAME: **Turkey Vulture, *Cathartes aura***
RANGE: **temperate and tropical N. and South America**
HABITAT: **plains, desert, forest**
SIZE: 66–132 cm (26–52 in)

Also known as the turkey buzzard, this most widespread New World vulture soars over open country in search of carrion. It feeds on waste of all sorts, including sea lion excrement, rotten fruit and vegetables and carrion of small animals. Turkey vultures have been trapped and destroyed in many parts of their range because they are mistakenly believed to carry anthrax and other diseases of livestock. They are, however, pests on some Peruvian guano islands, where they take eggs and young birds.

At night groups of 30 or more birds roost together, but this is really the only time that turkey vultures are social. No real nest is made at breeding time; the female lays her 2 eggs in a cave or in a hollow log on the ground. Both parents incubate the eggs and care for the young.

## SAGITTARIIDAE: Secretary Bird Family

This family contains only 1 species, an eaglelike bird with a distinctive crest, elongated tail feathers and long legs. Male and female look alike, but females are slightly smaller.

NAME: **Secretary Bird, *Sagittarius serpentarius***
RANGE: **Africa, south of the Sahara**
HABITAT: **open, grassy country**
SIZE: **150 cm (59 in)**

The secretary bird spends most of its time on the ground, walking with long strides, and may cover 30 km (20 mi) or so every day. It can run to catch prey, which it takes with a swift thrust of its head; it kills larger animals by stamping on them. Small mammals, insects, some birds and eggs, reptiles, in fact almost anything crawling on the ground, are the secretary bird's prey.

In the breeding season, pairs are strongly territorial and chase intruders off their breeding range. The nest is usually on top of a tree and is made of sticks and turf, lined with grass and leaves. The female incubates the 2 or 3 eggs.

## PANDIONIDAE: Osprey Family

This family contains only 1 species, the hawklike osprey. Male and female look alike.

NAME: **Osprey, *Pandion haliaetus***
RANGE: **almost worldwide**
HABITAT: **lakes, rivers, coasts**
SIZE: **53–62 cm (21–24 in)**

The osprey, or fish hawk, feeds almost exclusively on fish; the soles of its feet are studded with small spikes to help grip the slippery prey. When hunting, the osprey flies over water and, when it sights a fish, may hover briefly. It then plunges into the water, feet forward, sometimes completely submerging, sometimes alighting quite gently. It grasps the fish in both feet and returns to feed at its perch. If fish are not available, the osprey feeds on small mammals and wounded birds.

At breeding time, the pair makes a large nest on the ground, using sticks, seaweed and other debris. The same nest may be repaired and used year after year and becomes huge. A clutch of 2 to 4 eggs, usually 3, is incubated mainly by the female. The male brings food during incubation and for the first 4 weeks of the fledgling period. After breeding, northern populations migrate south for the winter.

California Condor

Turkey Vulture

Osprey

Secretary Bird

King Vulture

# Hawks

**NAME: Egyptian Vulture,** *Neophron percnopterus*
**RANGE: S. Europe, Africa, Middle East, India**
**HABITAT: open country**
**SIZE: 60–70 cm (23½–27½ in)**

The Egyptian vulture is a small species which defers to larger vultures at a carcass and so must often be content with scraps. It also feeds on insects and on ostrich and flamingo eggs and is one of the very few creatures to use a tool: in order to break into a huge ostrich egg, the vulture will drop rocks on it until it cracks open. This vulture often scavenges on all kinds of refuse, including human excrement.

Display flights of swoops and dives precede mating, and the pair builds a nest on a crag or on a building. The female lays 1 or 2 eggs, which both parents incubate for about 42 days.

**NAME: Lammergeier/Bearded Vulture,** *Gypaetus barbatus*
**RANGE: S. Europe, Africa, India, Tibet**
**HABITAT: mountains**
**SIZE: 95–105 cm (37–41 in)**

An uncommon and magnificent bird, the lammergeier descends from the mountains only to forage for food. It spends most of its day on the wing, soaring with unequaled grace. It feeds on carrion of all sorts, including human, but defers to larger vultures at carcasses. As one of the last in line, the lammergeier is often left with the bones, and it has developed the knack of dropping them on rocks to split them and reveal the marrow.

Each breeding pair holds a large territory, and the birds perform spectacular diving and swooping flight displays. They nest in cliff niches or on ledges and lay 1 or 2 eggs, which are incubated for 53 days. Normally only 1 chick is reared.

**NAME: Lappet-faced Vulture,** *Torgos tracheliotus*
**RANGE: Africa**
**HABITAT: bush, desert**
**SIZE: 100–115 cm (39–45 in)**

The lappet-faced is a typical Old World vulture with perfect adaptations for a scavenging life. Its powerful hooked bill cuts easily into carrion, and its bare head and neck save lengthy feather-cleaning after plunging deep into a messy carcass. The immense broad wings, with widely spaced primary feathers, are ideal for soaring and gliding for long periods, using few wing beats. No real mating display has been observed. A huge stick nest is made at the top of a tree or on a crag, and the female lays 1 egg.

## ACCIPITRIDAE: Hawk Family

This is the largest family in the Falconiformes order and contains about 217 species of diverse predatory and carrion-eating birds. Representatives occur in almost all regions of the world except Antarctica, northern parts of the Arctic and small oceanic islands.

It is hard to generalize about the typical accipiter since the family contains so many different types and sizes of bird, and, in addition to the predatory forms, the family also includes the 14 or so carrion-feeding Old World vultures. Apart from the vultures, the family includes the "true hawks" (including buzzards and eagles), harrier eagles and serpent eagles, harriers, kites and fish eagles, honey buzzards and a few other specialized types.

Among these birds, the female is significantly larger than the male in almost every case, excluding the vultures. Characteristic physical features of this family are the down-curved, pointed beak, the base of which is covered with a fleshy cere carrying the external nostrils, and large wings with rounded tips and often barred or streaked underparts. All the birds have widely spaced toes and long, sharp, curving claws. On the soles of the feet are roughened, bulging pads to facilitate the seizing of prey.

Most species nest in trees, while some of the larger eagles and buzzards use cliff ledges. These large species are long-lived birds which reach breeding maturity slowly. They have small clutches of only 1 or 2 eggs.

**NAME: Honey Buzzard,** *Pernis apivorus*
**RANGE: Eurasia, Indonesia**
**HABITAT: woodland**
**SIZE: 52–61 cm (20½–24 in)**

The honey buzzard has broad, barred wings, a long tail and specially adapted feathers to protect it from the stings of bees and wasps whose nests it attacks. Larvae and honey are a major food source for this bird, and it also feeds on live wasps, skillfully nipping off the sting before swallowing them. Some small vertebrates and flying termites also feature in the honey buzzard's diet.

A mating pair holds a home territory, and the male performs a distinctive display flight, striking his wings together above his head. They make a tree nest of sticks and leaves. Both parents incubate the clutch of 1 to 3 eggs for 30 to 35 days and feed the young. Northern Eurasian populations migrate south to Africa in winter.

**NAME: Red Kite,** *Milvus milvus*
**RANGE: Europe, W. Asia, N. Africa**
**HABITAT: woodland, open country**
**SIZE: 61–66 cm (24–26 in)**

The red kite is a large bird with long wings and a distinctive, deeply forked tail. It breeds in woodland but hunts in open country. As it flies low over fields, it searches for prey. It can hover briefly and pursues its quarry with great agility. Small mammals up to the size of a weasel, birds, reptiles, frogs, fish, insects and carrion are all eaten, and red kites also kill domestic poultry.

A breeding pair nests in a tree, often adding sticks and oddments to an old nest. Between 1 and 5 eggs, usually 3, are laid, and the female undertakes most of the 28- to 30-day incubation; the male brings her food and takes over from time to time.

**NAME: Brahminy Kite,** *Haliastur indus*
**RANGE: India, S. China, Australasia**
**HABITAT: near water, coasts**
**SIZE: 46 cm (18 in)**

The brahminy kite feeds on frogs, crabs, snakes, fish, insects and some carrion. It also scavenges around human habitation for all kinds of scraps and refuse. At the breeding site the birds perform display flights before starting to build a nest. The nest is made of sticks and lined with leaves and is sited in a tree or among mangroves. The female lays 1 to 4 eggs, which she incubates for 26 or 27 days while her mate keeps her supplied with food.

**NAME: Everglade/Snail Kite,** *Rostrhamus sociabilis*
**RANGE: USA: Florida; Caribbean, Mexico, Central and South America**
**HABITAT: freshwater marshes**
**SIZE: 38 cm (15 in)**

The Everglade kite feeds solely on water snails of the genus *Pomacea*; the elongated upper bill is an adaptation for this curious diet. The kite flaps slowly over the water on its large broad wings. When it sights a snail, it swoops down, grasps it with one foot and takes it back to a perch. Standing on one foot, the kite holds the snail in such a way that it can emerge from the shell. The instant the snail appears, the kite strikes it with its sharp bill; the blow damages the snail's nervous system and its impaled body goes limp. The kite shakes the snail free, and the empty shell falls to the ground.

Nests of breeding pairs are simple structures in marsh grass or bushes. The female lays 3 or 4 eggs, and both parents incubate the clutch and care for the young. This unusual bird is now rare, particularly in Florida, and is protected by conservation laws.

Red Kite

Lammergeier

Brahminy Kite

Honey Buzzard

Lappet-faced Vulture

Everglade Kite

Egyptian Vulture

# Hawks

**NAME: Bald Eagle,** *Haliaeetus leucocephalus*
**RANGE: N. America**
**HABITAT: coasts, rivers and lakes**
**SIZE: 81–102 cm (32–40 in)**

The national symbol of the USA, the bald eagle is one of 8 species of eagle in the genus *Haliaeetus*, all with a liking for fish. Most of the others are called "sea" or "fish" eagles and are coastal birds. Dead and dying fish are the staple diet of the bald eagle, but it also takes live fish from the water and catches some birds and mammals. Groups of these impressive birds gather where food is available, particularly by rivers near the Alaskan coast, where they prey on exhausted salmon migrating upriver.

Bald eagles breed in northern North America on inland lakes, migrating south, if necessary, in the winter to find food. Pairs remain together and reestablish bonds each year with spectacular courtship displays, when the birds lock talons in midair and somersault down together. The nest is made of sticks and sited in a large tree or on rocks. It is added to, year after year, and can be as large as 2.5 m (8 ft) across and 3.5 m (11½ ft) deep, one of the largest of all birds' nests. Most of the time the female incubates the 1 to 3 eggs, but the male takes an occasional turn. The young remain in the nest for 10 or 11 weeks and are aggressive and competitive. Often the youngest of the brood is starved or killed.

All populations of this fine eagle have declined, seriously in some areas. It has suffered from the contamination of its habitat and prey by toxic chemicals, and with its slow breeding rate, it is hard for the species to recover.

**NAME: Palm-nut Vulture,** *Gypohierax angolensis*
**RANGE: Africa, south of the Sahara**
**HABITAT: forest, mangrove swamps, savanna**
**SIZE: 71 cm (28 in)**

This curious bird resembles both vultures and sea eagles, and some authorities believe it to be a link between them. It feeds almost exclusively on the husk of the fruit of the oil palm, *Elaeis guineensis*, and its distribution virtually coincides with that of the plant. The diet is supplemented with fruit of the raphia palm, crabs, mollusks, snails and locusts, but all are rejected in favor of oil palm. A sedentary bird, the palm-nut vulture tends to stay around the same haunts and may remain near its breeding grounds all year. A pair builds a nest in a tree, using sticks and pieces of oil palm, or repairs an old nest. The female lays 1 egg, which is incubated for about 44 days.

**NAME: Bateleur,** *Terathopius ecaudatus*
**RANGE: Africa, south of the Sahara**
**HABITAT: savanna and plains**
**SIZE: 80–85 cm (31½–33½ in)**
**wingspan: 170–180 cm (67–71 in)**

The most interesting bird in a group of birds of prey known as snake eagles or snake hawks, the bateleur has an unmistakable flight silhouette, with its exceptionally long wings and very short tail; its feet project beyond the tail tip in flight. Unlike other snake eagles, the bateleur feeds mostly on carrion but also kills for itself. It makes fierce attacks on other carrion-feeding birds, robbing them of their spoils. A spectacular bird in flight, it soars effortlessly for hours and probably travels about 320 km (200 mi) every day. Once it gets aloft by means of rapid flapping, the bateleur makes scarcely a wing beat, and it performs aerobatic feats such as complete rolls.

Breeding pairs nest in trees and make compact, cup-shaped nests of sticks. A third adult is often present throughout the whole breeding cycle — an unusual occurrence in the bird world which has not been fully explained. The third adult does not incubate or visit the actual nest but roosts nearby with the male and appears at the nest if an intruder troubles the parents. This habit may be a development of the tendency of juvenile and subadult birds to stay near the parents' nest during breeding. The single egg is normally incubated by the female for about 42 days. The young bird is particularly weak at first but has a long fledgling period, during which it is fed by both parents.

**NAME: Crested Serpent Eagle,** *Spilornis cheela*
**RANGE: India to S. China; S.E. Asia, Indonesia**
**HABITAT: forest**
**SIZE: 51–71 cm (20–28 in)**

The crested serpent eagle is a variable species and the many races differ in size and plumage tones. The birds soar above the land, calling occasionally, but do not hunt in the air; they generally catch prey by dropping down on it from a perch. Like other snake eagles, the crested serpent eagle feeds mainly on reptiles, particularly tree snakes; its feet, with short, strong, rough-surfaced toes, are adapted for grasping its slippery prey.

A pair often remains together all year. In the breeding season, the birds perform flight displays, then build a small nest of sticks in a tree. The female incubates her 1 egg for about 35 days, and the male supplies her with food.

**NAME: African Harrier Hawk,** *Polyboroides typus*
**RANGE: Africa, south of the Sahara**
**HABITAT: forest**
**SIZE: 63 cm (25 in)**

The African harrier hawk is a long-tailed, long-legged bird with a bare-skinned face. The young of other birds are its main source of food, although it also eats other creatures and the fruit of the oil palm. It clambers about on trees with great agility, searching for nests, and even hangs upside down, with wings flapping, to attack pendulous weaver-bird nests. The hawks' own nest is built in a tree, and both parents incubate the 1 to 5 eggs for about 40 days.

**NAME: Northern Harrier/Marsh Hawk,** *Circus cyaneus*
**RANGE: Holarctic**
**HABITAT: moors, marshes, plains**
**SIZE: 44–52 cm (17–20½ in)**

A widely distributed bird, the northern harrier breeds in North America, Europe and Asia, then migrates south of its breeding grounds in winter. There are 10 species of harrier, all in the genus *Circus*. All hunt by flying low over the ground, carefully searching the area for prey. Once a creature is spotted, the harrier drops down on it and kills it on the ground.

Northern harriers feed on small mammals, birds, including those wounded by hunters, and some reptiles, frogs and insects. A nest is made on the ground in marshy land or among low vegetation, and the average clutch contains 4 to 6 eggs. The female incubates the eggs and the male brings food, both during this period and after the chicks hatch.

**NAME: Dark Chanting Goshawk,** *Melierax metabates*
**RANGE: W. central Africa; Middle East**
**HABITAT: bush, scrub**
**SIZE: 38–48 cm (15–19 in)**

The handsome dark chanting goshawk perches on a vantage point in a tree or bush ready to glide swiftly down to take prey on the ground. The bird's long legs enable it to pursue quarry on the ground too, where it runs quickly, like a small secretary bird. Lizards, snakes and insects are the chief prey, but small mammals and ground birds are also caught.

At the onset of the breeding season, the male bird chants his melodious song to attract the female, and the two fly together over the breeding site. A small nest of sticks and mud is built in a tree, and the female lays 1 or 2 eggs.

The habits of the closely related pale chanting goshawk, M. *canorus*, are almost identical.

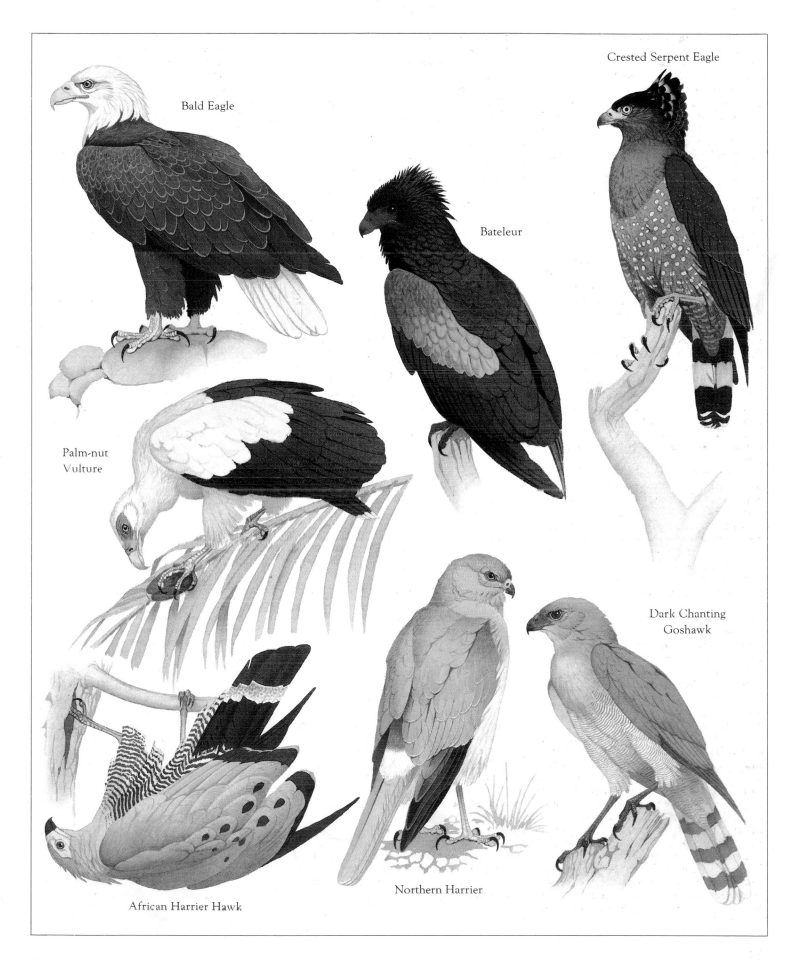

Bald Eagle

Crested Serpent Eagle

Bateleur

Palm-nut
Vulture

Dark Chanting
Goshawk

African Harrier Hawk

Northern Harrier

# Hawks

NAME: Goshawk, *Accipiter gentilis*
RANGE: N. America, Europe, Iran, Tibet, Japan
HABITAT: forest, woodland
SIZE: 51–66 cm (20–26 in)
  wingspan: 120 cm (47¼ in)

These aggressive hawks are the largest birds in the genus *Accipiter* and are efficient killers. They fly through the forest, weaving skillfully in and out of trees, and sometimes soar over the tree-tops. They kill prey with a viselike grip of the powerful talons, then pluck it (if a bird) and eat it on the ground. A goshawk is capable of killing birds as large as pheasant and grouse and mammals the size of rabbits and hares. The birds are often trained for falconry.

Goshawk pairs usually mate for life. They winter alone and in the spring meet at the breeding grounds, where they perform flight displays. A new nest is made in a tree or an old nest is repaired. The pair roost together while building the nest and perform a screaming duet each day before sunrise. They mate about 10 times a day during the egg-laying period, which lasts 6 to 8 weeks.

The clutch contains from 1 to 5 eggs, usually 3, but the number is affected by the availability of suitable prey. The female incubates the clutch for 36 to 38 days; the male brings her food and takes over occasionally. Some northern populations of goshawks migrate south after breeding.

NAME: Cooper's Hawk, *Accipiter cooperii*
RANGE: S. Canada, USA, N. Mexico
HABITAT: woodland
SIZE: 36–51 cm (14–20 in)

Cooper's hawk is a medium-sized bird with rounded wings and tail and is a typical accipiter in its habits. It lives in the cover of woodland and ventures out to find prey. When hunting, Cooper's hawk usually perches and watches for prey, waits until its quarry is looking away, then quickly swoops down and seizes it. Bobwhites, starlings, blackbirds, chipmunks and squirrels are common prey. The hawk also pursues creatures on the ground, half running and half flying.

At the breeding site, the male defends a territory, and when a female appears, he feeds her; both then perform courtship flights. The clutch is usually 4 or 5 eggs, sometimes 6, and the female does most of the incubation. An attentive mother, she helps the chicks to emerge from their shells and feeds and guards them closely in the first weeks of life. Some northern populations migrate south after breeding.

NAME: Fishing Buzzard, *Busarellus nigricollis*
RANGE: tropical lowlands, Mexico to Paraguay and Argentina
HABITAT: open country near water
SIZE: 46–51 cm (18–20 in)

A specialized hawk, the fishing buzzard has long, broad wings, a short, broad tail and a slightly hooked bill. The bottoms of its toes are covered with tiny prickly spines — an adaptation for catching and holding fish. In open areas the fishing buzzard can swoop down and catch its prey while scarcely wetting its plumage; elsewhere it will plunge into the water to fish, then sit drying its wings.

NAME: Buzzard, *Buteo buteo*
RANGE: breeds in Europe, Asia to Japan; winters in E. Africa, India, Malaya and S. China
HABITAT: woodland, moorland
SIZE: 51–56 cm (20–22 in)

The buzzard is not a bold hunter and spends more time perching than on the wing; once aloft it soars well. It feeds mainly on small ground mammals up to the size of rabbits, reptiles, insects, carrion and some ground birds. It kills most of its prey by dropping on it from its perch or from hovering flight and nearly always kills on the ground.

The size of the buzzard's breeding territory varies from year to year, according to food supplies. Courtship flights are uncharacteristically energetic, and the birds dive and swoop with vigor. A nest is made on a tree or crag, and the female lays 2 to 6 eggs.

NAME: Red-tailed Hawk, *Buteo jamaicensis*
RANGE: N. and Central America, West Indies
HABITAT: varied: deserts, forest, mountains
SIZE: 46–61 cm (18–24 in)

A powerful, thickset, aggressive bird with a loud voice and a distinctive chestnut tail, the red-tailed hawk tolerates a wide variety of habitats, probably more than any other North American hawk. It is an opportunistic hunter, and although its staple diet is rodents and rabbits, it also eats snakes, lizards, birds and insects. It hunts on the wing or from a perch, swooping down on prey.

Pairs display over the breeding territory. A nest is made of twigs high in a tree or, in the desert, on a cactus plant. The female hawk remains on or near the nest for some weeks before laying her clutch of 1 to 4 eggs. Her mate feeds her throughout this period. Both parents share the incubation, which lasts from 28 to 32 days. The young birds are able to feed themselves at 4 or 5 weeks.

NAME: Harpy Eagle, *Harpia harpyja*
RANGE: S. Mexico to N. Argentina
HABITAT: lowland rain forest
SIZE: 90 cm (35½ in)                    ®

A formidable bird, the harpy is the world's largest eagle. It has huge feet, each the size of a man's hand, equipped with lethally sharp talons. Its broad wings are short for a bird of its size and enable it to maneuver through dense forest. The harpy flies from tree to tree, looking and listening for prey, and can give chase through the branches with great agility. Arboreal mammals, such as monkeys, sloths, opossums, coati and tree porcupines, are its primary source of food, and it occasionally catches large birds.

The harpy's nest is a platform of sticks placed high in the tallest trees. Because these nests are perhaps 45 m (150 ft) up from the forest floor, observations of egg-laying and care of the young are few, but the bird is believed to lay 2 eggs. The young birds remain with their parents for a long time, perhaps a year, and it seems certain that harpy eagles breed only every other year. Now rare, harpy eagles have declined in numbers, largely because of the destruction of vast areas of their habitat. They have also been relentlessly shot by hunters. Although nominally protected by law, any measures are difficult to enforce in the remote areas where the harpy is likely to occur.

NAME: Golden Eagle, *Aquila chrysaetos*
RANGE: Holarctic, as far south as N. Africa and Mexico
HABITAT: moor, mountain forest
SIZE: 76–89 cm (30–35 in)

These magnificent birds are probably the most numerous large eagles in the world. The golden eagle is a formidable predator, equipped with huge feet with long curved claws, a hooked bill and exceptionally sharp-sighted eyes. When hunting, the golden eagle soars for long periods searching for prey, then makes a rapid dive down to seize and kill the animal with its crushing talons. Most food is taken on the ground, and mammals such as hares and rabbits are the chief prey. Grouse and other birds are also caught, and carrion is an important food source.

Golden eagles perform spectacular flight displays over the nest site. The nest is made high on a ledge or tree and is often repaired and reused. Some pairs have several nests, used in rotation. The 2 eggs are usually incubated by the female, but the male takes an occasional turn. In 80 percent of observed cases, the first chick to hatch killed the younger, unhindered by the mother.

Cooper's Hawk

Goshawk

Buzzard

Fishing Buzzard

Red-tailed Hawk

Harpy Eagle

Golden Eagle

# Falcons

NAME: **Caracara,** *Polyborus plancus*
RANGE: **S. USA; South America**
HABITAT: **open country**
SIZE: **56–61 cm (22–24 in)**

Caracaras are a group of neotropical birds quite unlike the rest of the falcons. They eat all kinds of animals, from insects to mammals, and also scavenge on carrion. Both members of a breeding pair build the nest, usually in a tree or on the ground. The female lays 2 to 4 eggs, and both parents incubate the eggs for a total of 28 days and care for the young. The young remain in the nest for 2 or 3 months, being fed by their parents.

NAME: **Barred Forest Falcon,** *Micrastur ruficollis*
RANGE: **S. Mexico to N. Argentina**
HABITAT: **forest**
SIZE: **33–38 cm (13–15 in)**

One of a group of 5 neotropical forest falcons, the barred forest falcon is well adapted for life in dense jungle. A long-legged, short-winged bird, it flies deftly through the trees and waits in cover to attack prey. It feeds on small mammals, lizards and birds and often hunts the birds that follow army ants. Little is known of its breeding habits.

NAME: **Collared Falconet,** *Microhierax caerulescens*
RANGE: **Himalayas, N. India, S.E. Asia**
HABITAT: **forest**
SIZE: **19 cm ($7\frac{1}{2}$ in)**

The 8 species of falconet are the smallest birds of prey. All have similar habits. The collared falconet hunts its food more in the manner of a flycatcher than a true falcon; it makes short flights from a perch to catch insects and, occasionally, small birds. It lays 4 to 5 eggs in a hole in a tree.

NAME: **Kestrel,** *Falco tinnunculus*
RANGE: **Europe, Asia, Africa**
HABITAT: **open country, plains, cultivated land**
SIZE: **34–38 cm ($13\frac{1}{4}$–15 in)**

Kestrels hunt over open ground and are the hovering specialists. They fly some 10 to 15 m (30 to 50 ft) above ground to search an area, hover and watch and, if something is sighted, drop gently down on it. The staple diet of kestrels consists of small mammals, but they also catch small birds, reptiles and insects. The clutch of 4 to 9 eggs is laid on a ledge, in a hole in a tree or in the old nest of another bird. The female does the greater share of the incubation, which lasts 27 to 29 days. She remains with the chicks when they are first hatched and the male brings food, but later she leaves them to assist her mate.

## FALCONIDAE: Falcon Family

The 60 species of falcon are all daytime-hunting birds of prey. They are found nearly all over the world. In appearance they are close to similar-sized accipiters, having sharp curved claws and powerful hooked beaks. Most species, however, have long pointed wings in contrast to the more rounded, slotted outlines of accipiters. There are also specific skeletal differences between the groups, such as details of skull structure and breastbones. Many falcons have so-called "tomial" teeth — cutting edges on the upper bill with corresponding notches in the lower bill. Males and females look similar, but females are generally larger.

The family is divided into 4 subfamilies: caracaras, laughing falcons, forest falcons, and the main subfamily, Falconinae, which includes falconets, pygmy falcons and the typical falcons of the genus *Falco*, of which there are some 37 species. Falcons (except caracaras) do not build nests.

NAME: **Hobby,** *Falco subbuteo*
RANGE: **Britain to China; winters in Africa and the Far East**
HABITAT: **open country, bush, savanna**
SIZE: **30–36 cm (12–14 in)**

Hobbies are small, long-winged falcons found all over the Old World. All are exceedingly swift in flight and catch almost all their prey on the wing. They are specialists in taking flying prey (birds, insects, bats) from a swarm or flock and can even catch swallows and swifts. In the breeding season, pairs perform mutual aerobatic displays with great speed and agility. The 2 or 3 eggs are laid in an old abandoned nest of another bird. The female does most of the incubation, and her mate feeds her.

NAME: **Brown Falcon/Hawk,** *Falco berigora*
RANGE: **Australia, New Guinea, Tasmania, Dampier Island**
HABITAT: **open country**
SIZE: **40–51 cm ($15\frac{3}{4}$–20 in)**

The brown falcon is one of the commonest birds of prey in Australia. Its appearance and behavior are more like those of an *Accipiter* hawk than a falcon, hence its name. Less active than other falcons, it spends much time perching but is capable of swift flight. It kills prey on the ground, mammals such as rabbits, young birds, reptiles, insects and some carrion making up its diet. The female lays her 2 to 4 eggs in the abandoned nest of another bird, and both parents incubate.

NAME: **Gyrfalcon,** *Falco rusticolus*
RANGE: **Arctic Europe, Asia, N. America, Greenland, Iceland**
HABITAT: **mountains, tundra**
SIZE: **51–63 cm (20–25 in)**

An impressive bird and the largest of the falcons, the gyrfalcon has a stockier build than the peregrine. Plumage can be dark, white or gray. Most breed north of the timberline and remain in the Arctic all year, but some populations migrate south for the winter. When hunting, the gyrfalcon flies swiftly near the ground. It can make rapid dives on prey, like the peregrine, but this is less characteristic. Birds are its main prey, although it feeds on some mammals, particularly in winter. Rock ptarmigan and willow grouse make up the bulk of the gyrfalcon's diet, and their numbers can affect its breeding rate. In years when these birds are abundant, gyrfalcons produce large clutches, but in years of scarcity they lay only a couple of eggs or do not breed at all.

Gyrfalcons perform display flights when courting. The female lays 2 to 7 eggs on a ledge or in an old cliff nest. She incubates the clutch for 27 to 29 days, during which her mate brings her food. When the young hatch, both parents bring food to them.

NAME: **Peregrine Falcon,** *Falco peregrinus*
RANGE: **almost worldwide**
HABITAT: **varied, often mountains and sea cliffs**
SIZE: **38–51 cm (15–20 in)** Ⓥ

The 17 races of this widespread bird vary greatly in plumage color. The peregrine's wings are tapered and pointed and its tail slim and short; it is virtually without equal in the speed and precision of its flight. Birds are its chief prey. The peregrine makes a dramatic, high-speed, near-vertical dive at its prey, then kills it outright with its talons or seizes it and takes it to the ground to eat. The peregrine can also chase prey through the air, changing direction with supreme ease. It is the most highly prized bird for falconry.

At the onset of the breeding season, peregrines perform spectacular flight displays. The 2 to 6 eggs are laid on a ledge site, on the ground or even on a city building. The female does most of the incubation, but the male takes an occasional turn and brings food for his mate. When the young are 2 weeks old, the female leaves them in the nest and helps the male find food for them. The young fly at about 40 days old. These birds are seriously declining in numbers, partly because of the incidental ingestion of pesticides, which reach them via insect-feeding birds.

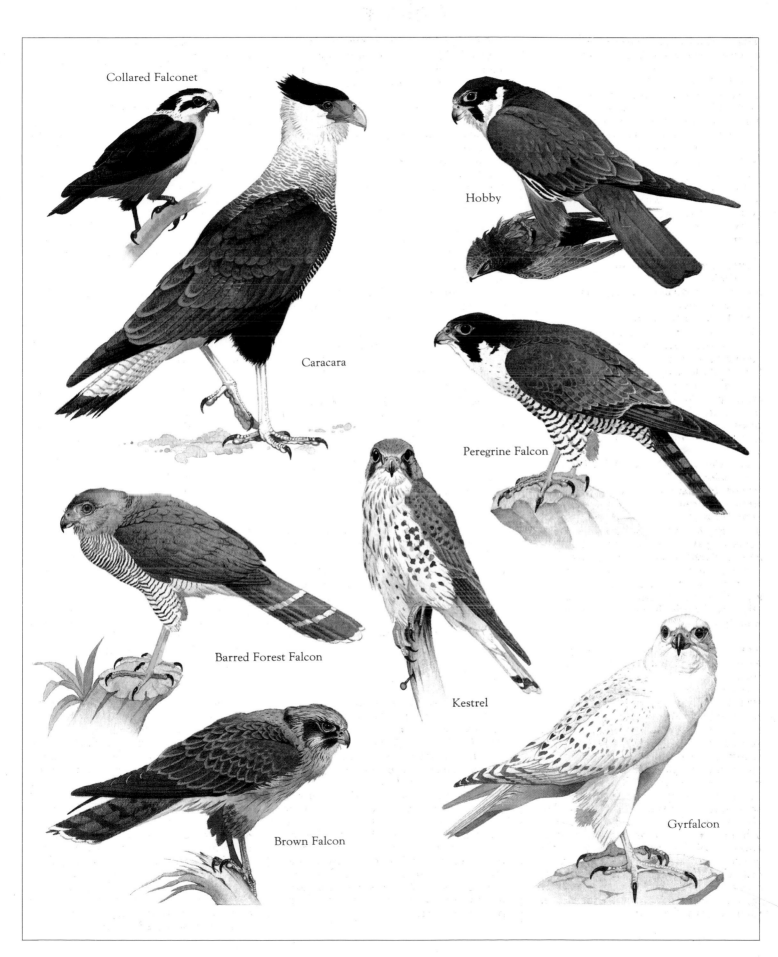

Collared Falconet

Caracara

Hobby

Peregrine Falcon

Barred Forest Falcon

Kestrel

Brown Falcon

Gyrfalcon

# Megapodes, Curassows, Hoatzin

## ORDER GALLIFORMES

This order includes the megapodes, curassows, hoatzin, and pheasants and their relatives. Most are ground-living birds, but curassows and hoatzins are arboreal.

## MEGAPODIIDAE:
### Megapode Family

The 12 species in this family all occur in Australasia and Indonesia. Males and females look more or less alike, and all have large, strong legs and feet. They feed on insects, small vertebrate animals, seeds and fruit.

Megapodes do not brood their eggs in the normal way but lay them in mounds of decaying vegetation or sand and allow them to be incubated by natural heat.

NAME: **Malleefowl,** *Leipoa ocellata*
RANGE: **S. Australia**
HABITAT: **mallee (arid eucalyptus woodland)**
SIZE: **55–61 cm (21½–24 in)**

Despite its arid habitat, the male malleefowl manages to create an efficient incubator mound, which he is engaged in tending for much of the year. In winter, he digs a pit and fills it with plant material. Once this has been moistened by the winter rains, he covers it with sand, and the sealed-off vegetation starts to rot and build up heat. The malleefowl keeps a constant check on the temperature by probing the mound with his beak and keeps it to about 33°C (91°F). He controls any fluctuations by opening the mound to cool it or by piling on more sand.

The laying season lasts some time, since the female lays her 15 to 35 eggs one at a time, at intervals of several days, in holes made in the mound by the male. The chicks hatch about 7 weeks after laying and struggle out unaided. They are wholly independent and can fly within a day.

NAME: **Common Scrubfowl,** *Megapodius freycinet*
RANGE: **E. Indonesia to Melanesia; N. and N.E. Australia**
HABITAT: **rain forest and drier areas**
SIZE: **45 cm (17¾ in)**

An active, noisy bird, the scrubfowl seldom flies but seeks refuge in trees if disturbed. In some areas these birds make simple incubation mounds in sand, which are then warmed by the sun or, on some islands, by volcanic activity. In rain forest, they make huge mounds, up to 5 m (16 ft) high, containing decomposing plant material. The eggs are laid in tunnels dug into the mound.

## CRACIDAE: Curassow Family

There are about 44 species in this family, found in the neotropical zone from south Texas to Paraguay. All are nonmigratory forest birds, often adapted for a tree-dwelling life. Many species have crests or casques on their heads.

NAME: **Great Curassow,** *Crax rubra*
RANGE: **Mexico to Ecuador**
HABITAT: **tropical rain forest**
SIZE: **94 cm (37 in)**

Great curassows roost and nest in trees but also spend a good deal of time on the ground. They feed on fruit, leaves and berries. The males have a loud, booming ventriloquial call that seems to be amplified by the elongated trachea. This call is used in courtship display and to threaten other males.

Curassows make an untidy nest of twigs and leaves in a bush or tree. Both parents feed and care for the 2 chicks.

NAME: **Nocturnal Curassow,** *Nothocrax urumutum*
RANGE: **South America: upper Amazon basin**
HABITAT: **tropical rain forest**
SIZE: **66 cm (26 in)**

The nocturnal curassow is, in fact, active during the day, searching for its food. It sings only at night, however, making a booming call, and in males the voice is amplified by means of an extended trachea. The sexes look alike, with bare, brightly colored faces, ample crests and brown and rufous plumage.

NAME: **Crested Guan,** *Penelope purpurascens*
RANGE: **Mexico, south to Venezuela, Ecuador**
HABITAT: **lowland rain forest and drier areas**
SIZE: **89 cm (35 in)**

Primarily tree-living birds, crested guans forage in small groups up in the treetops, walking slowly along the branches and leaping across gaps. They will, however, come down to the ground to collect fallen fruit and seeds and to find drinking water. Male and female birds look alike.

In the breeding season, guans perform a wing-drumming display. While in flight, the bird begins to beat its wings at twice the normal speed, producing a whirring sound that is maintained for several seconds. A bulky nest, sited in a tree, is made from twigs and lined with leaves. The usual clutch is 2 or 3 eggs, and the female guan does most of the incubation.

NAME: **Chachalaca,** *Ortalis vetula*
RANGE: **USA: extreme S. Texas; Mexico, Central America**
HABITAT: **brush, thickets in rain forest; drier areas**
SIZE: **51–61 cm (20–24 in)**

The chachalaca's common name is derived from its three-syllable call, "cha-cha-lak," and, like the curassow's, its voice is amplified by its elongated trachea. Groups of birds set up a deafening chorus, morning and evening.

Primarily a tree-dwelling bird, the chachalaca feeds on berries, fruit, leaves and shoots and some insects. It also comes down to the ground to search for some of its food. A small, frail nest is made of twigs, up in a tree or bush, and the female incubates the clutch of 3 or 4 eggs. Male and female chachalacas look alike.

## OPISTHOCOMIDAE:
### Hoatzin Family

The hoatzin is the sole species in this family. It has some similarity to Galliformes, so has been placed in this order, but the grouping has recently been challenged, and because of its unique characteristics, it is suggested that the hoatzin be placed on its own.

NAME: **Hoatzin,** *Opisthocomus hoazin*
RANGE: **South America: Amazon and Orinoco basins**
HABITAT: **wooded riverbanks**
SIZE: **61 cm (24 in)**

The hoatzin is an unusual-looking bird, with large wings and tail, a long neck and a small head for its size, topped with a ragged crest. Male and female look alike. An arboreal bird, it is a poor flier and uses its wings more for support and balance when climbing and perching than for flying. Hoatzins live in flocks of 10 to 20 individuals and are most active in the mornings and evenings. They feed on fruit and leaves, particularly the tough leaves of mangrove and arum; their digestive tracts are enlarged, which enables them to cope with this bulky vegetation.

The hoatzin builds its untidy stick nest in a tree overhanging water so that, if threatened, the young birds, which can swim, can drop down into the water and so escape danger. There are 2 or 3 eggs in a clutch, and both parents are believed to incubate. The young hoatzin possesses a unique adaptation for arboreal life: there is a pair of hooked claws on the bend of each wing, which help the young bird to clamber nimbly among the trees. These claws are lost as the bird matures.

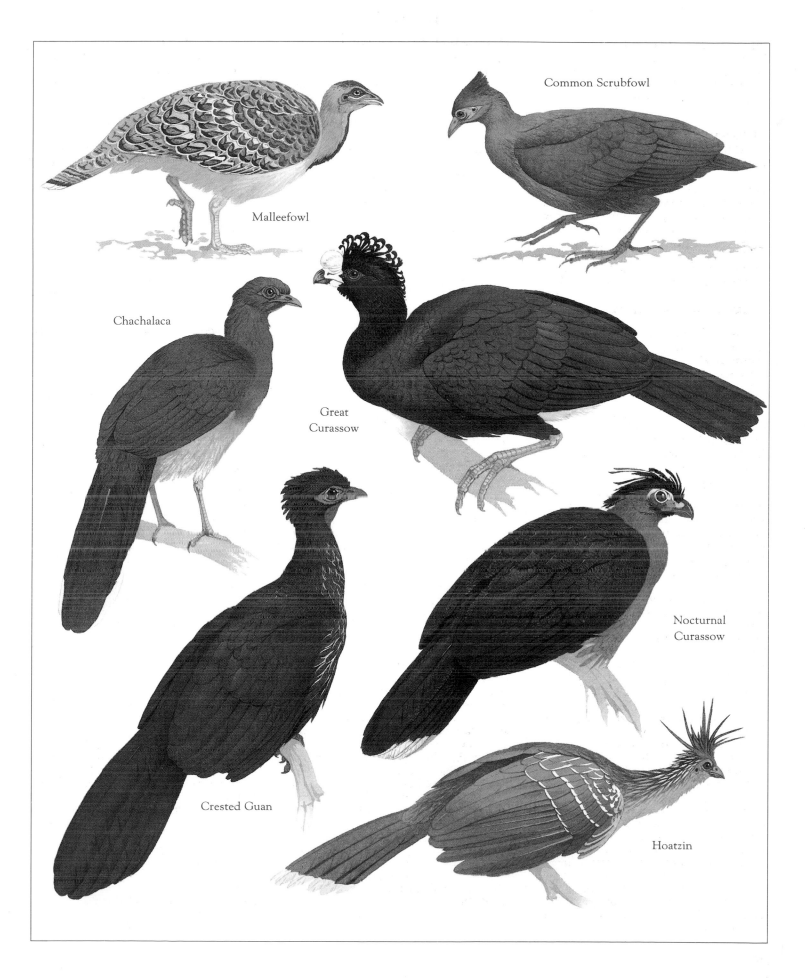

Common Scrubfowl

Malleefowl

Chachalaca

Great
Curassow

Nocturnal
Curassow

Crested Guan

Hoatzin

# Pheasants

NAME: **European Quail,** *Coturnix coturnix*
RANGE: **Europe, Asia, east to Lake Baikal, N. India; Africa; winters Mediterranean coast, Africa, Asia to S. India, Thailand**
HABITAT: **grassland, farmland**
SIZE: **18 cm (7 in)**

One of the smallest birds in the pheasant family, the quail is a neat, rounded bird with a weak bill and legs. The female resembles the male in build but has an unmarked buff throat and a closely spotted breast. A rarely seen bird, the quail forages in the undergrowth and tends to run through vegetation to escape danger, rather than to fly, although it can fly considerable distances when migrating. It feeds mainly on seeds but eats some small invertebrates, particularly in the summer.

Breeding takes place in early summer, and the female lays one clutch of 9 to 15 eggs in a plant-lined scrape on the ground. She incubates her eggs for 16 to 21 days.

NAME: **Painted Quail,** *Excalfactoria chinensis*
RANGE: **India to S.E. China, Malaysia, Indonesia, Australia**
HABITAT: **swamp, grassland**
SIZE: **15 cm (6 in)**

A tiny but distinctive bird, the painted quail is typical of the eastern quails, which are more boldly patterned than the European birds. The female painted quail has duller plumage than the male, mainly buff-colored with a barred breast. Painted quails forage in vegetation and feed on seeds and insects.

The female lays 4 to 8 eggs in a shallow scrape on the ground. She incubates the clutch for about 16 days.

NAME: **Himalayan Snowcock,** *Tetraogallus himalayensis*
RANGE: **W. Himalayas**
HABITAT: **mountain slopes**
SIZE: **72 cm (28¼ in)**

The Himalayan snowcock is one of 7 species of snowcock, all found at high altitudes in Asia. Typical of its group, it is a large bird, with coloration which blends well with its environment. In the early morning, pairs or groups of up to 5 snowcocks fly down the hillsides from their roosts to find water to drink. The rest of the day is spent slowly coming back up, feeding on the way on roots, tubers, green plants, berries and seeds.

Breeding takes place between April and June. The courting males are particularly noisy at this time, making loud five-note whistles. The female lays 5 to 7 eggs in a hollow she scrapes in the ground among stones and rocks. She incubates the clutch for 27 or 28 days.

## PHASIANIDAE: Pheasant Family

This large family contains 5 subfamilies: the grouse, guineafowl, turkey and American quail subfamilies (shown on p.232) and the largest, the pheasant subfamily.

There are about 154 species in the pheasant subfamily (Phasianinae), divided into 3 main groups: partridges, including snowcocks and francolins, Old World quails and the true pheasants. Most are plump, rounded birds which usually feed and nest on the ground but often roost for the night in trees. Their wings are short and powerful and capable of strong but not sustained flight. Most are seed-eating birds which scratch around for food with their stout, unfeathered legs and strong claws, but many also eat insects and other small invertebrates, as well as fruit and berries.

Males and females have different plumage coloration in many species, particularly the larger pheasants. Some of the smaller, plainer birds are monogamous, while in the more ornate species, the males tend to be polygamous. The nest is usually simple, often a scrape on the ground; chicks are born fully covered with down and can leave the nest soon after hatching.

The pheasant subfamily is an Old World group, but many species have been successfully introduced in areas outside their native range. Some are well known as game birds, hunted for sport and eaten by humans.

NAME: **Red-legged Partridge,** *Alectoris rufa*
RANGE: **S.W. Europe to S.E. France, N. Italy, Corsica; introduced in Britain, Azores, Madeira and Canary Islands**
HABITAT: **scrub, moorland, farmland**
SIZE: **32–34 cm (12½–13¼ in)**

A typical partridge, with a larger bill, stronger legs and longer tail than the quails, the red-legged partridge is distinguished by the white stripe above each eye, the black-bordered white throat and red bill and legs. Males and females look alike, but juveniles are less vividly colored. These birds roost in trees and bushes but feed on the ground, mainly on plants, although they occasionally eat insects and frogs. Reluctant to fly, they prefer to escape danger by running.

Breeding begins in April or May. Red-legged partridges are monogamous birds and make long-lasting pair bonds. The female lays 10 to 16 eggs in a shallow scrape, which the male makes on the ground and lines with leaves. The clutch is incubated by both parents for about 23 or 24 days.

NAME: **Red-necked Francolin,** *Francolinus afer*
RANGE: **Africa, south of the equator, except S.W.**
HABITAT: **bush, cultivated land, savanna**
SIZE: **41 cm (16 in)**

The francolins are all large game birds, with strong bills and characteristic patches of bare skin on head or neck. Mainly African birds — over 30 species occur in Africa — a few francolins live in Asia. The red-necked francolin, with the distinctive red skin around its eyes and on its neck, is typical of the group. Its breast is covered with broad dark streaks which help to camouflage it in the open bush country it frequents. Males and females look alike.

In small family groups, francolins forage for plant food and insects. They fly well and take refuge in trees if disturbed. They nest on the ground and females lay 5 to 9 eggs.

NAME: **Red Spurfowl,** *Galloperdix spadicea*
RANGE: **India**
HABITAT: **cultivated land, stony hills**
SIZE: **36 cm (14¼ in)**

A type of partridge, the male red spurfowl has distinctive scalloped plumage and naked red skin around each eye. The female's grayish plumage is barred and spotted with black. Pairs or groups of up to 5 spurfowl forage together, scratching in the undergrowth for seeds, tubers and berries, as well as slugs, snails and termites.

The timing of the breeding season varies from area to area, according to conditions; although this is usually between January and June, it can be at any time of year. The nest is a shallow scrape on the ground among bamboo or scrub, scantily lined with a few leaves or blades of grass. The female lays 3 to 5 eggs which she incubates alone. The male helps to care for the young.

NAME: **Roulroul Partridge,** *Rollulus roulroul*
RANGE: **Burma to Sumatra and Borneo**
HABITAT: **floor of dense forest on lowland or hills**
SIZE: **25.5 cm (10 in)**

The roulroul is the most attractive and unusual of the wood partridges. The male is instantly recognizable by his red, brushlike crest; he also has red skin around the eyes and a red patch on his bill. The female bird has a few long feathers on her head but lacks the crest.

These partridges move in mixed groups of up to 12, occasionally more, feeding on seeds, fruit, insects and snails. Little is known about their breeding habits, but they are thought to lay 5 or 6 eggs.

Red Spurfowl (male)

Red-legged Partridge

Himalayan Snowcock

Painted Quail (male)

Roulroul
Partridge (male)

Red-necked
Francolin

European Quail (male)

# Pheasants

NAME: **Temminck's Tragopan,** *Tragopan temminckii*
RANGE: mountains of W. China, N. Burma and S.E. Tibet
HABITAT: forest
SIZE: 64 cm (25¼ in)

Like all the 5 species of tragopan, the male Temminck's tragopan is a striking bird, with beautiful, elaborate plumage. The female is much plainer, with rufous to grayish-brown plumage on the upperparts and a buff or white throat and light-brown underparts. This tragopan is even more unsocial and more arboreal than other tragopans and prefers cool, damp forest. It feeds on seeds, buds, leaves, berries and insects.

At the start of the breeding season, the male courts his mate, displaying his brilliant plumage. The nest is made in a tree, and the female lays 3 to 6 eggs.

NAME: **Red Junglefowl,** *Gallus gallus*
RANGE: Himalayas to S. China, S.E. Asia, Sumatra, Java; introduced in Sulawesi, Lesser Sunda Islands
HABITAT: forest, scrub, cultivated land
SIZE: 43–76 cm (17–30 in) including tail of 28 cm (11 in) in male

The ancestor of the domestic fowl, the red junglefowl is a beautiful, colorful bird. The female is much smaller and duller than the striking male, however, with mainly brown plumage and some chestnut on the head and neck. Over the range, several races of red junglefowl occur which vary slightly in appearance. They are gregarious birds, gathering in flocks of up to 50 or so to feed on grain, grass shoots and crops, fruit, berries, insects and their larvae.

The breeding season is usually March to May. The female scrapes a hollow in the ground near a bush or bamboo clump and lines it with leaves. She incubates the clutch of 5 or 6 eggs for 19 to 21 days.

NAME: **Gray Peacock Pheasant,** *Polyplectron bicalcaratum*
RANGE: Himalayas to Hainan; S.E. Asia: Burma, Thailand, Indo-China
HABITAT: forest
SIZE: 56–76 cm (22–30 in)

The gray peacock pheasant is one of 6 species in the genus *Polyplectron*, all of which occur in India, Southeast Asia or Sumatra. The female is smaller than the decorative male and has fewer, smaller eyespots, which are black with white borders. They are secretive, yet noisy, birds and feed on grain, fruit, berries and insects.

The male displays to his mate, calling as he spreads his tail and wing coverts. The female lays 2 to 6 eggs in a nest on the ground and incubates the clutch for about 21 days.

NAME: **Golden Pheasant,** *Chrysolophus pictus*
RANGE: W. China; introduced in Britain
HABITAT: scrub on rocky hillsides; introduced in woodland
SIZE: male: 98–108 cm (38½–42½ in)
female: 63–65 cm (24¾–25½ in)

A spectacularly beautiful bird, the male golden pheasant has brilliant plumage and a crest of golden feathers. The female bird is much plainer, with various shades of brown plumage, streaked with black. In the wild, golden pheasants move in pairs or alone and are shy birds, alert to any danger. They have short wings and are reluctant to fly, preferring to run from any threat. Seeds, leaves, shoots and insects are their main foods.

Little is known of the breeding habits of this pheasant in its natural habitat, but in Britain, it makes a shallow scrape on the ground and lines it with plant material. The female lays 5 to 12 eggs, which she incubates for 22 days, apparently hardly ever, if at all, leaving the nest during this period.

NAME: **Ring-necked Pheasant,** *Phasianus colchicus*
RANGE: Caspian area, east across central Asia to China, Korea, Japan and Burma; introduced in Europe, N. America, New Zealand
HABITAT: woodland, forest edge, marshes, agricultural land
SIZE: male: 76–89 cm (30–35 in)
female: 53–64 cm (20¾–25¼ in)

Extremely successful as an introduced species, the ring-necked pheasant is probably the best known of all game birds. So many subspecies have now been introduced and crossed that the plumage of the male is highly variable, but a typical bird has a dark-green head and coppery upperparts, with fine, dark markings; many have a white collar. The female is less variable and has brown plumage.

In the wild, ringnecks feed on plant material, such as seeds, shoots and berries, and on insects and small invertebrates. They are ground-dwelling birds and spend much of their time scratching for food in undergrowth.

Male ringnecks are polygamous and have harems of several females. The female scrapes a shallow hollow in the ground, usually in thick cover, which she lines with plant material. She lays 7 to 15 eggs on consecutive days and begins the 22- to 27-day incubation only when the clutch is complete. The young are tended and led to food by the female, rarely with any help from the male. Ringnecks produce only one brood a season.

NAME: **Indian Peafowl,** *Pavo cristatus*
RANGE: India, Sri Lanka
HABITAT: forest, woodland, cultivated land
SIZE: male: 92 cm–1.2 m (3–4 ft) without train; 2–2.25 m (6½–7¼ ft) in full plumage;
female: 86 cm (33¾ in)

The magnificent Indian peafowl is so widely kept in captivity and in parks and gardens outside its native range that it is a familiar bird in much of the world. The cock is unmistakable, with his iridescent plumage, wiry crest and glittering train, adorned with eyespots. The smaller female, or peahen, has brown and some metallic green plumage and a small crest.

Outside the breeding season, peafowls live in small flocks of 1 male and 3 to 5 hens, but, after breeding, they may split into groups made up of adult males or females and young. They feed in the open, early in the morning and at dusk, and spend much of the rest of the day in thick undergrowth. Seeds, grain, groundnuts, shoots, flowers, berries, insects and small invertebrates are all eaten by these omnivorous birds, and they may destroy crops.

In the breeding season, the male bird displays, fully spreading his erect train to spectacular effect by raising and spreading the tail beneath it. With his wings trailing, he prances and struts in front of the female, periodically shivering the spread train and presenting his back view. The female may respond by a faint imitation of his posture. In the wild, the nest scrape is made in thick undergrowth, and the female incubates her 4 to 6 eggs for about 28 days.

NAME: **Congo Peacock,** *Afropavo congensis*
RANGE: Africa: Congo basin
HABITAT: dense rain forest
SIZE: 60–70 cm (23½–27½ in)

First described in 1936, the Congo peacock is the only native African game bird larger than a francolin. The male bird has dark, glossy plumage and a crest of black feathers on the head, behind a tuft of white bristles. The female has a crest, but no bristles, and is largely rufous brown and black, with some metallic green plumage on her upperparts. The habits of Congo peacocks in the wild have seldom been documented, but they are believed to live in pairs and to take refuge and to roost in trees. They feed on grain and fruit.

Congo peacocks are monogamous in captivity and build a nest of sticks in a tree. The female incubates the 3 or 4 eggs for about 26 days.

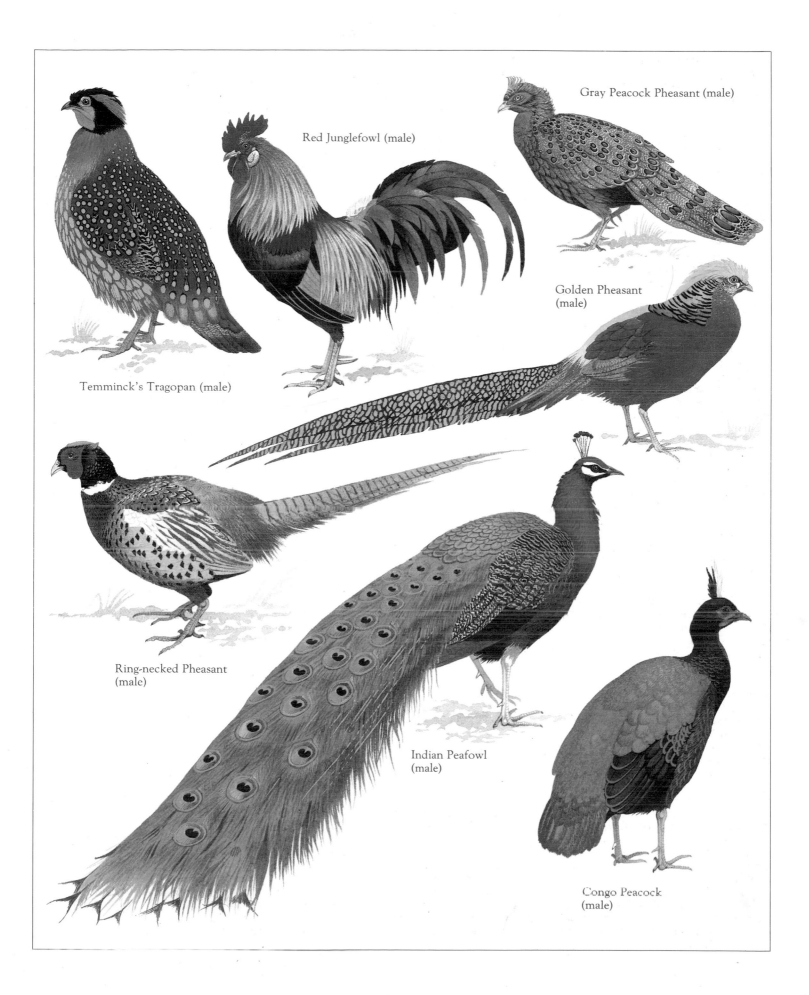

Gray Peacock Pheasant (male)

Red Junglefowl (male)

Golden Pheasant
(male)

Temminck's Tragopan (male)

Ring-necked Pheasant
(male)

Indian Peafowl
(male)

Congo Peacock
(male)

# Grouse, Turkeys, Guineafowl, American Quail

## TETRAONINAE: Grouse Subfamily

The 18 species of grouse are all plump, rounded birds, found in temperate regions of North America, northern Europe and Asia. Many species are hunted for sport and eaten by man. Grouse have short wings and are capable of strong but not prolonged flight; their legs, and sometimes their toes, are feathered. They feed mostly on plant material and some insects.

Many species perform elaborate courtship displays, often communally. Sexes look different in some species. The young are born in a well-developed state, able to leave the nest only hours after hatching, and they require little attention from the parent birds.

NAME: **Black Grouse,** *Tetrao tetrix*
RANGE: **N. Europe, N. Asia**
HABITAT: **moor, forest**
SIZE: **41–51 cm (16–20 in)**

Social display is a particularly well-developed activity in the black grouse. In spring males, or blackcocks, gather at a traditional display ground, known as a lek and used year after year. Each day about sunrise, the males call, dance and posture — each in his own patch of the lek — to attract the watching females. The male black grouse has a distinctive lyre-shaped tail, which he spreads and displays in courtship. Females, or gray-hens, are smaller than males and have mottled brown plumage and forked tails.

Black grouse are polygamous birds, and a successful dominant male may mate with many females. Each female lays a clutch of 6 to 11 eggs in a shallow, leaf-lined hollow on the ground. She incubates the eggs for 24 to 29 days.

NAME: **Greater Prairie Chicken,** *Tympanuchus cupido*
RANGE: **central N. America**
HABITAT: **prairie**
SIZE: **42–46 cm (16½–18 in)**

This increasingly rare bird was once common over a large area of North America. Male and female birds look similar, but females have barred tail feathers and smaller neck sacs. Prairie chickens feed on plant matter, such as leaves, fruit and grain, and in the summer they catch insects, particularly grasshoppers. Male birds perform spectacular courtship displays, inflating their orange neck sacs and raising crests of neck feathers. They give booming calls and stamp their feet as they posture, to make the display even more impressive. Female birds lay 10 to 12 eggs and incubate them for 21 to 28 days.

NAME: **Rock Ptarmigan,** *Lagopus mutus*
RANGE: **Holarctic**
HABITAT: **forest, tundra**
SIZE: **33–39 cm (13–15½ in)**

The ground-dwelling rock ptarmigans depend on camouflage for defense, and to achieve this in the changing background of their northerly range, they adopt different plumages. The summer plumage is mottled to blend with the forest, while during the winter snows ptarmigans have white plumage, only the tail feathers remaining dark. Rock ptarmigans feed on leaves, buds, fruits and seeds and on some insects in the summer.

They are monogamous birds; the male defends a small territory at the breeding grounds. The female lays 6 to 9 eggs in a leaf-lined hollow on the ground and incubates them for 24 to 26 days.

## MELEAGRIDINAE: Turkey Subfamily

There are 2 species of wild turkey. Both are large birds with bare skin on head and neck. Males and females look similar, but females are smaller and have duller plumage and smaller leg spurs.

NAME: **Turkey,** *Meleagris gallopavo*
RANGE: **USA, Mexico**
HABITAT: **wooded country**
SIZE: **91–122 cm (36–48 in)**

The wild turkey has a lighter, slimmer body and longer legs than the domesticated version. Turkeys are strong fliers over short distances. They roost in trees but find most of their food on the ground and eat plant matter, such as seeds, nuts and berries, as well as some insects and small reptiles.

A breeding male has a harem of several females. Each female lays her eggs in a shallow, leaf-lined nest on the ground; sometimes two or more females use the same nest. The female incubates the clutch of 8 to 15 eggs for about 28 days and cares for the young. The sexes segregate after breeding.

## NUMIDINAE: Guineafowl Subfamily

The 7 species of guineafowl are heavy-bodied, rounded game birds with short wings and bare heads. Males and females look virtually alike. All species occur in Africa and Madagascar. The helmeted guineafowl is the ancestor of the domestic guineafowl.

NAME: **Helmeted Guineafowl,** *Numida meleagris*
RANGE: **E. Africa**
HABITAT: **forest, dry brush**
SIZE: **63 cm (25 in)**

The helmeted guineafowl, named for the bony protuberance on its crown, has the distinctive spotted plumage of most species of guineafowl. It feeds on insects and on plant material such as seeds, leaves and bulbs. The female lays 10 to 20 eggs in a hollow scraped in the ground. She incubates the eggs and her mate helps care for the young.

## ODONTOPHORINAE: American Quail Subfamily

There are about 33 species of American quail, distributed from Canada to northeast Argentina. Many are hunted for sport and food. They are larger, more diverse and more strikingly colored than the Old World quails and differ from them in certain anatomical features, the most important of which is the stronger, serrated bill, typical of the American birds.

NAME: **Bobwhite,** *Colinus virginianus*
RANGE: **USA to Guatemala; introduced in West Indies**
HABITAT: **brush, open woodland, farmland**
SIZE: **23–27 cm (9–10½ in)**

Bobwhites are gregarious birds for much of the year, moving in coveys of 30 or so. In spring the coveys break up, and the birds pair for mating. The nest is a hollow in the ground. The average clutch is 14 to 16 eggs, and both parents incubate the eggs. Male and female birds look alike, but the male has striking face markings, while the female's face is buff-brown. The common name of this species is an imitation of its call.

NAME: **California Quail,** *Lophortyx californica*
RANGE: **W. USA**
HABITAT: **rangeland and agricultural land**
SIZE: **24–28 cm (9½–11 in)**

The state bird of California, this quail is an attractive bird with a characteristic head plume. Females look similar to males and have head plumes but lack the black and white facial markings; they have buff-brown heads and chests. California quail move in flocks, mostly on foot; they do not fly unless forced to do so. They feed on leaves, seeds and berries, and some insects. The female lays her 12 to 16 eggs in a leaf-lined hollow on the ground, and generally she incubates them for 18 days.

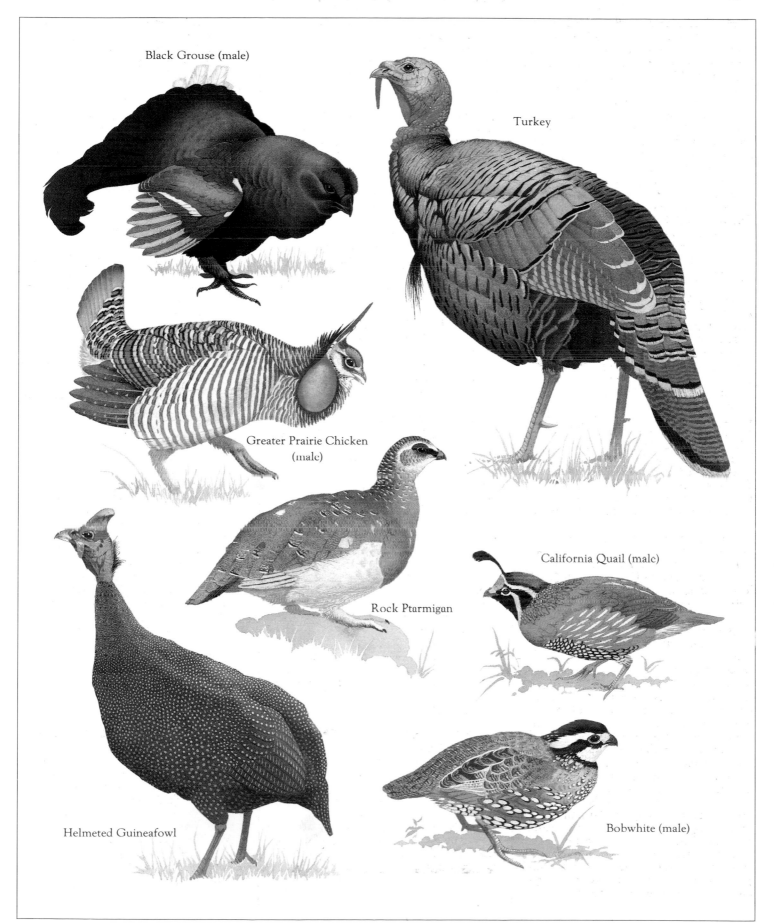

Black Grouse (male)

Turkey

Greater Prairie Chicken
(male)

Rock Ptarmigan

California Quail (male)

Helmeted Guineafowl

Bobwhite (male)

# Cranes and relatives

## ORDER GRUIFORMES
A diverse assemblage of wading and ground-living birds, this order contains 12 families, several of which contain only 1 species.

## MESITORNITHIDAE: Mesite Family
The 3 species of mesite all live in Madagascan forests. They run well but rarely fly, and 1 species, Bensch's mesite, *Monias benschi*, has yet to be seen in flight. Males and females look alike in 2 species, but unalike in Bensch's mesite.

NAME: **White-breasted Mesite,** *Mesitornis variegata*
RANGE: **N.W. Madagascar**
HABITAT: **dry forest**
SIZE: **25.5 cm (10 in)**  ®

The white-breasted mesite is a ground-dwelling bird and spends much of its life searching the forest floor for insects and seeds. Mesites generally move in pairs, heads bobbing as they walk.

The nest is made in a bush or low tree so the birds can climb up to it. It consists of a platform of twigs, lined with leaves; 1 to 3 eggs are laid. There is some doubt as to whether the male or female incubates the eggs.

## TURNICIDAE: Buttonquail Family
The 14 species of buttonquail and hemipode are dumpy, ground-living birds which closely resemble quails but have only three toes on each foot. Their wings are short and rounded, and the birds seldom fly. Females are larger and more brightly plumaged than males. All species occur in tropical and subtropical regions of the Old World.

NAME: **Andalusian Hemipode/Little Buttonquail,** *Turnix sylvatica*
RANGE: **S. Spain, Africa; S. Asia to Indonesia, Philippines**
HABITAT: **grassland, scrub**
SIZE: **15 cm (6 in)**

A shy, secretive bird, the Andalusian hemipode spends much of its time in the undergrowth, although it is able to fly. It feeds on plants, seeds and insects. The female bird takes the dominant sexual role, displaying to the male and competing with other females. Both birds make the nest, which is usually a hollow in the ground, lined with grass. From 3 to 8 oval eggs, usually 4, are laid, and the male incubates the clutch for an average of 13 days — one of the shortest incubation periods for any bird.

## PEDIONOMIDAE: Plains-wanderer Family
The single species in this family is related to the buttonquails and was formerly included in that family. The plains-wanderer, however, has four toes on each foot and lays pointed, not oval, eggs. These and some structural differences are sufficient to place it in a separate family.

NAME: **Plains-wanderer/Collared Hemipode,** *Pedionomus torquatus*
RANGE: **S.E. Australia**
HABITAT: **open grassland**
SIZE: **15–17 cm (6–6¼ in)**

A small, compact bird with short rounded wings, the female plains-wanderer has a chestnut-colored breast and a distinctive collar of black spots. Plains-wanderers seldom fly, but search for their food — insects, seeds and plants — on the ground. The nest is a simple hollow in the ground, lined with grass. The female lays 3 or 4 eggs, which are incubated by the male.

## GRUIDAE: Crane Family
The 15 species of crane are splendid, long-legged, long-necked birds, often with brightly colored bare skin on the face and decorative plumes on the head. The larger species stand up to 1.5 m (5 ft) tall. They are found over most of the world, except in South America, Madagascar, Malaysia, Polynesia and New Zealand.

Except during the breeding season, when they consort only in pairs, they are gregarious birds, and after breeding, they migrate in large flocks, flying in V-formation or in line, with necks extended and legs trailing. Males and females have similar plumage.

NAME: **Whooping Crane,** *Grus americana*
RANGE: **N. America**
HABITAT: **wetlands in prairies and other open habitats**
SIZE: **1.2–1.4 m (4–4½ ft) tall**  Ⓔ

Exceedingly rare birds in the wild, whooping cranes have been at the point of extinction, although vigorously protected, since the 1930s, when they almost disappeared. They breed in Canada and winter on the Texas Gulf Coast, and their migrations are carefully monitored.

An omnivorous bird, the whooping crane feeds on grain, plants, insects, frogs and other small animals. It lays 2 eggs on a flat nest of sticks on the ground. Both parents incubate the eggs and care for the young.

NAME: **Crowned Crane,** *Balearica pavonina*
RANGE: **Africa, south of the Sahara**
HABITAT: **swamps**
SIZE: **1 m (3¼ ft) tall**

The common name of this elegant bird is derived from the magnificent crest of yellow feathers on its head. All cranes perform ceremonial dances in the breeding season and, in a simpler form, throughout the year; the crowned crane is particularly spectacular as it postures with wings outstretched to display its feathers, struts about and jumps into the air. Both parents incubate the clutch of 2 or 3 eggs and care for the young.

## ARAMIDAE: Limpkin Family
The single species in this family is a marsh bird with similarities to both cranes and rails. It is now protected by law in the USA, after having been hunted almost to extinction early this century. Males and females look alike.

NAME: **Limpkin,** *Aramus guarauna*
RANGE: **USA: S. Georgia, Florida; Mexico, Central and South America; Caribbean**
HABITAT: **swamps**
SIZE: **59–71 cm (23¼–28 in)**

A long-legged bird, with long toes and sharp claws, the limpkin flies slowly and infrequently. It is most active at dusk and at night, when it uses its sensitive, slightly curved beak to probe the mud for freshwater snails.

Limpkins breed between January and August, depending on area, but in the USA the nesting season is usually March or April. A shallow nest is made of sticks, usually on the ground near water, and both parents incubate the 4 to 8 eggs.

## PSOPHIIDAE: Trumpeter Family
The 3 species of trumpeter are soft-plumaged, largely black birds, with weak, rounded wings. They rarely fly, but run swiftly on their long legs. Males look like females but make loud, trumpeting calls.

NAME: **Common Trumpeter,** *Psophia crepitans*
RANGE: **South America: Amazon basin**
HABITAT: **forest**
SIZE: **53 cm (20¾ in)**

Common trumpeters are gregarious birds which move in flocks around the forest floor, feeding on fruit, berries and insects. Trumpeters perform dancelike courtship movements and are believed to nest in holes in trees. The 6 to 10 eggs are incubated by the female.

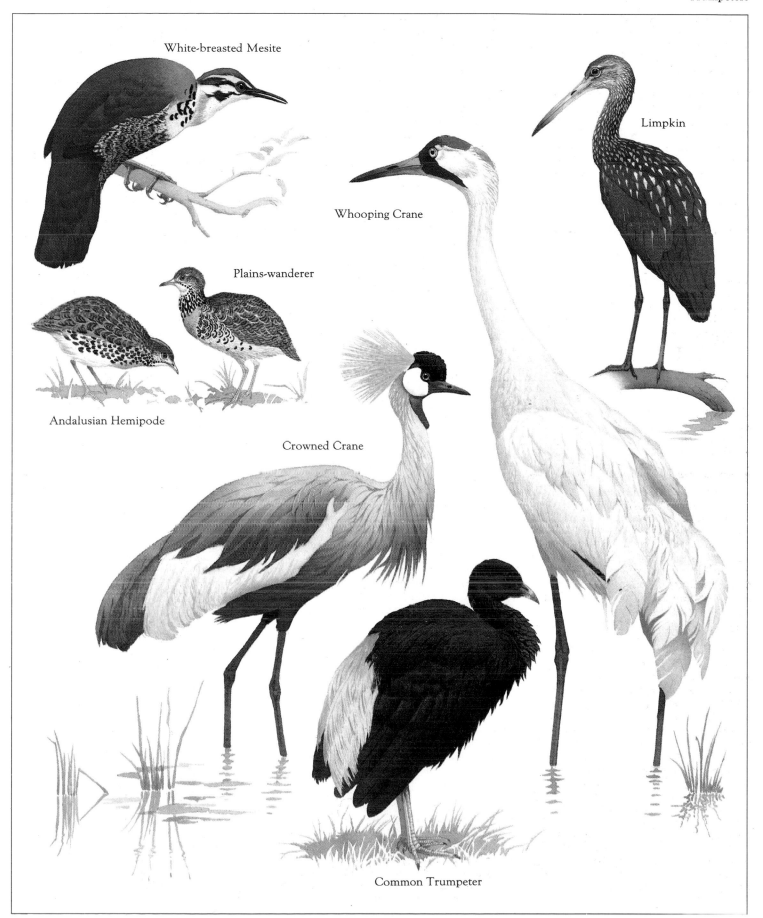

White-breasted Mesite

Limpkin

Whooping Crane

Plains-wanderer

Andalusian Hemipode

Crowned Crane

Common Trumpeter

# Rails

NAME: **Takahe,** *Notornis mantelli*
RANGE: **New Zealand: now confined to Murchison Mountains, South Island**
HABITAT: **high valleys at 750–1,200 m (2,500–4,000 ft)**
SIZE: **63 cm (24¾ in)**　　　　Ⓔ

First discovered in 1849, the takahe was sighted only four times in the next 50 years and was assumed to be extinct until its rediscovery in 1948. Despite careful conservation, however, there were thought to be only 100 pairs alive in 1977. Competition from introduced deer for the plants it feeds on and predation by introduced ermines are major reasons for its decline.

A stout bird, the takahe runs well but is flightless. It may venture into shallow water but does not swim as a rule. It feeds on the coarse fibrous vegetation of its habitat, particularly on snow grass (*Danthonia*), taking the seed heads and stems. Holding down the clump with one foot, it cuts out stems with its heavy beak and consumes their tender bases.

Pairs remain together for life when possible and usually breed in November. After several trial nests, a nest of grass stalks is made between or under clumps of grass which give some shelter. Both parents incubate the 2 eggs for up to 28 days, but many nests are destroyed by bad weather or predators and only 1 chick from each clutch is ever reared.

NAME: **Common Moorhen/Common Gallinule,** *Gallinula chloropus*
RANGE: **worldwide (not Australasia)**
HABITAT: **swamps, marshes, ponds, slow rivers with cover on banks**
SIZE: **33 cm (13 in)**

A familiar water bird, the moorhen is one of the most adaptable, successful members of its family. It frequents almost any fresh water and adjacent land and readily adapts to man-made environments such as urban parks and farms. It is a lively, active bird, far less secretive than the rail or crake, and swims freely on open water. Plant matter, such as pond weeds, berries and fallen fruit, makes up the bulk of the moorhen's diet, but it also eats a small amount of insects.

In the breeding season, the timing of which varies over its vast range, the moorhen pair defends a territory and performs intricate displays on both land and water. Both sexes help to build a nest of dead reeds and other aquatic plants among reeds or in a bush at the water's edge. The 5 to 11 eggs are laid on consecutive days and incubated for 19 to 22 days by both parents. Some pairs may produce a second brood during the season. Northernmost populations migrate south in winter.

## RALLIDAE: Rail Family

There are 132 species of rail, crake, wood rail, gallinule and coot in this distinctive, cosmopolitan family. They are ground-living birds, often found in or around water and marshy areas, and are well adapted for life in dense vegetation. Typical species are small to medium-sized birds — 14 to 51 cm (5½ to 20 in) long — with moderately long legs and toes and short rounded wings. Their bodies are laterally compressed, enabling them to squeeze through clumps of vegetation. Males and females look alike or nearly so in most species, although males are sometimes larger. Most are solitary, secretive birds.

There are two groups within the family: first, the rails, crakes and wood rails, with their camouflaging mottled plumage; and second, the darker gallinules and coots, which are much more aquatic in their habits. Most species fly reasonably well but may ordinarily be reluctant to take to the air, although many make long migrations between winter and summer habitats. Island-dwelling rails have been particularly prone to becoming flightless, which has then led to their extinction.

Diet is varied in the rail family. Species with long, thin bills probe in soft soil and leaf litter for insects, spiders, mollusks, worms and other invertebrates, while species with shorter, thicker bills feed on vegetation. Coots are aquatic feeders and dive or up-end for a variety of underwater plants and animals.

NAME: **Water Rail,** *Rallus aquaticus*
RANGE: **Europe, N. Africa, N. Asia to Japan**
HABITAT: **marshes, reedbeds**
SIZE: **28 cm (11 in)**

The slim-bodied water rail moves easily and skillfully through the tangled aquatic vegetation which it frequents. A shy bird, it runs for cover when alarmed, but is less retiring than the small rails and will come onto open land when the marshes freeze over in winter. It swims short distances near cover. Its varied diet includes plant material, such as roots, seeds and berries, as well as insects, crustaceans, small fish and worms.

April to July is the normal breeding season in most of the rail's range, and it sometimes produces two broods. The nest, made of dry reeds and other plants, is situated on the marsh. Both parents share the 19- to 21-day incubation of the 6 to 11 eggs.

NAME: **Giant Wood Rail,** *Aramides (= Eulabeornis) ypecaha*
RANGE: **South America: E. Brazil, Paraguay, Uraguay, E. Argentina**
HABITAT: **marshes, reedbeds, rivers**
SIZE: **53 cm (20¾ in)**

A large, handsome bird, the giant wood rail is an abundant species in its range. These birds feed alone during the day on plant and animal material, but at night they gather in small groups in the marshes and call in chorus.

The nest is made of grass and plant stems in a low bush just above the marsh surface. About 5 eggs are laid.

NAME: **American Coot,** *Fulica americana*
RANGE: **central and S. Canada, USA, Central and South America along Andes; Hawaiian Islands, Caribbean, Bahamas**
HABITAT: **marshes, ponds, lakes, rivers**
SIZE: **33–40 cm (13–15¾ in)**

A dark-plumaged, ducklike species with a white bill, the American coot is a conspicuous, noisy water bird. Its flight is strong and swift, although it seldom flies far unless migrating. It is a strong swimmer and good walker; as with all coots, its toes are lobed, which improves its swimming abilities.

Water plants are its main food, but it also eats aquatic insects, mollusks and some land plants. The coots often feed in flocks on the water, hundreds of birds swimming together like a moving black island.

In North America, the birds breed from April to May. After prolonged courtship rituals, a cup-shaped nest is made of dried marsh plants in a reedbed or on floating vegetation. The 8 to 12 eggs are incubated by both male and female for 21 or 22 days. Northernmost populations migrate south in winter.

NAME: **Corncrake,** *Crex crex*
RANGE: **Europe, W. Asia**
HABITAT: **grassland, cultivated land**
SIZE: **26.5 cm (10½ in)**

This small, slender rail seldom flies in its everyday life, although it migrates several thousand miles to winter in tropical Africa. It is a land-dwelling rail and runs swiftly through vegetation in search of seeds, grain and insects to feed on. Dawn and dusk are the corncrake's main periods of activity, but in spring the male makes his rasping call day and night. Only seen alone or in pairs, it is not a gregarious species except when migrating south.

The female corncrake constructs the nest, which is made on the ground from grass and weeds, and she incubates the 8 to 12 eggs for 14 to 21 days. The young birds are fed for a few days by the female or by both parents.

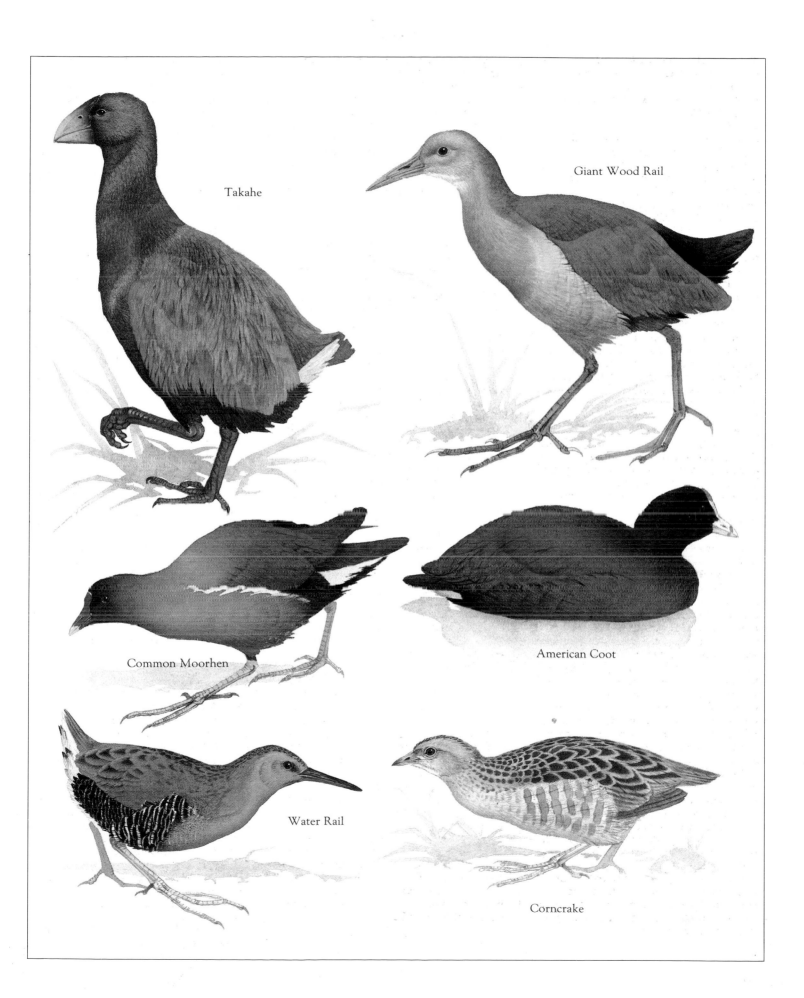

Takahe

Giant Wood Rail

Common Moorhen

American Coot

Water Rail

Corncrake

# Finfoots, Bustards and relatives

## HELIORNITHIDAE: Finfoot Family

There are 3 species of finfoot, one in each of the world's major tropical areas: Central and South America, Africa and Asia (India to Sumatra). They are probably the last relics of a once large, wide-ranging family. Male and female look more or less alike, but females may be smaller and differ slightly in plumage.

NAME: **African Finfoot**, *Podica senegalensis*
RANGE: **Africa, south of the Sahara**
HABITAT: **wooded streams, pools, mangrove swamps**
SIZE: **53–63.5 cm (20¾–25 in)**

An aquatic bird, the finfoot skulks at the edges of well-wooded streams, among overhanging vegetation. It swims low in the water, sometimes with only its head and neck visible, and dives well. Once aloft, it flies strongly and also leaves the water to clamber around in vegetation and climb trees. Insects and small invertebrates, amphibians and fish are its main foods. Male and female birds look similar, but the male is larger and has buff-gray plumage on the front of the neck, while the female's throat and neck are whitish.

The nest is made of twigs and rushes on a branch overhanging water or else among flood debris. The female lays 2 eggs.

NAME: **Sungrebe**, *Heliornis fulica*
RANGE: **S. Mexico, through Central and South America to N. Argentina**
HABITAT: **stagnant streams, wooded rivers**
SIZE: **28 cm (11 in)**

Although smaller than the African finfoot, the sungrebe has the same elongate body and lobed toes. Its common name is particularly unsuitable, since the bird frequents shady overgrown margins of streams and rivers and is rarely seen in the open. It feeds on insects, especially larvae found on leaves, and on small invertebrates, amphibians and fish. It flies strongly but tends to take cover in undergrowth to escape danger, rather than to fly.

The 4 eggs are laid in a bush or tree overhanging water.

## EURYPYGIDAE: Sunbittern Family

The sunbittern, found in Central and South America, is the sole member of its family. It is related to rails and bustards, but its exact affinities are uncertain. Male and female look alike.

NAME: **Sunbittern**, *Eurypyga helias*
RANGE: **Central America, South America to Brazil**
HABITAT: **forest streams and creeks**
SIZE: **46 cm (18 in)**

The sunbittern is an elegant bird, with a long bill, slender neck and long legs. It frequents the well-wooded banks of streams, where it is perfectly camouflaged in the dappled sunlight by its mottled plumage. Fish, insects and crustaceans are its main foods, which it hunts from the bank or seizes with swift thrusts of its bill, while wading in the shallows.

In courtship display, the beautifully plumaged wings are fully spread, revealing patches of color, and the tips are held forward, framing the head and neck. The birds also perform a courtship dance, with tail and wings spread. Both partners help to build the large domed nest in a tree and incubate the 2 or 3 eggs for about 28 days.

## RHYNOCHETIDAE: Kagu Family

The classification and relationships of the kagu, the sole member of its family, have been the subject of much dispute.

NAME: **Kagu**, *Rhynochetos jubatus*
RANGE: **New Caledonia**
HABITAT: **forest**
SIZE: **56 cm (22 in)**　　　　Ⓔ

Once abundant, the nocturnal, virtually flightless kagu is now rare, largely due to the onslaught by introduced dogs, cats and rats. The kagu feeds on insects, worms and snails, which it finds on or in the ground by probing with its long, pointed bill. Male and female look more or less alike.

In display, the two birds face each other, spreading their wings to show off the black, white and chestnut plumage. They may perform remarkable dances, whirling round with the tip of the tail or wing held in the bill. A nest is made on the ground, and both parents incubate the single egg for about 36 days.

## CARIAMIDAE: Seriema Family

The 2 species of seriema are long-legged, ground-living birds, both of which occur in South America. They are believed to be the only surviving descendants of some long-extinct carnivorous ground birds, known from fossils. Males and females look alike or nearly so.

NAME: **Red-legged Seriema**, *Cariama cristata*
RANGE: **E. Bolivia, Brazil, Paraguay, Uruguay, N. Argentina**
HABITAT: **grassland**
SIZE: **76–91 cm (30–35¾ in)**

A tall, graceful bird, the red-legged seriema runs fast but rarely flies, tending to rely on its speed on land to escape from danger. The sharp, broad bill, under the tufty crest, is powerful, reminiscent of the bill of a bird of prey, and is used to kill reptiles and amphibians, as well as for feeding on insects, leaves and seeds.

The nest is made of sticks and built in a tree. Both parents incubate the 2 or 3 eggs for 25 or 26 days.

## OTIDIDAE: Bustard Family

Bustards are heavily built, ground-dwelling birds, which tend to run or walk rather than fly, although they are capable of strong flight. The majority of the 24 species occur in Africa, but there are bustards in southern Europe, Asia and Australia. Male birds are more boldly plumaged than females.

NAME: **Great Bustard**, *Otis tarda*
RANGE: **scattered areas of S. and central Europe, east across Asia to Siberia and E. China**
HABITAT: **grassland, grain fields**
SIZE: **75 cm–1 m (29½ in–3¼ ft)**

The male great bustard is a large, strong bird, with a thick neck and sturdy legs. The female is smaller and slimmer, lacking the male's bristly "whiskers" and chestnut breast plumage. Insects and seeds are their main foods, but they are omnivorous.

The male bustard performs a remarkable courtship display, raising his wings and tail and puffing himself out until he resembles a moving, feathery ball. The 2 or 3 eggs are laid in an unlined scrape on the ground and incubated by the female for 25 to 28 days.

NAME: **Little Black Bustard/Black Korhaan**, *Afrotis atra*
RANGE: **South Africa**
HABITAT: **grassland, bush**
SIZE: **53 cm (20¾ in)**

Male little black bustards are showy, conspicuous birds, with distinctive markings on the head and neck. Females are duller, with much of the plumage mottled with black, tawny and rufous spots and only the underparts pure black. They generally live in pairs in a well-defined territory and feed mainly on vegetable matter and some insects.

The female usually lays only 1 egg on the ground and incubates it herself.

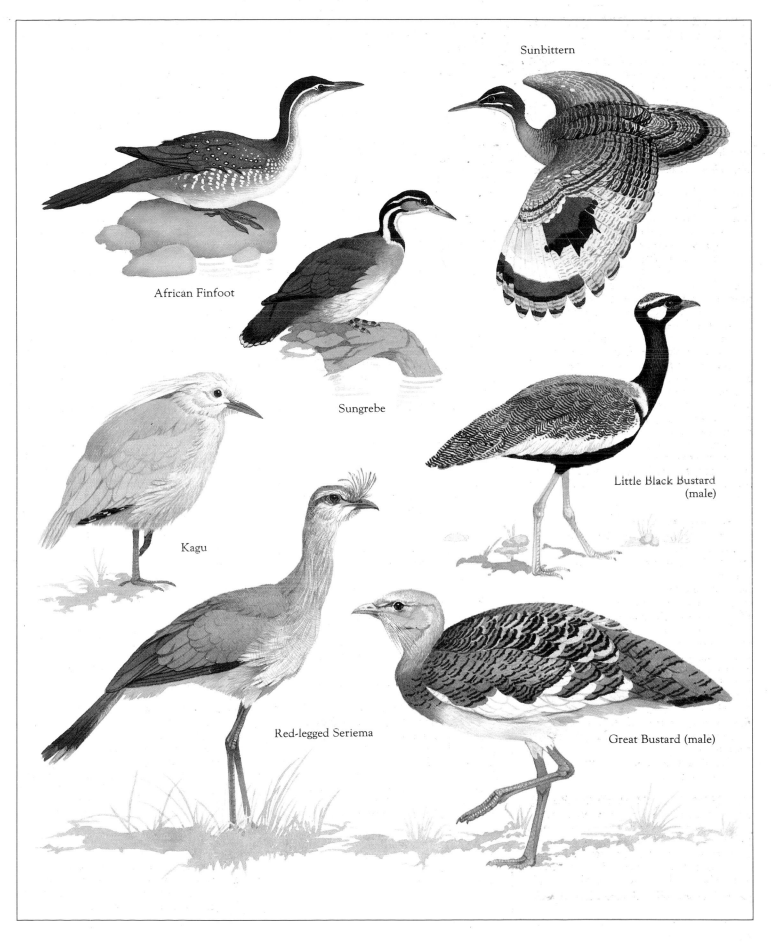

Sunbittern

African Finfoot

Sungrebe

Little Black Bustard
(male)

Kagu

Red-legged Seriema

Great Bustard (male)

# Jacanas, Plovers, Painted-snipes, Oystercatchers

## ORDER CHARADRIIFORMES

This order contains over 300 species in 15 families grouped into 3 suborders. The first contains all the shorebirds, or waders, such as plovers, sandpipers and jacanas. In the second group are skuas, gulls and terns, and skimmers. The third suborder has a single family, the auks.

## JACANIDAE: Jacana Family

The 8 species of jacana are all long-legged water birds found in tropical and subtropical areas worldwide. They have extraordinary feet which are an adaptation for their habit of moving over floating vegetation: their toes and claws are so exceedingly long that their weight is well distributed over a large surface area, and they are able actually to walk over precarious floating lily pads. Males and females look alike, but females are slightly larger.

NAME: **North American Jacana, *Jacana spinosa***
RANGE: **Central America, Greater Antilles, USA: S. Texas**
HABITAT: **lakes, ponds**
SIZE: **25 cm (9¾ in)**

North American jacanas feed on insects and other aquatic life and on the seeds of water plants, all of which they take from the water surface or vegetation. They swim and dive well but fly slowly. A nest is made of aquatic plants, and the clutch of 3 to 5, usually 4, eggs is incubated by both parents for a total of 22 to 24 days.

## CHARADRIIDAE: Plover Family

This family contains about 63 species of small to medium-sized, fairly plump wading birds. The typical plover has a short straight bill, round head and short legs. Males and females look alike or nearly so, but some species have seasonal differences in plumage.

NAME: **Lapwing, *Vanellus vanellus***
RANGE: **Europe, W. and N. Africa, Asia**
HABITAT: **grassland, farmland**
SIZE: **30 cm (12 in)**

A distinctive bird with a crested head and broad rounded wings, the lapwing is also known as the peewit, after the cry it makes in flight. Lapwings feed mostly on insects but also on worms, snails and some plant matter. The male makes a ceremonial nest scrape to initiate breeding behavior in the female. She completes the nest and lays 3 to 5 eggs. The clutch is incubated for 24 to 31 days.

NAME: **American Golden Plover, *Pluvialis dominica***
RANGE: **N. America, Asia; winters in South America, Hawaii and other Pacific islands, Australia, New Zealand, S. Asia**
HABITAT: **marshes, fields, open country**
SIZE: **23–28 cm (9–11 in)**

One of the champion long-distance migratory birds, this plover flies to wintering grounds 12,800 km (8,000 mi) south of its breeding grounds on the tundra of North America and Siberia.

American golden plovers feed on insects and some mollusks and crustaceans. They lay 3 or 4 eggs in a shallow dip in the tundra, lined with moss and grass. Both parents incubate, the male during the day and the female at night, for a total of 20 to 30 days. In winter this plover loses its distinctive facial markings, and its head and breast are a speckled golden color.

NAME: **Wrybill, *Anarhynchus frontalis***
RANGE: **New Zealand**
HABITAT: **riverbeds, open country**
SIZE: **20 cm (8 in)**

The wrybill is a small plover with a unique bill, the tip of which turns to the right. To find its insect food, the wrybill tilts its head to the left and sweeps the tip of its bill over the mud with a horizontal scissoring action. Wrybills winter in North Island and travel to South Island to breed. They nest in large estuaries on a particular type of shingle, the stones of which are similar in color to the wrybill and its eggs, thus providing camouflage. The female lays 2 or 3 eggs among the shingle in October.

NAME: **Ringed Plover, *Charadrius hiaticula* (conspecific with Semipalmated Plover)**
RANGE: **N. Europe, W. Asia, N. America**
HABITAT: **seashore**
SIZE: **19 cm (7½ in)**

A common northern shorebird, the ringed plover has distinctive head and breast markings in its summer plumage. It feeds on mollusks, insects, worms and some plants. The female lays 3 to 5 eggs and will defend eggs or young with a distraction display technique used by many plover species. If a predator approaches the nest, the parent bird flaps awkwardly away as if injured and unable to fly, all the time leading the enemy away from the young. Once the predator is well away from the nest, the plover flies up suddenly and escapes, to return to the nest later.

## ROSTRATULIDAE: Painted-snipe Family

There are only 2 species in this family, one in the Old World and the other, the lesser painted-snipe, *Nycticryphes semicollaris*, in South America. It is an unusual family in that the normal sexual roles are reversed.

NAME: **Greater Painted-snipe, *Rostratula benghalensis***
RANGE: **Africa, south of the Sahara; Madagascar, S. Asia, Australia**
HABITAT: **marshes**
SIZE: **24 cm (9½ in)**

The greater painted-snipe is a secretive crepuscular bird, rarely seen in the open. It feeds on insects, snails and worms, most of which it finds in muddy ground with its sensitive bill, and some plant matter.

The female bird is the showy partner, the male is smaller with brownish plumage. She performs an impressive courtship display, spreading her wings forward and expanding her tail to show the spots on the feathers. Females will fight over males. The male bird makes a pad of grass as a nest, and when the female has laid the 3 or 4 eggs, he incubates the clutch and cares for the young.

## HAEMATOPODIDAE: Oystercatcher Family

Oystercatchers are large, noisy, coastal birds found throughout the world, except on oceanic islands and in polar regions. There is only 1 genus, with about 8 closely related species. There are only slight sexual and seasonal plumage differences.

NAME: **European Oystercatcher, *Haematopus ostralegus***
RANGE: **virtually worldwide**
HABITAT: **coasts, estuaries**
SIZE: **46 cm (18 in)**

The European oystercatcher is by far the most widespread of its family, and there are several races. Like all oystercatchers, it has a long, blunt, flattened bill, which it uses to pry shellfish off rocks. Mollusks and crustaceans are its main food, but this bird has also learned to seek insects and worms on farmland farther inland.

Oystercatchers are gregarious birds and live and move in large flocks. Their nest is a hole in the ground, often lined with grass or decorated with moss. The female lays 2 to 4 eggs, and both partners incubate them for 24 to 27 days.

North American Jacana

Lapwing

Greater Painted-snipe
(female)

American Golden Plover
(summer plumage)

European
Oystercatcher

Wrybill

Ringed Plover
(summer plumage)

# Sandpipers

NAME: **Whimbrel**, *Numenius phaeopus*
RANGE: **breeds in Canada, Alaska, Asia, N. Europe; winters in S. America, Africa, S.E. Asia, Australasia**
HABITAT: **breeds on moors, tundra; winters on muddy and sandy shores, estuaries, marshes**
SIZE: **40 cm (15¾ in)**

One of the group of birds known as curlews, the whimbrel has a distinctively striped crown and a long, curving bill. It feeds on small invertebrates, including crabs, which it often partially dismembers before swallowing. In spring and summer, it eats many insects, and berries are also an important food.

Whimbrels breed in subarctic and subalpine tundra and arrive at breeding grounds in the spring, often returning to the same territory year after year. As the snows disperse, males begin their courtship displays. The nest is made on the ground, usually in the open, and the female bird lays 4 eggs, which are incubated for 27 or 28 days by both parents. Once the chicks are fully fledged, at 5 or 6 weeks, the adults leave almost immediately, starting the migration south to wintering areas. The young birds follow a few weeks later.

NAME: **American Woodcock**, *Scolopax minor*
RANGE: **N. America: breeds from Manitoba to Louisiana and Florida; winters from southern part of breeding range to Gulf Coast**
HABITAT: **woodland, young forest**
SIZE: **28 cm (11 in)**

Woodcocks are inland wood and forest birds, far less aquatic than most others of their family. The American woodcock is a shy, secretive bird, with a long bill, rounded wings and chunky body. It finds its food by probing the soil with its slender bill, the tip of which is very flexible and can be opened under the soil. It prefers areas with low, shrubby vegetation where there are plenty of earthworms, for they constitute two-thirds of its total intake, although it also feeds on beetle and fly larvae.

Males generally arrive at breeding grounds in March and April, slightly before females, in order to establish display territories that are sufficiently large to allow their courtship flights. Females are attracted to the display area by the males' calls, and a male will mate with several females. The female bird makes a nest under a small tree or bush and lays 4 eggs. She incubates the clutch for 21 days, leaving the nest only once a day at dusk to feed. Chicks are almost fully grown at about 4 weeks. If a woodcock's chicks are in danger, the mother can take them, one at a time, between her legs and fly to a safe refuge.

## SCOLOPACIDAE:
## Sandpiper Family

There are about 82 species in this, the most diverse of all the families in the Charadriiformes order. Under a wide range of common names, such as sandpiper, curlew, turnstone, snipe, woodcock and redshank, species are found worldwide, on every continent and on almost every island of any size. Most species are ground-living wading birds that find much of their food in water. Males and females generally look alike, but some species develop special breeding plumage.

NAME: **Redshank**, *Tringa totanus*
RANGE: **breeds in Europe, N. USSR; winters in S. Europe, N. Africa, S. Asia**
HABITAT: **breeds on moorland, marshes; winters on mud flats, meadows, estuaries, shores**
SIZE: **28 cm (11 in)**

An abundant and widespread sandpiper, the redshank adapts well to almost any habitat near water. The bright red legs identify this species immediately; it also has dark stripes on head and neck, which become paler in winter. Insects predominate in its diet, but it also eats mollusks and crustaceans.

Redshanks arrive at breeding grounds between March and May and pair off after courtship displays. The 4 eggs are laid in a cup-shaped nest on the ground and are incubated for 23 days.

NAME: **Common Snipe**, *Gallinago gallinago*
RANGE: **breeds in Canada, N. USA, Europe to N.E. Asia; winters in Central and South America, Africa, India, Indonesia**
HABITAT: **marshes, wet meadows, moors**
SIZE: **25.5 cm (10 in)**

A shy, secretive bird, the common snipe has rather pointed wings, a long bill and striped and barred plumage, which provides effective camouflage among vegetation. Insects, particularly fly and beetle larvae, are the snipe's most important food items, but it also eats earthworms, small crustaceans, snails and small quantities of plant material.

Males arrive at breeding grounds before females and establish territories for display. In the most common display, the male dives through the air at great speed, causing a drumming sound as air rushes through his outer tail feathers. The nest is made on dry ground when possible and near clumps of grass, which the birds pull down over it. The 3 or 4 eggs are incubated for 17 to 19 days, usually by the female alone.

NAME: **Ruff**, *Philomachus pugnax*
RANGE: **breeds in N. Europe, Asia; winters in Europe, Africa, S. Asia**
HABITAT: **tundra, grassland, marshes**
SIZE: **23–30.5 cm (9–12 in)**

Male ruffs perform complex communal displays to attract mates. In the breeding season, males develop large frills of feathers around their heads and necks and gather at a traditional display ground, called a lek; there is great individual variation in the color of frills. Each older, dominant male holds an area within the lek and may be attended by several males, who must display with him and pay court to him in the hope of a chance to mate with one of his females.

Once mated, the female bird, called a "reeve," leaves the display ground and makes a nest in long grass. She incubates her 4 eggs for 20 to 23 days.

NAME: **Ruddy Turnstone**, *Arenaria interpres*
RANGE: **circumpolar: breeds on arctic coasts; winters south of breeding range**
HABITAT: **breeds on marshes, tundra; winters on rocky shores**
SIZE: **18–23 cm (7–9 in)**

In the breeding season, the turnstone has bold black, white and reddish-brown markings, which become duller in winter. Insects, particularly midges, and some plant material are its main food in summer, but in winter it forages on seashores, turning over stones and other debris with its bill to find mollusks, crustaceans and even carrion.

Breeding birds arrive from wintering areas in late May or early June. The 4 eggs are laid in a grass-lined hollow on the ground and incubated by both parents for 21 to 23 days.

NAME: **Red Phalarope**, *Phalaropus fulicarius*
RANGE: **breeds in N. America: Alaska to Hudson Bay and arctic islands; winters off W. Africa and Chile**
HABITAT: **breeds in tundra and wet meadows; winters at sea**
SIZE: **18 cm (7 in)**

The only swimming bird in its family, the toes of the phalarope are adapted for swimming, having flattened fringing scales, and it comes ashore only to breed. The female is the brightly colored sex in this species, with her breeding plumage of reddish throat and underparts, while the male is smaller and duller. In winter both sexes have grayish plumage. Phalaropes feed on beetles, flies, crustaceans and small fish.

Normal sexual roles are reversed in phalaropes, and the showy female takes the initiative in courtship and mating. The male incubates the 4 eggs for about 19 days and cares for the young.

Ruddy Turnstone (breeding plumage)

Whimbrel

Redshank

Common Snipe

Ruff (variations in male breeding plumage)

American Woodcock

Red Phalarope
(female in breeding plumage)

# Avocets, Crab Plover, Thick-knees

## IBIDORHYNCHIDAE: Ibisbill Family

The ibisbill, the single species in this family, differs from the avocets and stilts, with which it is sometimes grouped, both in its northerly, high-altitude habitat and in its downward-curving bill.

NAME: Ibisbill, *Ibidorhyncha struthersii*
RANGE: high plateaus of central Asia; Himalayas
HABITAT: shingle banks, shingle islands in mountain streams
SIZE: 38 cm (15 in)

The ibisbill uses its down-curving bill to probe for food under stones in the shingly riverbeds it frequents. It often wades into the water and submerges its head and neck. Small groups of ibisbills generally live and feed together. The female bird lays 4 large eggs in a ground nest, and the clutch is incubated by both parents.

## RECURVIROSTRIDAE: Avocet Family

This family includes 13 species of long-billed, long-legged wading birds, which are found throughout much of the world, except in northernmost regions. These birds fly and sometimes swim well and generally live near water. Their feet are usually at least slightly webbed. Aquatic insects, mollusks, fish, frogs and some plant matter are the main items of their diet. Many species have black and white plumage, and male and female look more or less alike.

NAME: Black-winged Stilt, *Himantopus himantopus*
RANGE: Old World, to about 50°N
HABITAT: mainly freshwater swamps, marshes, lagoons
SIZE: 38 cm (15 in)

This distinctive stilt has long pink legs, longer in proportion to its body size than those of any bird except the flamingo; in flight, its legs project far beyond the tail. Stilts walk quickly, taking long strides, and wade into water to pick insects and small aquatic animals off vegetation and off the water surface. The long slender bill is ideally adapted for this purpose.

Colonies of stilts nest together near water. Some nests are substantial structures, built up in shallow water from sticks and mud; others are small flimsy ground nests. Between April and June the female lays 3 to 5 eggs, which both parents incubate for 26 days. The young leave the nest soon after hatching.

NAME: Avocet, *Recurvirostra avosetta*
RANGE: Europe, W. and central Asia; northern populations winter in W. Africa and S. Asia
HABITAT: mud flats, estuaries, sandbanks
SIZE: 42 cm (16½ in)

An unmistakable bird, the avocet has striking black and white plumage and a long bill that curves upward. In flight, the long legs usually project beyond the tail. Avocets feed on insects, small aquatic animals and some plant matter, all of which they find by sweeping their bills from side to side at the surface of mud or shallow water. In deeper water, the avocet dips its head below the surface and will swim and up-end like a duck.

Avocets breed colonially; pairs mating after displays involving both partners. The nest is usually a simple scrape near water in which the female lays 3 to 5 eggs. Both parents incubate the eggs and later guard their chicks against predators. Juveniles have some brownish plumage but are otherwise similar to adults. The American avocet, *R. americana*, resembles this avocet, but has cinnamon plumage on head, neck and breast during the breeding season.

## DROMADIDAE: Crab Plover Family

The sole species in this family, the crab plover may be related to stone curlews and thick-knees, which it resembles to some degree. However, the bird has several unique features, so it is at present placed in its own family. Female crab plovers are slightly smaller than males and have shorter black feathers.

NAME: Crab Plover, *Dromas ardeola*
RANGE: breeds on islands from E. Africa to the Persian Gulf; winters on coasts and islands of the W. Indian Ocean
HABITAT: estuaries, reefs
SIZE: 38 cm (15 in)

A stocky bird with a heavy, compressed bill, the crab plover flies strongly and runs swiftly. Its black and white markings are striking and distinct in flight; the legs are long and the toes are partially webbed. Crabs are, indeed, the main item of its diet, but it also feeds on other crustaceans and on mollusks, which it breaks open with its strong, pointed bill. Crab plovers are noisy, gregarious birds and they nest in colonies. The female lays her single egg at the end of a burrow in a sandbank, often in a crab burrow. Although it is able to run around soon after hatching, the chick is cared for by both parents and fed in the burrow.

## BURHINIDAE: Thick-knee Family

The 9 species in this family have a variety of common names, such as thick-knee, stone curlew and dikkop, and all have characteristic thickened joints between tarsus and shin. These birds are ploverlike in appearance but also resemble the bustards, Otididae, in some respects. They have three toes only on each foot, and these are partially webbed. Thick-knees are active at dusk and at night, and their unusually large yellow eyes are an adaptation for nocturnal activity. Male and female birds look alike. The family is widely distributed in the Old World, and there are 2 species in Central and South America.

NAME: Great Shore Plover, *Esacus magnirostris*
RANGE: India, Sri Lanka; Australia and New Caledonia
HABITAT: coasts and rivers
SIZE: 50 cm (19¾ in)

A sturdy, large-headed bird, this thick-knee has a strong, slightly upturned bill and large yellow eyes. It feeds mostly at night on insects, worms, mollusks and crustaceans, and on some small vertebrate animals. Like all thick-knees, it runs fast, but in short dashes, and is a reluctant but strong flier. To avoid danger, it may crouch down or even flatten itself on the ground, head and neck outstretched.

In the breeding season, the great shore plover lays 2, or sometimes 3, eggs in a shallow hollow in the ground; these are incubated by the female, with some assistance from the male. Both parents care for the chicks which are, however, able to fend for themselves almost immediately.

NAME: Stone Curlew, *Burhinus oedicnemus*
RANGE: S. England, Europe, N. Africa, S.W. Asia; winters to the south of its range
HABITAT: open country, heath, farmland
SIZE: 41 cm (16 in)

Although only some populations migrate, the stone curlew is nevertheless the only migratory thick-knee, northern birds wintering in East Africa. Like all its family, the stone curlew's plumage blends well with its surroundings, providing camouflage, but it has two bold wing bars which are conspicuous in flight. Its bill is short and straight, and it feeds mainly on invertebrates and on snails and worms. The female lays her 2 eggs on the ground in a hollow and incubates them with some assistance from her mate.

Avocet

Crab Plover

Black-winged Stilt

Great Shore Plover

Ibisbill

Stone Curlew

# Pratincoles, Seedsnipes, Sheathbills

## GLAREOLIDAE: Pratincole Family

This family contains 16 species: pratincoles, coursers and the Egyptian plover. All are fairly small, ploverlike birds with sharply pointed bills. The pratincoles and coursers differ in some general respects: the former have short beaks, narrow, pointed wings, forked tails, short legs and feet with four toes; the latter have longer bills, broader wings and tails and longer legs with three-toed feet (they have no hind toes). Birds of both groups feed on insects, mollusks, leeches, small lizards and seeds. The species occur in warmer areas of the Old World, including Australia. Males and females have similar plumage but may differ in size.

---

NAME: **Cream-colored Courser,**
 *Cursorius cursor*
RANGE: **Africa, Canary and Cape Verde Islands; S.W. Asia, W. India**
HABITAT: **desert and semidesert**
SIZE: **23 cm (9 in)**

A slender, pale-plumaged bird with distinctive eye stripes, the cream-colored courser merges well with its desert surroundings. Although its flight is rapid, it tends to run rather than fly, often crouching down on the ground between bursts of movement.

Cream-colored coursers do not make regular migrations but do wander out of their range, often flying into Europe, although they do not breed there. The female lays 2 or 3 eggs on the ground, on sand or rock. She incubates the eggs at night, when the desert temperature drops, but may need to stand above them during the day to shield them from the sun.

NAME: **Egyptian Plover,** *Pluvianus aegyptius*
RANGE: **N.E., W. and W. central Africa**
HABITAT: **shores and sandbanks of rivers and lakes**
SIZE: **20 cm (7¾ in)**

The Egyptian plover differs, in its more striking plumage and rather short legs, from the coursers, with which it belongs. It is usually found near water, and for centuries has been known as the crocodile bird because of the belief that it will feed on the debris and food particles remaining in the mouth of a basking crocodile. This behavior is unconfirmed, although the bird does often feed near crocodiles and on their body parasites; its main food is insects.

The female Egyptian plover lays 2 or 3 eggs, which it covers lightly with sand while they incubate; it will also cover chicks temporarily, to hide them from potential danger.

NAME: **Collared Pratincole,** *Glareola pratincola*
RANGE: **S. Europe, S.W. Asia, Africa**
HABITAT: **open land, sun-baked mud flats, freshwater banks**
SIZE: **25 cm (9¾ in)**

The collared pratincole, with its deeply forked tail, is ternlike in its swift, agile flight, but can run easily on the ground like a plover. It has a characteristic creamy, black-bordered throat, but the border is less distinct in winter. Pratincoles are gregarious birds, and flocks gather at dusk to feed on insects which they chase and catch in the air, often in the vicinity of water.

They breed in colonies of anything from a few pairs to hundreds of birds and generally nest after the rainy or flood season in their area. Their 2 to 4 eggs are laid on the ground and are well camouflaged by their blotched, neutral coloration, which blends with the background, whether soil, sand or rock. Both parents incubate the eggs for a total of 17 or 18 days. The young are able to run around immediately after hatching. After breeding, European collared pratincoles migrate to Africa, south of the Sahara.

---

## THINOCORIDAE: Seedsnipe Family

The 4 species of seedsnipe all live in South America. The common name derives from the fact that all are seed-eating birds that have the rapid zigzagging flight of the snipes.

Seedsnipes are rounded, ground-feeding birds which range in size from 17 to 28 cm (6¾ to 11 in). The wings are long and pointed, the tail short and the bill strong and conical. The plumage is cryptic and partridgelike, and males and females show some differences in plumage.

---

NAME: **Least Seedsnipe,** *Thinocorus rumicivorus*
RANGE: **Andes: Ecuador to Tierra del Fuego; east to Patagonia and Uruguay; Falkland Islands**
HABITAT: **dry plains, coastal and inland**
SIZE: **17 cm (6¾ in)**

The smallest of the seedsnipes, the least seedsnipe has the mottled, camouflaging plumage typical of its family; male birds have black markings which give a "necktie" effect. Primarily a ground-living bird, it can run rapidly, despite its short legs, and it blends so well with its surroundings that, if threatened, it will remain still and almost invisible, taking to the air at only the last minute.

The nesting season varies according to latitude. The 4 eggs are laid on the ground in a shallow hollow and are incubated by the female. If she has to leave the eggs for a time, she will half bury them in the sand. The young are able to run around soon after hatching.

---

## CHIONIDIDAE: Sheathbill Family

The 2 species of sheathbill are medium-sized — 35.5 to 43 cm (14 to 17 in) — white-plumaged, shore-living birds, found on the islands of the far southern oceans. They are squat and heavy-bodied, resembling pigeons in build, and have a comblike covering over the upper beak which gives them their common name. Their legs are short and stocky and their feet powerful. Male and female sheathbills look alike, but females are usually smaller.

Ornithologists consider the sheathbills to resemble the common ancestors of the gulls and waders and to be a link between the two families.

---

NAME: **Snowy/Yellow-billed Sheathbill,** *Chionis alba*
RANGE: **subantarctic islands of the S. Atlantic Ocean, extending to Graham Land and southern South America when not breeding.**
HABITAT: **coasts**
SIZE: **39 cm (15¼ in)**

Snowy sheathbills are gregarious and pugnacious birds, and except during the breeding season, they live in small flocks, feeding together and often fighting. Although they fly well and will make long journeys, even over sea, they spend most of their time on the ground. They swim well although their feet have only rudimentary webs. Sheathbills are avid scavengers and haunt seal and penguin colonies to seize afterbirths or weak young. They also search the shore for all kinds of fish, invertebrates, carcasses and almost any other debris that they can eat. They consume quantities of seaweed for the invertebrates that it harbors.

Sheathbills nest in isolated pairs in a crevice or among rocks. The 2 or 3 eggs are laid on feathers, seaweed and other soft material. Both male and female incubate the eggs for a total of 28 days, but it seems as if only 1 chick is actually reared as a general rule.

In winter, sheathbills in the extreme south of the range migrate north, but those on subantarctic islands usually remain there. The other species in this family, the black-billed sheathbill, *C. minor*, occurs in the subantarctic sector of the Indian Ocean.

Collared Pratincole

Cream-colored Courser

Snowy Sheathbill

Egyptian Plover

Least Seedsnipe (male)

# Skuas, Gulls, Skimmers

## STERCORARIIDAE: Skua Family
There are about 5 species of skua, or jaeger, as some are called in North America. They are dark-plumaged, gull-like seabirds, characterized by their piratical method of obtaining food: they chase other seabirds, such as gulls and terns, in the air and force them to disgorge their prey. Males and females are outwardly alike, but the females are sometimes larger.

NAME: **Skua,** *Catharacta skua*
RANGE: **N. Atlantic Ocean: Iceland, Faeroes, Shetland and Orkney Islands; winters as far south as the Tropic of Cancer**
HABITAT: **oceanic, coastal waters**
SIZE: **51–56 cm (20–22 in)**

A strongly built bird with a hooked bill and sharply curved claws, the skua not only attacks other birds to steal their prey but also kills and eats ducks and gulls and preys on eggs and young at breeding grounds. It also follows ships to feed on scraps thrown overboard and takes carrion.

An otherwise solitary bird, it nests in colonies. A shallow scrape is made on a rocky slope or at the foot of a cliff, and 1 to 3 eggs, usually 2, are laid. Both partners incubate the eggs for 26 to 29 days and care for the chicks.

## LARIDAE: Gull Family
This family of about 90 species of white seabird with black or gray markings is distributed worldwide. The family divides into two distinct groups: gulls and terns. Gulls are the classic shoreline birds; they seldom dive and few species catch fish. Powerfully built, with heavy bills and bodies, they have long wings which are broader and blunter than those of the terns. Terns are smaller, graceful birds, often with deeply forked tails. They dive for fish, and most species also catch insects in the air or on the water.

NAME: **Ivory Gull,** *Pagophila eburnea*
RANGE: **Arctic coasts and islands; winters among ice floes, sometimes south of the Arctic Circle**
HABITAT: **coasts, pack ice**
SIZE: **35.5–43 cm (14–17 in)**

The only gull with all-white plumage, the ivory gull is a striking, plump-bodied bird with black legs. It seldom swims but can run over ice. It feeds on fish and invertebrates and scavenges on carrion and refuse. It breeds in colonies and lays 2 eggs on the ground or on a cliff ledge.

NAME: **Herring Gull,** *Larus argentatus*
RANGE: **most of northern hemisphere**
HABITAT: **coasts, estuaries; inland water and fields**
SIZE: **55–66 cm (21½–26 in)**

The commonest coastal gull in North America and Europe, the herring gull feeds on small surface fish, scavenges on waste and sewage, steals eggs and preys on young birds and small mammals. It also flies inland to feed on worms and other invertebrates.

Herring gulls nest in colonies on cliff slopes, islands or beaches. The nest is usually made of weeds and grass in a hollow in the ground or is sometimes built in a tree or even on a building. The 2 or 3 eggs are incubated for 25 to 27 days by both parents. In their first year, the young have dark-brown plumage, and they do not attain full adult plumage for 3 years. Male and female adult birds look alike, but males are often larger.

NAME: **Black-headed Gull,** *Larus ridibundus*
RANGE: **Iceland, N. Europe and Asia; winters south of range to N. Africa, S. Asia and Philippines**
HABITAT: **coasts, inland marshes**
SIZE: **35.5–38 cm (14–15 in)**

A small, active gull, the black-headed gull is often seen inland in winter (when it is not black-headed), and thrives in freshwater habitats, where it feeds on insects and invertebrates. It scavenges, especially at refuse dumps, and also feeds on the coast like other gulls.

Black-headed gulls breed colonially on marshes, moors and coasts in the spring. A pair builds a nest, usually on the ground and made of plant material, and the female lays 3 eggs, which are incubated for 20 to 24 days.

NAME: **Black-legged Kittiwake,** *Rissa tridactyla*
RANGE: **N. Pacific, N. Atlantic Oceans, parts of Arctic Ocean**
HABITAT: **oceanic**
SIZE: **41–46 cm (16–18 in)**

This kittiwake is much more oceanic in its habits than the *Larus* gulls and normally comes ashore only to breed. It seldom walks, so its legs are much shorter than those of most gulls, and it has only three toes on each foot. It feeds on fish, small mollusks and crustaceans and also scavenges the waste dumped from fishing boats.

These kittiwakes nest in huge colonies of thousands of birds, normally on high cliffs. A pair builds a nest from plants, seaweed and guano, cementing it to the cliff ledge with mud. The usual clutch is 2 eggs, which are incubated for 23 to 32 days by both parents.

NAME: **Common Tern,** *Sterna hirundo*
RANGE: **eastern N. America, N. Europe, Asia; winters south of range to the tropics**
HABITAT: **coastal islands, coasts; inland rivers and lakes**
SIZE: **33–41 cm (13–16 in)**

A common and widespread coastal bird, the common tern feeds on small fish and other marine creatures, which it catches by hovering over the prey and then diving rapidly into the water to seize it with its bill.

Terns nest in colonies of hundreds of thousands on isolated beaches, islands or cliffs. A pair scrapes a hollow in the ground which is then lined with vegetation. Both parents take turns, incubating the 2 or 3 eggs for 21 to 26 days.

NAME: **Brown Noddy,** *Anous stolidus*
RANGE: **tropical oceans**
HABITAT: **offshore waters, islands**
SIZE: **41–43 cm (16–17 in)**

The 5 species of noddy tern are all birds of tropical seas. The noddy seldom dives, but will float on the surface of the water or perch on buoys, driftwood or reefs, watching for prey. It often flies just above the water and snatches small fish when they are driven to the surface by larger fish.

Brown noddies make their untidy twig nests in bushes or on the ground. Both parents incubate the single egg.

## RYNCHOPIDAE: Skimmer Family
There are 3 species of skimmer: 2 are tropical freshwater birds; the third, from the Americas, is coastal in its habits. Skimmers have eyes with slitlike pupils, unique among birds.

NAME: **Black Skimmer,** *Rynchops niger*
RANGE: **USA; winters in S. USA, Central and South America**
HABITAT: **coastal waters, rivers and lakes with sandbanks**
SIZE: **41–51 cm (16–20 in)**

Skimmers possess a unique structural modification: the lower half of the bill, which is laterally flattened and considerably longer than the upper half, is an adaptation for a special method of fishing. The skimmer flies just above a smooth water surface, with its bladelike lower bill cleaving a straight furrow through the water. When the bill strikes a small fish or crustacean, the skimmer clamps down its upper bill and pulls its head back to swallow the prey, while continuing to fly.

Black skimmers breed in spring in colonies of as many as 200 pairs. They scrape hollows in the sand, and the female lays 2 to 4 eggs.

Skua (arctic form)

Black-legged Kittiwake

Ivory Gull

Herring Gull

Common Tern

Black-headed Gull
(breeding plumage)

Brown Noddy

Black Skimmer

# Auks

**NAME: Common Murre,** *Uria aalge*
**RANGE: N. Atlantic, N. Pacific Oceans**
**HABITAT: offshore waters, oceanic**
**SIZE: 41–43 cm (16–17 in)**

One of the most common species in this family, the common murre has a longer, narrower bill than is usual for auks and a less bulky body. In breeding plumage, the head, neck and upperparts are dark brown, but in winter, the throat and front and sides of face and neck are white, with dark stripes extending back from the eyes. These birds feed on fish, mollusks and worms which they catch underwater.

At the end of May, colonies of birds gather in breeding areas on top of rocks or on cliffs. Each female lays 1 egg on bare rock; the egg is pear-shaped, and this led to the long-held belief that, if it moves, it rolls around in a circle, rather than off the ledge. However, this is probably not so, and the reason why the egg is this shape may well be related to its large size and the narrow pelvis of the mother bird. The eggs vary enormously in color and pattern, and this may help the birds to recognize their own eggs in the crowded breeding colony. Both parents incubate the egg for 28 to 30 days. In winter, the birds migrate south of their normal breeding range.

**NAME: Common Puffin,** *Fratercula arctica*
**RANGE: N. Atlantic Ocean: arctic coasts of eastern N. America and W. Eurasia**
**HABITAT: open sea, rocky coasts**
**SIZE: 29–36 cm (11½–14¼ in)**

A small, round-bodied auk with a large head, the common puffin has a spectacular striped bill, which it uses to catch food and in display. In summer, the puffin's bill is colorful, the upper parts of the body and collar are black and the underparts white. In winter, the face is grayish and the bill smaller and duller. Young birds resemble adults in winter plumage, but have smaller, darker bills. The puffin feeds on fish and shellfish and can carry several items at a time in its capacious bill as it flies back to its nest. Its flight is strong and fast, but, like all auks, it has short legs set well back on the body and waddles along clumsily on land.

Common puffins breed from late May in colonies on turfed cliff tops or on islands. The female lays 1 egg, rarely 2, in a burrow abandoned by a shearwater or rabbit or in a hole which she digs herself with her feet. Both parents incubate the egg for 40 to 43 days. After breeding, most puffins winter at sea, offshore from the breeding range, but some populations migrate southward.

## ALCIDAE: Auk Family

The auks are a small family of short-tailed, short-necked diving seabirds, found in the North Pacific, North Atlantic and Arctic oceans and along their coasts. They are truly marine birds, only coming to land to breed on coasts. The 22 species include the guillemots, razorbills, auklets, puffins, murres and auks. All have dark-brown or black plumage, usually with white underparts. Auks swim well and dive from the surface to pursue prey underwater, propelling themselves with their short, narrow wings. They stand upright on land, and this, combined with their general body shape and marine habits, makes them the northern equivalents of the penguins, found in the southern hemisphere.

Indeed, the name penguin was first applied by early mariners to the largest member of the family, the great auk; it was only later used for the similarly adapted birds we know today as penguins. The great auk was flightless, its short, powerful wings of use only for underwater propulsion. Because of this it could not easily escape from man, so great auks were constantly slaughtered for food and have now been extinct for more than a century.

Auks are not, however, closely related to penguins: the resemblance is an example of two groups of birds adapting in a similar way to fill the same niche in northern and southern hemispheres.

Gregarious birds, auks nest in colonies of hundreds or even thousands of birds on cliff tops and rocks. They fly fast, with rapid wing beats, but some of the small species are better adapted for swimming than flying. Some species migrate south of the normal range in winter. Males and females look alike, but there are some seasonal plumage changes. In their annual molt, most species lose all the flight feathers at once and are temporarily flightless.

**NAME: Crested Auklet,** *Aethia cristatella*
**RANGE: N. Pacific Ocean, Bering Sea**
**HABITAT: ocean, sea cliffs**
**SIZE: 24–27 cm (9½–10½ in)**

In the breeding season, the crested auklet has a dark crest of long plumes that fall forward over its bright bill and white plumes behind the eyes. In winter, the crest and eye plumes are smaller, and the bill a dull yellow. Young birds have no crests. These small auklets feed mainly on crustaceans.

Colonies of crested auklets gather on cliffs to breed, and the female lays 1 egg in a rock crevice or among stones.

**NAME: Razorbill,** *Alca torda*
**RANGE: N. Atlantic Ocean**
**HABITAT: coasts, open sea**
**SIZE: 40–42 cm (15¾–16½ in)**

A well-built auk, with a heavy head and a thick neck, the razorbill has a stout, compressed bill with distinctive white markings. In summer, the razorbill's head, neck and upper parts are black, with prominent white lines from bill to eyes. In winter, the cheeks and forehead are white. Razorbills feed on fish, crustaceans and mollusks.

Colonies of razorbills nest on sea cliffs and rocky shores on the Atlantic coasts of Europe and North America, often near guillemot colonies. The breeding season starts about mid-May, and the female lays 1 egg, rarely 2, in a hole or crevice. Both parents incubate the egg for about 25 days, and the young leaves the nest after about 15 days.

**NAME: Dovekie,** *Alle alle*
**RANGE: Arctic Ocean; winters in N. Atlantic Ocean**
**HABITAT: coasts, open sea**
**SIZE: 20 cm (7¾ in)**

The smallest auk, the dovekie is a squat, rounded bird, with a short thick neck and a stout, strong bill. In winter the throat and breast, which are dark in summer plumage, become white. The dovekie feeds on crustaceans, small fish and mollusks. An excellent swimmer, it dives rapidly if alarmed.

From mid-June, thousands of dovekies gather in crowded colonies on arctic coasts and cliffs. They do not make nests, and the female lays 1 egg, occasionally 2, in a crack in the rock. Both sexes take turns to incubate the egg for 24 to 30 days. Dovekies spend the winter at sea, moving as far south as Iceland and Norway. They may even appear inland in particularly bad weather. This species occurs in vast numbers in its arctic habitat and is believed to be one of the most abundant birds in the world.

**NAME: Marbled Murrelet,** *Brachyramphus marmoratus*
**RANGE: N. Pacific Ocean**
**HABITAT: coasts, islands**
**SIZE: 24–25 cm (9½–9¾ in)**

In the breeding season, the marbled murrelet has distinctly barred and speckled underparts, which become white in winter. It feeds, like the rest of the auks, on fish and other marine animals and, when on water, holds its slender bill and tail pointing upward.

Unusually for an auk, it flies inland to breed in mountains or forest areas and lays 1 egg on a twig platform, on moss, or in a nest abandoned by another species of bird.

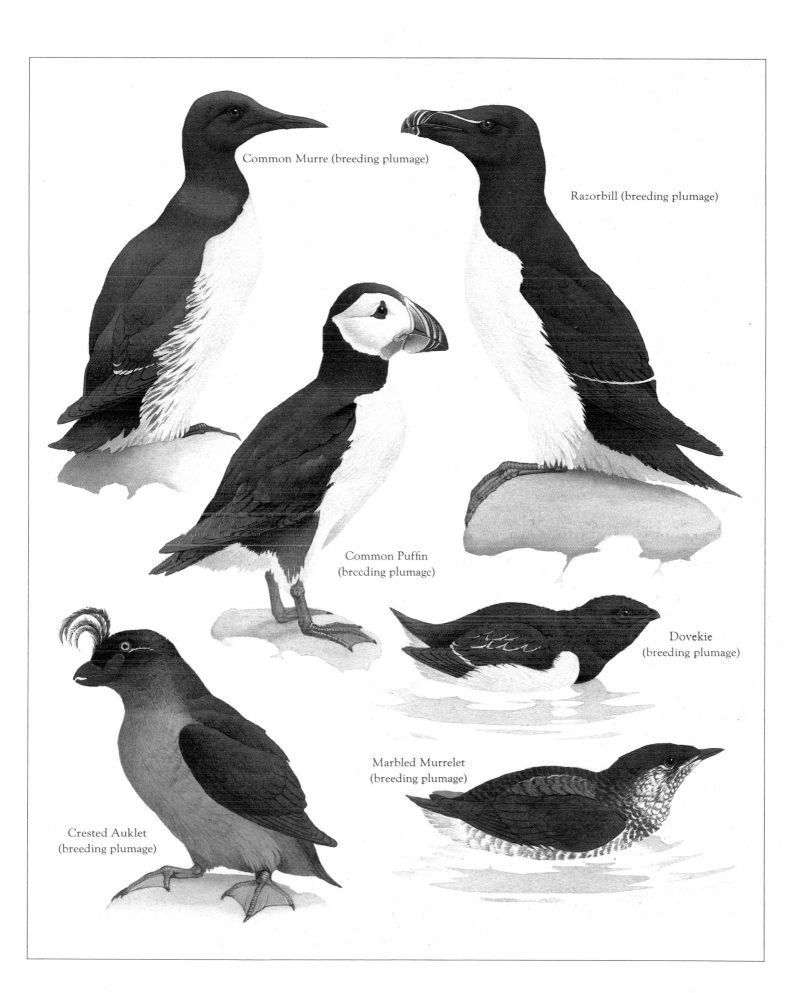

Common Murre (breeding plumage)

Razorbill (breeding plumage)

Common Puffin
(breeding plumage)

Dovekie
(breeding plumage)

Marbled Murrelet
(breeding plumage)

Crested Auklet
(breeding plumage)

# Sandgrouse, Pigeons

## ORDER COLUMBIFORMES

This order includes 2 living families — the sandgrouse and the pigeons — and the now extinct dodo family.

## PTEROCLIDIDAE: Sandgrouse Family

The 16 species of sandgrouse are all terrestrial birds, found in south Europe, Asia and Africa. Despite their name, they are not related to grouse. Sandgrouse are sturdy birds, with short necks, small heads and long, pointed wings; their legs are short and they cannot run but move fast with a waddling gait. Most are sandy colored, with many spotted and barred feathers, which provide good camouflage in the deserts and open plains in which they live. Females are usually smaller than males.

NAME: **Pallas's Sandgrouse,** *Syrrhaptes paradoxus*
RANGE: **central Asia, S. Siberia, S. Mongolia to N. China**
HABITAT: **high-altitude semidesert, steppe**
SIZE: **35–40 cm ($13\frac{3}{4}$–$15\frac{3}{4}$ in)**

Pallas's sandgrouse is a rounded, short-legged bird about the size of a small pigeon. The central tail and outer wing feathers are long and pointed, an indication that it is a strong, fast flier. It is distinguished from other sandgrouse by the black patch on the belly. Adults feed on hard seeds and shoots of desert plants and also take much hard grit.

These sandgrouse nest in large colonies from April to June, laying 3 or 4 eggs in a scrape on the ground. Both parents incubate the eggs for 22 to 27 days and feed the young by regurgitation. There are probably two or three clutches a year.

## COLUMBIDAE: Pigeon Family

There are about 295 species of pigeon and dove, found in most parts of the world except the Antarctic and some oceanic islands. The greatest variety occurs in Asia and Australasia, where there are many extremely beautiful species. The name "pigeon" is generally used to describe larger birds in the family, while "dove" is applied to smaller forms, but there are exceptions to this rule, such as the rock dove, which is pigeonlike in every way.

Pigeons and doves vary in size from birds about the size of a sparrow to a few almost as large as a turkey. Most have dense, soft plumage, rounded, compact bodies and relatively small heads. Male and female look alike in most species, but in a few birds, the male has more striking plumage. Both share an unusual reproductive feature: the lining of the crop secretes "pigeon milk," with which they feed their young for the first few days. This nutritious fluid is high in protein and fats and smells like cheese. Pigeons and doves generally lay only 1 or 2 eggs in a flimsy, but effective, nest, made of sticks.

Many pigeons and doves spend much of their lives in and around trees, feeding on seeds, fruit, buds and other plant material. Others are ground-dwelling but have much the same diet. Pigeons and doves are strong fliers, with excellent homing abilities.

NAME: **Ground Dove,** *Columbina passerina*
RANGE: **S. USA; Mexico, south to central Ecuador, N. Brazil; West Indies**
HABITAT: **open scrub, cultivated land**
SIZE: **15–17 cm ($6$–$6\frac{3}{4}$ in)**

These tiny, ground-living doves walk about briskly in pairs or small groups, with heads nodding, picking up seeds, waste grain, insects and small berries and even scraps of human food. The ground dove is a plump, compact bird with a short, broad tail and rounded wings. The female is much duller than the male.

Mating takes place from February to October over the range. The male courts the female on the ground, pursuing her with his expanded neck bobbing in time to his monotonous cooing. A flimsy nest is made in a low bush or tree or on the ground, and 2 eggs are laid. They are incubated by both parents for 13 or 14 days.

NAME: **Rock Dove/Pigeon,** *Columba livia*
RANGE: **islands and coasts of W. Britain, countries bordering Mediterranean; E. Europe, east to India and Sri Lanka**
HABITAT: **sea and inland cliffs; fields**
SIZE: **33–35.5 cm (13–14 in)**

This species is the ancestor of all the domestic pigeons, including the homing pigeon, and of the feral pigeons (wild birds descended from birds bred in captivity) found in towns almost worldwide. Rock doves generally move in pairs or small groups, although large flocks are quite frequent. They feed on open ground, mainly on seeds, especially cultivated grains, but also on grasses, snails and other mollusks.

Mating takes place throughout the year, after much bowing, nodding, billing and cooing. The nest is flimsily made of twigs and grass on a sheltered cliff ledge or in a hole in a cliff, building or, occasionally, a tree. Two eggs are laid, which are incubated for 17 or 18 days.

NAME: **Band-tailed Pigeon,** *Columba fasciata*
RANGE: **western N. America, south to Mexico; Central America, Colombia**
HABITAT: **coniferous forest, oak woodland in mountainous areas**
SIZE: **36–39 cm ($14\frac{1}{4}$–$15\frac{1}{4}$ in)**

This is a heavily built pigeon. The tail, which is notable in flight and gives the bird its common name, is distinctly banded, with a pale end, a dark band across the middle and a blue-gray base. The band-tailed pigeon flies strongly and swiftly and spends much time perching in trees, where it also seeks most of its food: nuts, berries, seeds, buds and blossoms. It also eats grasshoppers and other insects and, in the autumn, gorges on acorns.

Depending on area, the pigeons mate from March to September, and the female lays 1 egg, occasionally 2, which both parents incubate for 18 to 20 days.

NAME: **Mourning Dove,** *Zenaida macroura*
RANGE: **temperate areas in Canada; USA: all states; Mexico, Bahamas, Cuba, Hispaniola**
HABITAT: **woodland, grain fields with trees, semidesert, suburbs**
SIZE: **28–33 cm (11–13 in)**

The mourning dove has short legs, a rounded body, a neat head and a thin, delicate-looking bill. The central tail feathers are very long in the male, and the wings are long and pointed. The birds generally move in pairs or small groups, but large numbers may gather at feeding grounds. Ground-living birds, they eat mainly weed seeds or grain spilled in harvesting but also take snails and other invertebrates.

The common name derives from the sweet, melancholy cooing of the male, which is followed by a courtship flight. Mating begins in January in the south of the range to April in the north. The nest is loosely constructed of twigs in a tree or bush, a roof gutter or chimney corner or even on the ground. The female lays 2 eggs, which are incubated by both birds for 14 or 15 days.

NAME: **Blue-headed Quail-dove,** *Starnoenas cyanocephala*
RANGE: **Cuba, formerly Jamaica**
HABITAT: **lowland forest and shrubbery; locally highland forest**
SIZE: **30.5–33 cm (12–13 in)**

Numbers of this medium-sized dove are becoming fewer, owing to destruction of its habitat, and little is known about it. It feeds on the ground in areas where it can walk freely, taking mainly seeds, snails and berries. The nest is made low in a tree or shrub or on the ground, and usually 2 eggs are laid.

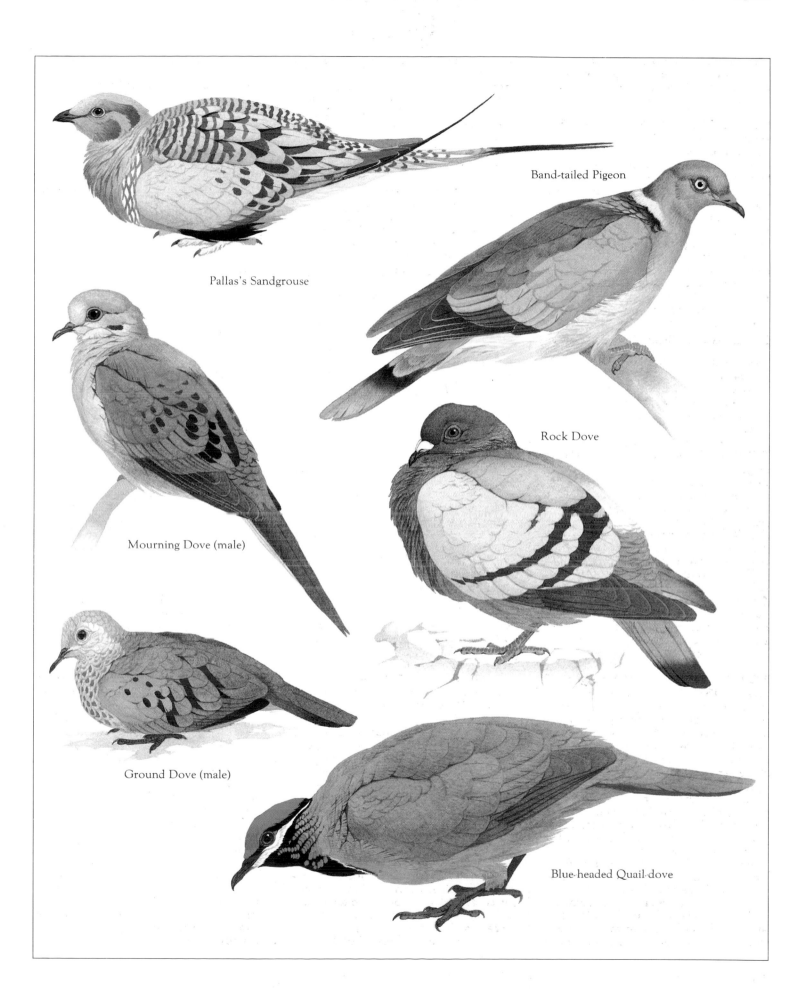

Band-tailed Pigeon

Pallas's Sandgrouse

Rock Dove

Mourning Dove (male)

Ground Dove (male)

Blue-headed Quail-dove

# Pigeons

NAME: **Collared Dove,** *Streptopelia decaocto*
RANGE: **Ireland, Britain, W. Europe (not Spain, Portugal); India, Sri Lanka, Burma; introduced in Middle East, China, Japan.**
HABITAT: **towns, villages, farmland; arid scrubland, palm groves (in India)**
SIZE: **31.5 cm (12½ in)**

This species has enormously expanded its range over recent years by adapting to live in close association with man in both towns and countryside. It now breeds regularly in Great Britain and can be identified by its gray-brown coloration and by its proportionately long white-edged tail and dark primary feathers. Ground-feeding birds, collared doves feed chiefly on seeds, often spilled grain, but take also human food, berries and other plant material. In Europe, to the dismay of fruit-growers, they raid cherry orchards.

In India, these birds breed throughout the year, whenever food supplies are plentiful; in Europe, from March to October. The male makes frequent and showy display flights, rising up with clapping wings then gliding down, often in a spiral, with its wings and tail spread out. The scanty twig nest is made in a tree or bush or on a ledge on a building, and the female lays 2 eggs which are incubated for 14 to 16 days.

NAME: **Nicobar Pigeon,** *Caloenas nicobarica*
RANGE: **Andaman and Nicobar Islands, east to Philippines, New Guinea and Solomon Islands**
HABITAT: **small, off-lying wooded islands**
SIZE: **40 cm (15¾ in)**

The Nicobar pigeon is quite a large bird, with long legs, a short white tail and heavy bill. Its stance is rather like that of a vulture, and unlike most pigeons, it has short, hard plumage, except on the neck, where the feathers are elongated to form hackles that cover most of the body. The female is slightly smaller than the male, with a smaller bill cere, and the juvenile looks like the female, but duller and without the white tail.

These birds are found throughout their range only on small islands and tiny islets off larger islands, but their flight is swift and strong and they wander freely between groups of islands. Little is known about their habits, but they appear to be ground feeders, feeding on seeds, fruit and some invertebrates, mainly at dusk, or by day in the gloom of the forest. The white tail and large eyes seem to be adaptations for this way of life.

Nicobar pigeons may nest in large colonies, building their nests in trees or bushes. The female lays a single egg.

NAME: **Yellow-legged Green Pigeon,** *Treron phoenicoptera*
RANGE: **India, Sri Lanka, S.E. Asia to Vietnam (not Malaysia)**
HABITAT: **forest, scrubland, fruiting trees in open country, parks and gardens**
SIZE: **33 cm (13 in)**

This colorful bird is about the size of a feral pigeon but is rather more heavily built. Females look similar to males but are not quite as bright, while juveniles have no mauve shoulder patches and are much duller and paler. Yellow-legged green pigeons are swift, strong fliers and usually move about in groups of up to 10 birds, although they will gather in trees in huge flocks to feed. They clamber about the branches, clinging to them and even hanging upside down to reach particularly succulent berries and fruit (especially wild figs), buds and shoots. They also drink by clinging to branches which overhang or trail into the water.

In India, green pigeons breed from March to June. Before mating, the male parades up and down in front of the female with feathers puffed out, calling with a tuneful sequence of notes rather like a human whistle. The usual twiggy nest is built in a shrub or tree, often close to other green pigeons' nests, and the female lays 2 eggs which are incubated for about 14 days.

NAME: **Nutmeg/Torres Strait Pigeon,** *Ducula spilorrhoa*
RANGE: **New Guinea, islands and archipelagos to N.E. and E. Australia**
HABITAT: **woodland, mangrove swamps, savanna, forest edge, plantations, gardens**
SIZE: **39–44.5 cm (15¼–17½ in)**

Nutmeg pigeons roost and breed in large numbers on small off-lying islands, but parties of them daily fly long distances over the sea to feed on larger islands or in coastal areas of the mainland. They search among the branches of trees and shrubs for fruit and berries, and as their name suggests, they eat wild nutmegs, although these are not an important part of their diet. Observations indicate that birds breeding on islands of the Great Barrier Reef off Australia fly high in large flocks when going to feed but return in the evening, just skimming the water, in a stream of small parties.

Flying also plays a part in the mating behavior of these birds, when males display to females by bowing and then shooting swiftly up into the air to glide down, time and again. The breeding season appears to be from September to January in New Guinea and October and November in Australia. The birds build a twiggy nest in a shrub or tree, and the female lays 1 egg, which is incubated by both parents for 26 to 28 days.

NAME: **Superb Fruit Dove/ Purple Crowned Pigeon,** *Ptilinopus superbus*
RANGE: **Sulawesi, Sulu Archipelago, islands and archipelagos of W. Papua and New Guinea to N.E. Australia**
HABITAT: **forest, forest edge, riverbanks, cultivated land with trees**
SIZE: **22–24 cm (8½–9½ in)**

This compact, medium-sized dove is truly superb, with its green and coppery plumage but, despite this, is remarkably inconspicuous when sitting in the tree-tops. The female is a more uniform blue-green, while the feathers of the juvenile are yellow-green. Superb fruit doves fly with a whirring flight from tree to tree, usually singly or in pairs, but dozens may congregate to feed on berries and small fruit as it ripens.

The nest is normally a small collection of twigs, set low in a tree or shrub, and the female lays a single egg. Both parents incubate the egg for about 14 days, the male during the day and the female at night.

NAME: **Diamond Dove,** *Geopelia cuneata*
RANGE: **N. and inland Australia; sometimes coastal areas of S. Australia**
HABITAT: **open woodland, mulga (acacia) scrub, open land with trees, near water**
SIZE: **19–21.5 cm (7½–8½ in)**

A delicate-looking, rather plump little bird about the size of a house sparrow, the diamond dove is the smallest pigeon of all. Diamond doves are gregarious birds and are only rarely seen alone. Normally they move about in pairs, not always of opposite sexes, or in groups of up to 20 or so. Although they usually roost and nest in trees, they feed on the ground and walk around with a quick toddling action, searching for tiny seeds of grasses and herbaceous plants. They also eat the larger seeds of the *Acacia* and probably leaves and shoots of weeds and grasses. They are great sun lovers and will often rest in the sunshine, even in the heat of the day. Characteristically their flight is fast and swooping, rather like that of parakeets.

Mating is accompanied by unusual behavior by the male: he displays to the female by lifting his wings, then mounts her and immediately dismounts and strikes above her head with his wing. He remounts and repeats the action on the other side of the female; he then mounts her for the third time and copulates. Once again, he appears to attack the female but does not actually touch her. The nest is a typical pigeon nest, although small, usually low down in a bush or tree or a tangle of fallen branches and dry grass, in which the female lays 2 eggs. The eggs hatch after 12 or 13 days, and the young can fly 11 or 12 days later.

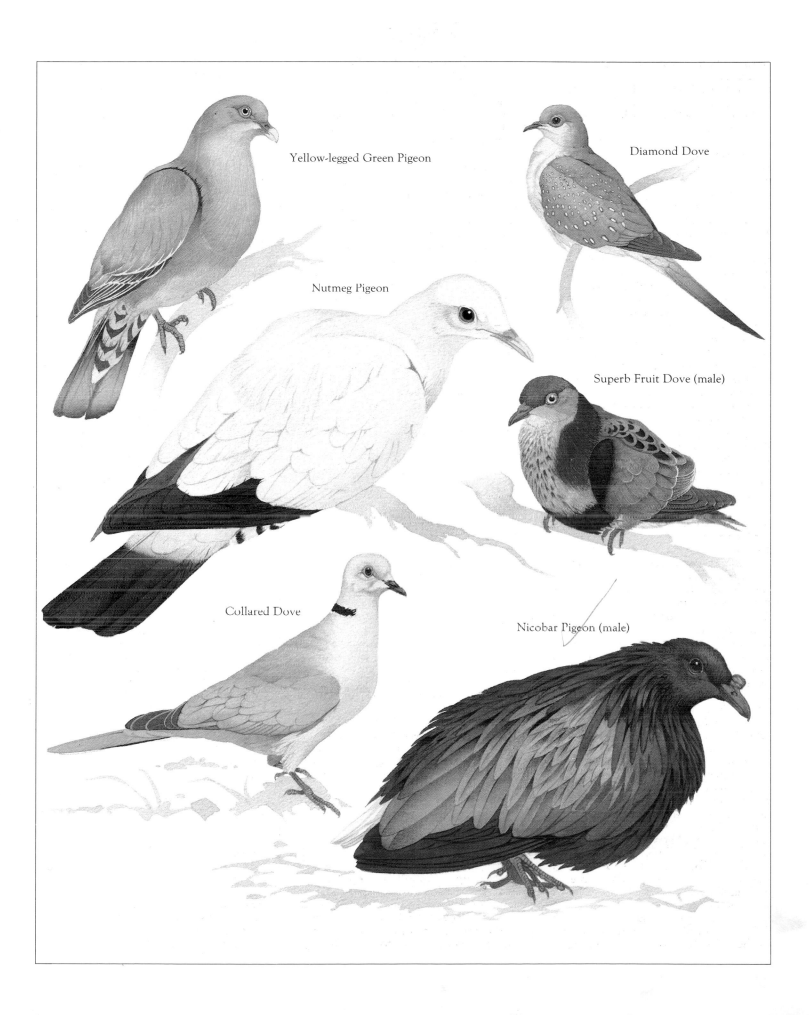

Yellow-legged Green Pigeon

Diamond Dove

Nutmeg Pigeon

Superb Fruit Dove (male)

Collared Dove

Nicobar Pigeon (male)

# Pigeons

NAME: **Large Brown Cuckoo Dove/ Brown Pigeon,** *Macropygia phasianella*
RANGE: **E. Australia; Java and Sumatra and adjacent islands; N. Borneo to the Philippines**
HABITAT: **glades and clearings in forest**
SIZE: **38–43.5 cm (15–17 in)**

The large brown cuckoo dove has rich, reddish-brown plumage with faint gray barring and spotting on the neck, breast and underparts; the speckling is more marked in the female, and the juvenile is even more noticeably barred. In eastern Australia, this is one of the commonest pigeons in the remaining pockets of rain forest, but populations are being reduced by forest clearance and by hunting. The long tail gives the bird an awkward appearance when it is flying among the trees, but, in fact, it seems to be an adaptation to the bird's largely arboreal way of life, since the spread tail is often used as a balancing aid. Cuckoo doves eat fruit and berries, which they take from the ground, as well as from trees and shrubs.

In Queensland, Australia, where breeding has been observed, mating takes place between July and January. The female lays 1 egg which is incubated for 16 to 18 days.

NAME: **Crested Pigeon,** *Ocyphaps lophotes*
RANGE: **Australia**
HABITAT: **arid areas: lightly wooded grassland, open country and agricultural land with some trees and shrubs, near water**
SIZE: **31–35 cm (12¼–13¾ in)**

This slimly built pigeon, with its longish tail, long dark crest, like that of a lapwing, and strikingly barred wing coverts, has a sprightly air. The impression of jauntiness is emphasized by its swift, distinctive flight, in which several rapid wing beats alternate with periods of gliding, with the wings held still and almost horizontal. Since these birds live in arid country, reliable watering places, such as steady streams, dams or even cattle troughs, are essential to them. They normally come to drink before feeding, about an hour after sunrise, and in dry periods a flock of up to a thousand may gather. Generally, however, crested pigeons move about in pairs or in groups of from 4 to 30 individuals, feeding on the ground on seeds of herbaceous plants and *Acacia* trees, young green shoots and small bulbs.

They nest mainly in spring and summer, but breeding can take place almost year-round, usually after heavy rains. The female lays 2 eggs which are incubated for 18 days. There may be up to 7 successive broods.

NAME: **Luzon Bleeding-heart Pigeon,** *Gallicolumba luzonica*
RANGE: **Philippines: islands of Luzon and Polillo**
HABITAT: **forest**
SIZE: **30.5 cm (12 in)**

The most striking characteristic of this pigeon is the patch of hairy, blood-red feathers in the middle of the breast that gives the bird its common name. The illusion that the breast of the bird is bleeding is enhanced by the fact that the red feathers of the "wound" form an indentation in the surrounding white feathers. Both male and female have this "bleeding-heart." The bleeding-heart pigeon has a plump, compact body, short to medium-length wings and tail, and long legs. When alarmed, it tends to fly only a short distance and then to land and run rapidly, or to crouch with its head lowered and tail raised. Although it roosts in trees, it is mainly a ground-living bird and feeds on seeds, fallen berries and probably many insects and other invertebrates: the pigeons in this genus appear to take more animal food than most other pigeons.

They are thought to nest fairly low down in bushes, trees or vines and to lay 2 eggs to a clutch.

Other closely related species of *Gallicolumba* are found on neighboring islands. There are 3 species in New Guinea, but generally most islands and archipelagos support only one species.

NAME: **Victoria Crowned Pigeon,** *Goura victoria*
RANGE: **N. New Guinea: Siriwo River to Astrolabe Bay; introduced (?) in Japen and Biak Islands**
HABITAT: **rain forest, muddy lowland flats**
SIZE: **58.5–73.5 cm (23–29 in)**

The 3 species of crowned pigeon are remarkable chiefly for their size — about that of a large domestic fowl — and for their erect, laterally compressed, fan-shaped crests of feathers. These feathers are long, with slightly separated barbs at the ends, which give them a beautiful lacelike appearance. Male and female look alike; juveniles are duller.

Little is known of the habits of the Victoria crowned pigeon in the wild, but it probably behaves in much the same way as other closely related species in the same area, spending most of its time on the ground, feeding on fallen fruit, berries and possibly small invertebrates. In captivity, it will also eat lettuce, corn, carrots and peanuts and is particularly fond of wild figs. It perches on branches and flies up into trees when alarmed.

Courtship display seems to consist of bowing and "dancing" by the male bird.

The female responds by spreading her wings and raising them up high; she also runs around the male, with slightly bent legs, uttering short hissing cries. The proportionately large nest is built among the branches of a tree and is more compact and less makeshift than a typical pigeon nest. In captivity, the female has been observed to lay 1 egg, which was incubated by both parents for 30 days. The young bird left the nest at about 4 weeks but was fed by both parents until it was 13 weeks old.

NAME: **Tooth-billed Pigeon,** *Didunculus strigirostris*
RANGE: **Samoa: Upolu and Savaii Islands**
HABITAT: **wooded mountainsides**
SIZE: **38 cm (15 in)** Ⓥ

This species takes its name from its unique bill, which is strong and curved, with two notches and three projections — or teeth — on each side of the lower mandible. The scientific name, *strigirostris*, means "owl bill." The tooth-billed pigeon is a thick-set bird about the size of a feral pigeon, with a short tail, rather long legs and tight plumage, which has a silvery sheen, on head and breast. In the female, the feathers have less sheen; the juvenile is much browner and its plumage is more barred.

These birds live on the ground, feeding on seeds, fruit, berries and the mountain plantain which grows in their habitat. When eating, they hold their food down with their feet and, with the bill, tear it apart or nibble it into pieces before swallowing it. It is thought that the shape of the bill may have evolved as a response to these specialized feeding habits. When numbers of these birds were still plentiful, they were usually found in groups of 10 to 20.

When flushed, tooth-billed pigeons will fly, with loudly beating wings, for about 30 m (100 ft), beneath the lowest branches of tall trees, and then glide for a comparable distance before settling in a tree. They fly with agility among undergrowth and perch in low trees, although they seem to roost in tall ones. It is said that formerly these birds nested on the ground, but they now nest in trees because of the destruction wrought by introduced pigs. No definite information about their nesting habits is available.

Large Brown
Cuckoo Dove (male)

Luzon Bleeding-heart Pigeon

Tooth-billed Pigeon

Crested Pigeon

Victoria Crowned Pigeon

# Lories, Cockatoos, Parrots

## ORDER PSITTACIFORMES

The 315 or so species of parrot make up one of the most easily identified groups of birds. Despite a size range of between 10 and 101 cm (4 and 40 in), all types have a general similarity of outward appearance and inner structure. There are 3 families within the order: first, the brush-tongued lories; second the cockatoos; and third, the parrots proper.

Most parrots are brightly colored tree-living birds. Their beaks are short, powerful and strongly hooked, with a bulging base, or cere. The upper part of the parrot's bill is hinged and moved by muscles, and the flexibility that this gives allows the bill to become almost like a third manipulative limb, which is used in climbing and feeding. Although many birds have hinged bills, this feature is more marked in the short-billed parrots. Males and females look alike in most species, but there are plumage differences in a few instances.

Parrots are distributed throughout the tropical and subtropical zones of both hemispheres, with the largest number of species found in Australasia and in the Amazon area of South America. In the forests of these regions, parrots feed largely on fruit, nuts, seeds, nectar and fungi. They manipulate their foods with their feet and with their beaks and strong, mobile tongues. Many parrots are extremely gregarious and vocal, making screaming and discordant calls. Although renowned as mimics in captivity, they are not known to mimic sounds in the wild.

### LORIIDAE: Lory Family

Known as lories or lorikeets, the 54 species in the lory family are characterized by their brush-tipped tongues, with which they extract pollen and nectar from flowers. They are all gregarious, arboreal birds.

NAME: Black-capped Lory, *Lorius lory*
RANGE: New Guinea, Papuan Islands
HABITAT: forest
SIZE: 31 cm (12¼ in)

Several races of this lory, with slight plumage differences, occur on the various islands in its range. Shy birds, black-capped lories frequent the upper levels of the forest, usually moving in pairs or small groups of up to a dozen. They feed on pollen, nectar, flowers and fruit, and on insects and their larvae. Little is known of the breeding habits of this lory, but from the few observed cases, it appears that the female lays 2 eggs, which she incubates for a period of about 24 days.

NAME: Rainbow Lory/Lorikeet, *Trichoglossus haematodus*
RANGE: E. and N. Australia, Tasmania; Bali, east to New Hebrides
HABITAT: forest, coconut plantations, gardens, parks
SIZE: 26 cm (10¼ in)

One of the most attractively plumaged birds in the parrot order, the adaptable rainbow lorikeet inhabits almost any wooded land, even near human habitation. Usually seen in pairs or flocks of anything from 3 or 4 to 100 birds, rainbow lorikeets are active and noisy and continually fly about the trees, searching for food and calling loudly. Pollen, nectar, fruit, berries, seeds, leaves, insects and larvae are all included in their diet, and they will feed on grain crops and invade orchards.

Rainbow lorikeets nest in holes in trees, high above the ground. The female lays 2 eggs, rarely 3, which she incubates for about 25 days. Both parents feed the chicks, which stay in the nest until they are about 7 or 8 weeks old.

### CACATUIDAE: Cockatoo Family

The 18 species of cockatoo are distinguished from other parrots mainly by skull characteristics, but their most obvious external feature is the erectile crest on the head. A cockatoo raises its crest when alarmed and when alighting.

NAME: Cockatiel, *Nymphicus hollandicus*
RANGE: Australia
HABITAT: open country
SIZE: 32 cm (12½ in)

The slender cockatiel has long wings and tail and a tapering crest on its head. Males and females differ slightly in plumage, males having brighter markings than females. In pairs or small flocks, cockatiels forage on the ground for grass seeds and also feed in the trees on fruit and berries.

Breeding usually takes place between August and December, but the exact timing depends on the conditions, particularly on rainfall. The 4 to 7 eggs are laid in a hole in a tree and are incubated by both parents for 21 to 23 days. The young leave the nest at 4 or 5 weeks, and males acquire their bright facial markings at about 6 months.

NAME: Sulphur-crested Cockatoo, *Cacatua galerita*
RANGE: New Guinea and offshore islands, Aru Islands, N. and E. Australia, Tasmania; introduced in New Zealand
HABITAT: forest, savanna, farmland
SIZE: 50 cm (19¾ in)

Noisy, gregarious birds, sulphur-crested cockatoos move in pairs or family groups in the breeding season, but join in flocks for the rest of the year. In open country, these flocks may number hundreds of birds. Each flock has a habitual roosting site, which the birds leave at sunrise to fly to daytime feeding grounds, where they eat seeds, fruit, nuts, flowers, leaves, insects and larvae.

After a brief courtship display, culminating in a spell of mutual preening, the sulphur-crested cockatoos nest in a hole in a tree. Both parents incubate the 2 or 3 eggs for about 30 days, and the young stay in the nest for 6 to 9 weeks.

### PSITTACIDAE: Parrot Family

With about 243 species, this is the largest of the 3 families in the parrot order. It includes a wide variety of forms, none of which has a crest or a brush-tipped tongue.

NAME: Kea, *Nestor notabilis*
RANGE: New Zealand: South Island
HABITAT: forest, open country
SIZE: 48 cm (18¾ in)

The kea is a bold, stocky bird with a long, curving upper bill; the female's bill is shorter and less curved. Keas fly strongly, wheeling in wide arcs, even in stormy, windy weather. They feed in trees and on the ground on fruit, berries, leaves, insects and larvae. They will also scavenge on refuse dumps and eat carrion. The belief has long persisted that keas attack and kill sheep, and many birds have been destroyed by farmers for this reason. Although they may well attack sick, injured or trapped sheep, these activities are thought to have been exaggerated, and keas are now protected by law.

Nesting can take place at almost any time of year but usually occurs between July and January. Males are polygamous and may mate with several females. The nest is made in a crevice, under rocks, among the roots of a tree or in a hollow log. The female lays 2 to 4 eggs which she incubates for 21 to 28 days.

NAME: Red-breasted Pygmy Parrot, *Micropsitta bruijnii*
RANGE: Buru, Ceram, New Guinea, Bismarck Archipelago, Solomon Islands
HABITAT: mountain forest
SIZE: 9 cm (3½ in)

In pairs or small groups, these tiny parrots clamber over branches of trees, busily feeding on the lichens and fungus prevalent in high forest. The short tail has stiff shafts and can be used as a prop, in the manner of a woodpecker. Pygmy parrots may also feed on other plant material and insects.

Kea (male)

Sulphur-crested
Cockatoo

Black-capped
Lory

Red-breasted
Pygmy Parrot

Cockatiel (male)

Rainbow Lory

# Parrots

NAME: **Eclectus Parrot,** *Eclectus (=Larius) roratus*
RANGE: **New Guinea to Solomon and Sumba Islands; Australia: extreme N. Queensland;**
HABITAT: **lowland forest**
SIZE: **35 cm (13¾ in)**

Male and female eclectus parrots differ so radically in plumage that for years they were thought to be separate species. Both are glossy, brilliant birds, males with primarily green plumage and females with red. The body is stocky and the tail short and square. They are noisy, gregarious birds, roosting in groups of as many as 80 and flying off at sunrise in pairs or small groups to feed on fruit, nuts, seeds, berries, leaves, flowers and nectar.

The nest is made high up in a tree at the edge of the forest or in a clearing. The 2 eggs are laid in a hole in the tree trunk, and the female incubates them for about 26 days.

NAME: **Gray Parrot,** *Psittacus erithacus*
RANGE: **central Africa: W. coast to Kenya and N.W. Tanzania**
HABITAT: **lowland forest, savanna, mangrove swamps**
SIZE: **33 cm (13 in)**

Flocks of gray parrots roost together in tall trees at the forest edge or on small islands in rivers and lakes. At sunrise they fly off swiftly in pairs or small groups to find food, following regular routes to and from the roosting area. Climbing from branch to branch, gray parrots feed in the trees on seeds, nuts, berries and fruit, particularly the fruit of the oil palm.

The timing of the breeding season varies according to area, and there may occasionally be two broods a year. There have been few observations of nesting in the wild, but the female is believed to lay 3 or 4 eggs in a hole in a tree and to incubate them herself.

NAME: **Peach-faced Lovebird,** *Agapornis roseicollis*
RANGE: **S.W. Africa: Angola, Namibia, S. Africa: N. Cape Province**
HABITAT: **dry open country**
SIZE: **15 cm (6 in)**

Flocks of these noisy, abundant lovebirds maneuver skillfully and swiftly among the trees and bushes. They eat seeds and berries and never move far from some form of water supply. Lovebirds are so called because of their conspicuous mutual preening habits.

Colonies of lovebirds nest in crevices in cliffs or in buildings, or take over large parts of the communal, many-chambered nests of weaver birds. The female is thought to lay 3 to 6 eggs, which she incubates for 23 days.

NAME: **Kakapo/Owl Parrot,** *Strigops habroptilus*
RANGE: **New Zealand: formerly all islands, now parts of South and Stewart Islands (least threatened on Stewart Island)**
HABITAT: **mountain forest (all altitudes to 1,250 m (4,100 ft)**
SIZE: **64 cm (25¼ in)** Ⓔ

Although the highest priority has been given to its protection, the kakapo is in serious danger of extinction. The population has declined steadily over the last 1,000 years, with the settlement of New Zealand, the resulting land clearance and the introduction of predators such as ermines and rats. Efforts are being made to establish kakapos on offshore islands, which are free from predators.

A most unusual parrot, the kakapo is a ground-living, flightless, nocturnal bird. During the day it shelters among rocks or bushes or in a burrow and emerges at dusk to feed on fruit, berries, nuts, seeds, shoots, leaves, moss and fungi. The kakapo climbs well, using its beak and feet, and can flap its wings to help balance itself as it climbs or jumps from trees.

Courtship habits, too, are different from those of other parrots, for the males display communally in traditional areas, or leks. Each male excavates several shallow, bowl-shaped areas in which he displays: the bowl helps to amplify the booming calls which accompany his show. The nest is a burrow, made among rocks or tree roots, and 1 or 2, rarely 3, eggs are laid. The female is thought to incubate the clutch and care for the young alone. Kakapos do not appear to breed every year, and breeding may be linked to the availability of food.

NAME: **Rose-ringed Parakeet,** *Psittacula krameri*
RANGE: **central Africa, India to Sri Lanka; introduced in Mauritius, Middle East, Singapore**
HABITAT: **woodland, cultivated land**
SIZE: **40 cm (15¾ in)**

The bold, noisy rose-ringed parakeets are usually seen in small flocks, although they may gather in hundreds at feeding or roosting sites. They fly well but tend not to travel far afield. Seeds, berries, fruit, flowers and nectar are the main items of their diet, and they are relentless in their search, invading orchards and plantations, decimating sunflower crops and rice paddies and even ripping open bags of stored grain.

Males and females differ slightly in plumage: the female lacks the pink collar and black facial markings and has shorter central tail feathers. At the onset of the breeding season, the pair perform

their courtship ritual, the female rolling her eyes and head until the male approaches, rubs bills with her and feeds her. They nest in a hole in a tree, which they excavate or take over from woodpeckers or barbets, or under the roof of a building. The female lays 3 to 5 eggs, which she incubates for 22 days. The young leave the nest about 7 weeks after hatching.

NAME: **Crimson Rosella,** *Platycercus elegans*
RANGE: **E. and S.E. Australia; introduced in New Zealand and Norfolk Island**
HABITAT: **coastal and mountain forest, gardens, parks**
SIZE: **36 cm (14¼ in)**

Crimson rosellas are bold, colorful birds, abundant in most of their range. Adults live in pairs or groups of up to 5, while juveniles band together in larger groups. Much of their day is spent feeding, mainly on seeds but also on fruit, blossoms, insects and larvae, on the ground or in the treetops.

The breeding season starts in late August or early September. In his courtship display, the male lets his wings droop while he fans his tail out, moving it from side to side. The female nests in a hole in a tree and lays 5 to 8 eggs, which she incubates for 21 days, leaving the nest only briefly each morning to be fed by her partner. The young leave the nest at about 5 weeks but remain with their parents for another 5 weeks before joining a flock of other young rosellas.

NAME: **Budgerigar,** *Melopsittacus undulatus*
RANGE: **Australia (interior); introduced in USA: Florida**
HABITAT: **scrub, open country**
SIZE: **18 cm (7 in)**

So popular as a cage bird, with its many color variations, the budgerigar is a small parrot with predominantly green plumage in the wild. Its numbers vary with conditions, but it is generally common and, in years of abundant food supplies, is one of the most numerous Australian species. Active mainly in the early morning and late afternoon, flocks of budgerigars search on the ground for grass seeds, their main food. They are swift, agile birds in the air, and flocks are nomadic, continually moving from one area to another in search of food and water.

Breeding takes place at any time of the year, usually after rains which ensure food supplies. A nest is made in a hollow in a tree stump or log, and 4 to 6, sometimes 8, eggs are laid and incubated by the female for 18 days. The young leave the nest after about 30 days.

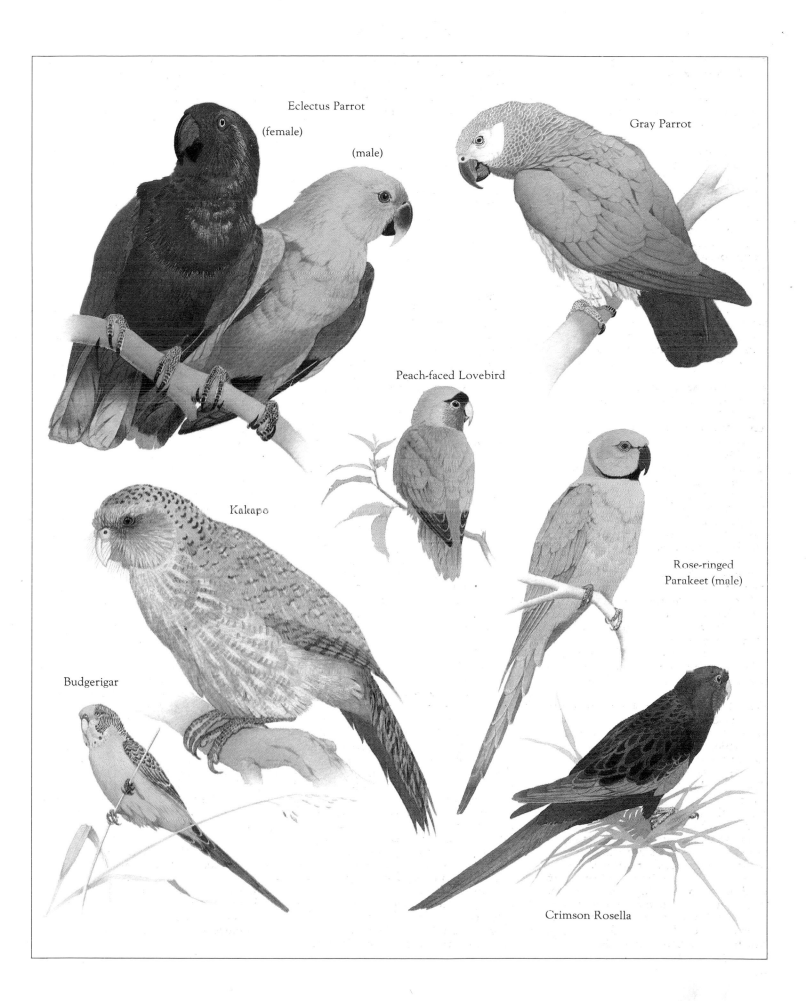

Eclectus Parrot
(female)
(male)

Gray Parrot

Peach-faced Lovebird

Kakapo

Rose-ringed
Parakeet (male)

Budgerigar

Crimson Rosella

# Parrots

NAME: **Scarlet Macaw,** *Ara macao*
RANGE: **Mexico, Central America,**
**northern South America to Brazil**
HABITAT: **forest, savanna, plantations**
SIZE: 85 cm (33½ in)

A spectacular, brilliantly plumaged bird, the scarlet macaw is one of the largest and most striking members of its family. A frequently photographed and painted species and the most familiar of South American parrots, it is nevertheless declining in numbers because of the widespread destruction of its rain forest habitat and the collection of large numbers of young birds and nestlings for the lucrative cage-bird trade. It is already rare in some parts of its range.

Scarlet macaws maintain strong pair bonds and are generally seen in pairs, family groups or flocks of up to 20. As they make their daily journeys from roosting areas to feeding grounds, pairs will fly together, wings almost touching. They feed up in the trees on seeds, fruit, nuts, berries and other plant matter and, although they eat in silence, they fly off, squawking noisily, at any disturbance.

Surprisingly little is known of the breeding habits of these splendid birds. Nests have been observed in holes in tree trunks well above the ground, but there is little reliable information on clutch size or incubation.

NAME: **Spectacled Parrotlet,** *Forpus*
*conspicillatus*
RANGE: **Central and South America:**
**E. Panama, Colombia (not S.E.),**
**W. Venezuela**
HABITAT: **open forest, thornbush**
SIZE: 12 cm (4¾ in)

About 3 races of this little parrotlet occur within the range, all with slight plumage differences. Generally, however, males have dull, greenish upperparts, with yellow markings on the forehead, cheeks and throat and some blue markings. Females have brighter green upperparts than males and lack the blue markings. Out of the breeding season, spectacled parrotlets move in small flocks of 5 to 20, making constant chattering calls. Busy, active birds, they forage in trees and bushes for berries, fruit, buds and blossoms or search on the ground for the seeds of grasses and herbaceous plants. Their flight is swift and erratic.

During the breeding season, the parrotlets associate in pairs. Little is known of their breeding habits, but it is likely that they make their nests in natural holes in trees or posts. The female is believed to lay 2 to 4 eggs. There are several species of parrotlet in the genus *Forpus*, all with similar habits and appearance.

NAME: **Sun Conure,** *Aratinga solstitialis*
RANGE: **South America: Guyana,**
**Suriname, French Guiana, N.E. Brazil**
HABITAT: **open forest, savanna**
SIZE: 30 cm (11¾ in)

A beautiful bird, with vibrant yellow plumage, the sun conure is not a common species, and little is known of its habits. Generally seen in small flocks, sun conures are noisy birds which make frequent screeching calls. They feed on seeds, fruit, nuts and berries, usually up in the treetops.

According to the few observations of breeding habits, the female lays 3 or 4 eggs and incubates them for 4 weeks. Both parents feed the chicks, which remain in the nest for about 8 weeks.

The golden-capped conure, *A. auro-capilla*, and the jendaya conure, *A. jendaya*, are both similar to the sun conure and may even be races of the same species.

NAME: **Yellow-headed Parrot/Yellow-**
**crowned Amazon,** *Amazona*
*ochrocephala*
RANGE: **Mexico, Central America, south**
**to E. Peru, N. Bolivia and N. Brazil;**
**Trinidad**
HABITAT: **forest, wide range of wooded**
**habitats**
SIZE: 35 cm (13¾ in)

The yellow-headed parrot is one of the 29 or so species in the genus *Amazona*, all sometimes referred to as "amazons." Most are medium-sized parrots with predominantly green plumage and some brilliant markings. Like many amazons, this species is declining in numbers both because of the destruction of its forest habitat in some areas and because of the collection of large numbers of young for the cage-bird trade. Yellow-headed parrots are particularly sought after because of their reputation as good mimics and talkers.

During the day small groups of these parrots feed in the treetops on fruit, seeds, nuts, berries and blossoms and will also come down to within 2 m (6½ ft) of the ground to find food. They are strong fliers and travel well above the trees except when going only short distances. At dusk they return to regular roosting areas.

A breeding pair finds a hollow in a tree trunk, which both enlarge, and the female lays 3 or 4 eggs. She incubates them for 29 days, during which the male remains nearby. Twice a day the female leaves the eggs briefly to join her mate, who feeds her by regurgitation.

NAME: **Monk Parakeet,** *Myiopsitta*
*monachus*
RANGE: **South America: central Bolivia,**
**S. Brazil to central Argentina;**
**introduced in Puerto Rico and**
**N.E. USA**
HABITAT: **open woodland, palm groves,**
**cultivated land, eucalyptus plantations**
SIZE: 29 cm (11½ in)

A popular cage bird and abundant in the wild, the monk parakeet is a medium-sized parrot, with long tail feathers and a heavy bill. It is an adaptable species and readily inhabits trees planted by man in orchards or on ranchland, even when near to human habitation. The highly gregarious monk parakeets occur in flocks of 10 to 100 or more and build enormous communal nests, unique in the parrot order. The nest is used for breeding and for roosting and so is inhabited throughout the year and is always the center of much activity as the birds come and go, shrieking noisily.

Monk parakeets leave the nest in small groups to find food, and if they are feeding in open country or fields, a few birds will sit up in nearby trees to act as sentinels. At the first sign of danger, they call a warning, and the feeding birds quickly disperse. Seeds, fruit, berries, nuts, blossoms, leaves, insects and larvae are all eaten, and monk parakeets can cause much damage by feeding on cereal crops and in orchards.

Although the nest is used all year round, at the start of the breeding season in October the birds add to it and repair any damage. The nest is usually situated at the top of a tree and is made of twigs, particularly thorny twigs, which hold together well and deter predators. It may start with only a few compartments, but it is gradually added to until it has anything up to 20 compartments, each occupied by a pair of birds. Each compartment has its own entrance at the bottom of the nest, leading into the brood chamber. The whole structure is so strong that other birds may nest on top of it.

The female parakeet lays 5 to 8 eggs, but because of the obvious difficulties of observing behavior in such a structure, little is known of the incubation of the clutch or the care of the chicks. The young birds leave the nest at about 6 weeks old.

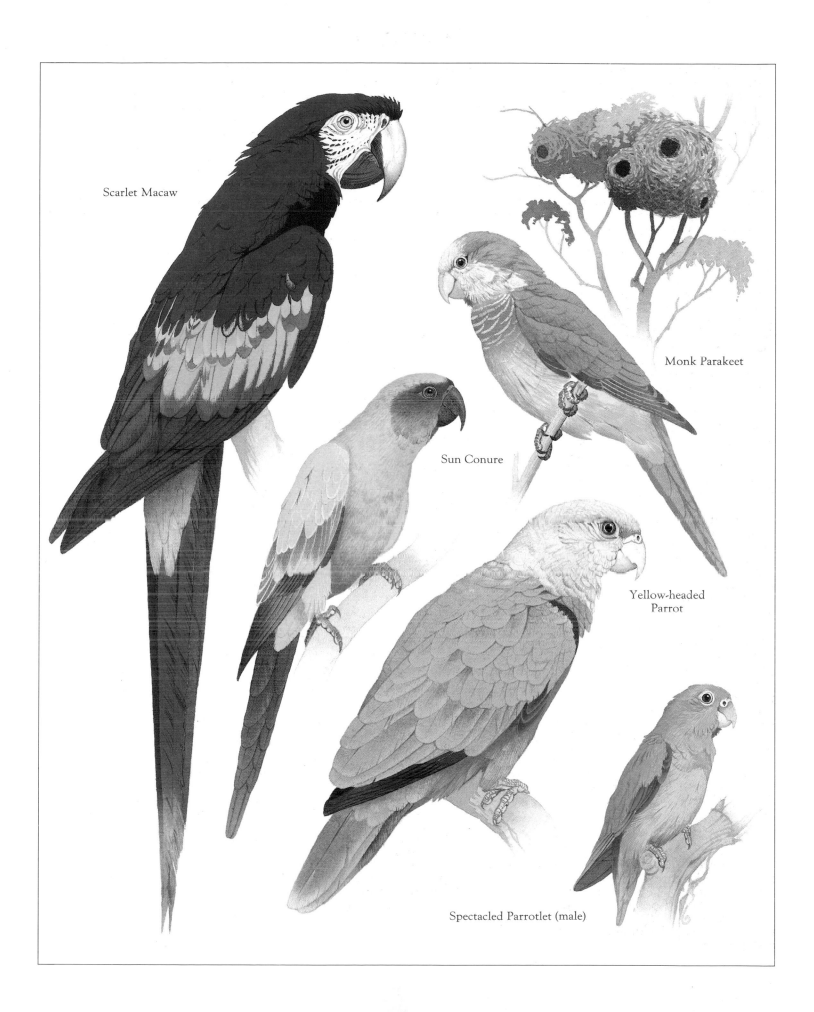

Scarlet Macaw

Monk Parakeet

Sun Conure

Yellow-headed
Parrot

Spectacled Parrotlet (male)

# Cuckoos

**NAME: Common Koel,** *Eudynamys scolopacea*
**RANGE: India, Pakistan, Sri Lanka, S. China, S.E. Asia, New Guinea, Australia**
**HABITAT: forest edge, scrub, cultivated land, gardens**
**SIZE: 43 cm (17 in)**

The koel is a solitary bird, keeping to leafy trees and seldom descending to the ground. It feeds on fruit, particularly figs, but also eats insects and small invertebrates such as snails. Male and female look unalike: the male is black and glossy, while the female has brownish plumage, spotted and barred with white and buff.

The female koel lays her eggs in the nest of the house crow, *Corvus splendens*, or of a friarbird or honey eater. Birds which use the crow as a foster parent lay several eggs which resemble those of the host but are smaller. The young koels are black like young crows.

**NAME: Drongo Cuckoo,** *Surniculus lugubris*
**RANGE: India, S.E. Asia, S. China, Indonesia**
**HABITAT: forest, scrub, cultivated land**
**SIZE: 25.5 cm (10 in)**

The drongo cuckoo resembles the drongo, *Dicrurus macrocercus*, in its plumage and forked tail, unique among cuckoos, and uses it as a foster parent in some areas. A solitary, mainly nocturnal bird, it feeds on insects, particularly grasshoppers and caterpillars, and on fruit such as figs. It also catches winged insects by leaping up into the air after them in the manner of the drongo.

The female lays her eggs in the nests of various drongo species and in those of other birds. Juveniles have white flecks in their black plumage, which disappear as the birds mature.

**NAME: Channel-billed Cuckoo,** *Scythrops novaehollandiae*
**RANGE: Australia to New Guinea, Indonesia**
**HABITAT: forest, woodland**
**SIZE: 63.5 cm (25 in)**

The largest cuckoo of the Australasian region, the channel-billed cuckoo, with its large, deep bill, is reminiscent of a toucan or hornbill. It will devour almost anything, but insects, fruit and berries are its preferred foods.

Channel-billed cuckoos migrate north in March, returning south in September to breed. The female lays 2 or more eggs in the nest of a crow, magpie or currawong. The 2 blind, naked cuckoo chicks attempt to push one another out of the nest at first, but are usually unable to do so, and normally both are reared.

## ORDER CUCULIFORMES

This order contains only 2 families: the cuckoos and the turacos.

---

## CUCULIDAE: Cuckoo Family

The 50 species of true cuckoo are the best-known members of this family, largely because of the practice of brood parasitism. The female bird lays her eggs in the nest of another species, which then incubates and rears her young. In some species this habit is now highly developed, and the cuckoo's eggs resemble those of the host species. Since parasitic cuckoos generally lay in the nests of much smaller passerine birds, their eggs must be smaller and hatch more quickly than those of the nonparasitic cuckoos.

There are 127 species in the family, including the Old World cuckoos, many of which are brood parasites, and the New World cuckoos, which, for the most part, are not. Other forms are the social-nesting guira, the anis, roadrunners, couas and coucals.

The family as a whole has a cosmopolitan distribution and contains many migratory forms. Cuckoos and their relatives range in size between 15 and 71 cm (6 and 28 in) in length, and most are slender bodied, with long tails and short legs. Males and females look alike in most species.

---

**NAME: Cuckoo,** *Cuculus canorus*
**RANGE: Europe, N. Africa, N. and S.E. Asia; winters south of range in Africa and S. Asia**
**HABITAT: forest, woodland, moors**
**SIZE: 33 cm (13 in)**

The male cuckoo's familiar song, the origin of its common name, heralds the arrival of spring, when the bird flies north to breed in Europe and Asia. A slim, long-tailed bird, it leads a solitary life outside the breeding season and haunts trees, hedges and thickets, where it feeds on large insects, particularly hairy caterpillars.

Breeding starts in mid-May, and each female has a well-defined territory in which she searches for nests in which to lay her eggs. She uses the same host species, usually small passerine birds such as dunnocks, wagtails or redstarts, throughout her life. The species she chooses is probably that of her own foster parents. On alternate days, she lays a single egg, each in a different nest, at the same time removing one of the host's eggs, until she has laid a total of 8 to 12 eggs. She must lay her egg stealthily, without the host bird's knowledge, for, if it is alarmed, it may reject the whole clutch. The young cuckoo hatches in about 12 days; since it is much the bigger, stronger and faster-growing bird, it is able to oust the hosts' own young from the nest and claim all its foster parents' attention. The hosts have to work extremely hard in order to satisfy the demands for food made by the young cuckoo, which is much larger than they are.

**NAME: African Emerald Cuckoo,** *Chrysococcyx cupreus*
**RANGE: Africa, south of the Sahara**
**HABITAT: forest edge and clearings**
**SIZE: 20 cm (7¾ in)**

A shy bird, which haunts the dense foliage of tall forest trees, the emerald cuckoo is more often heard than seen, for it darts for cover at the slightest hint of danger. Considered to be one of the most beautiful of African birds, the male has a golden-yellow belly and an emerald-green back. The female has moss-green upperparts, a brown crown and a white belly, barred with moss-green. Emerald cuckoos feed on a variety of insects, including caterpillars, ants and beetles.

The female lays her eggs in the nests of such birds as bulbuls, orioles, puffback shrikes and black-headed weavers.

The emerald cuckoo is thought to be migratory. A smaller relative, the shining cuckoo, *C. lucidus*, migrates some 3,200 km (2,000 mi) across the southwest Pacific Ocean from New Zealand to the Solomon Islands.

**NAME: Yellow-billed Cuckoo,** *Coccyzus americanus*
**RANGE: breeds from Canada to Mexico and Caribbean islands; winters in Central and South America**
**HABITAT: woodland, orchards, thickets**
**SIZE: 28–33 cm (11–13 in)**

A secretive, shy bird, the yellow-billed cuckoo frequents undergrowth and brush, searching for hairy caterpillars (its preferred food) and beetles, grasshoppers, tree crickets, army ants, wasps and flies. It also feeds on summer fruit and small frogs and lizards.

A nonparasitic cuckoo, it builds its own nest of sticks in a tree or bush and lines it with dry leaves, grass or even pieces of rag. The female lays 3 or 4 eggs, one every 2 or 3 days, and both parents incubate the eggs, each of which hatches 14 days after laying. The nestlings are almost naked when they hatch, with only a sparse covering of down. Both parents feed and tend the young.

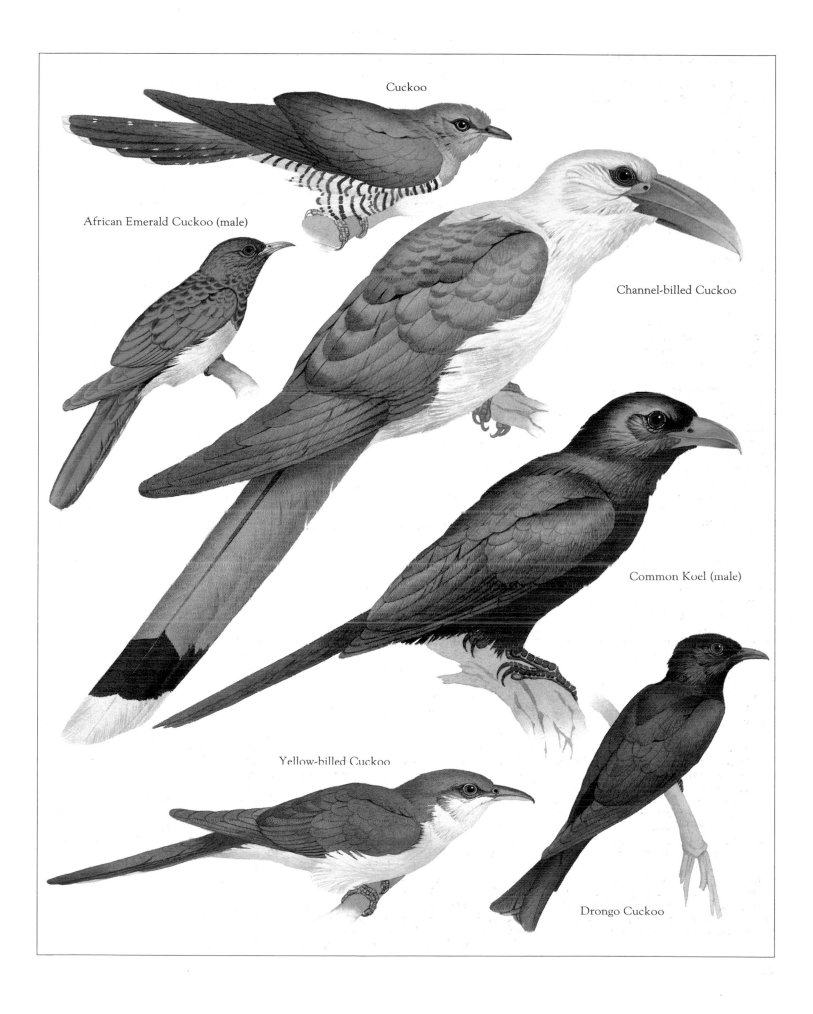

Cuckoo

African Emerald Cuckoo (male)

Channel-billed Cuckoo

Common Koel (male)

Yellow-billed Cuckoo

Drongo Cuckoo

# Cuckoos, Turacos

NAME: **Roadrunner,** *Geococcyx californianus*
RANGE: **S.W. USA: S. California, Utah, Kansas, south to Mexico**
HABITAT: **semiarid open country**
SIZE: **50–60 cm ($19\frac{3}{4}$–$23\frac{1}{2}$ in)**

A slender, fowl-like bird, with a small shaggy crest, a long tail and long legs, the roadrunner is a fast-running ground-bird which can attain speeds of 24 km/h (15 mph) or more. But its short, rounded wings are functional, and it can fly, albeit clumsily. Like its cousin, the lesser roadrunner, *G. velox*, of Mexico and Central America, it lives in dry, open places and feeds on ground-living insects, such as crickets and grasshoppers, and on other small invertebrates, bird's eggs, lizards, snakes (even rattlesnakes) and fruits such as prickly pear. It usually kills by making a sudden pounce on prey. True to its name, this shy bird is often seen on roads, but if surprised, it runs rapidly away.

Roadrunners form permanent pair bonds and live in their territory all year round. They build neat, shallow nests of sticks, lined with leaves and feathers, in trees or cactus clumps. The female lays 2 to 6 eggs in April or May; they are incubated for about 20 days. The eggs hatch over several days, and if food supplies are scarce, the larger nestlings take all there is, leaving the younger, smaller birds to starve. Both parents care for the young, which hatch naked and helpless. Their eyes open after about 7 days, and they are able to feed themselves at about 16 days.

NAME: **Smooth-billed Ani,** *Crotophaga ani*
RANGE: **Central and South America, West Indies**
HABITAT: **forest edge, grassland, pasture**
SIZE: **33 cm (13 in)**

Anis are nonparasitic cuckoos, with long square-ended tails, heavy hooked bills and short wings. Their flight is weak, so they feed mainly on the ground on insects and some fallen fruit and berries. Anis are often seen on ranches near grazing cattle because the animals disturb ground insects, and this association helps the anis to find three times more food than they otherwise would.

Smooth-billed anis are gregarious birds, living in flocks of up to 25 and even building a communal nest, which is a bulky structure, made of sticks, weeds and grass and situated low in a small tree or bush. A group of females, each laying 3 or 4 eggs, fills the nest with 20 or more and will then share the incubation of the clutch. The young birds hatch after about 14 days, and the whole flock helps to feed them.

NAME: **Small Green-billed Malkoha,** *Rhopodytes viridirostris*
RANGE: **S. India, Sri Lanka**
HABITAT: **forest, scrub, bamboo forest**
SIZE: **38 cm (15 in)**

Also known as the blue-faced malkoha, this distinctive cuckoo, with its green bill and sky-blue eye patch, is a common Indian species. It flies feebly and reluctantly and spends most of the time under cover of bushes and undergrowth. Large insects, such as grasshoppers, mantids and caterpillars, form the bulk of its diet, and it occasionally catches small lizards.

A nonparasitic species, it builds a shallow nest, made of sticks and lined with leaves. The female lays 2 eggs.

NAME: **Running Coua,** *Coua cursor*
RANGE: **S.W. Madagascar**
HABITAT: **arid brush**
SIZE: **36 cm ($14\frac{1}{4}$ in)**

The running coua is a terrestrial bird and usually moves on foot, although it can fly reasonably well, if laboriously. Single birds or small groups walk about looking for insects such as caterpillars; if alarmed, they run quickly, periodically interrupting their stride with hops.

Although a member of the cuckoo family, the coua builds its own nest, but little is known about its breeding habits.

NAME: **Buff-headed Coucal,** *Centropus milo*
RANGE: **Solomon Islands**
HABITAT: **forest**
SIZE: **66 cm (26 in)**

One of the largest cuckoos, the buff-headed coucal has short wings, a long tail and a big, curved bill. A poor flier, it spends most of its time on the ground and even there moves awkwardly. It will sometimes flap up into a tree, moving from branch to branch and then gliding clumsily down. It feeds on large insects, frogs and reptiles.

The coucal's nest is a rounded, domed structure, made of grass and built in the undergrowth just above ground level. The female lays 3 to 5 eggs.

NAME: **Striped Cuckoo,** *Tapera naevia*
RANGE: **S. Mexico, Central America, South America to N. Argentina**
HABITAT: **savanna, swamps**
SIZE: **30.5 cm (12 in)**

The striped cuckoo is a shy bird that perches on a tree, calling for hours at a time, often during the hottest part of the day. Its call is a melancholy, carrying whistle, which sounds like "sa-ci." The striped cuckoo is one of the 3 American cuckoos to have parasitic breeding habits, but little is known about them.

## MUSOPHAGIDAE: Turaco Family

The 19 species of turaco are fowl-like, tree-dwelling birds of tropical Africa. Except for the go-away birds, which are gray and white, turacos are glossy and brightly colored, with long, broad tails and short, rounded wings. Many species have hairy crests and bare skin around the eye area. The brilliant red of the head and wing feathers of some species is the result of a copper complex pigment, unique in the animal kingdom, which is soluble in alkalis. The quite different green pigment is also unique.

Turacos have short, stout bills and feed largely on insects and fruit. Males and females look alike.

NAME: **Red-crested Turaco,** *Tauraco erythrolophus*
RANGE: **Africa: Angola, Zaire**
HABITAT: **woodland, savanna**
SIZE: **40.5 cm (16 in)**

The red-crested turaco is a fruit-eating bird, which lives in trees and seldom descends to the ground. Like other turacos, it is a poor flier but is agile and swift in the trees and can run, hop and climb among the branches. In addition to fruit, it eats seeds, insects and snails.

This turaco is almost identical in appearance to Bannerman's turaco, *T. bannermani*, and the most obvious distinguishing feature is the nostrils: rounded in the red-crested and slit-shaped in Bannerman's turaco. Nothing is known of the breeding habits of either species.

NAME: **Common Go-away Bird,** *Corythaixoides concolor*
RANGE: **Africa: Tanzania, Congo River basin to South Africa**
HABITAT: **open bush, acacia scrub**
SIZE: **51 cm (20 in)**

Although wary, the common go-away bird is not timid, and at the hint of anything suspicious, it alerts all the animals in the area with its penetrating call, which sounds like "g'away, g'away." In pairs or small groups, the go-away birds perch on treetops or fly clumsily from one tree to another; they feed on berries, fruit and insects.

The breeding season is between October and January. The birds display, one partner perching in a treetop and the other hovering above it, and both help to build a nest of sticks in dense creepers or up in an acacia tree. The female lays 2 or 3 large eggs, which both parents incubate for, it is thought, a total of about 18 days.

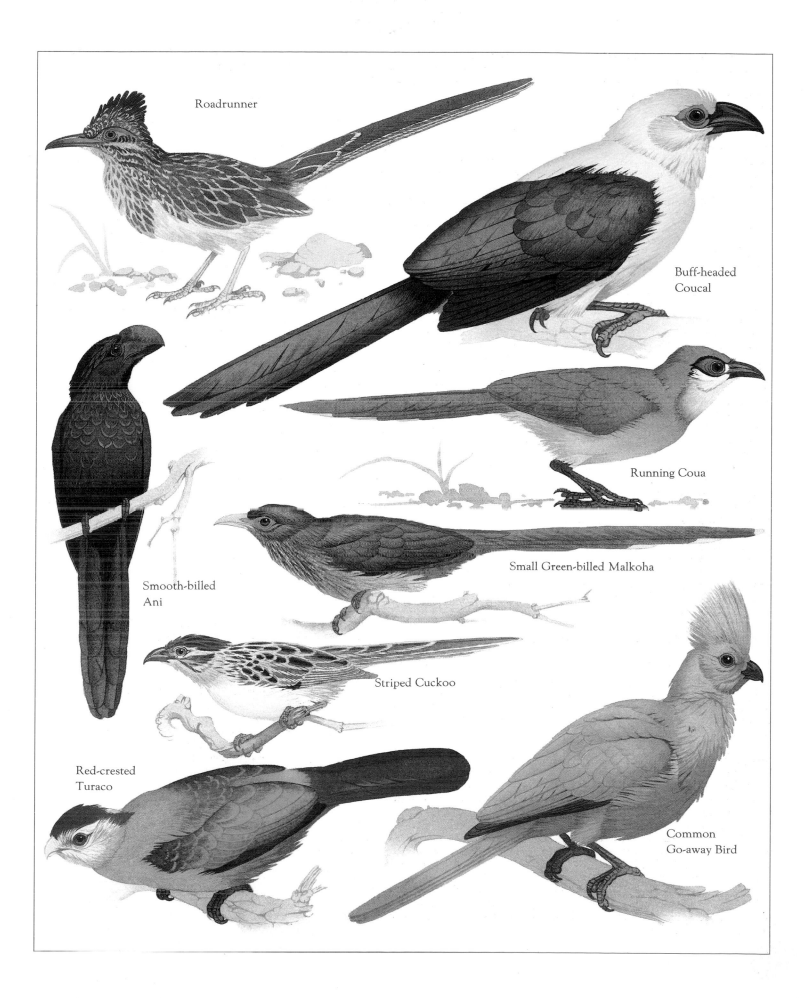

Roadrunner

Buff-headed
Coucal

Running Coua

Smooth-billed
Ani

Small Green-billed Malkoha

Striped Cuckoo

Red-crested
Turaco

Common
Go-away Bird

# Barn Owls, Owls

## ORDER STRIGIFORMES

Within this order are 2 very similar families of owls. With their flattened faces, enormous eyes, taloned feet and predatory, usually nocturnal habits, owls represent the nighttime equivalent of the hawks, eagles and falcons.

Owls kill with their talons: each toe is tipped with a sharp, hooked claw. They then swallow their prey whole and regurgitate the indigestible bones, fur and feathers in the form of pellets. Males and females look alike in most species, although the females are sometimes larger.

## TYTONIDAE: Barn Owl Family

The 12 species of barn and bay owl differ from the typical owls in many minor details. They can be distinguished by the heart-shaped facial disk, relatively small eyes and long, slender legs. The long, hooked beak is mostly concealed by feathers, and the toes are strong with sharp, curved claws. All barn owls are nocturnal hunters.

NAME: **Oriental Bay Owl,** *Phodilus badius*
RANGE: **N. India, Sri Lanka, S.E. Asia, Greater Sunda Islands**
HABITAT: **forest**
SIZE: **29 cm (11½ in)**

The oriental bay owl is similar in shape and appearance to the barn owl with which it is now grouped. It is strictly nocturnal and is believed to feed mostly on insects, which it hunts in and around the trees. It lays 3 to 5 eggs, usually in a hole in a tree. An African species of bay owl has been discovered only recently.

NAME: **Barn Owl,** *Tyto alba*
RANGE: **worldwide, except temperate Asia and many Pacific islands**
HABITAT: **open country, woodland, inhabited areas**
SIZE: **34 cm (13¼ in)**

The barn owl is a long-legged, usually pale-plumaged bird with a white face. There are over 30 subspecies over its wide range, differing mainly in intensity of plumage coloration. Barn owls generally live alone or in pairs and roost during the day in farm buildings, hollow trees or caves. At night, they emerge to hunt, feeding primarily on small rodents, which they catch and kill on the ground, and also on small birds.

Breeding usually starts in April in the north. The female nests in an old building, a hollow tree trunk or a rock crevice and lays 4 to 7 eggs, which she incubates for about 33 days. The male brings food to her during this period, and both parents care for the young.

## STRIGIDAE: Owl Family

The 134 species of typical owl are distributed all over the world, except on some oceanic islands. They are soft-feathered, short-tailed birds, with big heads and enormous eyes set in a circular facial disk. In all species the beak is hooked and partly hidden by feathers.

Most owls hunt at night and all feed entirely on animals, from insects and invertebrates to birds and medium-sized mammals such as rabbits. They have exceptionally keen eyesight and excellent hearing.

NAME: **Brown Fish Owl,** *Ketupa zeylonensis*
RANGE: **Middle East to S. China, Sri Lanka, S.E. Asia**
HABITAT: **forested streams and lakes**
SIZE: **56 cm (22 in)**

A specialized, semiaquatic owl, the brown fish owl is always found near water and feeds on fish, as well as on the more typical prey of owls. Its feet and ankles are unfeathered, an adaptation which allows it to wade in the shallows to catch fish without the plumage getting wet.

The breeding season of this species begins in February or March. It makes a nest platform in a tree by joining some branches together, or nests on a ledge or rock. Only 1 or 2 eggs are laid and are then incubated by both parents for a total of about 35 days.

NAME: **Elf Owl,** *Micrathene whitneyi*
RANGE: **S.E. USA, Mexico**
HABITAT: **wooded canyons, deserts with saguaro cactus**
SIZE: **12.5–15 cm (5–6 in)**

One of the smallest owls in the world, the elf owl is distinguished by its short tail from other small owls in its range. During the day, it roosts in a tree or bush and comes out at dusk to hunt. Insects are its main prey, many being caught in the owl's feet while it is in flight. It will also hover over foliage or dart out from a perch after prey like a flycatcher. Beetles, moths, grasshoppers, crickets and scorpions (the sting is removed or crushed) are frequent prey, and it occasionally catches small snakes and lizards.

Elf owls nest in deserted woodpecker holes in cactus plants or tree trunks. The male finds a suitable site and sings to attract a female, who responds and enters the nest. In April or May, she lays 1 to 5 eggs, which she incubates for 24 days. The male feeds the female while she incubates and also brings food for her to give to the young when they have hatched.

NAME: **Screech Owl,** *Otus asio*
RANGE: **N. America: Canada to Mexico**
HABITAT: **open woodland, cactus desert**
SIZE: **18–25.5 cm (7–10 in)**

A small owl with conspicuous ear tufts, the screech owl roosts during the day in a hollow tree or old building and starts to hunt at dusk. It catches insects and mice, shrews and other small mammals, as well as frogs, lizards and some birds. Breeding starts from February to July, according to area. Screech owls nest in a hole in a tree, such as an abandoned woodpecker hole, usually without any nesting material. Normally 4 or 5 eggs are laid, but there may be as many as 8. The male brings food while the female incubates, but once the eggs hatch, both parents feed the young.

NAME: **Snowy Owl,** *Nyctea scandiaca*
RANGE: **circumpolar: arctic Canada, Greenland, N. Eurasia**
HABITAT: **tundra, marshes, coasts**
SIZE: **52–65 cm (20½–25½ in)**

The snowy owl is a large species with distinctive, mainly white plumage; females have more dark, barred markings than males. It usually hunts during the day and takes prey up to the size of arctic hares and lemmings, as well as smaller rodents and birds such as ducks and gulls.

The snowy owl begins nesting in mid-May. It makes a shallow scrape in the ground or on a rock, lines it with moss and feathers and lays 4 to 10 eggs. Up to 15 eggs may be laid if food supplies are particularly good. The male brings food to the female while she incubates the eggs for 32 or 33 days.

NAME: **Great Horned Owl,** *Bubo virginianus*
RANGE: **N., Central and South America**
HABITAT: **varied: woodland, forest, city parks, suburbs**
SIZE: **46–64 cm (18–25¼ in)**

The great horned owls are among the biggest and most powerful of American owls. Their prominent ear tufts are simply feathers and are not connected with the hearing apparatus. They roost in trees, and while they do most of their hunting at night, they may hunt by day in unpopulated regions. They catch mammals up to the size of cats, birds, insects and reptiles.

The timing of nesting depends on area, but it can be as early as January or February. The owl uses the old nest of another bird species or nests in a cave, a hollow in a tree or on a cliff ledge. Usually 3 eggs are laid, but there can be as many as 6. The eggs are incubated for 30 to 35 days by both parents, who then feed and vigorously defend their young.

Barn Owl

Elf Owl

Great Horned Owl

Screech Owl

Oriental Bay Owl

Snowy Owl (male)

Brown Fish Owl

# Owls

NAME: **Morepork/Boobook,** *Ninox novaeseelandiae*
RANGE: **New Zealand, Australia, S. New Guinea, Lesser Sunda Islands**
HABITAT: **forest, scrub, open country with caves for roosting**
SIZE: **29 cm (11½ in)**

The morepork is the most widely distributed owl in New Zealand and Australia. It is usually seen at dusk when it begins to hunt for its food, which consists largely of insects, particularly moths, as well as spiders, lizards, small birds, rats and mice. It occasionally hunts during the day. The common names are derived from one of its calls, which sounds like "morepork" or "boobook." One subspecies, the Norfolk boobook, is now listed as rare.

The morepork nests in November and lays 3 or 4 eggs in a nest in a hollow tree or in a patch of thick vegetation. The female begins her 30- to 31-day incubation after laying the first egg, but lays the rest later, at 2-day intervals. After hatching, the young remain in the nest for about 5 weeks, guarded and fed by their parents.

NAME: **Long-eared Owl,** *Asio otus*
RANGE: **N. America, Europe, Asia**
HABITAT: **coniferous forest, woodland, parks**
SIZE: **33–40.5 cm (13–16 in)**

The long-eared owl is of a slenderer build than the tawny owl and has distinctive ear tufts; these tufts are simply feathers and have no connection with the actual ears. In flight, the long-eared owl keeps its ear tufts flat against its head. One of the most nocturnal of owls, it preys on rats, mice, shrews, moles, bats, squirrels, rabbits and other small mammals, as well as on birds and insects. During the day, long-eared owls roost in trees, their mottled brown plumage helping them to blend with the surroundings.

Long-eared owls roost from March to May, according to area; when food supplies are abundant they may produce two broods. The female lays 3 to 10 eggs, usually 4 or 5, in an old nest of another bird species or even in a squirrel's nest. If no such nest is available, she will lay her eggs on the ground under a tree or bush. She incubates the eggs for 26 to 28 days, and her partner brings food to her both during this period and once the chicks are hatched. The young leave the nest 3 to 4 weeks after hatching.

Some northern populations of long-eared owls migrate south of their breeding areas in winter, to Mexico, northern Egypt and India, and northward again in spring.

NAME: **Hawk Owl,** *Surnia ulula*
RANGE: **Canada, extreme N. USA, N. Asia, Scandinavia**
HABITAT: **open areas in coniferous forest**
SIZE: **36–43 cm (14¼–17 in)**

The hawk owl is easily recognized by its tail, which is longer than usual for owls, and by its pale facial disk, bordered with black. Its wings are fairly short and pointed, giving it a hawklike appearance in flight. It hunts by day, watching from a perch in the trees then flying down after prey. It feeds on mice, lemmings, squirrels and other small mammals, as well as on birds and some insects.

Nesting takes place from April to June, depending on the area, and the clutch size varies annually according to the food supply. The female lays her eggs, usually 5 or 6 but sometimes up to 9, in the hollow top of a tree stump or in an abandoned nest or woodpecker hole. The eggs are incubated for 25 to 30 days, mostly by the female.

NAME: **Eurasian Pygmy Owl,** *Glaucidium passerinum*
RANGE: **N. Europe, east through USSR and central Asia to China**
HABITAT: **open forest**
SIZE: **16 cm (6 in)**

The smallest European owl, the pygmy owl has a small head and a long tail for its size. Its facial disk is less apparent than that of most owls. It hunts mainly at night and feeds on small rodents and on birds, many of which it catches in flight.

Pygmy owls breed from March to May and often nest in disused woodpecker holes. The male brings food to the female while she incubates the 2 to 7 eggs for about 28 days and to the young once they are hatched.

NAME: **Little Owl,** *Athene noctua*
RANGE: **Europe, Africa, W. and central Asia, east to China; introduced in Britain and New Zealand**
HABITAT: **forest, open country, urban land**
SIZE: **21 cm (8¼ in)**

A small owl, with a flat-topped head, low forehead and large yellow eyes, the little owl has a stern, frowning expression. It is often active in the daytime. Insects and small rodents are its main foods, but it occasionally eats small birds and even carrion.

In Europe, the little owl nests from mid-April onward in a hole in a tree, on rocks or buildings, or even in an abandoned burrow or old nest of another bird. The female lays 3 to 5 eggs and incubates them for about 29 days. The male must bring all the food when the young are first hatched, but later both parents take a share in the hunting.

NAME: **Tawny Owl,** *Strix aluco*
RANGE: **Britain, Europe, N. Africa, W. and central Asia to Korea**
HABITAT: **woods, gardens, parks, urban areas**
SIZE: **38 cm (15 in)**

The tawny owl is a strongly built bird, with mottled plumage, a rounded head and black eyes. One of the most common European owls, it is distinguished from the long- and short-eared owls by its lack of ear tufts and its dark eyes. It is strictly nocturnal, roosting in a tree during the day and hunting small rodents, birds and some insects at night.

Breeding starts in late March. The tawny owl nests in a hole in a tree or occasionally on the ground or in an old nest of another species. Usually 2 to 4 eggs are laid, but there can be as many as 8. The female alone incubates the clutch for 28 to 30 days. The male brings food for the newly hatched young for the first few weeks, but then both parents go out hunting. The young leave the nest at about 5 weeks.

NAME: **Burrowing Owl,** *Speotyto cunicularia*
RANGE: **S.W. Canada, W. USA and Florida; Central and South America**
HABITAT: **semidesert, grassland without trees**
SIZE: **23–28 cm (9–11 in)**

The burrowing owl is a small, ground-living owl with a short tail and long legs, well suited to its terrestrial habits. It often lives in the abandoned burrows of prairie dogs and other mammals and usually adapts the burrow to its needs by digging with its feet to enlarge the hole and make a nesting chamber. Where there is a complex of burrows, such as those left by prairie dogs, a number of owls will take over, forming a colony. Contrary to popular belief, the owls do not share the burrows with prairie dogs.

Although burrowing owls usually hunt in the evening, they are often seen during the day standing at the burrow entrances. They feed on insects, such as moths, dragonflies, grasshoppers, beetles and crickets, and on small rodents, birds, frogs and reptiles. They frequently follow moving animals, such as dogs or horses, presumably to catch any prey the animals disturb.

Burrowing owls nest from March to July. The female lays 6 to 11 eggs, usually 8 or 9, in a chamber at the end of the burrow, which may be lined with dried animal droppings. Both parents incubate the eggs for about 28 days. Northern populations of burrowing owls migrate south of their breeding range in winter.

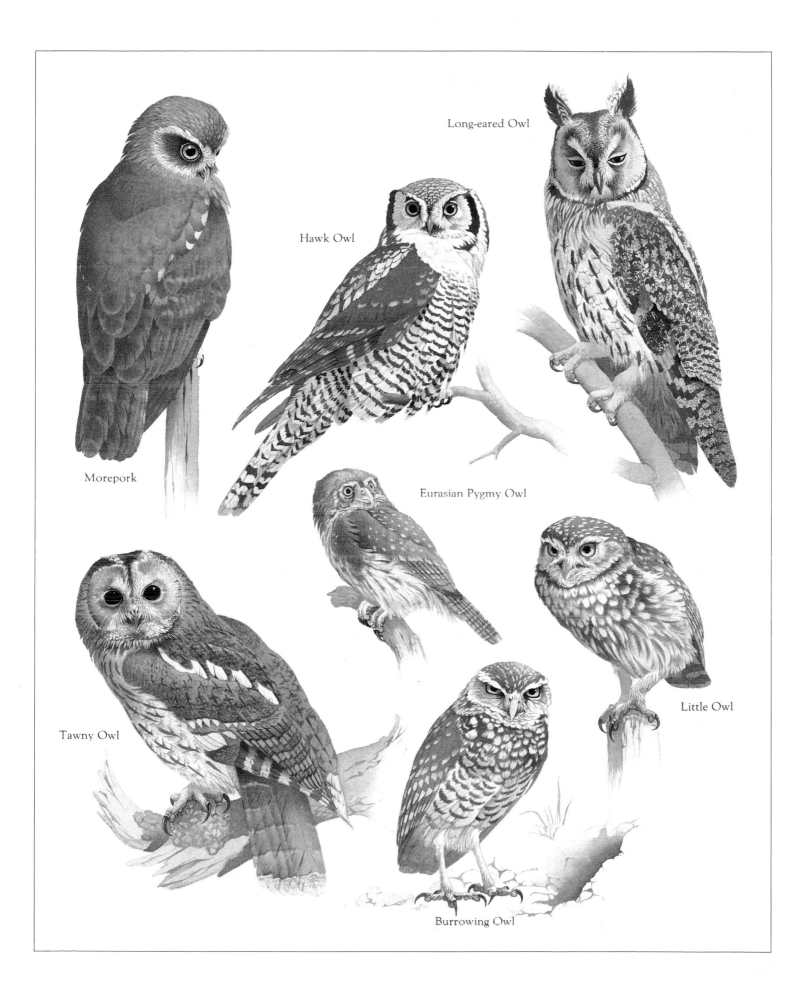

Morepork

Hawk Owl

Long-eared Owl

Eurasian Pygmy Owl

Tawny Owl

Little Owl

Burrowing Owl

# Frogmouths, Potoos and relatives

## ORDER CAPRIMULGIFORMES
This order comprises 5 families: the oil-bird, frogmouths, potoos, nightjars and owlet-nightjars. Most of these birds are nocturnal.

## PODARGIDAE: Frogmouth Family
The 13 species of frogmouth occur from India through Southeast Asia to New Guinea and Australia. Poor fliers, they have short, rounded wings and stumpy tails and tend to catch their prey by jumping onto it from a tree. They have large, flat bills with an enormous gape. Males and females look more or less alike.

NAME: Tawny Frogmouth, *Podargus strigoides*
RANGE: **Australia, Tasmania**
HABITAT: **forest, open woodland, trees in scrub, gardens, parks**
SIZE: 33–47 cm (13–18½ in)

The nocturnal tawny frogmouth spends the day resting in a tree, where its mottled, streaked plumage blends perfectly with the lichen-covered branches. At any hint of danger, the bird stretches out its body, with head and bill pointing upward, and in this posture it is almost indistinguishable from a broken branch or stump. Much of the frogmouth's hunting is done at dusk, when it watches for prey from a tree or post, then descends silently to seize it on the ground. Insects, snails, frogs and even small mammals and birds are all included in its diet. There are at least 7 subspecies of tawny frogmouth, all varying slightly in size and shade of plumage.

The nest is a flimsy platform of sticks and leaves, made on a forked branch, or an old nest of another species may be used. The female incubates the 2 eggs for about 30 days, and both parents feed the young.

NAME: Ceylon Frogmouth, *Batrachostomus moniliger*
RANGE: **Sri Lanka, S.W. India**
HABITAT: **forest**
SIZE: 19–23 cm (7½–9 in)

The Ceylon frogmouth is a tree-dwelling bird but takes most of its food on the ground after short flights from a perch; frogmouths of this genus seem to be more skillful in flight than those of the genus *Podargus*. Insects and small invertebrates are its main food. Like all frogmouths, this bird has mottled gray-brown plumage, which provides excellent camouflage as it sits on branches.

A single egg is laid in a small padlike nest, made from the bird's own down with a covering of lichen and cobwebs.

## STEATORNITHIDAE: Oilbird Family
The single species of oilbird is sufficiently unusual to merit its own family. A large-eyed nocturnal bird, it has a patchy distribution in northern South America. Male and female birds look alike.

NAME: Oilbird, *Steatornis caripensis*
RANGE: **locally in Peru, through Ecuador, Colombia and Venezuela to French Guiana; Trinidad**
HABITAT: **seaside and mountain caves**
SIZE: 43 cm (17 in)

A long-winged, long-tailed bird, the oilbird has small, almost useless legs and feet. It lives in deep, totally dark caves, where even its large eyes, specialized for nighttime vision, are ineffective. However, it can nest and fly about in these caves with ease by means of a system of echolocation similar to that used by bats. As it flies, the bird makes a series of high-pitched clicking sounds, which bounce off the walls of the cave and enable it to navigate. After dark, the oilbird emerges to feed on fruit, particularly that of palms. It seizes the fruit in its strong bill, swallows it whole and digests the entire night's intake the following day, back in its roost. The oilbird has a well-developed sense of smell and probably uses this, as well as its good nighttime vision, to find ripe fruit.

Oilbirds live in colonies of up to 50 pairs. The nest is made on a ledge from droppings, mixed with regurgitated fruit, and the female lays 2 to 4 eggs. Both parents incubate the eggs for about 33 days and feed the young on palm fruit. During their period on the nest, the young oilbirds become enormously fat, weighing at least half as much again as an adult, since they are not able to fly until they are about 4 months old. Local people used to capture these fledglings and render their fat for use as cooking oil — hence the common name — but this practice is now prohibited by law in most areas.

## NYCTIBIIDAE: Potoo Family
The 5 species of potoo occur in the West Indies and adjacent areas of Central and South America. Although related to nightjars and similar to them in appearance, potoos feed like flycatchers, darting out from a perch to catch insects. Males and females look alike or nearly so.

NAME: Common Potoo, *Nyctibius griseus*
RANGE: **Jamaica, Hispaniola, Trinidad and Tobago; Mexico, Central America, tropical South America**
HABITAT: **forest edge, open forest, cultivated land with trees**
SIZE: 41 cm (16 in)

The common potoo has a long tail, sometimes as much as half of its total length, and very short legs. Its grayish-brown plumage is heavily mottled and streaked, rendering it almost invisible among the lichen-covered branches of its habitat. During the day it sits in an extremely upright posture, often on a broken branch or stump, with its head and bill pointing upward so that it looks like part of the tree. At night, the potoo hunts for food, flying out from a perch to catch insects and returning to the same spot to consume them.

The single egg is laid on top of a tree stump and is incubated by both parents. If disturbed, the sitting bird adopts the upright posture and freezes or may retaliate by opening its eyes and bill wide and fluffing out its plumage in threat. Both parents feed the young, which sit in the upright posture in the nest. The young fly about 44 days after hatching.

## AEGOTHELIDAE: Owlet-nightjar Family
Owlet-nightjars are small, dumpy birds, which resemble the related nightjars in many respects but have the flat-faced look of owls. They hunt at dawn and dusk, catching insects in the air or, more often, on the ground, where they move easily. There are 8 species, found in New Guinea, Australia and some nearby islands.

NAME: Australian Owlet-nightjar, *Aegotheles cristatus*
RANGE: **Australia, Tasmania, S. New Guinea**
HABITAT: **forest, woodland, scrub**
SIZE: 20–24 cm (7¾–9½ in)

A shy, solitary bird, the Australian owlet-nightjar spends the day perched in an upright posture on a branch, disguised by its mottled and barred plumage. It starts to hunt for insects and invertebrates at dusk, taking much of its prey on the ground but also chasing aerial insects. Its bill is small and flat, but with a large gape, and is almost obscured by erect bristles.

The clutch of 3 or 4 eggs is laid in a hole in a tree or bank, lined with green leaves. The lining is renewed as the leaves wither. There may be more than one brood in a year.

Common Potoo

Tawny Frogmouth

Ceylon Frogmouth

Oilbird

Australian
Owlet-nightjar

# Nightjars

NAME: **Common Poor-will,**
*Phalaenoptilus nuttallii*
RANGE: **breeds S.W. Canada, W. USA;**
**winters S. USA, Mexico**
HABITAT: **arid bush on hills and**
**mountains**
SIZE: **18–21.5 cm (7–8½ in)**

A small, short-tailed nightjar, the common poor-will flits around at night, hunting moths, beetles and grasshoppers on or near the ground. During the day, it roosts in shrubbery or tall woods, at dawn and dusk calling out its cry of "poor-will" or "poor-jill."

The poor-will is the only bird known to hibernate. Each October it seeks out a rock crevice in which to spend the winter, often returning to the same spot year after year. Its body temperature falls from 40° to 41°C (104° to 106°F) to 18° to 19°C (64° to 66°F), and its heart and breathing rates drop to almost undetectable levels as its energy requirements drop to a minimum.

In early summer, poor-wills breed; the female lays 2 eggs on bare ground or gravel. The clutch is incubated by both parents.

NAME: **Lyre-tailed Nightjar,** *Uropsalis*
*lyra*
RANGE: **South America: Andes in**
**Venezuela, Colombia, Ecuador, Peru**
HABITAT: **mountain forest, savanna, open**
**woodland**
SIZE: **male: 79 cm (31 in);**
**female: 25.5 cm (10 in)**

The male lyre-tailed nightjar has two extremely long outer tail feathers, which account for up to 66 cm (26 in) of his total length. As the common name implies, these feathers are lyre-shaped and they are thought to be used in the male's courtship display. The female lacks these specialized features.

A solitary, nocturnal bird, this nightjar perches on low branches, often near water, and calls at dusk. Little is known of its feeding or breeding habits, but they are probably similar to those of other nightjars.

NAME: **Greater Eared Nightjar,**
*Eurostopodus macrotis*
RANGE: **India: Assam to S.E. Asia,**
**Philippines, Sulawesi**
HABITAT: **forest, scrub**
SIZE: **41 cm (16 in)**

Mainly solitary birds, these large nightjars occasionally gather in small groups. They feed on insects caught in the air. Flying high around the treetops at dawn or dusk, they perform skillful aerobatics as they pursue their prey and call constantly, with a clear whistle. The female lays 1 egg on dead leaves, often in the shade at the foot of a tree.

## CAPRIMULGIDAE:
### Nightjar Family

Approximately 67 species of this specialized family of nocturnal birds are distributed almost worldwide: only New Zealand and some Pacific islands lack an example. They do not occur at high latitudes. Many have evocative names, such as nightjar, goatsucker, whip-poor-will and chuck-will's-widow, which are usually derived from their loud, repetitive calls.

Nightjars have long, pointed wings, and large eyes for good nighttime vision. The bill is short and weak, but it opens extremely wide and is fringed by sensory bristles. Most nightjars call for a period each evening at dusk, before they begin their aerial hunting. Flying silently and slowly, but making sudden darts after prey, they capture insects, which the bristles help to funnel into their wide, open mouths, and occasionally young birds. Nightjars are masterly in flight but have short, weak legs and avoid walking far on the ground.

During the daytime, nightjars roost in trees or on the ground, hidden from predators by their supremely efficient camouflaging plumage. In trees, they perch with their bodies lengthwise along the branch. All species have finely mottled gray, black and brown heads and backs, which blend perfectly with foliage or ground vegetation. Male and female look unalike in most species, having some plumage differences.

NAME: **Standard-winged Nightjar,**
*Macrodipteryx longipennis*
RANGE: **Africa: Chad, Sudan, Ethiopia,**
**N. Uganda, Kenya**
HABITAT: **savanna, scrub**
SIZE: **23 cm (9 in)**

The standard-winged nightjar feeds on insects, which it catches in the air. A migratory species, it breeds in the southern part of its range from January to March and then moves north to Chad and northern Sudan.

In the breeding season, the male nightjar develops one elongated flight feather on each wing that grows to about 23 cm (9 in) in length. These are used in courtship displays, when the male flies around the female, raising his elongated feathers and arching and vibrating his wings. The male is believed to mate with more than one female, each of which lays 2 eggs on the ground; several birds may lay in the same area. The male bird then migrates, leaving the females to incubate the eggs and care for the young.

NAME: **Pauraque,** *Nyctidromus albicollis*
RANGE: **S.W. USA; Mexico; Central and**
**South America to N.E. Argentina**
HABITAT: **semiopen scrub, woodland**
**clearings**
SIZE: **28 cm (11 in)**

Perching in a tree at night, the pauraque watches for prey, then launches into the air and flies close to the ground to catch insects, such as moths, wasps, bees and beetles, in its wide, gaping bill. During the day it roosts, hidden among the dead leaves on the woodland floor where it is virtually invisible. Male and female have some plumage differences: the female's outer wing and tail feathers are black, barred with rufous brown, while the male's are brown, barred with white, and are conspicuous in flight.

Pauraques live alone or in pairs. The female lays 2 eggs on bare ground, under the cover of bushes, and both parents incubate the clutch. They feed the nestlings by inserting the tip of the bill into a gaping mouth and regurgitating insects from the throat. The young birds begin to hop out of the nest at 2 or 3 days old, although they are not yet able to fly.

NAME: **(European) Nightjar,**
*Caprimulgus europaeus*
RANGE: **breeds in Europe, N. Africa,**
**W. and central Asia; winters in**
**tropical Africa**
HABITAT: **open country, forest edge,**
**moors, heaths, semidesert**
SIZE: **26 cm (10¼ in)**

This long-winged, long-tailed bird is the only nightjar widespread in Europe, and it tolerates many different habitats. The male bird has some white spots on the outer wing tips and his tail feathers are tipped with white, but the sexes are otherwise similar in plumage.

After spending an inactive day perching on a branch, or on the ground, the nightjar takes wing at sunset and can be seen wheeling and gliding in the air and making sudden darts after moths and other nocturnal insects. It makes a churring call — the "jar" of its name.

The breeding season starts in mid-May. The male courts the female by clapping his wings together, and both birds sway their tails from side to side before mating. The female lays 2 eggs in a slight scrape on the ground or on top of vegetation. Both parents incubate, the female during the day and the male at night, and the eggs hatch after 18 days. Both parents care for the young, which are able to fly at about 17 or 18 days old. There are 2 broods in a season.

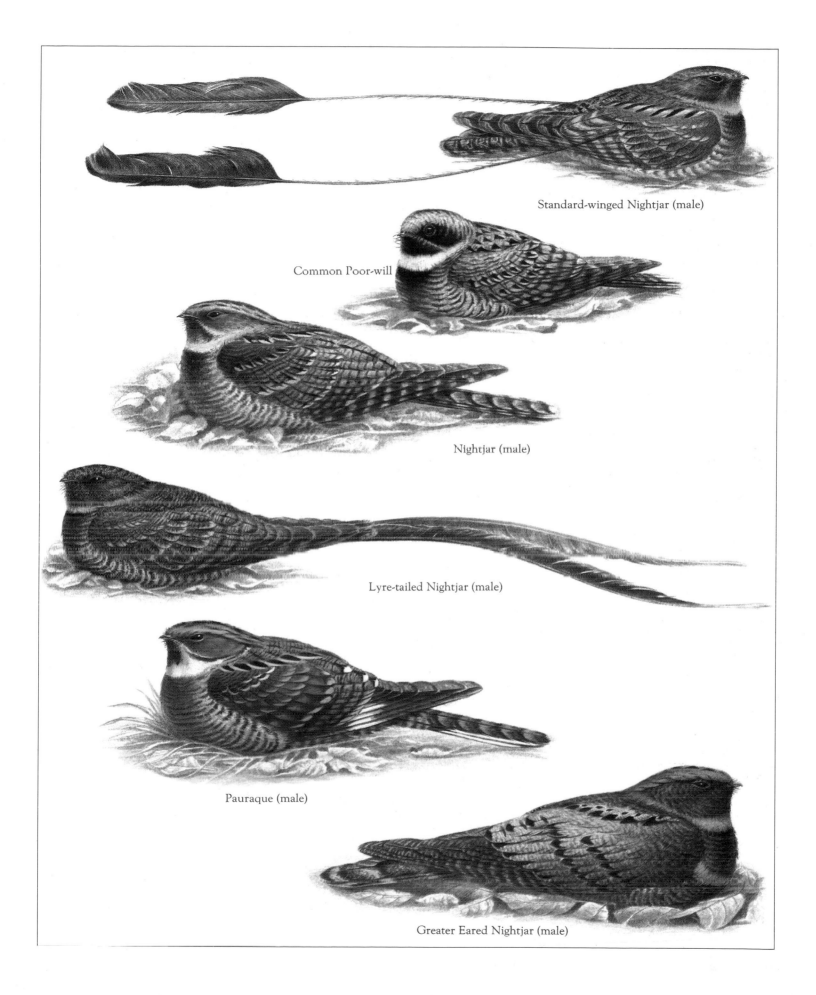

Standard-winged Nightjar (male)

Common Poor-will

Nightjar (male)

Lyre-tailed Nightjar (male)

Pauraque (male)

Greater Eared Nightjar (male)

# Swifts, Crested Swifts

## ORDER APODIFORMES

This order includes 3 families: swifts, crested swifts and hummingbirds. All are birds with highly developed flight abilities.

## APODIDAE: Swift Family

Swifts are the most aerial of birds. The 67 species in this fast-flying family seem to be able to carry out every avian activity on the wing, other than nesting. They catch food, eat, drink, collect material for nest construction and even copulate while flying. Some species may also be able to sleep aloft. Although they can take off with difficulty from flat ground, swifts normally alight only on vertical surfaces, such as cliffs or buildings, and they cannot perch. They are usually active in the daytime and feed on insects.

Swifts range in length between 9 and 25.5 cm (3½ and 10 in), and male and female look alike. Owing to similarity of habits rather than close relationship, swifts have a superficial resemblance to swallows and martins, for they possess the same narrow, pointed, although longer, wings and short, normally forked tails. Their legs and feet are tiny since they seldom, if ever, walk, but they have strong, curved claws for gripping landing and nesting surfaces. In most species, all four toes point forward. The beak is typically short and slightly down-curving and has a wide gape.

All swifts glue their nests together with glutinous saliva from specialized salivary glands.

NAME: **Brown Needletail, *Chaetura gigantea***
RANGE: **India through S.E. Asia to the Philippines**
HABITAT: **forest up to 1,800 m (6,000 ft)**
SIZE: **25.5 cm (10 in)**

One of the fastest-flying bird species, the brown needletail can reputedly attain speeds of 250 to 300 km/h (155 to 185 mph). It feeds on insects and will hover motionless, like a hawk, watching for prey. The female lays 3 to 5 eggs in a nest made on the ground.

NAME: **White-throated Swift, *Aeronautes saxatalis***
RANGE: **W. Canada and USA to Mexico and El Salvador**
HABITAT: **vicinity of mountain and coastal cliffs, canyons, rugged foothills**
SIZE: **15–18 cm (6–7 in)**

The white-throated swift attains speeds of up to 300 km/h (185 mph) and is probably the fastest-flying bird in North America. It catches insects, such as flies, beetles, bees, wasps, flying ants and leaf-hoppers, on the wing. The swifts court in flight and copulate either on the wing, with bodies pressed together as they tumble downward, or in a nesting site. The nest, made in a crack or crevice in a coastal cliff or mountainside, is cup shaped and constructed of feathers and grass, glued together with saliva. The 4 or 5 eggs are laid in May and June and incubated by both parents.

NAME: **Palm Swift, *Cypsiurus parvus***
RANGE: **W. Africa**
HABITAT: **open country**
SIZE: **18 cm (7 in)**

Palm swifts are gregarious birds which move in flocks and are easily distinguished by their unusually long tails. They are especially active at dusk, when many insects swarm.

The palm swift nests on the underside of a palm frond. The breeding pair makes a pad of feathers, which are glued together and to the leaf with saliva. They then glue the 1 or 2 eggs to the nest, also with saliva. Assuming a vertical posture and gripping the sides of the nest with their claws, both partners take turns at incubating the eggs. When the chicks hatch, they must immediately cling on to the nest with their claws and maintain their hold until they are fully fledged and ready to fly.

NAME: **Edible-nest Swiftlet, *Collocalia fuciphaga***
RANGE: **Andaman and Nicobar Islands, S.E. Asia, Philippines**
HABITAT: **coasts, islands; feeds over forest and scrub**
SIZE: **12.5 cm (5 in)**

This swiftlet is one of 20 or more similar species in the genus *Collocalia*, all of which are found in Southeast Asia and the islands of the Pacific. The differentiation of the species is extremely difficult but has now been clarified by considering nest construction and sites and the ability to echolocate.

The swiftlets build their nests in caves, often in colonies of many thousands, and find their way in the darkness of the deeper caves by using echolocation, a rare ability among birds. As they fly, they make rapid clicking sounds and use the high-frequency echoes off the cave walls to navigate.

All swiftlets use saliva to make their nests and to glue them to cave walls, but the edible-nest swiftlet's nests are made almost entirely from hardened saliva with only a few feathers included — probably by accident. And it is these nests which give the bird its common name, for they are harvested in huge numbers to make the bird's-nest soup which Chinese gourmets consider a delicacy. The female lays 2 or 3 eggs.

NAME: **Common Swift, *Apus apus***
RANGE: **breeds in Europe, east to China; N.W. Africa; winters in Africa**
HABITAT: **over open country, fresh water, urban areas**
SIZE: **16 cm (6¼ in)**

A common, gregarious bird, this swift is almost always seen in the air and only occasionally alights on walls, rocks or buildings. Uttering harsh, screaming cries, it flies in search of aerial insects, alternating rapid wing beats with long spells of gliding flight.

The breeding season starts in mid-May. The swifts select nest sites under the eaves of buildings or in rock crevices and make shallow, cup-shaped nests of grass and feathers, glued together with saliva. There are usually 3 eggs in a clutch, laid at 2- or 3-day intervals, and they are incubated for 14 to 20 days. Both parents feed the young, but may leave them for several days at a time. When this happens, the young burn up their fat stores and development slows down. If the fast is prolonged, the nestlings' body temperature may drop as much as 27.5°C (50°F), and they lapse into torpor, without any ill effects, until food is once again available.

## HEMIPROCNIDAE: Crested Swift Family

The 4 species of crested swift all have crests and long, deeply forked tails. Their plumage is softer and brighter than that of other swifts, and they are less aerial in their habits. Unlike true swifts, they are able to perch. Males and females have some slight plumage differences. Crested swifts occur in India and Southeast Asia, south to the Solomon Islands.

NAME: **Crested Swift, *Hemiprocne longipennis***
RANGE: **India, S.E. Asia, Indonesia to Sulawesi**
HABITAT: **forest edge, open woodland**
SIZE: **20.5 cm (8 in)**

The crested swift can perch on branches and telephone wires, from which it swoops down to feed on airborne insects. Males and females look similar, but the male has a chestnut patch behind the eye, while in the female this plumage is green.

The nest of the crested swift is a tiny, cup-shaped structure, made of thin flakes of bark, glued together with saliva and attached with saliva to the branch of a tree. There is just room on it for the 1 egg, which both parents take turns to incubate by sitting on the branch and puffing up their breast feathers to cover the egg. Both parents care for the chick.

Edible-nest
Swiftlet

Palm Swift

Common Swift

Brown
Needletail

White-throated
Swift

Crested Swift
(male)

# Hummingbirds

NAME: **Sword-billed Hummingbird,** *Ensifera ensifera*
RANGE: **Andes: Venezuela, Colombia, Ecuador, Peru, Bolivia**
HABITAT: **shrubby slopes at 2,500–3,000 m (8,200–10,000 ft)**
SIZE: **bird: 7.5 cm (3 in) bill: 12.5 cm (5 in)**

The sword-billed hummingbird has the longest bill, relative to body size, of any bird. This bill allows the bird to probe deep into trumpet-shaped flowers to obtain nectar and to capture insects, which are themselves feeding on the nectar.

NAME: **White-tipped Sicklebill,** *Eutoxeres aquila*
RANGE: **Costa Rica, Panama, Colombia, Ecuador, N.E. Peru**
HABITAT: **forest**
SIZE: **12.5 cm (5 in)**

This little hummingbird's strongly downward-curving bill is adapted to obtaining nectar from irregularly shaped flowers such as *Coryanthes* orchids. The bird will also cling awkwardly to *Heliconia* flowers and probe the blossoms with its bill.

NAME: **Ruby-throated Hummingbird,** *Archilochus colubris*
RANGE: **breeds in S.E. Canada, E. USA; winters in Mexico, Central America and West Indies**
HABITAT: **woodland, gardens**
SIZE: **9 cm (3½ in)**

This tiny bird migrates 800 km (500 mi) or more across the Gulf of Mexico to its wintering grounds — an extraordinary feat for such a small bird. The male has a distinctive ruby-red throat, and the female has white throat plumage and a rounded tail.

NAME: **Bee Hummingbird,** *Calypte helenae*
RANGE: **Cuba, Isle of Pines**
HABITAT: **forest**
SIZE: **5.7 cm (2¼ in)**

The smallest bird in the world, the bee hummingbird's actual body measures only 1.25 cm (½ in), and its bill, of similar size, and tail make up the total length. It weighs only 2 g (1/14 oz). Its tiny wings beat 50 to 80 times a second as it hovers to feed from flowers.

NAME: **Giant Hummingbird,** *Patagona gigas*
RANGE: **Ecuador to Chile and Argentina**
HABITAT: **arid land**
SIZE: **21.5 cm (8½ in)**

The largest hummingbird, this species weighs 20 g (⅔ oz). It beats its wings only 8 or 10 times a second, and although it feeds at flowers, it also catches insects in flight.

## TROCHILIDAE:
## Hummingbird Family

Named for the drone produced by the extremely rapid beating of their wings, the spectacular hummingbirds occur all over the Americas, from Alaska to Tierra del Fuego and high in the Andes, but mainly in the tropics. The 319 or so species include the smallest, and some of the most striking, birds known.

Hummingbirds range in length from 5.7 to 21.5 cm (2¼ to 8½ in), but the tail often makes up as much as half of this length. Their wings are long and narrow relative to body size, and hummingbirds are quite unsurpassed in their aerial maneuverability. They can hover motionless in front of a flower, their wings beating so fast that they are virtually invisible; they can fly upward, sideways, downward and, uniquely, backward. The keel of the breastbone in a hummingbird is proportionately bigger than that of any other bird, to support the massive flying muscles needed to power their movements.

The hummingbird's main foods are insects and nectar, which it obtains by plunging its long, slender, often curved bill (which has become specially adapted for the task) deep inside the flower. It uses its tubular tongue to extract the nectar, and the shapes of both bill and tongue are often closely related to those of particular flowers.

There is a great variety of tail shapes among male hummingbirds, and these decorative feathers are used in courtship display; females have duller plumage than males and lack the ornamental tail feathers. Except in the breeding season, hummingbirds are solitary and defend their territory aggressively, even against much larger birds. The female builds a cup-shaped nest, which is placed on a branch or palm frond or on a rock, and normally lays 2 eggs. In all but 1 species, she alone incubates the eggs and cares for the young.

NAME: **Frilled Coquette,** *Lophornis magnifica*
RANGE: **E. and central Brazil**
HABITAT: **forest, scrub**
SIZE: **7 cm (2¾ in)**

The brilliant frilled coquette can easily be mistaken for a butterfly, either as it hovers, feeding from a flower, or when pairs are courting, for the male chases the female until she slows down, and they then hover together, fluttering up and down. The female builds a cup-shaped nest among low vegetation and covers the outside with cobwebs, pieces of bark and plant fibers, which camouflage it.

NAME: **Ruby-topaz Hummingbird,** *Chrysolampis mosquitus*
RANGE: **Colombia, Venezuela, the Guianas, Brazil, N.E. Bolivia**
HABITAT: **forest, scrub, savanna**
SIZE: **9 cm (3½ in)**

The male of this species has glittering, colorful plumage, while the female's feathers are greenish and gray.

The birds feed on nectar and insects, both in low vegetation and tall trees.

NAME: **Marvelous Spatule-tail,** *Loddigesia mirabilis*
RANGE: **Andes in Peru**
HABITAT: **forest at 2,300–2,600 m (7,500–8,500 ft)**
SIZE: **body: 12.5 cm (5 in) tail: 14 cm (5½ in)**

The male of this little-known hummingbird species has an extraordinary tail, with only four feathers, two of which are greatly elongated and wirelike and expanded into racket shapes at the ends. During his courtship display, the male bird frames his iridescent throat plumage with his decorative tail feathers and flies back and forth in front of his prospective mate.

NAME: **Long-tailed Sylph Hummingbird,** *Aglaiocercus kingi*
RANGE: **Venezuela to Bolivia, Peru and Ecuador**
HABITAT: **forest, scrub**
SIZE: **male: 18 cm (7 in) female: 9.5 cm (3¾ in)**

The outer tail feathers of the male of this species are almost 12.5 cm (5 in) long and are used in courtship display. The female's tail feathers are not elongated, and she has a buff-white throat and cinnamon underparts.

NAME: **Crimson Topaz,** *Topaza pella*
RANGE: **the Guianas, Venezuela, Brazil**
HABITAT: **rain forest**
SIZE: **20 cm (7¾ in)**

A glittering, colorful bird, the male crimson topaz has two elongated black tail feathers, which are 6 cm (2¼ in) longer than the rest of the tail. The female is less startling, but she, too, has some gleaming green and red plumage, as well as bronze and violet tail feathers.

NAME: **Andean Hillstar,** *Oreotrochilus estella*
RANGE: **Andes: from Ecuador to Argentina and Chile**
HABITAT: **rocky slopes**
SIZE: **12 cm (4¾ in)**

The neck and throat plumage of the male of this species varies but usually includes some glittering green or violet and sometimes both. The female bird has a dull olive-green back and head, white throat and grayish underparts.

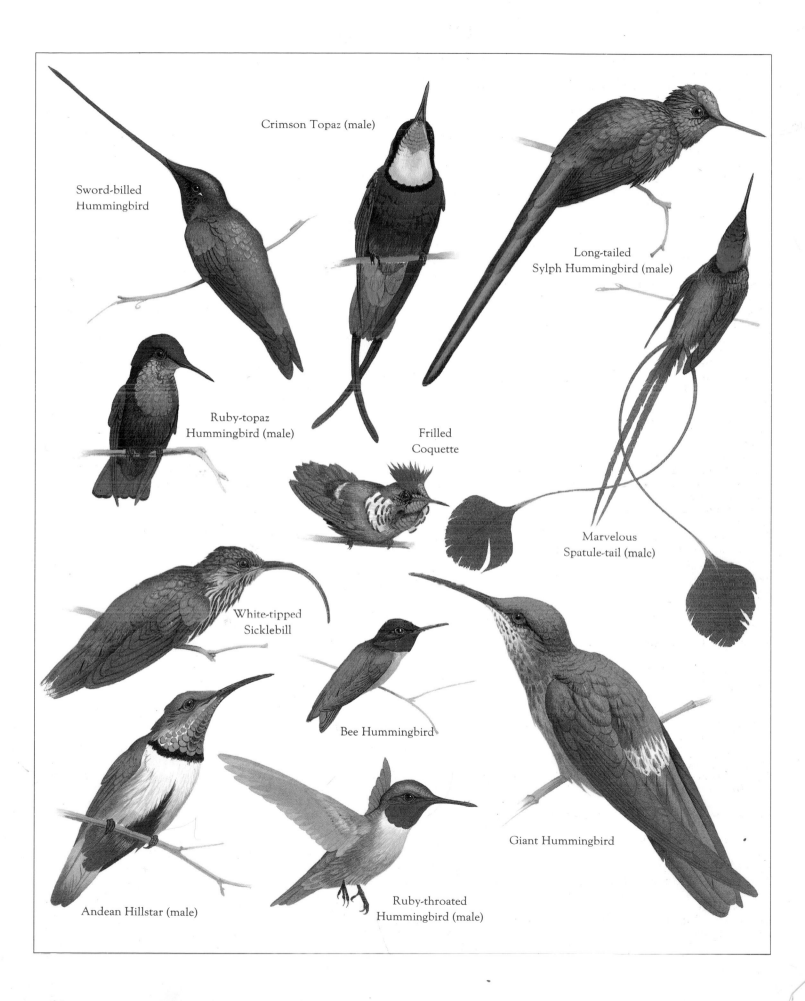

Sword-billed
Hummingbird

Crimson Topaz (male)

Long-tailed
Sylph Hummingbird (male)

Ruby-topaz
Hummingbird (male)

Frilled
Coquette

Marvelous
Spatule-tail (male)

White-tipped
Sicklebill

Bee Hummingbird

Giant Hummingbird

Andean Hillstar (male)

Ruby-throated
Hummingbird (male)

# Trogons, Mousebirds

## ORDER TROGONIFORMES
### TROGONIDAE: Trogon Family

The trogons make up a family that is placed in its own order. The 35 or 36 species of trogon are among the most resplendently colorful birds in the world; males are always more brilliantly marked than females. They are found in forest habitats in three quite separate tropical areas: the southern regions of Africa; India and Southeast Asia; and Central and South America.

Trogons are between 23 and 35.5 cm (9 and 14 in) in length and possess short, rounded wings and long tails. Their feet are zygodactyl, that is, they have two toes pointing forward and two pointing backward, an adaptation possessed by many tree-living birds. However, in trogons the first and second digits point forward, while in all other birds with such feet, it is the first and fourth digits that do so.

Primarily woodland and forest birds, trogons spend much of their time perching in trees. They feed on insects and other small invertebrates and also on berries and fruit.

---

**NAME: Quetzal, *Pharomachrus mocinno***
**RANGE: Mexico, Central America**
**HABITAT: high-altitude rain forest**
**SIZE: 30 cm (11¾ in)**
**tail feathers: 61 cm (24 in)** Ⓥ

The strikingly colored quetzal has greatly extended upper tail coverts (feathers overlying the tail), which form a magnificent train and are shed and regrown after each breeding season. These feathers were highly prized for ceremonial use by ancient Mayan and Aztec civilizations, and the quetzal itself was regarded as a sacred bird and was associated with the plumed serpent god, Quetzalcoatl. The quetzal is now the national bird of Guatemala. Females are plainer than males, and their upper tail coverts extend only to the end of the tail proper and do not form a train.

Quetzals are arboreal, somewhat solitary birds which inhabit the lower layers of the tropical forest trees. They feed on fruit, of which they seem particularly fond, as well as on insects, small frogs, lizards and snails, and flutter from branch to branch, seizing food items as they go.

They nest in a hole in a tree and 2 or 3 eggs are laid. The male bird takes his turn at incubating the clutch and must sit on the nest with the tail plumes bent forward over his head and hanging out of the hole. By the end of the breeding season, the feathers are damaged and broken from many maneuvers in and out of the nest.

**NAME: Elegant/Coppery-tailed Trogon, *Trogon elegans***
**RANGE: extreme S.W. USA to Costa Rica**
**HABITAT: forest, woodland**
**SIZE: 28–30.5 cm (11–12 in)**

This brilliantly plumaged trogon has a stout yellow bill and a distinctive broad, blunt tail. The tail is coppery-red, seen from above, but gray and white below, with a black band at the base. The female bird is patterned like the male but is duller, with a brownish head. This is the only species in the trogon family to occur in the USA.

Elegant trogons are solitary, generally quiet birds, but they do make monotonous, froglike calls. They perch for long periods in the trees and then take to the air to dart about the branches in search of insects, small animals and fruit. Most of their feeding is done in flight, and the birds will sometimes hover in front of a cluster of leaves to glean food from their surfaces. The trogon's legs and feet are weak and are used almost entirely for perching, only rarely for walking.

Both partners of a breeding pair help to excavate a hole in a tree for use as a nest, or they take over an existing hollow or an abandoned woodpecker hole. The 3 or 4 eggs are incubated by both male and female, probably for a total of 17 to 19 days. The young hatch naked and helpless and are cared for and fed by both parents. They leave the nest when 15 to 17 days old.

**NAME: Red-headed Trogon, *Harpactes erythrocephalus***
**RANGE: Nepal: Himalayas, S. China; S.E. Asia, Sumatra**
**HABITAT: forest**
**SIZE: 34 cm (13¼ in)**

There are 11 species of trogon in Asia, all in the genus *Harpactes*. All are beautiful birds with broad, squared-off tails. The male red-headed trogon has distinctive dark-red plumage on its head, while the female has a brownish head, throat and breast. Like the American trogons, they are mainly solitary birds which perch on trees and dart out to catch food. Insects form the bulk of their diet, but they also eat leaves, berries, some frogs, and lizards; they do not appear to eat fruit. Twilight is their main period of activity.

The 3 or 4 eggs are laid in an unlined hole in a tree, usually an existing hollow, and are incubated by both parents for about 19 days.

**NAME: Narina Trogon, *Apaloderma narina***
**RANGE: southern Africa: S. and E. coastal regions**
**HABITAT: forest, scrub**
**SIZE: 29 cm (11½ in)**

One of the 3 African trogon species, the narina trogon lives in the lower levels of dense forest and will perch for long periods on a branch or creeper in a characteristically hunched posture. It feeds mainly on insects, which it catches among the branches or by darting out from the perch, and only rarely eats fruit.

The 2 or 3 eggs are laid in a hollow tree trunk and are incubated for about 20 days.

---

## ORDER COLIIFORMES
### COLIIDAE: Mousebird Family

The 6 species of mousebird, or coly, constitute a distinctive family that modern taxonomists place in an order of its own. All the forms are of very similar appearance, and the sexes look alike in all species. The body of the mousebird is about the size of that of a house sparrow, but it has extremely long tail feathers of graduated lengths. The plumage is soft and loosely attached to the skin. All species have crests, and their bills are short, curved and quite strong.

Mousebirds are distributed in the savanna regions of Africa, south of the Sahara. They are sociable birds which live in small groups and roost together, huddling close for warmth.

---

**NAME: Speckled Mousebird, *Colius striatus***
**RANGE: Africa, south of the Sahara**
**HABITAT: savanna, dense forest**
**SIZE: body: 12 cm (4¾ in)**
**tail: 18–20 cm (7–7¾ in)**

The speckled mousebird has a tail almost twice the length of its body. It spends much of its life in trees and climbs expertly among the branches, using its strong, adaptable feet — the hind toes can be turned forward — and long, sharp claws. Like all mousebirds, this species is extremely gregarious and feeds and roosts in small groups. Fruit and any soft vegetable matter, particularly young shoots, are its normal diet, but it occasionally eats insects.

The speckled mousebird makes a nest of twigs and rootlets, lined with leaves, in a tree or bush. Usually 3 eggs are laid, and they are then incubated by both parents for a total of 12 to 14 days. Young are able to leave the nest a few days after hatching and fly at 16 to 18 days old.

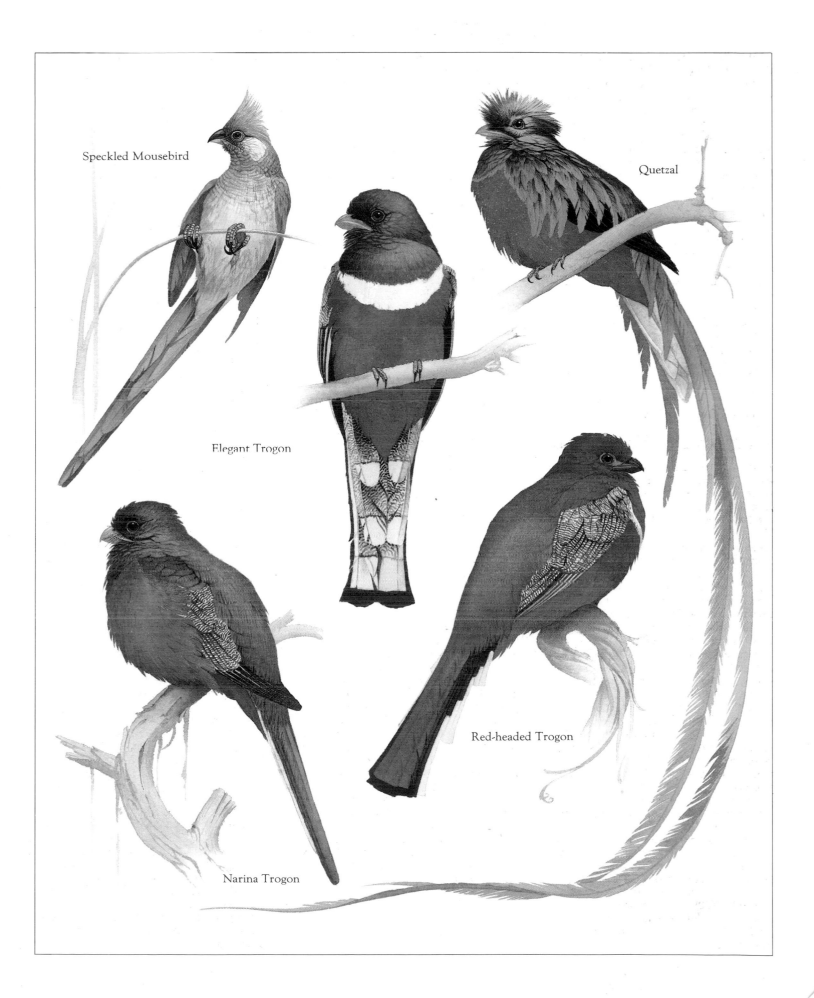

Speckled Mousebird

Quetzal

Elegant Trogon

Narina Trogon

Red-headed Trogon

# Kingfishers

NAME: Kingfisher, *Alcedo atthis*
RANGE: Europe, N. Africa to Asia, New Guinea and Solomon Islands
HABITAT: inland waterways, marshes. mangrove swamps, seashores
SIZE: 16 cm (6¼ in)

The only European kingfisher, this bird has a wide range and is unmistakable, with its brilliant plumage and long, daggerlike bill. A solitary bird, it lives in the vicinity of water. When hunting, it perches on branches overhanging the water, watching for prey, or flies low over it, often hovering for a few seconds before diving for fish and other small aquatic animals.

In the breeding season, a pair makes a slightly upward-sloping tunnel, up to 61 cm (24 in) long, in the bank of a stream, with a nesting chamber about 15 cm (6 in) across at the end of it. They start the tunnel by repeatedly hurling themselves against the riverbank so that their sharp bills always strike the same spot. Here the female lays 4 to 8 eggs which both parents incubate in shifts for 19 to 21 days. They share in the care and feeding of the young.

NAME: Shovel-billed Kingfisher, *Clytoceyx rex*
RANGE: New Guinea
HABITAT: forest
SIZE: 30.5 cm (12 in)

The soberly colored shovel-billed kingfisher is a solitary bird which inhabits forest at altitudes of up to 2,350 m (7,700 ft). It perches for long periods on tree stumps and branches, swooping down suddenly to catch large insects, larvae and small mice. Using its short, heavy bill as a shovel, it also probes in the mud beside streams and rivers, searching for worms, crabs and reptiles. Little is known about its breeding habits, but it is thought to make its nest on the ground.

NAME: White-collared/Mangrove Kingfisher, *Halcyon chloris*
RANGE: Ethiopia to India, S.E. China, Australia, S.W. Pacific islands
HABITAT: mangrove swamps, estuaries, rivers, forest clearings
SIZE: 25.5 cm (10 in)

This widely distributed kingfisher is found in a variety of habitats but most commonly in mangrove swamps. Perching on branches, it watches for prey, then swoops down to the swamp mud or dives into the water in pursuit of crabs and small fish, its main foods. Before swallowing a crab, the kingfisher will dash it against a branch a few times to crush the shell. These kingfishers nest in holes in trees, among the roots of an arboreal fern or in termite or ant nests. The female lays 3 or 4 eggs.

## ORDER CORACIIFORMES

There are 10 families in this order: kingfishers, todies, motmots, bee-eaters, rollers, cuckoo-rollers, ground rollers, hoopoes, woodhoopoes and hornbills. Most species in the order have large bills in proportion to their body size and brightly colored plumage.

## ALCEDINIDAE: Kingfisher Family

Although kingfishers are found all over the world, the majority of the 86 or so known species inhabit the hotter regions of the Old World. They range in length from 10 to 46 cm (4 to 18 in) and have stocky bodies, large heads and short necks. The beak is almost always straight, with a pointed tip, and is large in proportion to the body. Wings are short and rounded, and tail length is variable. Most kingfishers have multicolored plumage, with patches of iridescent blue, green, purple or red. Male and female differ slightly in appearance in some species.

As the group name suggests, several kingfishers are fish-eaters. They are usually found near inland waters and catch aquatic invertebrates as well as fish by diving headlong from a perch just above the water. Unusually for diving birds, they do not actually swim. The majority of species, however, feed on dry land on insects, lizards, snakes and even birds and rodents, catching prey by swooping down from a high vantage point.

Kingfishers nest in tunnels, often in riverbanks, or in cavities in trees or termite nests; there is little or no nesting material. Some northern populations migrate south in winter.

NAME: Beautiful/Common Paradise Kingfisher, *Tanysiptera galatea*
RANGE: New Guinea to the Moluccas
HABITAT: forest
SIZE: 28 cm (11 in)

This handsome kingfisher has greatly elongated tail feathers, thought to be used in courtship display. Deep in the forest understory, it perches on branches to watch for its prey, mainly millipedes and lizards but also insects and other invertebrates, and it may dig in the forest litter for earthworms.

Beautiful paradise kingfishers are normally solitary birds, but in the breeding season both partners of a breeding pair help to dig a hole in an arboreal termite nest in which to lay their eggs. Alternatively, the birds will nest in patches of vegetation at the forest edge. The female lays 3 to 5 eggs, which are incubated by both parents.

NAME: Laughing Kookaburra, *Dacelo novaeguineae*
RANGE: Australia; introduced in Tasmania
HABITAT: dry forest fringe, savanna, any open country with trees
SIZE: 46 cm (18 in)

The largest of the kingfishers, the kookaburra is renowned for its noisy, laughlike call; when one bird starts calling, all the others near by will join in, particularly at dawn or at dusk. Kookaburras eat practically anything, including large insects, crabs, small reptiles, mammals and birds, and are beneficial to humans in that they prey on rodents and other harmful vermin.

Kookaburras nest in holes in trees or sometimes in arboreal termite nests, in cavities in banks or even on buildings. The female lays 3 or 4 eggs.

NAME: African Pygmy Kingfisher, *Ispidina picta*
RANGE: Africa, south of the Sahara to Zambia
HABITAT: bush, woodland
SIZE: 12.5 cm (5 in)

One of the smallest kingfishers, this species has the curious habit of diving from its perch into grass, much as other kingfishers dive into water. Grasshoppers, caterpillars, beetles and other insects, as well as some lizards, make up its diet. The insects are caught in the air or on the ground. The pygmy kingfisher's nest is made at the end of a tunnel in a riverbank or in a termite mound or anthill, and the female lays 3 to 5 eggs.

NAME: Belted Kingfisher, *Ceryle alcyon*
RANGE: Alaska, Canada, USA, south to Mexico and Panama; West Indies
HABITAT: fresh water, coasts
SIZE: 28–35.5 cm (11–14 in)

The only American kingfisher to occur north of Texas and Arizona, this common bird inhabits any territory near water. Male and female birds look similar, but the female has a chestnut band across the breast and extending down the flanks, which the male lacks. Solitary birds out of the breeding season, each individual holds its own territory and has a series of habitual perches overlooking water. They feed on small fish, crabs, crayfish, tadpoles, frogs, lizards and some insects and generally hover above the water before diving for prey.

Using their bills and feet, both members of a breeding pair dig a nesting tunnel 1.2 to 2.4 m (4 to 8 ft) long in the riverbank, at the end of which they make a nesting chamber. The female lays 5 to 8 eggs, which are incubated for about 23 days.

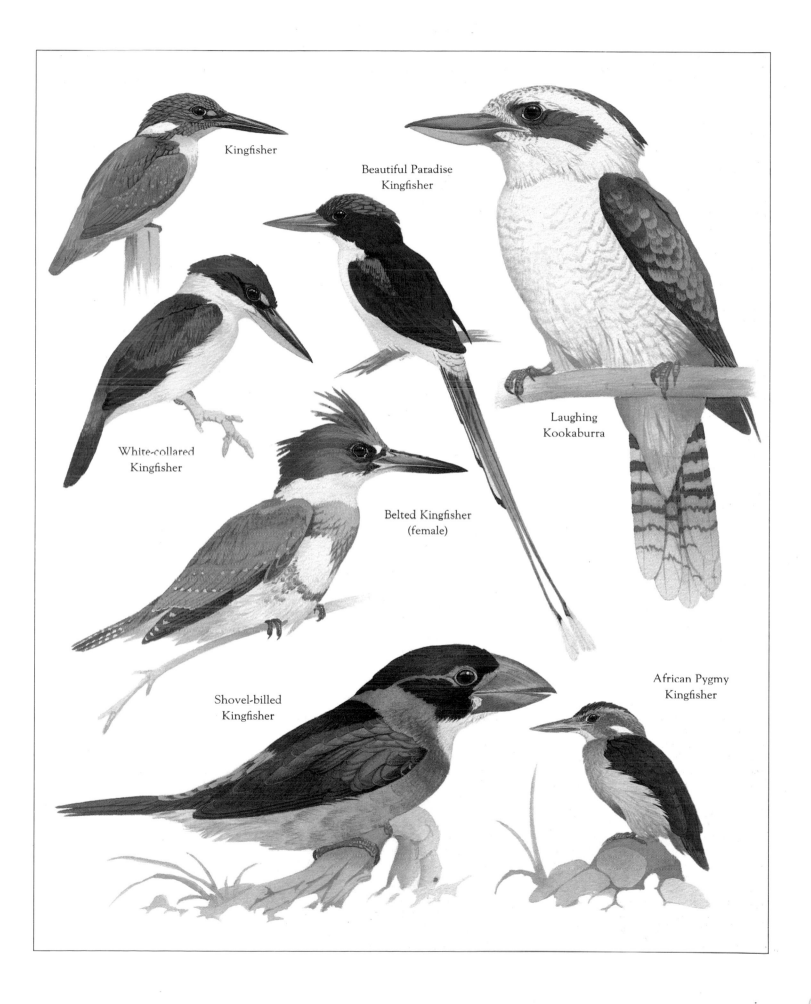

Kingfisher

Beautiful Paradise
Kingfisher

Laughing
Kookaburra

White-collared
Kingfisher

Belted Kingfisher
(female)

Shovel-billed
Kingfisher

African Pygmy
Kingfisher

# Motmots,
## Bee-eaters and relatives

### MOMOTIDAE: Motmot Family
Motmots are beautifully plumaged birds, with decorative, elongated tail feathers. There are 9 species of motmot, found from Mexico to northeastern Argentina. All have slightly downward-curving bills with serrated edges, which they use to seize prey from the dense vegetation among which they live. Male and female look alike or nearly so.

NAME: **Blue-crowned Motmot,** *Momotus momota*
RANGE: **Mexico, Central America, South America to N.W. Argentina; Trinidad and Tobago**
HABITAT: **rain forest, plantations**
SIZE: **38–41 cm (15–16 in)**

The blue-crowned motmot has two greatly elongated central tail feathers, with racket-shaped tips. Although the feathers are initially fully vaned, the vanes just above the ends of the feathers are loosely attached and fall away as the bird preens or brushes against vegetation, leaving the racket tips. The motmot perches to watch for prey, such as insects, spiders or lizards, often swinging its tail from side to side like a pendulum while it waits. It darts out from the perch to seize prey, then returns to consume the item, having briefly beaten it against a branch.

Motmots nest in a burrow, which is dug by both members of a breeding pair, in a bank or opening off the side of a mammal's burrow. The burrow may be up to 4 m (13 ft) long and have several sharp turns. In the enlarged chamber at the end of the tunnel, the female lays her 3 eggs on bare ground. Both parents incubate the eggs for about 21 days.

### MEROPIDAE: Bee-eater Family
The 24 species of bee-eater are brightly plumaged birds, with streamlined bodies, long wings and small, weak legs. They occur in tropical and warm temperate areas of the Old World. As their name suggests, they are adept at the aerial capture of insects, such as bees and wasps, which they seize with their long, downward-curving bills. While they are considered a menace by beekeepers, these birds are much appreciated in the tropics, where they consume large numbers of locusts.

Bee-eaters are gregarious birds, feeding together and nesting in colonies of sometimes hundreds of pairs. Males and females look alike. Many species are migratory.

NAME: **(European) Bee-eater,** *Merops apiaster*
RANGE: **breeds in Europe, USSR, N. Africa, S.W. Asia; winters in tropical Africa and Middle East**
HABITAT: **open country, woodland**
SIZE: **28 cm (11 in)**

One of the most tropical-looking European birds, the gaudy bee-eater makes swift darts from a perch to catch prey, mainly bees and wasps. It rubs its prey against a branch or the ground before swallowing it, presumably to destroy the sting.

Bee-eaters nest in colonies. Each pair makes a tunnel 1 to 3 m (3¼ to 9¾ ft) long, often in a riverbank. The female lays 4 to 7 eggs at the end of the tunnel, and both parents incubate the clutch for about 20 days. Together, they care for and feed their young.

### TODIDAE: Tody Family
The 5 species of tody all live in the West Indies and are extremely similar in size and appearance, with mostly green and red plumage. Males and females look alike. They are insect-eating birds which catch their prey, flycatcher-fashion, in the air.

NAME: **Jamaican Tody,** *Todus todus*
RANGE: **Jamaica**
HABITAT: **wooded hills and mountains**
SIZE: **10.75 cm (4¼ in)**

The Jamaican tody is typical of its family, with its small, compact body, relatively large head and long, sharp bill. It hunts close to the ground, catching flying insects and, occasionally, baby lizards.

Todies live in pairs or singly and are strongly territorial. They nest in burrows, which they dig with their bills, usually in the sides of banks. The nest tunnel is about 30 cm (11¾ in) long, with a tiny entrance just big enough for the birds to squeeze through, but it opens out at the end into a breeding chamber. The female lays 3 or 4 eggs, and both parents incubate the clutch and care for the young.

### CORACIIDAE: Roller Family
Most of the 11 species of roller live in Africa, although they occur in warm temperate and tropical parts of the Old World, from Europe to Australia. They are brightly colored, stocky birds, with large heads, long, downward-curving bills and long wings. Their common name originates from their tumbling, aerobatic courtship displays. Males and females look alike.

NAME: **Roller,** *Coracias garrulus*
RANGE: **breeds in Europe, N. Africa, S.W. Asia; winters in E. and S. Africa, Middle East**
HABITAT: **forest, woodland, open country**
SIZE: **30 cm (11¾ in)**

Robust, gregarious birds, rollers like to perch, particularly on telephone wires, to watch for prey such as insects, small lizards, frogs and birds, They dart out to seize the prey and return to the perch to feed. Fruit is also part of their diet.

The male roller courts his mate with extraordinary flight displays in which he dives to the earth from high in the air, tumbling and rolling as he descends. The nest is made in an existing hole in a tree, wall or bank, or an abandoned nest of another bird species may be used. Both parents incubate the 4 to 7 eggs for a total of 18 or 19 days and share the care of the young.

### LEPTOSOMATIDAE: Cuckoo-roller Family
The single species in this family is related to the true rollers and ground rollers. It differs from them, however, in that male and female look unalike.

NAME: **Cuckoo-roller,** *Leptosomus discolor*
RANGE: **Madagascar, Comoro Islands**
HABITAT: **forest, savanna**
SIZE: **41–46 cm (16–18 in)**

Cuckoo-rollers are noisy birds which live in trees, feeding on insects, especially hairy caterpillars, and on lizards. Their legs are short and weak, but they are strong fliers and perform spectacular maneuvers over the treetops. The female is plainer than the male, with rufous plumage and black markings.

### BRACHYPTERACIIDAE: Ground Roller Family
The 5 species of ground roller all live in Madagascar. Sometimes classified as a subfamily of rollers (Coraciidae), they differ from the latter in that they are ground-living rather than arboreal.

NAME: **Short-legged Ground Roller,** *Brachypteracias leptosomus*
RANGE: **E. Madagascar**
HABITAT: **dense forest to 1,800 m (6,000ft)**
SIZE: **25.5–30.5 cm (10–12 in)** ®

Typical of its family, the short-legged ground roller is a squat bird, with short wings, strong legs and a stout, downward-curving bill. It lives on the forest floor, feeding on insects and reptiles, and flies up into trees only when alarmed.

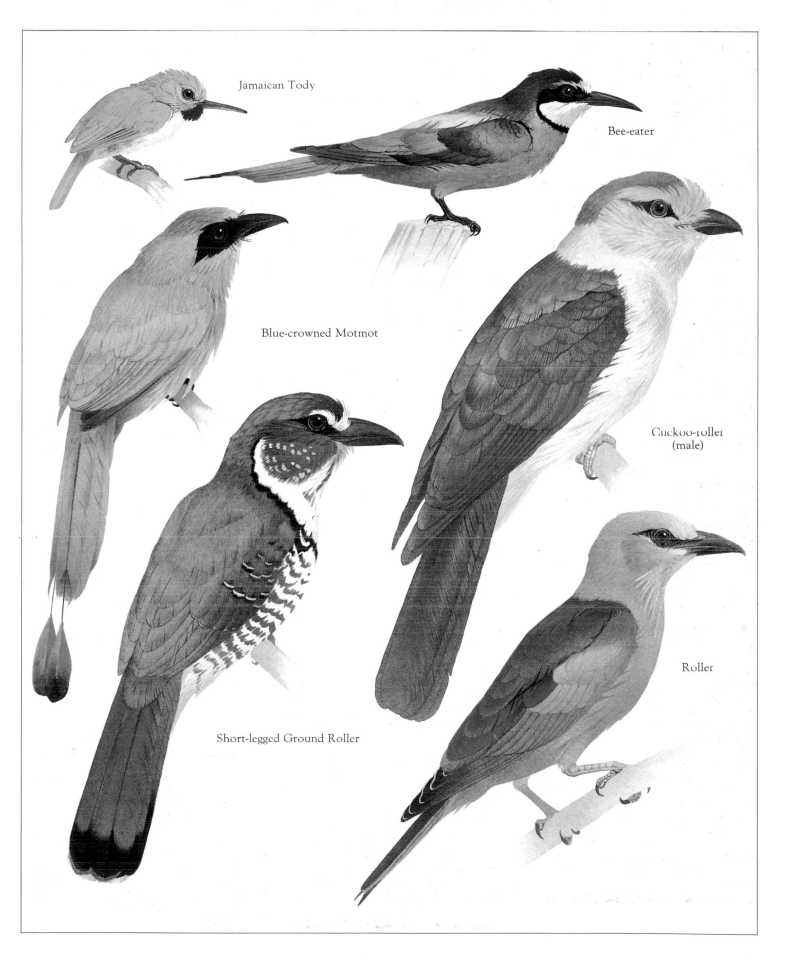

Jamaican Tody

Bee-eater

Blue-crowned Motmot

Cuckoo-roller
(male)

Short-legged Ground Roller

Roller

# Hoopoe, Woodhoopoes, Hornbills

## UPUPIDAE: Hoopoe Family

The single species of hoopoe is a ground-living bird, distinct enough in structure to merit a family of its own. Male and female birds look more or less alike, but females may sometimes be smaller and duller.

NAME: **Common Hoopoe,** *Upupa epops*
RANGE: **Europe (except Scandinavia and, usually, Britain), N. Africa, central and S. Asia; winters tropical Africa, S. Asia**
HABITAT: **open country with trees, forest edge, parks, gardens, orchards**
SIZE: **28 cm (11 in)**

An unusual, striking bird, the hoopoe has pinkish to cinnamon body plumage, boldly barred wings and tail and a huge crest, which is usually held flat. The hoopoe's legs are strong, and it walks and runs swiftly as it searches for worms, insects and invertebrates to eat, probing the ground with its curved, slender bill. Although primarily a ground bird, the hoopoe does perch and roost in trees and flies efficiently, if slowly, occasionally hunting insects in the air.

The female lays 5 to 8 eggs, sometimes as many as 12, in a hole in a tree, wall or building. The male bird feeds his mate while she incubates the clutch for 16 to 19 days.

## PHOENICULIDAE: Woodhoopoe Family

Wooded grassland, forest and forest edge in central and southern Africa are the habitats of the 8 species of woodhoopoe. Male and female birds look similar, but the female is often smaller and sometimes browner than the male.

NAME: **Green Woodhoopoe,** *Phoeniculus purpureus*
RANGE: **Africa, south of the Sahara**
HABITAT: **woodland, often near rivers, forest**
SIZE: **38 cm (15 in)**

The slender green woodhoopoe has glossy dark-green and purple plumage and a long, deep-purple tail; its distinctive red bill is long and downward-curving. Male and female look alike, but young birds have brownish neck and breast plumage and black bills. Noisy, gregarious birds, woodhoopoes fly from tree to tree in small parties, searching for insects to eat and calling harshly.

The female woodhoopoe lays her 3 to 5 eggs in a hole in a tree or may use an old woodpecker or barbet hole. She incubates the clutch, but her mate helps her tend and feed the young.

## BUCEROTIDAE: Hornbill Family

The 44 species of hornbill occur in Africa, south of the Sahara, and in tropical Asia, south to Indonesia. Most have brown or black and white plumage but are instantly recognizable by their huge bills, topped with horny projections, or casques. Despite its heavy appearance, the hornbill's beak is actually a light honeycomb of bony cellular tissue, encased in a shell of horn. While a few hornbills are ground-feeding birds of open country, most live and feed in trees in forest and savanna. Most are omnivorous, feeding on fruit, insects, lizards and even small mammals. Male and female look similar in some species but differ in others.

Hornbills are probably best known for their extraordinary nesting habits. Once the female has laid her eggs in a suitable nest hole, the entrance is walled up with mud, leaving a small slitlike opening. The male may do this or the female may barricade herself in, using material that the male brings her. She remains there throughout the incubation and part of the fledgling period, totally dependent on her mate for food supplies but perfectly protected from predators. The male brings food, which he passes to her through the slit — a task to which his long, laterally compressed bill is admirably suited.

While she is a captive, she undergoes a molt, but by the time the appetites of the young are too much for the male to cope with, her feathers have regrown. Using her beak, she hacks her way out of the nest, and the young repair the barricade. Both parents then bring food until the young hornbills are able to fly. Details vary slightly from species to species, but all hornbills keep their nests clean, throwing out food debris and excreting through the slit.

NAME: **Red-billed Hornbill,** *Tockus erythrorhynchus*
RANGE: **W., E. and S.E. Africa**
HABITAT: **bush, open woodland**
SIZE: **46 cm (18 in)**

Although brightly colored, the beak of the red-billed hornbill has little, if any, casque. Male and female look similar, with gray and brownish-black plumage and light markings on the wings. The female does not always have a black base to the lower bill. Usually in pairs or small family parties, red-billed hornbills feed on the ground and in trees on insects, such as grasshoppers, locusts and beetles, and on fruit.

The female lays her 3 to 6 eggs in a hole in a tree, which is barricaded with mud in the usual manner of hornbills.

NAME: **Southern Ground Hornbill,** *Bucorvus leadbeateri*
RANGE: **Africa: Lake Tanganyika, south to South Africa: Cape Province**
HABITAT: **open country**
SIZE: **107 cm (42 in)**

The southern ground hornbill and the closely related Abyssinian ground hornbill, *B. abyssinicus*, are the largest of the African hornbills. Both are primarily ground-living, turkey-sized birds, which walk about in pairs or small family parties, feeding on insects and small reptiles and other animals.

The female lays 1 to 3 eggs in a hole in a tree or stump, lined with leaves. She is not walled up in the nest and comes and goes freely, covering the eggs with leaves when she is not sitting.

NAME: **Helmeted Hornbill,** *Rhinoplax vigil*
RANGE: **Malaysian Peninsula, Sumatra, Borneo**
HABITAT: **forest**
SIZE: **1.2 m (4 ft)** Ⓘ

The greatly elongated central tail feathers of this huge hornbill may add as much as 50 cm (20 in) to its length. The female is slightly smaller than the male. This bird is unusual in that while all other hornbills have bills that are deceptively light, its casque is formed of solid ivory, making its skull the heaviest of any bird's. This heavy head could cause problems for the bird when in flight, but the elongated central tail feathers help to counterbalance the skull. Unfortunately the attributes of the helmeted hornbill have created much demand for it, and it has long been hunted both for its ivory casque and its tail feathers.

Helmeted hornbills feed on fruit, lizards, birds and their eggs. The breeding procedure is believed to be similar to that of other hornbills.

NAME: **Great Indian Hornbill,** *Buceros bicornis*
RANGE: **India, S.E. Asia, Sumatra**
HABITAT: **forest**
SIZE: **1.5 m (5 ft)**

Although a large bird, the great Indian hornbill has a top-heavy appearance, with its huge bill and casque. The female bird is much smaller, particularly her bill and casque, and has white instead of red eyes, but she is otherwise similar to the male. These hornbills spend much of their time in trees, feeding on fruit, especially figs, as well as on insects, reptiles and other small animals.

The female bird lays 1 to 3 eggs in an unlined hole in a tree and walls up the entrance from within, using her own feces and material brought to her by the male. She incubates the eggs for about 31 days.

Green Woodhoopoe

Red-billed Hornbill

Common Hoopoe

Helmeted Hornbill

Great Indian Hornbill

Southern Ground
Hornbill

# Jacamars, Barbets and relatives

## ORDER PICIFORMES

This order includes 6 families: jacamars, puffbirds, honey guides, woodpeckers, toucans and barbets. Most of the birds in these families are tree-dwelling and have in common a zygodactyl foot (a foot with two toes pointing forward and two pointing backward), which aids climbing up vertical tree trunks.

## GALBULIDAE: Jacamar Family

The 17 species of jacamar are graceful, long-billed birds, which resemble bee-eaters in appearance and in their technique of catching insects in the air, although they are unrelated. Males are usually brightly plumaged, with some glossy or iridescent feathers, while females are a little duller. Jacamars nest in tunnels, which they dig in the ground. They occur from Mexico to Brazil.

NAME: **Rufous-tailed Jacamar,** *Galbula ruficauda*
RANGE: **Mexico, Central America, through tropical South America to Brazil; Trinidad and Tobago**
HABITAT: **forest clearings, second-growth forest, scrub woodland**
SIZE: **23–28 cm (9–11 in)**

The rufous-tailed jacamar is a brightly plumaged bird, with gleaming, iridescent upperparts. The female differs in that she has a buff throat, and young birds are generally duller. Perching on a branch, the jacamar watches for insect prey to fly past, then darts after it in agile, swooping flight, snapping the insect out of the air with great expertise. It returns to its perch to consume the catch, and if the insect is large, beats it against the branch to kill it and to remove any hard, horny legs or wing cases before swallowing.

Jacamars excavate their own breeding tunnel in the ground, the female of the pair doing most of the work. Both birds share the incubation of 19 to 23 days, the female sitting at night, and the male taking over in the daytime. They feed their young until they are able to fly, about 3 weeks after hatching.

## BUCCONIDAE: Puffbird Family

Closely related to jacamars, the 34 species of puffbird and nunbird are also insect-eating birds, found from Mexico south through Central and tropical South America. Puffbirds are, however, stouter, more lethargic birds than the agile jacamars, although they do make aerial sallies after prey. Male and female look more or less alike, both with large heads for their size and sober plumage.

NAME: **White-necked Puffbird,** *Notharchus macrorhynchos*
RANGE: **Central and South America to N.E. Argentina**
HABITAT: **open forest, forest edge, savanna with trees**
SIZE: **25.5 cm (10 in)**

Like all puffbirds, this species has a habit of fluffing out its plumage as it perches watching for prey, thus creating a bulky appearance, which is the origin of the common name. Once an insect is sighted, the puffbird flies out to catch it in flight with its broad, hook-tipped bill.

Breeding white-necked puffbirds excavate a tunnel in the ground and then camouflage the entrance with leaves and twigs. The female lays 2 or 3 eggs in a leaf-lined chamber at the end of the tunnel, and both birds incubate the clutch.

NAME: **Black-fronted Nunbird,** *Monasa nigrifrons*
RANGE: **Colombia, east to the Andes, south to Bolivia, Brazil**
HABITAT: **forest**
SIZE: **29 cm (11½ in)**

Puffbirds of the genus *Monasa* have black or black and white plumage, hence their common name of nunbirds. Nunbirds are more gregarious than other puffbirds and often gather in flocks, but they are otherwise similar in their habits. They perch on branches to watch for insects and then fly out to seize the prey in the air.

Breeding pairs excavate tunnels in which to nest, and the female of this species is thought to lay 2 or 3 eggs.

## CAPITONIDAE: Barbet Family

The 81 species of barbet are chunky, generally brightly colored little birds, with large heads, and bills often fringed with tufts of bristles. They occur in tropical areas of the Americas, Asia and Africa, but the majority live in Africa. Most are solitary, tree-dwelling birds, and they feed on insects and fruit. Male and female look alike in most species.

NAME: **Double-toothed Barbet,** *Lybius bidentatus*
RANGE: **Africa: S. Sudan, Ethiopia, south to Uganda, W. Kenya, Tanzania**
HABITAT: **light forest, wooded savanna, cultivated land**
SIZE: **23 cm (9 in)**

Identified by its deep-red throat and breast, the double-toothed barbet feeds on fruit, particularly figs and bananas, and will invade plantations.

The nest is excavated in a dead branch of a tree, and the female is thought to lay 3 or 4 eggs. Like all barbets, both partners of a pair share the nesting duties.

NAME: **Coppersmith/Crimson-breasted Barbet,** *Megalaima haemacephala*
RANGE: **India, Sri Lanka, S.E. Asia, Sumatra, Java, Bali, Philippines**
HABITAT: **woodland, gardens, urban areas**
SIZE: **15 cm (6 in)**

A stocky bird, the coppersmith barbet is identified by the patches of bright red and yellow plumage on the throat and head, and the streaked belly. Alone, or sometimes in pairs or small groups, the coppersmith hunts in the trees for fruit, particularly figs, or may make clumsy aerial dashes after insects.

The breeding season lasts from January to June, and the barbets excavate a hole in a dead or rotting branch, which their beaks can penetrate easily. Both parents incubate the 2 to 4 eggs and tend the young birds.

## INDICATORIDAE: Honey Guide Family

There are 14 species of honey guide, found in Africa, Asia and Indonesia. Honey guides feed on wax and larval bees, and some species have developed the habit, for which the family is named, of leading man and other mammals to bee's nests in the hope that they will break the nests open. The birds are unique in being able to feed on wax, which they can digest by means of symbiotic bacteria in their intestines. They also feed on other insects, some of which they catch in the air. As far as is known, all species are brood parasites and lay their eggs in the nests of barbets and woodpeckers. Male and female look slightly different in most species.

NAME: **Greater/Black-throated Honey Guide,** *Indicator indicator*
RANGE: **Africa, south of the Sahara**
HABITAT: **varied: forest edge, arid bush, acacia woodland, cultivated land**
SIZE: **20 cm (7¾ in)**

The greater honey guide is one of the 2 species in the family that actively lead other creatures to bee's nests. Chattering loudly, the bird approaches a human being or another honey-eating mammal, such as the ratel, and having attracted the attention, leads the way to the nest, flying a short distance at a time. The honey guide needs the help of another creature to break open the nest and, once this has been done, will feed on the remains of the honey, the wax and larval bees. The skin of this bird is particularly thick and must guard it against stings. Like all honey guides, this bird also feeds on other insects.

The honey guide lays its eggs in the nests of other birds and its young are reared by their foster parents.

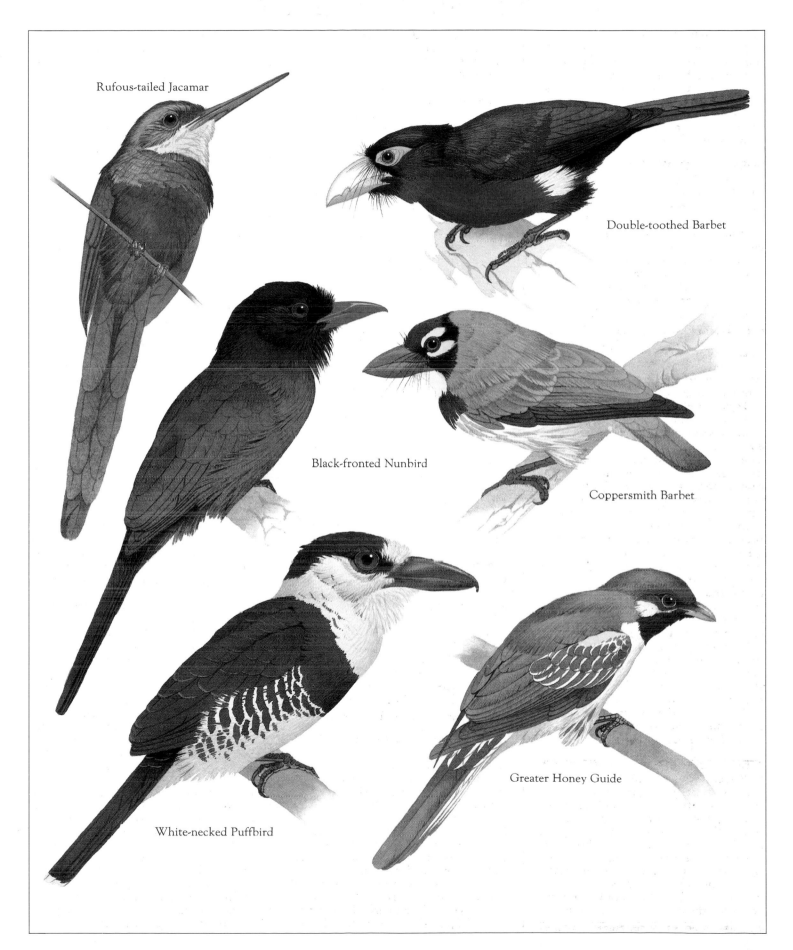

Rufous-tailed Jacamar

Double-toothed Barbet

Black-fronted Nunbird

Coppersmith Barbet

White-necked Puffbird

Greater Honey Guide

# Toucans

NAME: **Emerald Toucanet,**
　　*Aulacorhynchus prasinus*
RANGE: **S. Mexico to Nicaragua,**
　　**Venezuela, Colombia, Ecuador and**
　　**Peru**
HABITAT: **humid mountain forest, open**
　　**country with trees**
SIZE: **35.5 cm (14 in)**

The shy emerald toucanet lives at altitudes of between 1,800 and 3,000 m (6,000 and 10,000 ft). The birds sit inconspicuously among the foliage or fly for short distances in pairs or small groups to forage for food, calling to one another as they do so with a variety of noisy sounds. Their diet is wide-ranging and includes insects, small reptiles and amphibians, and the eggs and young of other bird species, as well as the more usual fruit and berries. Striking birds, emerald toucanets are unmistakable, with their bright green plumage and bold yellow and black bills.

The nest is made in a hole in a tree, often an old woodpecker hole; emerald toucanets have even been known to harass woodpeckers until they give up their nests. Both parents incubate the 3 or 4 eggs and bring food, mostly fruit, to the nestlings. The young of the emerald toucanet, like all toucans, hatch naked and develop their first feathers at about 2 weeks. Their beaks, however, grow faster than their bodies, and the young toucanet has a full-sized, 7.5-cm (3-in) bill before its body is even half the size of that of the adult.

NAME: **Saffron Toucanet,** *Baillonius*
　　*bailloni*
RANGE: **S.E. Brazil**
HABITAT: **forest**
SIZE: **35.5 cm (14 in)**

The saffron toucanet has fine, gold-colored plumage, which is especially lustrous on the cheeks and breast. Shy, graceful birds, they live in small groups and feed mainly on berries, preferring to forage high in the treetops rather than in the lower levels of the forest.

NAME: **Laminated Toucan,** *Andigena*
　　*laminirostris*
RANGE: **Andes in Colombia, W. Ecuador**
HABITAT: **forest**
SIZE: **43 cm (17 in)**

Also known as the plate-billed mountain toucan, this species lives at altitudes of between 1,000 and 3,000 m (3,300 and 10,000 ft). The bill is about 10 cm (4 in) long and extremely unusual in shape: on each side of the upper bill there is a horny yellow plate, which grows out from the base of the bill. The function of these plates is not clearly understood, since little is known of the habits of these toucans.

## RAMPHASTIDAE: Toucan Family

The toucans and aracaris are among the most extraordinary birds in the world. All 37 species are found living in the canopy layers of the dense rain forests of the Amazon basin and in neighboring forested areas of South America. They are medium-sized birds, ranging in size from 30 to 61 cm (12 to 24 in), and have enormous, boldly colored beaks that account for almost half the total body length. These bills are constructed of a honeycomb of bony material and are consequently light but very strong. The gaudy coloration varies greatly, not only between species but within a species. The plumage is usually dark, often black, with patches of boldly contrasting color on head and neck, which accentuates the bill colors. Toucans' wings are short and rounded and their flight weak. The legs are strong and the claws well adapted for grasping branches, with two toes pointing forward and two backward. Male and female look alike in most species.

The specific functions of the toucan's remarkable beak are poorly understood. It may act as an important visual signal in territorial or courtship behavior, or, it has been suggested, it may help the bird to obtain food otherwise out of its reach. Many other birds, however, manage without such bills. The bill may even help to intimidate other birds when the toucan raids their nests for young. Toucans feed on fruit of many types and on large, tree-living insects; occasionally they take larger prey such as nestling birds, eggs and lizards. The toucan seizes food with the tip of its bill and then throws its head back to toss the morsel into its mouth. An extremely long, narrow tongue with a bristlelike appendage at the tip aids manipulation of the food.

Toucans nest in tree cavities, either in natural holes or abandoned woodpecker holes. A few species line their nests with leaves, but in others, regurgitated seeds from fruit form a layer on the nest floor. The 2 to 4 eggs are incubated by both parents, who are able to flex their long tails forward over their backs to fit within the confines of the nesting cavity. Young toucans hatch naked and blind and develop slowly: at 3 weeks their eyes are only just opening, and they are not fully fledged for more than 6 weeks. They have specialized pads on their heels, on which they sit, which may be a form of protection against the rough floor of the nest. Both male and female feed and care for the young during this period.

NAME: **Spot-billed Toucanet,** *Selenidera*
　　*maculirostris*
RANGE: **tropical Brazil, south of the**
　　**Amazon to N.E. Argentina**
HABITAT: **lowland rain forest**
SIZE: **33 cm (13 in)**

An uncommon toucanet, this species has a patch of feathers, usually orange or yellow, behind each eye — a feature peculiar to the *Selenidera* genus and thought to be important in the male's courtship display. The bill of the male is distinctive, with a yellowish tip and black markings on the upper mandible; the female's bill is less clearly marked. This toucanet feeds on berries and large fruit, swallowing them whole and then disgorging the skins and stones. All toucans aid the seed dispersal of a number of fruit-bearing plants in this way.

Once their eggs are hatched, spot-billed toucanets often visit citrus plantations in groups to feed and find termites and other small insects to take to their young.

NAME: **Toco Toucan,** *Ramphastos toco*
RANGE: **E. South America: the Guianas**
　　**to N. Argentina**
HABITAT: **woodland, forest, plantations,**
　　**palm groves**
SIZE: **61 cm (24 in)**

A common toucan and one of the largest of its family, the toco toucan lives in small groups and frequents coconut and sugar plantations, as well as the normal toucan habitats. Its golden-yellow bill is about 19 cm (7½ in) long, and it feeds on a wide range of fruit but has a particular preference for capsicums. Toco toucans are not at all shy and will enter houses, steal food and tease domestic pets.

NAME: **Curl-crested Aracari,** *Pteroglossus*
　　*beauharnaesii*
RANGE: **Amazonian Peru, W. Brazil,**
　　**N. Bolivia**
HABITAT: **forest**
SIZE: **35.5 cm (14 in)**

This toucan is normally shy and nervous but can be aggressive and active. It has some curious plumage quite unlike that of any other toucan: the feathers on its crown are like shiny, curly scales, and those on the cheeks and throat have black scaly tips. Like other aracaris, it has pronounced jagged notches in its beak.

Groups of 5 or 6 adult aracaris roost together in an abandoned woodpecker hole or in a hollow in a tree, folding their tails over their backs to fit into the confined space.

Laminated Toucan

Curl-crested Aracari

Spot-billed Toucanet

Emerald
Toucanet

Toco Toucan

Saffron Toucanet

# Woodpeckers

NAME: **Wryneck,** *Jynx torquilla*
RANGE: **Europe, N. Africa, N. Asia;**
 **winters in Africa and S. Asia**
HABITAT: **open deciduous forest,**
 **cultivated land**
SIZE: **16–20.5 cm (6¼–8 in)**

A skulking, solitary bird, the wryneck is an unusual member of the woodpecker family, with a shorter, weaker bill than the true woodpeckers have. Although it can cling to tree trunks, it does not have the stiff, supporting tail of the typical woodpecker and more often perches. It does not bore into trees for its food but picks ants and other insects off leaves or from the ground, using its long, fast-moving tongue. The common name comes from its habit of twisting its head into strange positions while feeding and in courtship display.

The wryneck breeds in summer in Europe, north Africa and central Asia. It does not excavate its own nest but uses an existing cavity in a tree trunk, an abandoned woodpecker hole or a crevice in a wall or bank. The female lays 7 to 10 eggs, and both parents, but mainly the female, incubate the eggs for 13 days. Both parents feed insects and larvae to the young, which leave the nest about 3 weeks after hatching. After breeding, some populations of wrynecks migrate south to tropical Asia and Africa for the winter.

NAME: **Great Spotted Woodpecker,**
 *Picoides (= Dendrocopos) major*
RANGE: **Europe, N. Africa, Asia**
HABITAT: **mixed forest, woodland**
SIZE: **23 cm (9 in)**

The most common European woodpecker, the great spotted woodpecker is an adaptable species, living in all types of woodland, including parks and gardens. As it bores into tree trunks to extract its food — wood-boring insects and their larvae — it makes a characteristic drumming noise, which it also makes in spring in place of a courtship song. It supplements its diet with nuts, seeds and berries and has a habit of wedging a pinecone into a crevice and chipping out the kernels with its bill. The male bird has a red band at the back of his head, which the female lacks, and the juvenile has a red crown.

In Europe the breeding season begins in mid-May, and both partners help to excavate a hole in a tree, 3 m (10 ft) or more above ground. The female lays 3 to 8 eggs in this unlined nest and, with some assistance from the male, incubates them for 16 days. Both parents care for the young, bringing them insects in their bills. Most great spotted woodpeckers are resident birds, but some northern populations may migrate south in winter to find food.

## PICIDAE: Woodpecker Family

Woodpeckers and their relatives the wrynecks and piculets must be among the best-known of all specialized tree-living birds. There are about 208 species, found almost worldwide except in Madagascar, Australia, the Papuan region and most oceanic islands. Males and females have slight plumage differences in many species.

Woodpeckers are highly adapted for climbing in trees, extracting insects from bark and wood and making holes in tree trunks. The woodpecker clings tightly to the bark of the trunk with its sharply clawed feet, on which two toes face forward and two backward, giving it maximum grip. The stiff tail acts as an angled strut and gives the bird additional support as it bores into the wood with hammerlike movements of its strong, straight beak. A few woodpeckers are ground-living.

NAME: **Ivory-billed Woodpecker,**
 *Campephilus principalis*
RANGE: **S.E. USA, Cuba**
HABITAT: **swamps, forest**
SIZE: **51 cm (20 in)** Ⓔ

The largest North American woodpecker, this species is characterized by its pointed crest and long, ivory-colored bill. A seriously endangered species, it is now confined to a very few localities and may already be extinct in the USA.

It feeds on the larvae of insects, especially of the wood-boring beetles that live between the bark and wood of dying or newly dead trees, and also eats some fruit and nuts. Both members of a breeding pair help to excavate a nest cavity, and the female lays 1 to 3 eggs. The clutch is incubated for about 20 days, the male taking a turn at night, and both parents feed the young.

NAME: **White-barred Piculet,** *Picumnus*
 *cirratus*
RANGE: **South America: Guyana to**
 **N. Argentina**
HABITAT: **forest, woodland, parks**
SIZE: **9 cm (3½ in)**

A small, busy woodpecker, the white-barred piculet scrambles over trees, hanging upside down, moving over, under and around the branches in search of larvae to feed on. Predators are deterred from attacking this piculet because of its curious and particularly offensive odor.

The nest is made in a bamboo stem, and to excavate it, the piculet clings to the bamboo in true woodpecker fashion, speedily chipping it away with its beak.

NAME: **Rufous/White-browed Piculet,**
 *Sasia ochracea*
RANGE: **Himalayas, to mountains of**
 **S.E. Asia and S.E. China**
HABITAT: **woodland, especially bamboo**
 **forest**
SIZE: **9 cm (3½ in)**

This tiny, dumpy, stub-tailed woodpecker is an active, restless bird, usually seen singly or in pairs. With jerky movements, it creeps over thin twigs of low trees and bushes or hops around the litter of the woodland floor, searching for its food — mainly ants and their larvae. The female bird looks similar to the male but lacks his golden forehead.

The piculet's nest is a tiny hole about 2.5 cm (1 in) across, which is drilled in a decaying, hollow bamboo stem or an old tree. The female lays 3 or 4 eggs.

NAME: **Yellow-bellied Sapsucker,**
 *Sphyrapicus varius*
RANGE: **central Canada, E. USA; winters**
 **in Central America, West Indies**
HABITAT: **forest, woodland**
SIZE: **20.5 cm (8 in)**

The sapsucker migrates northward in the spring from its wintering grounds in Central America and the West Indies. On reaching its breeding range, it drills rows of holes in the bark of trees and returns from time to time to drink the oozing sap and to eat the insects that are attracted to it. The bird also collects many other insects in and around the trees, using its brushlike tongue.

A breeding pair bores a nest hole, usually in a dead tree, with the male doing most of the work. The female lays 5 to 7 eggs, which both birds incubate for about 12 days.

NAME: **Common Flicker (Yellow- and**
 **Red-shafted Flickers),** *Colaptes auratus*
RANGE: **Alaska to Mexico, Cuba, Grand**
 **Cayman Island**
HABITAT: **woodland, open country**
SIZE: **25.5–35.5 cm (10–14 in)**

The flicker is a ground-feeding bird which lives on ants and other insects; it also eats fruit and berries. There are 2 forms, now considered to be subspecies of the same species: the eastern birds have yellow wing linings, and the western birds red wing linings. The yellow-shafted flicker, *C. a. auratus*, is illustrated. In the Midwest, the forms meet and interbreed.

During courtship, or to communicate possession of its territory, the flicker drums with its bill on a tree or metal roofing. The male flicker selects a site for the nest hole, usually a hole in a tree trunk, stump or telephone pole, and does most of the excavation work. Both parents incubate the eggs.

Wryneck

Ivory-billed
Woodpecker

White-barred
Piculet

Rufous
Piculet
(male)

Great Spotted
Woodpecker
(male)

Common Flicker

Yellow-bellied Sapsucker

# Woodpeckers

NAME: **Green Woodpecker**, *Picus viridis*
RANGE: **Europe, N. Africa, Turkey to
Iran, W. USSR**
HABITAT: **open deciduous woodland,
gardens, parks**
SIZE: **32 cm (12½ in)**

A large, vividly plumaged woodpecker, this species has a short tail and a long, pointed bill. The male has a characteristic red mustache stripe with a black border; in the female the stripe is all black. Like other woodpeckers, the green woodpecker feeds in trees on the larvae of wood-boring insects, but it also feeds on the ground, where it hops along ponderously, searching for ants. It eats fruit and seeds as well. The flight of this species is typical of the woodpeckers, being deeply undulating, with long wing closures between each upward sweep.

The breeding season starts in April in the south of the range and May in the north. Both partners of a breeding pair help to excavate a nest cavity, often in a rotten tree trunk and usually at least 1 m (3¼ ft) above ground. The female lays 4 to 7 eggs, sometimes as many as 11, which both parents incubate for 18 or 19 days. The chicks hatch naked and helpless and must be fed by their parents on regurgitated food for about 3 weeks, when they are able to fend for themselves.

In a hard winter, as they do not migrate, green woodpeckers can suffer severe food shortages, which cause large drops in population.

NAME: **Golden-tailed Woodpecker,**
*Campethera abingoni*
RANGE: **Africa, south of the Sahara**
HABITAT: **woodland, brush, mountain
forest**
SIZE: **20.5 cm (8 in)**

The golden-tailed woodpecker can be identified by the broad black streaks on the white plumage from its chin to its belly and by the yellow-tipped tail feathers. There are some dark-red and black markings on the nape and head, and the rest of the plumage is largely green with white flecks. Usually seen in pairs, these woodpeckers are noisy birds and utter calls like derisive laughter; they also give a screeching alarm signal. They are restless birds, continuously on the move with swift, deeply undulating flight, searching for the arboreal ants and the larvae of other insects, such as beetles, that form their main foods.

The nest hole is usually excavated in the soft wood of a dead tree, and the female lays 2 or 3 eggs.

NAME: **Great Slaty Woodpecker,**
*Mulleripicus pulverulentus*
RANGE: **Asia: N. India to S.W. China,
Sumatra, Java, Borneo, Palawan**
HABITAT: **forest, swamp forest**
SIZE: **51 cm (20 in)**

The great slaty woodpecker is a large species that associates in groups of about 6 birds, which follow one another from one treetop to the next, calling noisily with loud cackles as they fly. Their flight is leisurely, without the normal woodpecker arcs and undulations. The larvae of wood-boring beetles and other insects are the main foods of this woodpecker, and it drills into trees with its powerful bill to find them. Both males and females of this species have some buffy-brown plumage on the chin and neck, but males also have mustache streaks, which the females lack. Juvenile birds resemble the female but are darker and duller in color, with more pale spots on the underparts.

In the breeding season, the groups break up into pairs, which then excavate their nests high up in tree trunks, often in dead or decaying wood. Both parents incubate the 3 or 4 eggs, which are laid in the unlined nest cavity, and share in the care and feeding of the nestlings.

NAME: **Ground Woodpecker,** *Geocolaptes
olivaceus*
RANGE: **South Africa**
HABITAT: **dry, open hill country**
SIZE: **28 cm (11 in)**

True to its name, this woodpecker lives almost entirely on the ground and hops everywhere. On the rare occasions when it does take to the air, it flies heavily and only for short distances, its red rump feathers showing conspicuously. Male and female look alike, with gray plumage on the head, olive-brown upperparts flecked with white, and rose-pink chest and belly. Juvenile birds are duller, with mottled olive and off-white plumage on the belly. Ground woodpeckers live in small groups of up to 6 or so and are usually found on high ground above 600 m (2,000 ft), where they perch on rocks or boulders or, very occasionally, on the low branches of trees and bushes. They feed on ants and other ground-living insects and their larvae, which they find by probing under rocks and stones. Their call is sharp and metallic, and they may also utter high-pitched whistles.

Unlike most woodpeckers, this species nests on the ground in a long tunnel that it excavates in a bank of clay or sand. Both partners of a breeding pair help to dig the burrow, which ends in a small chamber, where the female lays 4 or 5 eggs.

NAME: **Greater Goldenback/Large
Golden-backed Woodpecker,**
*Chrysocolaptes lucidus*
RANGE: **India, S.E. Asia to the
Philippines**
HABITAT: **woodland, forest fringe,
mangrove swamps**
SIZE: **33 cm (13 in)**

This medium-sized woodpecker is widespread in the wooded areas of India and Southeast Asia, where many races of the species inhabit a variety of forest types. Often found near flocks of other woodpeckers, drongos, bulbuls and babblers, these birds usually associate in pairs. After flying noisily from tree to tree, with characteristic woodpecker arcs and undulations, they alight on a trunk and, working their way up in jerky spirals, bore into the wood to feed on insect larvae. Goldenbacks have also been observed catching winged termites in the air. They seldom feed on the ground but are known to drink the nectar of some flowers. Although this is an extremely variable species, greater goldenbacks can generally be identified by the two black mustache streaks, separated by a patch of white plumage, on each side of the bill. The female bird lacks the male's distinctive red crest and has a flat black crown, spotted with white.

In the breeding season, the male drums particularly energetically as a courtship signal. The birds nest in a hole in a tree trunk, and the hole may be used many times; a fresh entrance to the breeding chamber is cut each season. It is not known whether the same birds return to the same hole every year. The female lays 4 or 5 eggs, which are incubated for 14 or 15 days, and the young woodpeckers remain in the nest until they are able to fly at 24 to 26 days old.

NAME: **Blond-crested Woodpecker,**
*Celeus flavescens*
RANGE: **South America: Amazonian
Brazil, E. Bolivia, Paraguay,
N.E. Argentina**
HABITAT: **forest**
SIZE: **28 cm (11 in)**

With its long, shaggy crest, this woodpecker appears rather larger than it is. The yellow feathers of the crest are narrow and soft, so that when erect they blow freely in the breeze. Particularly widespread in southeast Brazil, the blond-crested woodpecker is not confined to the lowlands but has been found at altitudes of up to 900 m (3,000 ft).

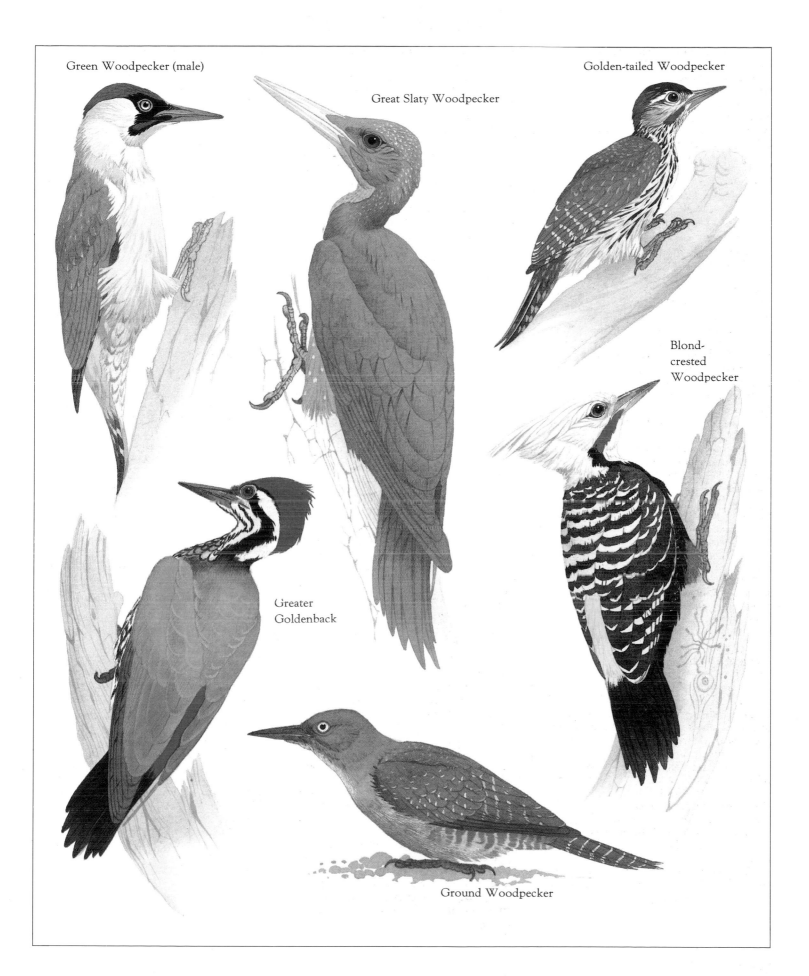

Green Woodpecker (male)

Great Slaty Woodpecker

Golden-tailed Woodpecker

Blond-crested Woodpecker

Greater Goldenback

Ground Woodpecker

# Ovenbirds

NAME: **Rufous Hornero,** *Furnarius rufus*
RANGE: **Brazil, Bolivia, Paraguay,**
   **Uruguay, Argentina**
HABITAT: **trees, often near habitation**
SIZE: **19–20.5 cm (7½–8 in)**

There has been an increasing tendency to refer to the ovenbirds by their South American name (hornero), to avoid confusion with an American wood warbler which is also called the ovenbird. The rufous hornero is a dignified-looking bird, which walks with long, deliberate strides, holding one foot aloft as it hesitates between steps. It feeds on insect larvae and worms and is vocal throughout the year.

Pairs stay together all year round, often for life, and breed during the wettest months. Each year they build a domed, ovenlike nest on a branch, post or building, using clay, with a little plant material mixed into it, which is then baked hard by the hot sun. A small entrance leads to the interior chamber, lined with soft grass, where up to 5 eggs are laid. Both parents incubate the clutch, and, after leaving the nest, the young birds stay with their parents for a few months.

NAME: **Plain Xenops,** *Xenops minutus*
RANGE: **S. Mexico, through Central and**
   **South America to N. Argentina**
HABITAT: **tall forest, plantations,**
   **clearings with scattered trees**
SIZE: **12.5 cm (5 in)**

One of several species of xenops, the plain xenops is distinguished by its unstreaked back. An active little bird, it forages in shrubs and thin branches of trees in search of insects to eat.

The nest is made by both partners of a breeding pair in a hole in an old, decaying tree and is lined with fine pieces of plant material. Alternatively, the birds may take over a hole abandoned by another bird. The 2 eggs are incubated by both parents for about 16 days.

NAME: **Stripe-breasted Spinetail,**
   *Synallaxis cinnamomea*
RANGE: **Venezuela, Colombia; Trinidad**
   **and Tobago**
HABITAT: **forest edge, coffee plantations**
SIZE: **16.5 cm (6½ in)**

Distinguished by its streaked cinnamon breast, this spinetail moves jerkily and makes low, short flights as it forages for small insects and spiders. It may also jump into the air to catch flying ants.

Both partners of a breeding pair help to build the nest, which is a round structure, made of twigs and placed in the fork of a branch in low scrub or on the ground. The nest is lined with soft plant material and has an entrance tunnel. The 2 or 3 eggs are incubated by both parents.

## ORDER PASSERIFORMES

Usually known as the perching birds, or songbirds, this is the largest of all bird orders. It includes about half of the approximately 8,600 living bird species. There are about 60 families in the order, and the most advanced 44 or so of these are grouped together as the oscine perching birds, or songbirds. The other families are known as the suboscines; these birds have a simpler organ of song. Perching birds are usually small — the lyrebirds are the largest species — but they have become adapted to almost all types of land-based habitat.

The group as a whole is identified by a number of structural and behavioral features. The foot is particularly characteristic and is excellently adapted for grasping any thin support such as a twig or grass stem: there are always four toes, all on the same level, with the hallux (big toe) pointing backward. The toes are never webbed.

Male perching birds are normally able to sing complex songs and give voice when courting mates or when defending territory.

## FURNARIIDAE: Ovenbird Family

The 219 or so known species in this family occur from southern Mexico through Central and South America, in a wide variety of habitats. As well as the ovenbirds proper, the family includes birds such as spinetails, plainsrunners and leafgleaners.

All the birds in the family have gray, brownish or russet plumage and are between 12 and 28 cm (4¾ and 11 in) long. They tend to be quick-moving, yet secretive birds, which generally remain well hidden within vegetation.

The diversity of this family is best shown by their breeding behavior. The true ovenbirds, for which the family is named, construct ovenlike mud nests, which are baked hard by the sun. Others build domed nests of grass or sticks, while some make well-lined nests in holes in the ground or in trees. Females generally lay from 2 to 5 eggs, and both parents care for the young. In most species, male and female look more or less alike.

NAME: **Red-faced Spinetail,** *Certhiaxis*
   (= *Cranioleuca*) *erythrops*
RANGE: **Costa Rica to Ecuador**
HABITAT: **humid mountain forest**
SIZE: **14–16.5 cm (5½–6½ in)**

Adult red-faced spinetails have reddish markings on the crown and sides of the head; juveniles have brownish crowns. They are active, acrobatic birds and much of their life is spent in the low levels of the forest, foraging in thickets and undergrowth for insects and other small invertebrates. They tend to move alone or in pairs but sometimes join in a flock of other highland birds.

The bulky, ball-shaped nest is made from vines and hangs from the end of a slender branch, well above ground. Both sexes incubate the 2 eggs and feed the young.

NAME: **Larklike Bushrunner,**
   *Coryphistera alaudina*
RANGE: **S. Brazil, Bolivia, Paraguay,**
   **Uruguay, N. Argentina**
HABITAT: **dry scrub regions**
SIZE: **15 cm (6 in)**

Identified by its prominent crest and streaked breast plumage, the larklike bushrunner generally moves in groups of 3 to 6, which are, possibly, family groups. Active both on the ground and in bushes and low trees, they stride along in the open, but if alarmed, they take to the trees and tall bushes.

A rounded nest is made in a low tree from interwoven thorny twigs. A small entrance tunnel leads to the central chamber, where the eggs are laid.

NAME: **Point-tailed/Pintailed**
   **Palmcreeper,** *Berlepschia rikeri*
RANGE: **Amazonian Brazil, Venezuela,**
   **Guyana**
HABITAT: **palm groves, often near water**
SIZE: **21.5 cm (8½ in)**

An elegant little bird, the point-tailed palmcreeper has distinctive black, white and chestnut plumage and pointed tail feathers. In pairs or small groups, it frequents palm trees of the genus *Mauritia* and forages for insects on the trunks and leaves of the trees. When it catches an insect, the palmcreeper bangs it sharply against the trunk or branch before swallowing it.

NAME: **Des Murs' Spinetail,**
   *Sylviorthorhynchus desmursii*
RANGE: **W. Argentina, adjacent Chile**
HABITAT: **humid forest with thick**
   **undergrowth**
SIZE: **24 cm (9½ in)**

Over two-thirds of the length of this species is taken up by its long and decorative tail, which consists of only two pairs of feathers, plus a vestigial pair. Otherwise this spinetail is an inconspicuous little bird, revealed only by its persistent calls. It frequents the densest parts of the forest and seems to move ceaselessly in search of food.

A globular nest is made just off the ground amid twigs and grass. It is constructed from dry plant material, lined with soft feathers, and has a side entrance. Usually 3 eggs are laid. The bird holds up its tail when in the nest.

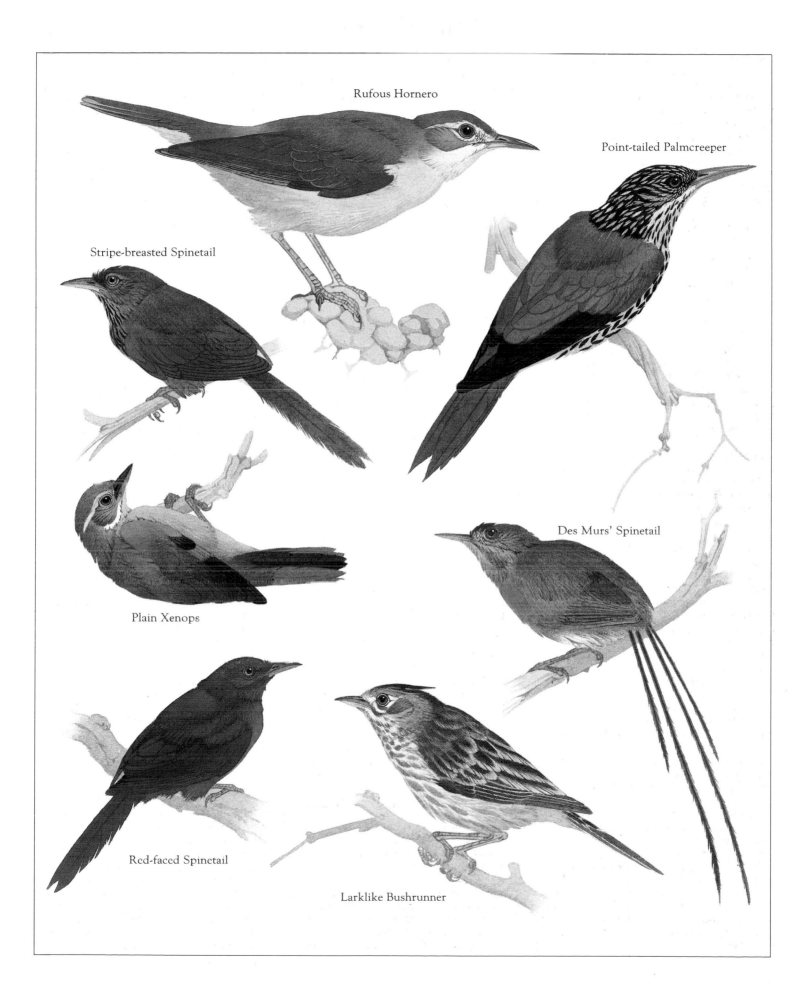

Rufous Hornero

Point-tailed Palmcreeper

Stripe-breasted Spinetail

Des Murs' Spinetail

Plain Xenops

Red-faced Spinetail

Larklike Bushrunner

# Antbirds

NAME: Ocellated Antbird, *Phaenostictus mcleannani*
RANGE: tropical Nicaragua to Panama; S. Colombia, N.W. Ecuador
HABITAT: undergrowth of humid, lowland forest
SIZE: 19–20 cm (7½–7¾ in)

The dark markings in the plumage of the ocellated antbird give it an overall spotted appearance, and it has a fairly long tail for its size. The eyes are surrounded with an area of bright-hued bare skin, and it is these two colored circles, one within the other, that give the bird its common name. Male and female look alike.

It is a generally uncommon, timid species and is often found in association with bicolored antbirds. It is seldom seen away from the columns of army ants that march through the forests of its habitat, for it feeds on the invertebrates, such as cockroaches and spiders, which are disturbed by their destructive passage. Its call is a fast series of whistles, running up the scale.

Ocellated antbirds form lasting pair bonds, and before mating, the male feeds the female with tidbits, at some distance from the nest.

NAME: **Bicolored Antbird, *Gymnopithys leucaspis***
RANGE: Honduras to Panama; N. Peru, Amazonian Brazil
HABITAT: forest undergrowth up to 2,000 m (6,600 ft)
SIZE: 14 cm (5½ in)

Although there is some disagreement, this bird is generally considered conspecific with the white-cheeked antbird, G. *bicolor*, of the western Amazon area. The plumage of male and female is alike, and there are patches of bare skin around the eyes. It is a fairly common species and usually the most numerous and noisy of the several that follow the army ants. It spends much of the time on the ground but will perch just above the forest floor, watching for insects, spiders and other invertebrates which are driven out of the leaf litter as the ants advance. It will occasionally even take a small frog.

The nest of the bicolored antbird is usually sited a few feet from the ground in the stump of a decaying palm tree and is made from small pieces of leaf, especially palm leaf, and lined with rootlets and plant fibers. The female lays 2 eggs, which both parents incubate for about 15 days.

## FORMICARIIDAE:
### Antbird Family

The antbirds are found exclusively in Central and South America, mostly on the floor and in the lower levels of the tropical rain forests of the Amazon basin, as well as in some drier and more open habitats. About 220 to 230 species of small to medium-sized birds are known. Many species of antbird do actually feed on ants and other social insects; some eat the invertebrates disturbed by columns of army ants which they follow through the forest, while others, although insectivorous, have no particular predilection for ants.

Their plumage is usually dull, and there are normally clear-cut differences between that of male and female birds. Little is known of their breeding biology, but open, cup-shaped nests seem to be the rule, and both sexes appear to incubate the clutch, which usually contains 2 eggs, for about 15 or 16 days.

NAME: **Chestnut-crowned Antpitta, *Grallaria ruficapilla***
RANGE: tropical and subtropical areas, Venezuela to N.W. Peru
HABITAT: dense cloud forest, damp woodland and open grassland
SIZE: 20 cm (7¾ in)

The chestnut-crowned antpitta is a long-legged bird, with a short tail and a noticeably large head; the feathers on head and neck are reddish brown, hence its common name. It is a ground-living bird, usually found alone, looking for the insects that make up its diet. Even though difficult to see, it is not shy, and its three-note call is often heard. In fact, it will respond to imitations of its call and has a number of local names that suggest it, such as "Seco estoy."

NAME: **Streaked Antwren, *Myrmotherula surinamensis***
RANGE: Amazonian Brazil, west to Pacific coast of South America
HABITAT: clearings in rain forest, forest edge, woodland
SIZE: 10 cm (4 in)

The male of this species is largely black and white, while the female has a bright orange-red head and nape and pale orange-buff underparts. Both sexes have two white bars on the wings. Streaked antwrens are fairly common birds, often found near rivers and on wet ground, where they can generally be seen in pairs, busily searching for grasshoppers and spiders among the undergrowth, vines and leaves. They have a fast, rising, chipping call.

The nest is made in a tree, and the female lays 2 eggs.

NAME: Great Antshrike, *Taraba major*
RANGE: tropical S. Mexico, Central and South America to N. Argentina
HABITAT: undergrowth in brush and grassland up to 2,000 m (6,600 ft)
SIZE: 20 cm (7¾ in)

The great antshrike is a fairly large bird with a thick, hooked bill and a crest; males and females have quite dissimilar coloration. Although common, these shy birds are usually found only in pairs or, occasionally, alone. They move stealthily through the bushes and low branches of small trees, searching for beetles, grasshoppers, bees and even small lizards to eat. When disturbed, the male performs a threat display, pointing his bill straight upward and raising his crest so that the normally concealed dorsal patch shows clearly.

The flimsy nest is cup shaped, made of dried grass and roots, sometimes lined with leaves, and is about 6.5 cm (2½ in) deep. The female lays 2 or 3 eggs, which both parents incubate for 2 to 3 weeks; they then feed the young until they are ready to leave the nest, about 2 weeks after hatching.

NAME: **Barred Antshrike, *Thamnophilus doliatus***
RANGE: tropical Mexico, Central and South America to N. Argentina; Trinidad and Tobago
HABITAT: varied: forest, brush, savanna, gardens; rarely above 2,000 m (6,600 ft)
SIZE: 15 cm (6 in)

As its name implies, the plumage of this antshrike is conspicuously barred and streaked. The male is mainly black and white, while the female is chestnut, shading to buff, with black barring. Both birds have a crest, which the male always carries partially erect, and a toothed beak. Barred antshrikes are common birds, usually found in pairs; but as they are always on the move through bushes and branches in thickets and forest edge about 4.5 m (15 ft) up, they are usually heard calling to one another before they are seen. They feed on insects, such as beetles, grasshoppers, bees and caterpillars, and on berries.

There seems to be no clearly defined mating season, but the male feeds the female during courtship and they may form a permanent pair bond. The female lays 2, rarely 3, eggs in a deep cup-shaped nest, made of grass and plant fibers and suspended by the rim in the fork of a low branch of a tree. Both parents incubate the eggs for about 14 days; only the female incubates at night. The young leave the nest 2 to 3 weeks after hatching.

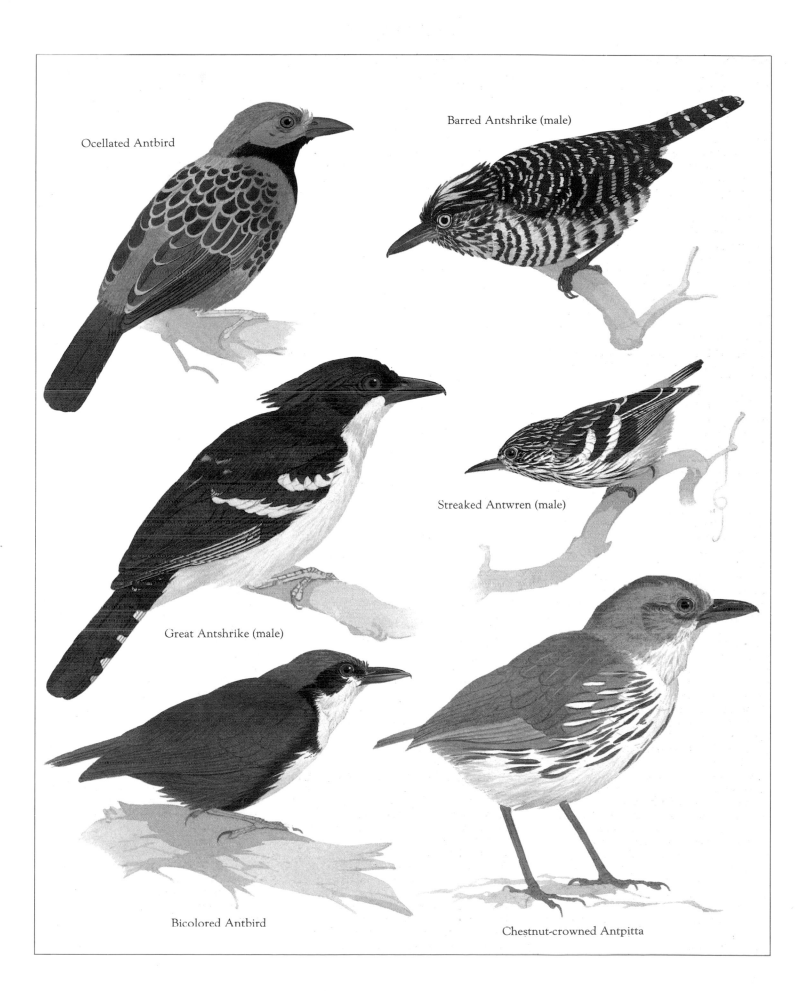

Ocellated Antbird

Barred Antshrike (male)

Great Antshrike (male)

Streaked Antwren (male)

Bicolored Antbird

Chestnut-crowned Antpitta

# Woodcreepers, Gnateaters, Tapaculos

## DENDROCOLAPTIDAE:
### Woodcreeper Family

The 48 species or so of woodcreeper, found in wooded areas of Central and South America, from Mexico to Argentina, are in many ways the New World equivalent of the treecreepers of the Old World. These birds, also known as woodhewers, vary in length from 15 to 38 cm (6 to 15 in), and male and female look very much alike. They have laterally compressed beaks, which range in shape from short and straight to long and curved, and strong legs and feet.

Woodcreepers are insectivorous and peck their food from crevices in the bark as they climb up the trunks of trees, with the aid of their sharp claws and the strong propping shafts of their tail feathers. They are generally solitary birds but may join in mixed flocks.

NAME: **Red-billed Scythebill,**
**Campylorhamphus trochilirostris**
RANGE: **E. Panama to N. Argentina**
HABITAT: **swampy and humid forest, woodland**
SIZE: **20.5–30.5 cm (8–12 in) including bill of 7.5 cm (3 in)**

These shy, arboreal birds live in the middle to upper stories of forest trees. They are usually found alone, although they may feed among other types of insectivorous birds. Their strong legs and stiff tail feathers help them to climb quickly, and with their long, curved bills, they probe for insects under the bark of trees and inside bromeliads.

The female scythebill lays 2 or 3 eggs in a hole in a tree or in a crevice, and they are incubated for about 14 days.

NAME: **Barred Woodcreeper,**
**Dendrocolaptes certhia**
RANGE: **tropical S. Mexico, through Central America to Bolivia, Amazonian Brazil**
HABITAT: **lowland rain forest to 1,400 m (4,600 ft), forest edge**
SIZE: **26.5 cm (10½ in)**

Both male and female barred woodcreepers are strongly built and have light olive-brown, barred plumage. The medium-length beak is heavy and slightly curved. These birds live in the undergrowth and tall secondary growth of the rain forest; they are not timid and can be seen alone or in twos and threes, feeding on the trunks of trees. Like the antbirds, they are constant followers of army ants and will come near the ground to feed on the insects disturbed by the ants' progress.

The female lays 2 eggs, in a hole or crevice in a tree; they are incubated for 14 or 15 days.

NAME: **Long-billed Woodcreeper, Nasica longirostris**
RANGE: **tropical northern South America to Brazil and Bolivia**
HABITAT: **rain forest at 100–200 m (330–650 ft)**
SIZE: **35.5 cm (14 in) including bill of 6.5 cm (2½ in)**

The solitary, long-billed woodcreeper is an agile bird that climbs about in the trees, looking for its insect food under the bark. It has a long, slightly curved bill, and male and female look similar.

The female makes her nest in a tree hole and lays 2 eggs, which are incubated for about 2 weeks.

NAME: **Olivaceous Woodcreeper,**
**Sittasomus griseicapillus**
RANGE: **tropical and subtropical Mexico, through Central and South America to N. Argentina; Tobago**
HABITAT: **deep forest, forest edge, open woodland, to 2,300 m (7,500 ft)**
SIZE: **15–16.5 cm (6–6½ in)**

These active little woodcreepers have buff bands on the wings that are conspicuous when they fly. Male and female look alike. They are more or less solitary, but may associate with other types of birds. They forage busily for insects on the trunks of trees with soft bark, in the under and middle stories of the forest, and will sometimes fly out and catch insects in the air.

Only one nest has been found, in a hole in a tree, but it contained no eggs.

## CONOPOPHAGIDAE:
### Gnateater Family

The gnateaters, or antpipits as they are sometimes called, are a small group of forest-dwelling birds, quite closely related to the antbirds and ovenbirds. Approximately 11 species are recognized, all living in Central and South America. Most are long-legged brown birds with round bodies and short tails. They live largely on the forest floor, capturing insect food on the ground with their flycatcherlike bills. Male and female are alike in some species but differ in others.

NAME: **Black-cheeked Gnateater,**
**Conopophaga melanops**
RANGE: **E. Brazil**
HABITAT: **rain forest**
SIZE: **12.5 cm (5 in)**

This South American gnateater has long legs and appears almost neckless; the female is more olive-brown than the male. The birds are quite tame but are not often seen because they prefer the undergrowth, where they find their insect food, mainly on the ground.

Black-cheeked gnateaters make an open, cup-shaped nest on the ground, using big leaves, and line it with plant fibers. The female lays 2 eggs, which both parents incubate. If danger threatens the bird on the nest, it will leave the eggs and lure the predator away by pretending to be injured.

## RHINOCRYPTIDAE:
### Tapaculo Family

The approximately 28 described species of tapaculo are found among low-growing plants in habitats as varied as dense forest, grassland and semiopen arid country in Central and South America. They are ground-living birds, with poor powers of flight, but can run fast on their strong legs. Tapaculos vary in size from 12.5 to 25.5 cm (5 to 10 in) and have rounded bodies; they often cock their tails vertically, as wrens do. They have a curious feature, to which the scientific name refers, of movable flaps covering the nostrils; the exact function of these is not known, but they are presumed to protect the openings against dust. Males and females look alike or nearly so.

NAME: **Elegant Crescentchest,**
**Melanopareia elegans**
RANGE: **W. Ecuador to N.W. Peru**
HABITAT: **arid scrub**
SIZE: **14 cm (5½ in)**

These small birds seldom fly, but they have long legs and large feet and run about rapidly, gathering up insects; when excited, they cock up their tails. Elegant crescentchests are shy birds that are not often seen, although their calls can be heard.

No information is available about the breeding biology of these birds.

NAME: **Chestnut-throated Huet-huet,**
**Pteroptochos castaneus**
RANGE: **Chile**
HABITAT: **forest**
SIZE: **25.5 cm (10 in)**

This is a medium-sized bird, with a rounded body, long legs and quite a long tail for its size — about 10 cm (4 in). The upperparts are mostly blackish-brown, but the throat and underparts are a dark reddish-brown, with some black and buff bars. Male and female look alike. These huet-huets are ground-dwellers which rarely fly, and they run, rather than hop, about looking for their insect food.

The nest is made from roots and soft grasses in a hole in the ground or in a tree stump, and the female lays 2 eggs.

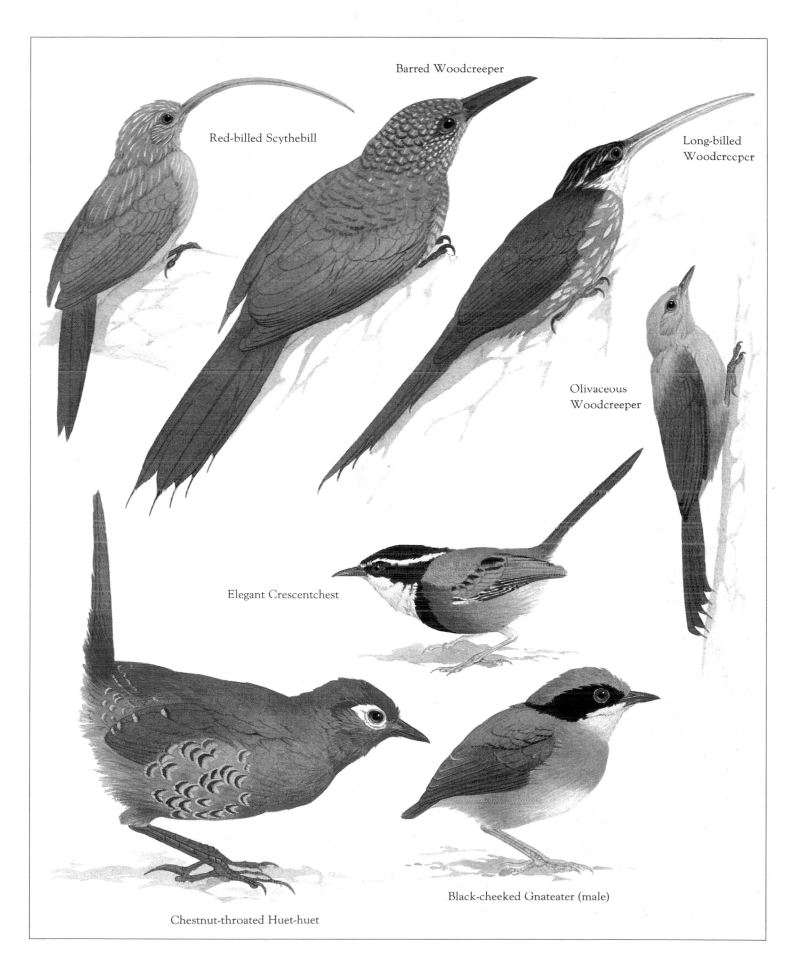

Barred Woodcreeper

Red-billed Scythebill

Long-billed
Woodcreeper

Olivaceous
Woodcreeper

Elegant Crescentchest

Black-cheeked Gnateater (male)

Chestnut-throated Huet-huet

# Manakins, Cotingas

## PIPRIDAE: Manakin Family

This intriguing and showy family contains about 56 species, all found in the tropical forests of Central and South America. They are small, colorful birds, rarely more than 12.5 to 15 cm (5 to 6 in) in length. Males and females are dramatically different in appearance. Males, typically, have a solid background color, commonly black, brilliantly counterpointed with areas of contrasting primary colors; females are generally olive-green. The decorative males utilize their plumage in intricate courtship dances.

NAME: **Blue-backed Manakin,** *Chiroxiphia pareola*
RANGE: **northern South America to S.E. Brazil, N. Bolivia; Tobago**
HABITAT: **rain forest, secondary growth**
SIZE: **10 cm (4 in)**

These lively, agile little birds forage in pairs or small groups for insects and fruit in low bushes, often near wet ground or streams. They are square tailed, with the male showing dazzling patches of pale blue and red feathers on back and crown.

Male manakins have display perches or "bowers," which they keep clear by plucking at the surrounding leaves while on the wing and pecking at the bark while perching. They wear the perch smooth by continually moving around. Before display, the dominant male summons a subordinate male by calling and then duets with him, the subordinate following a fraction of a second behind. The males dance together, but the dance only becomes fully developed if a female appears. The other bird drops out, leaving the dominant male to mate with the female after a quite different solo display. She lays 2 eggs in a nest, made of fine plant fibers, so cobwebby and transparent that eggs and young can be seen through it.

NAME: **Wire-tailed Manakin,** *Teleonoma* (= *Pipra*) *filicauda*
RANGE: **Venezuela to N.E. Peru, W. Brazil**
HABITAT: **rain forest, plantations**
SIZE: **11.5 cm (4½ in)**

The male wire-tailed manakin has dramatic black, red and yellow patches, typical of the family, and the tails of both male and female end in long wiry filaments, from which the common name is derived. These birds prefer humid areas and are found from the middle story to the forest canopy, as well as in clearings and cocoa plantations. Solitary birds, they forage alone for insects and fruit.

## COTINGIDAE: Cotinga Family

The 73 species of cotinga, all found in the New World, constitute a colorful and varied family, with common names such as bellbird, umbrellabird, tityra, fruiteater and cock-of-the-rock, as well as the cotinga itself. This variety of nomenclature mirrors an equal diversity in body form and habit.

Cotingas are nonmigratory birds in forested areas and often spend most of their time in the canopy layers, feeding on fruit and insects.

NAME: **Andean Cock-of-the-rock,** *Rupicola peruviana*
RANGE: **Andes, N. Venezuela to N. Bolivia**
HABITAT: **forest along river gorges**
SIZE: **38 cm (15 in)**

The male of this species is one of the most brilliantly colored of all birds, with its flashing orange or red plumage and strong, golden-colored beak. On its head is a crest of feathers that almost conceals the beak. Both male and female have powerful legs and sharp claws.

The Andean cock-of-the-rock lives in the lower levels of the forest, where its swift, weaving flight and good maneuverability enable it to move about easily as it searches for fruit to eat. Females also catch frogs and lizards to feed to their young. The males live an independent existence — they roost alone at night, forage in pairs and display in pairs at dawn and dusk at traditional leks, where each male has his own place near to that of his paired male. Only the dominant male of the lek mates with females. The female alone builds the nest — on a rocky cliff face — and often several nests are grouped together. The nest is a large truncated cone, made of mud, with a deep, 6.5 cm (2½ in), lined nest cup, in which 2 eggs are laid.

NAME: **Barred Fruiteater,** *Pipreola arcuata*
RANGE: **Andes, N.W. Venezuela to N.W. Bolivia**
HABITAT: **cloud forest at 1,200–3,350 m (4,000–11,000 ft)**
SIZE: **21.5 cm (8½ in)**

This heavy-bodied bird is the largest of the fruiteaters and is found at higher altitudes than any other. The male's coloration is striking, while the female is mostly olive-green; both birds have rather weak, slightly hooked beaks and red legs and feet. Barred fruiteaters live in the middle and lower layers of the forest, where they feed mainly on fruit and some insects, either singly or in pairs. No information is available about breeding and nesting behavior.

NAME: **Bearded Bellbird,** *Procnias averano*
RANGE: **parts of Colombia, Guyana, Venezuela, N. Brazil; Trinidad**
HABITAT: **high-altitude forest**
SIZE: **25.5 cm (10 in)**

The fringe of black wattles hanging from the throat of both male and female gives this species its common name. They are shy birds, feeding singly or in pairs on large, single-seeded berries, particularly laurel, which they take on the wing and then sit on a branch to eat.

In the breeding season, male bearded bellbirds display to other males and to females on special "visiting" perches in the lower forest layers. They jump as high as 1.2 m (4 ft) into the air and land crouched, on another perch, with tail spread. After mating, the female builds a light, thin, cup-shaped nest of twigs from specific trees, about 2.4 to 15.25 m (8 to 50 ft) up, in the horizontally forked outer branch of a tree. She lays 1 egg, which she incubates for about 23 days.

NAME: **Spangled Cotinga,** *Cotinga cayana*
RANGE: **Amazon and Orinoco basins; the Guianas**
HABITAT: **forest up to 1,200 m (4,000 ft)**
SIZE: **21.5 cm (8½ in)**

The blue plumage of the male spangled cotinga is iridescent, hence the name. These are gregarious birds, usually feeding in groups on large berries, sometimes with birds of other species.

The female alone builds the flimsy, shallow nest, using twigs and rootlets and coating the whole structure in white fungal threads. She lays and then incubates 1 large egg, sometimes 2.

NAME: **Amazonian/Ornate Umbrellabird,** *Cephalopterus ornatus*
RANGE: **northern South America to Amazonian Brazil, N. Bolivia**
HABITAT: **virgin forest to 1,400 m (4,600 ft), islands in larger rivers**
SIZE: **40.5–48 cm (16–19 in)**

The largest of the cotingas, the ornate umbrellabird is distinguished by its erect crest of long, silky feathers and by the wattle at the base of the neck. The female is much duller than the male, with a smaller wattle and "umbrella." The wings are short. These strange birds live in the forest canopy and spring noisily through the branches, looking for fruit and insects.

Males have their preferred calling trees, where they perch, spread their umbrellas and, filling two specially modified sacs in the trachea with air, make loud booming noises. The shallow, open nest is built of twigs in the fork of a fairly low tree, and the female lays 1 egg, which she incubates alone.

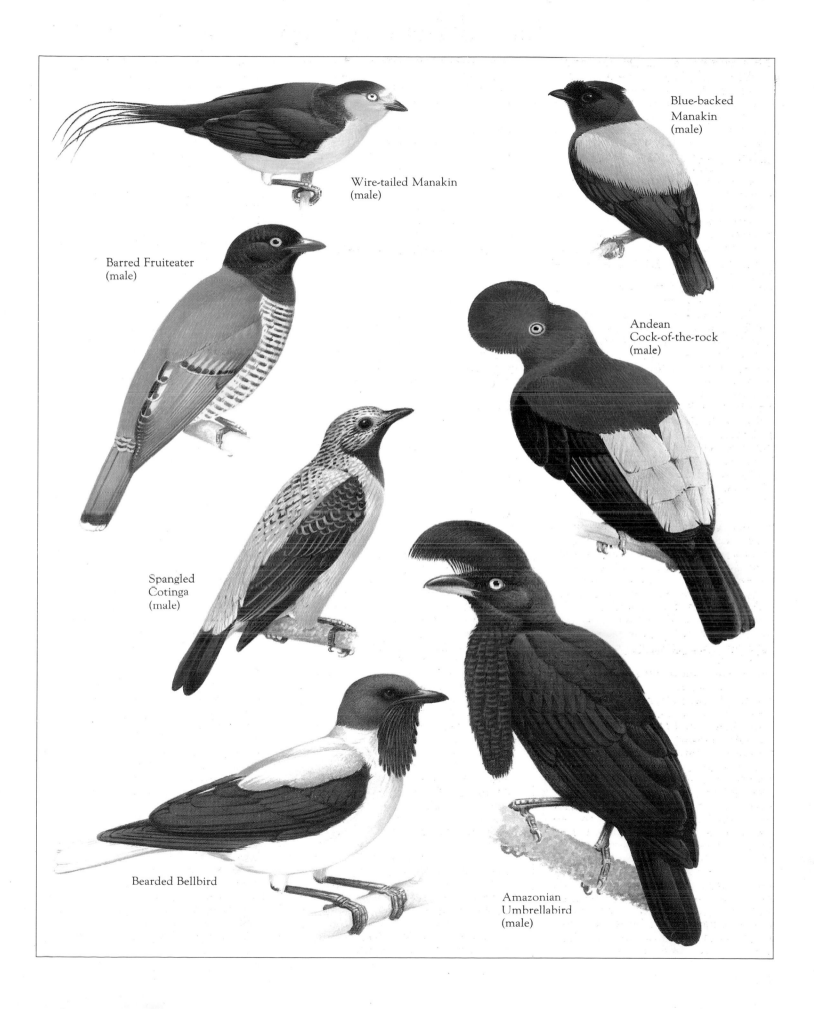

Wire-tailed Manakin
(male)

Blue-backed
Manakin
(male)

Barred Fruiteater
(male)

Andean
Cock-of-the-rock
(male)

Spangled
Cotinga
(male)

Bearded Bellbird

Amazonian
Umbrellabird
(male)

# Sharpbill, Plantcutters, Tyrant Flycatchers

## OXYRUNCIDAE: Sharpbill Family
The sharpbill family contains only 1 species, which is a neotropical form, found in the upper layers of humid forests from Costa Rica south to Paraguay.

NAME: **Sharpbill,** *Oxyruncus cristatus*
RANGE: **patchy distribution in Costa Rica, Panama to Paraguay, Amazonian Brazil**
HABITAT: **humid tropical forest**
SIZE: **16.5–18 cm (6½–7 in)**
The sharpbill has a straight, pointed beak, which gives it its common name. It is a strong flier, with rather rounded, long wings. Male and female look similar, but the male has a black and scarlet crest, bordered with black, while the female may have a pale crest. Sharpbills are secretive birds which forage actively for fruit in the middle to canopy layers of the forest.

## PHYTOTOMIDAE: Plantcutter Family
The 3 known species of plantcutter are found in the more open areas of western South America. They form a small, homogeneous family, closely related to the cotinga family (Cotingidae). In appearance, however, with their strong, conical beaks, they bear more resemblance to the finches of the Old World. The edges of their bills are finely serrated and used for cropping the buds, fruit and leaves that make up much of their diet. The plantcutters' fruit-eating habits mean that they are often regarded as pests by fruit farmers. Male and female do not look alike.

NAME: **Rufous-tailed Plantcutter,** *Phytotoma rara*
RANGE: **central Chile, Argentina**
HABITAT: **open scrub, orchards, gardens, mountain valleys**
SIZE: **20.5 cm (8 in)**
These short-legged birds have bright reddish-orange eyes and stout, serrated beaks. The male has reddish-chestnut underparts and tail; the female is paler, with a buff throat and underparts. Plantcutters are usually seen singly or in small groups, flying sluggishly among fruit trees, where they eat the buds, shoots and young leaves and often destroy the fruit. In spring, the plantcutters move to high mountain valleys, where they mate between October and December.

The female lays 2 to 4 eggs in a cup-shaped nest, made of twigs and lined with fine twigs and rootlets.

## TYRANNIDAE: Tyrant Flycatcher Family
The 370 species of tyrant flycatcher constitute one of the largest families of perching birds. They are found only in the Americas, where they replace, and in several respects are similar to, the Old World flycatchers, Muscicapinae. The center of the wide range of the family is within the rain forests of the Amazon basin, but species have spread wherever food is available; consequently forms are found as far apart as Alaska and Tierra del Fuego.

Most species catch insects on the wing, but forms are known which feed on fruit, small mammals, reptiles, amphibians and fish, as well as on insects. The insect-eaters' beaks are rather flattened and slightly hooked, with well-developed bristles at the base. The sexes look alike in most species.

NAME: **Scissor-tailed Flycatcher,** *Muscivora forficata*
RANGE: **south-central USA; winters S. Texas, Mexico to Panama**
HABITAT: **open grassland (prairie), ranchland**
SIZE: **28–38 cm (11–15 in) including tail of up to 23 cm (9 in)**
When these elegant birds fly, the black feathers of their remarkably long tails open and close like the blades of a pair of scissors; but when they perch, the birds close up the blades. The female is smaller than the male, with a shorter tail. Scissor-tailed flycatchers spend much of their time perching on fences, telephone wires and trees, darting out swiftly to catch insects in the air or on the ground. They take mainly grasshoppers and crickets, which make up 50 percent of their food, but also eat bees, wasps, moths, caterpillars and spiders, as well as berries and seeds.

The bulky nest is built from weeds, rootlets and cotton, lined with hair and rootlets. The female lays 4 to 6 eggs, usually 5, and incubates them for about 14 days.

NAME: **White-headed Marsh Tyrant,** *Arundinicola leucocephala*
RANGE: **South America, east of the Andes, to N. Argentina; Trinidad**
HABITAT: **riverbanks, marshes, wet grassland**
SIZE: **11.5 cm (4½ in)**
Sociable birds, these marsh tyrants live in pairs or family groups and feed on insects, which they catch on the wing. They make their nests in low bushes or clumps of grass, using boll cotton in their construction. The female lays 2 or 3 eggs.

NAME: **Eastern Phoebe,** *Sayornis phoebe*
RANGE: **eastern N. America; winters in S. USA and Mexico**
HABITAT: **woodland near water, rocky ravines, wooded farmland**
SIZE: **16–18.5 cm (6¼–7¼ in)**
The distinguishing features of this flycatcher are its erect posture and the way it appears to wag its tail when it alights, sweeping it from side to side. Its name is derived from its frequently repeated two-note call, "fee-bee." Phoebes are not timid birds and, in summer, can be seen on farmland and wooded country roads, searching for the beetles, ants, bees, wasps and other invertebrates that make up their diet.

Their cup-shaped nests are made from mud and moss and sited on rocky ledges, or even on rafters or window sills in farm buildings. The female lays 3 to 8 eggs, usually 5, which are incubated for 16 days.

NAME: **Kiskadee Flycatcher,** *Pitangus sulphuratus*
RANGE: **S.E. Texas, Central and South America to central Argentina**
HABITAT: **groves, orchards, wooded banks of streams**
SIZE: **23–26.5 cm (9–10½ in)**
A large bird with a big head, the kiskadee flycatcher is active and noisy, advertising its presence with its loud call, "kis-ka-dee." It is conspicuous at dawn and dusk and behaves much like a kingfisher, perching quite still above water and then plunging into it after fish and tadpoles. Its plumage needs to dry out after three dives, so it turns to catching flying insects such as beetles and wasps. In winter; when these are scarce, it feeds on fruit and berries.

Kiskadee flycatchers make their large, oval nests about 6 m (20 ft) up in trees. The female lays 2 to 5 eggs, usually 4.

NAME: **Eastern Kingbird,** *Tyrannus tyrannus*
RANGE: **central Canada, through USA to Gulf of Mexico; winters in Central and South America to N. Argentina**
HABITAT: **open country with trees, orchards, gardens**
SIZE: **20.5–23 cm (8–9 in)**
The eastern kingbird is a noisy and aggressive bird and will attack other birds, such as hawks, vultures and crows, sometimes landing on the other bird's back. It has even been known to attack low-flying aircraft. It has been observed to eat more than 200 types of insect, which it takes in the air or from the ground or scoops up from water. It will also pick berries, while hovering.

Both male and female kingbirds incubate the 3 to 5 eggs for about 2 weeks and both feed the young.

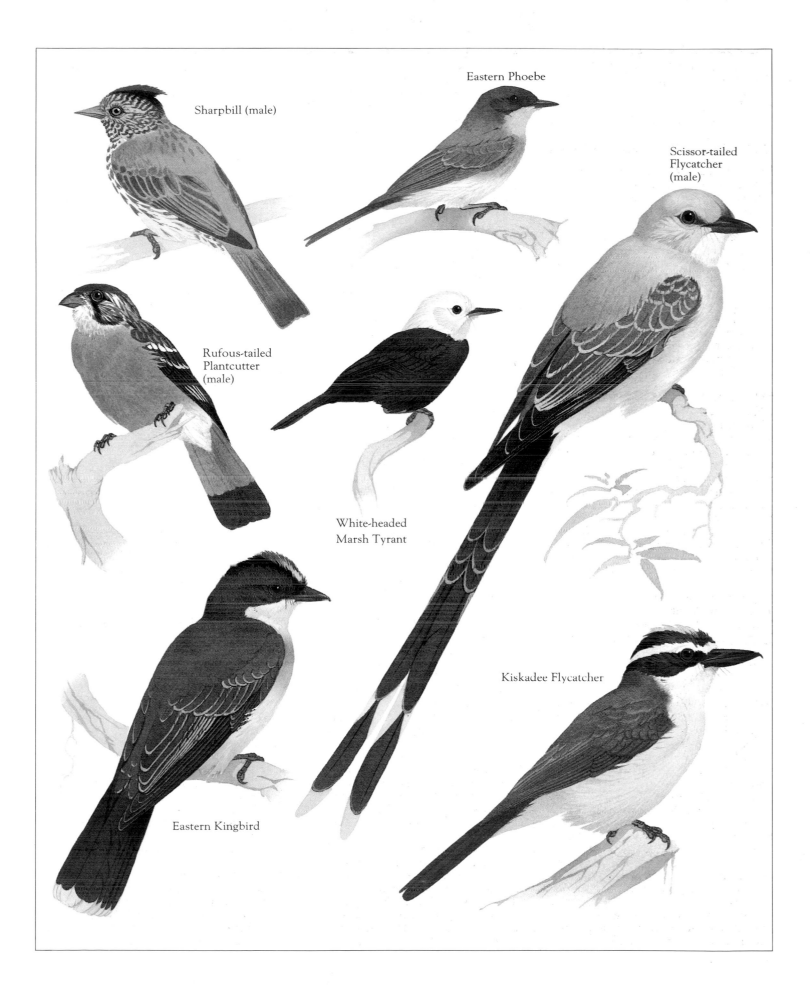

Sharpbill (male)

Eastern Phoebe

Scissor-tailed
Flycatcher
(male)

Rufous-tailed
Plantcutter
(male)

White-headed
Marsh Tyrant

Kiskadee Flycatcher

Eastern Kingbird

# Tyrant Flycatchers

NAME: **Willow Flycatcher,** *Empidonax traillii*
RANGE: **S. Canada, USA: Maine to Virginia, west to Arkansas and California**
HABITAT: **open country near water to 2,400 m (7,900 ft)**
SIZE: **13.5–15 cm (5¼–6 in)**

True to its common name, this bird is most frequently encountered where willow trees abound — on islands in rivers, in shrubs along streams and in beaver meadows. In appearance it is similar to the alder flycatcher (*E. alnorum*), but it has a slightly longer bill and more rounded wings. It is a prodigious insect-eater and is known to catch at least 65 species of beetle, as well as aphids, scale insects, bees, wasps and crane flies, all of which it takes in flight. It also eats caterpillars, spiders and millipedes, as well as some berries.

Willow flycatchers usually build their nests about 2.5 m (8 ft) above the ground in the upright fork of a bush or tree, in an area where willows or plants of the rose family grow. The shredded bark of milkweed, cattail and the silky catkins of aspen and willow are used in its construction, and it is softly lined with grass and feathers. The female lays 3 or 4 eggs, which are incubated for about 12 days. The young leave the nest when they are about 2 weeks old.

NAME: **Many-colored Rush-tyrant,** *Tachuris rubrigastra*
RANGE: **South America: Peru, S.E. Brazil, Paraguay, Uruguay, Argentina, Chile**
HABITAT: **fields, meadows near water, swampy ground**
SIZE: **10.5 cm (4¼ in)**

There are seven colors visible in the plumage of these pretty little birds — yellow, blue, white, bronze, black, carmine and green. The birds are sprightly and flit about constantly among the stems of tall grasses, particularly cattails, searching for small insects to eat. Although they are so active, many-colored tyrants are seldom seen and often can be located only by their frequently repeated, sharp, ringing calls.

The cone-shaped nest is attached to the stalk of a cattail or reed, 50 to 80 cm (20 to 30 in) above the water. It is intricately woven from small pieces of dry reed, with the point of the cone at the bottom, and the reeds are cemented with a sticky substance, which gives the nest a smooth, shiny surface. The female lays her eggs in multiples of three: 3, 6 or 9.

NAME: **Royal Flycatcher,** *Onychorhynchus coronatus*
RANGE: **South America: Amazon basin**
HABITAT: **rain and cloud forest, forest edge**
SIZE: **16.5 cm (6½ in)**

The royal flycatcher is a showy bird, with a large crest of crimson feathers that end in disks with a metallic blue luster; in the female the crest is orange. Normally the crest lies flat, but in display it is opened and closed like a fan. The bill is broad and flat and quite wide, well suited to the bird's diet of insects, which they take on the wing. These flycatchers are usually found singly or in pairs in secondary growth or at the forest edge.

The long, bag-shaped nest is built in a tree, often near a stream, and the female lays 2 eggs.

NAME: **Eastern Wood Peewee,** *Contopus virens*
RANGE: **breeds S.E. Canada, E. USA; winters Central America, northern South America**
HABITAT: **deciduous or mixed woodland, tall shade trees in gardens**
SIZE: **15–17 cm (6–6¾ in)**

The eastern wood peewee is so similar in appearance to the western species (*C. sordidulus*) that in western Manitoba and Nebraska, where their ranges overlap, it is possible to distinguish it only by its plaintive, whistling call. It perches in the deep shade of tall trees, darting out to catch flying insects, beetles and treehoppers.

Eastern wood peewees build thick-walled, cup-shaped nests high up on the horizontal branches of trees. The nest is made of weeds and fibers, lined with wool, grass and hair, and well covered with lichen, which makes it invisible from the ground. Normally 3 eggs are laid, which are incubated until they hatch after about 13 days.

NAME: **Short-tailed Pygmy-tyrant,** *Myiornis ecaudatus*
RANGE: **northern South America, east of the Andes, Amazonian Brazil; Trinidad**
HABITAT: **high open rain forest, clearings in forest, plantations**
SIZE: **6.5 cm (2½ in)**

The smallest of the tyrants, this tiny bird has an exceptionally short tail, scarcely longer than the tail coverts. Male and female look alike. Alone or in pairs, the birds dart about in the forest trees, from the bottom branches to the canopy, looking for insects to feed on. Pygmy-tyrants are not shy, but because they live in such dense vegetation, they are hardly ever seen, and no information is available about their breeding or nesting behavior.

NAME: **White-crested Spadebill,** *Platyrinchus platyrhynchos*
RANGE: **northern South America to Amazon basin**
HABITAT: **rain forest, forest edge**
SIZE: **7.5 cm (3 in)**

A tiny, stout-bodied bird, with a round head and a wide, short bill, the white-crested spadebill is distinguished by the white feathers on its head. Pairs remain together throughout the year, flitting busily through the bushes and the lower branches of forest trees in their search for insects and spiders to eat. Occasionally they may even be seen among the many birds that follow the columns of army ants.

The female spadebill builds a bulky, cup-shaped nest, rather like a hummingbird's, from tree ferns, plant fibers and cobwebs. The nest is usually sited in the vertical fork of a tree about 2 m (6½ ft) from the ground. Two eggs are laid, two days apart, and they are incubated for about 17 days by the female alone. Both parents feed the young, which can fly at about 2 weeks old.

NAME: **Yellow-bellied Elaenia,** *Elaenia flavogaster*
RANGE: **Central and South America: S. Mexico to N. Argentina; Trinidad, Tobago**
HABITAT: **shady pasture, savanna, parks, plantations, to 1,800 m (6,000 ft)**
SIZE: **16 cm (6¼ in)**

Despite its name, the most remarkable characteristic of this flycatcher is the double crest of stiff gray feathers that stands up on each side of the head, revealing the white patch between. The bird's breast and belly are pale yellow, the tail long and the bill short. Male and female look alike. Elaenias live in pairs all year round, always in open country with trees, where they feed on insects taken on the wing and on many different types of berries.

Both birds help to build the nest in the fork of a tree, generally about 2 to 4.5 m (6½ to 15 ft) above the ground. It is a shallow, open structure, made from rootlets, plant fibers and cobwebs, covered with lichen and moss and lined with feathers. The female lays 2 eggs, which she incubates for about 15 days. The nestlings are fed by both parents and leave the nest 17 or 18 days after hatching. There are often two broods produced in a year.

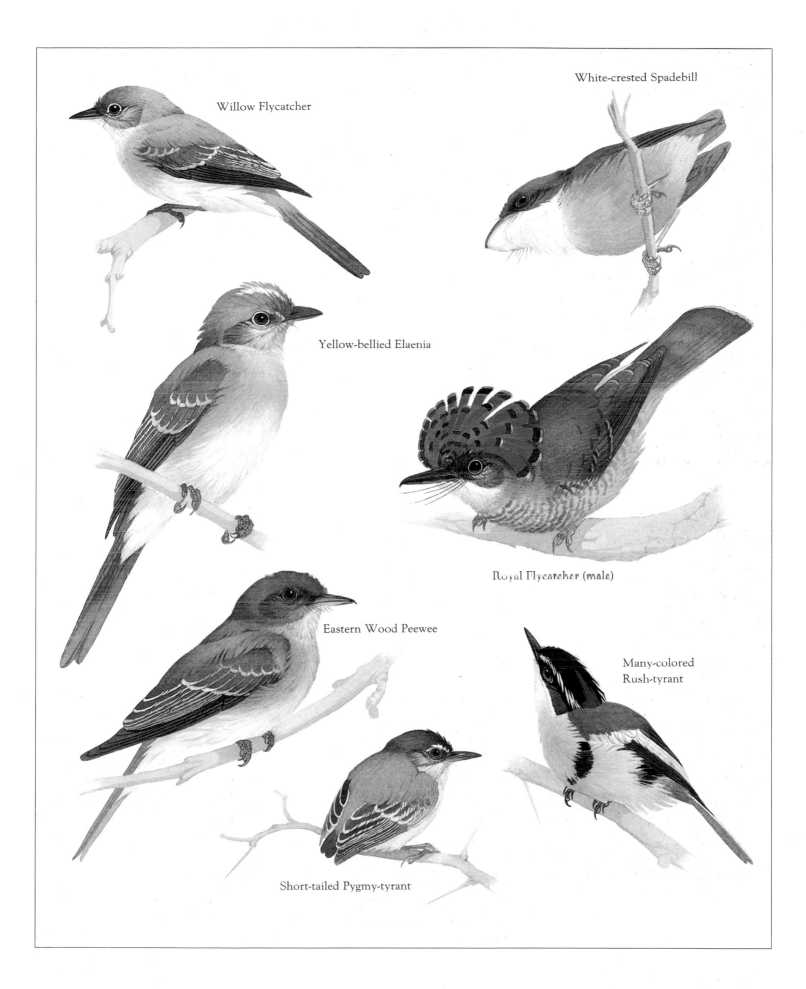

Willow Flycatcher

White-crested Spadebill

Yellow-bellied Elaenia

Royal Flycatcher (male)

Eastern Wood Peewee

Many-colored
Rush-tyrant

Short-tailed Pygmy-tyrant

# Tyrant Flycatchers

NAME: **Common Tody-flycatcher,** *Todirostrum cinereum*
RANGE: **S. Mexico, Central and South America to Bolivia and Brazil**
HABITAT: **open country, plantations, parkland**
SIZE: **10 cm (4 in)**

The long, straight bill and the narrow, graduated tail feathers make up over half of this bird's body length. Avoiding dense woodland, it feeds wherever there are scattered trees, making short darts from branch to branch and seizing insects and berries from foliage and bark. It hops sideways along branches, continuously wagging its tail as it goes. Male and female look alike and live in pairs throughout the year.

Both partners of a breeding pair help to make the nest, which is suspended from a slender twig or vine. They do not weave the nest but mat together plant fibers and then excavate an entrance hole and central cavity in the resulting mass. The female lays 2 or 3 eggs, which she incubates for 17 or 18 days, and both parents feed the young.

NAME: **Ocher-bellied Flycatcher,** *Pipromorpha oleaginea*
RANGE: **S. Mexico, through Central and South America to Peru and Brazil**
HABITAT: **forest, clearings**
SIZE: **12 cm (4¾ in)**

A slender, long-tailed bird, the ocher-bellied flycatcher is mainly olive-green, with grayish plumage on the throat and ocher-yellow underparts. Its bill is long and slender, with a hooked tip. An active little bird, it has a characteristic mannerism of constantly twitching its wings above its back, one at a time. Unlike other flycatchers, this species does not make aerial dashes after prey but seizes insects and spiders from foliage as it flits from tree to tree. It also feeds on fruit and berries, particularly mistletoe berries. An extremely solitary bird, it never gathers in flocks or even pairs, except during the brief period of courtship and mating.

Normally silent, in the breeding season male ocher-bellied flycatchers take up territories in which they perch and sing tirelessly to attract mates. Several males may sing within hearing of each other. They do not assist females in nest-building or rearing of young. A pear-shaped nest, covered with moss, is suspended from a slender branch or vine or from the aerial root of an air plant. It takes the female about 2 weeks to build this nest. She incubates the 2 or 3 eggs for 19 to 21 days and feeds the young for 2 to 3 weeks.

NAME: **Cliff Flycatcher,** *Hirundinea ferruginea*
RANGE: **northern South America to Brazil and N. Argentina**
HABITAT: **arid hillsides, ravines, cliffs, open woodland**
SIZE: **18.5 cm (7¼ in)**

A mainly brown and black bird, this flycatcher has bright chestnut underparts and wing patches, which are conspicuous in flight. Its wings are long and swallowlike, and it catches much of its insect prey in skillful aerial dashes.

The nest is made in a crevice in a rock or cliff.

NAME: **Great Shrike Tyrant,** *Agriornis livida*
RANGE: **South America: S. Argentina, Chile**
HABITAT: **open scrub, fields**
SIZE: **28 cm (11 in) including tail of 11 cm (4¼ in)**

This silent bird avoids woodland and populated regions and frequents lonely, open areas. It has a powerful beak and feeds on insects, small animals, such as newts, toads and mice, and eggs of other birds.

On the coast, the birds begin nesting in October, but farther inland, in the Andean foothills, breeding does not start until November. A bulky nest, made of grass and sticks and lined with sheep's wool, is built in a thick bush. The female lays 2 to 4 eggs, usually 3.

NAME: **Vermilion Flycatcher,** *Pyrocephalus rubinus*
RANGE: **S.W. USA, Mexico, Central and South America to Argentina; Galápagos Islands**
HABITAT: **scrub, desert**
SIZE: **14–17 cm (5½–6¾ in)**

A striking bird, the male vermilion flycatcher has a bright red head and underparts. The female is brownish above, with a lighter, streaked belly and breast. These flycatchers feed on flying insects, particularly bees, darting into the air from a high perch in pursuit of their prey. They also feed on the ground on grasshoppers and beetles, especially in areas of sparse vegetation.

The courting male flies up from a tree, singing ecstatically, his vermilion crest erect and his breast feathers puffed out. He hovers briefly, then flutters down to the female. A flattish, cup-shaped nest, made of twigs, grass and rootlets, is built on a horizontally forked branch. While the female incubates the 2 to 4 eggs, the male fearlessly defends the nest. The young leave the nest about 2 weeks after hatching.

NAME: **Piratic Flycatcher,** *Legatus leucophaius*
RANGE: **S. Mexico, Central and South America to N. Argentina**
HABITAT: **open woodland**
SIZE: **14.5 cm (5¾ in)**

A dully colored bird, the piratic flycatcher makes itself conspicuous by being one of the noisiest flycatchers, with a wide range of calls. It feeds on insects, especially dragonflies, caught on the wing, and berries.

Piratic flycatchers appear to be the only members of the tyrant flycatcher family to depart from normal nest-building habits, and this departure earns them their common name. They do not build their own nests but usurp the freshly built nests of other birds, often other species of flycatcher. Having chosen their victims, the pair of piratic flycatchers perch nearby to watch the building progressing. They chatter noisily and make their presence felt but do not usually attack until the nest is complete. Then they harass the rightful owners until they finally abandon the nest to their attackers. Any eggs are thrown out, and the female piratic flycatcher lays 2 or 3 eggs, which she incubates for about 16 days. Both parents feed the nestlings on berries and insects until they leave the nest almost 3 weeks after hatching. Central American and northern South American populations of piratic flycatchers migrate south after breeding.

NAME: **Torrent Tyranulet,** *Serpophaga cinerea*
RANGE: **Central and South America: mountains of Costa Rica and Panama, Andes from Venezuela to Bolivia**
HABITAT: **rocky streams**
SIZE: **10 cm (4 in)**

The torrent tyranulet lives amid the fast-flowing waters of mountain streams, and its gray and black plumage echoes its wild, rocky habitat. With great skill, it plucks insects not only from the air but also from slippery boulders surrounded by foaming water, often becoming drenched with spray in the process. It even alights on wet rocks to search for other tiny invertebrates. Male and female look alike and live together throughout the year, holding a stretch of river as their territory.

A cup-shaped nest, covered with moss, is made in vegetation overhanging water, rarely over the bank. The 2 eggs are incubated by the female for 17 or 18 days, but the male stays nearby. Both parents feed the young on insects for 2 or 3 weeks, and even after leaving the nest, the young birds stay with their parents for a further 5 or 6 weeks before seeking their own territory.

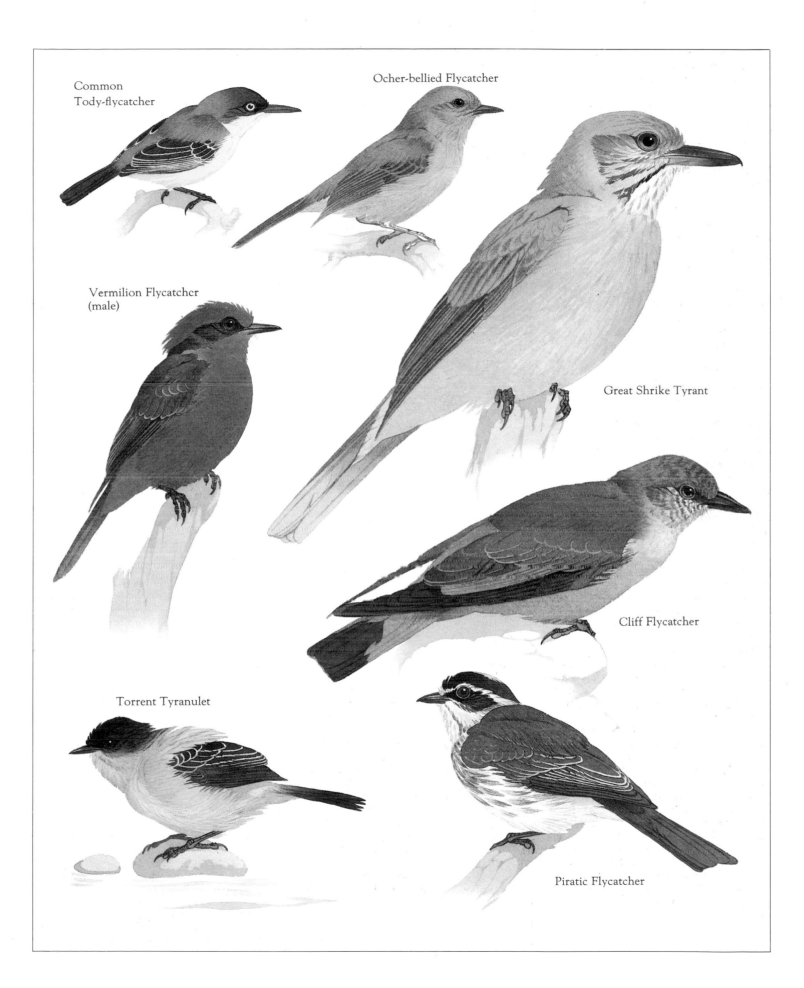

Common
Tody-flycatcher

Ocher-bellied Flycatcher

Vermilion Flycatcher
(male)

Great Shrike Tyrant

Cliff Flycatcher

Torrent Tyranulet

Piratic Flycatcher

# Broadbills, Pittas and relatives

## EURYLAIMIDAE: Broadbill Family

There are about 14 known species in the broadbill family, all found in Africa, southern and Southeast Asia in forest and woodland. They are rather rotund little birds, with bright plumage, heavy, wide bills and short legs and tails. Male and female look unalike in most species. Broadbills feed on insects, fruit, seeds and other plant material. Most build pear-shaped nests, suspended from branches or twigs, often over water.

NAME: **Green Broadbill**, *Calyptomena viridis*
RANGE: **Malaysia, Sumatra, Borneo**
HABITAT: **forest on lowland and hills**
SIZE: **19 cm (7½ in)**

The green broadbill spends much of its life foraging for fruit, its main food, high in the forest trees, where it is hard to spot among the leaves. The male is bright and iridescent, but the female is a duller green and often larger than the male.

The nest is made of coarse, matted plant fibers and is suspended from thin twigs just above the ground. It is wider at the top than at the bottom, and there is an entrance hole near the top. The female bird lays 2 eggs, which both parents are believed to incubate.

## PITTIDAE: Pitta Family

The 24 species of pitta occur in Africa, Asia and Southeast Asia to Australia. They are stout birds, with long legs, and most species have bright plumage. Male and female look alike in some species but differ in others.

NAME: **Indian Pitta**, *Pitta brachyura*
RANGE: **N. and central India; winters in S. India and Sri Lanka**
HABITAT: **varied, including semi-cultivated land and forest**
SIZE: **18 cm (7 in)**

This brightly plumaged little bird forages on or close to the forest floor, searching among leaves and debris for food such as insects and spiders; it will also eat worms and maggots found near excrement. If alarmed, it flies up into a tree with a whirring sound and then sits still, with only its tail moving slowly up and down.

The nest, built in a tree, is a domed, globular structure, made of moss and covered with twigs. It is lined with plant material and has a side entrance. Both parents incubate the 4 to 6 eggs and feed the helpless, naked young. Large flocks of Indian pittas migrate south in winter.

NAME: **Garnet Pitta**, *Pitta granatina*
RANGE: **Malaysia, Sumatra, Borneo**
HABITAT: **lowland forest, swamps**
SIZE: **15 cm (6 in)**

Both male and female garnet pittas have brilliant, jewel-like plumage, while juveniles are brownish and acquire the adult coloration only gradually. Much of the garnet pitta's life is spent running about on the ground, foraging for ants, beetles and other insects, as well as snails and seeds, but it will also fly short distances.

Its nest, typical of the pitta family, is made on the ground and is a domed structure of rotting leaves and fibers, roofed with twigs and leaves. There is a small entrance to the chamber in which the female lays 2 eggs.

## XENICIDAE:
### New Zealand Wren Family

This family of 4 species of small wren-like birds is confined to forest and scrubland in New Zealand.

NAME: **Rifleman**, *Acanthisitta chloris*
RANGE: **New Zealand and neighboring islands**
HABITAT: **forest and modified habitats with remnants of forest**
SIZE: **7.5–10 cm (3–4 in)**

The tiny rifleman feeds mainly in the trees, searching in crevices and over trunks and branches for insects and spiders; it may occasionally come down to the forest floor. Male and female differ in plumage, the female having dark- and light-brown striped upperparts, instead of yellowish-green.

The nest is made in a crevice in a tree, and both parents incubate the 4 or 5 eggs and feed the young.

## PHILEPITTIDAE: Asity Family

The 4 species in this family are divided into two distinct groups: the asities and the false sunbirds. They are plump, tree-dwelling birds, all found in Madagascar. Male and female differ in plumage.

NAME: **Wattled False Sunbird**, *Neodrepanis coruscans*
RANGE: **E. Madagascar**
HABITAT: **forest**
SIZE: **9 cm (3½ in)**

The long, downward-curving bill of the wattled false sunbird gives it a strong superficial resemblance to the true sunbirds (Nectariniidae), hence the common name. The bill is used for the same purpose, that is, to drink nectar from flowers. The false sunbird also feeds on fruit, insects and spiders.

## MENURIDAE: Lyrebird Family

The 2 species of lyrebird both live in the mountain forests of southeastern Australia. Both sexes have brownish plumage, but the males have extraordinarily long and elaborate tails.

NAME: **Superb Lyrebird**, *Menura novaehollandiae*
RANGE: **Australia: S.E. Queensland to Victoria; introduced in Tasmania**
HABITAT: **mountain forest**
SIZE: **male: 80–95 cm (31½–37½ in); female: 45–50 cm (17¾–19¾ in)**

Although male and female lyrebirds are similar in body size and general appearance, the male's tail is up to 55 cm (21½ in) long and is a flamboyant mix of boldly patterned, lyre-shaped feathers and fine, filamentous feathers. The lyrebirds are mainly ground-living and rarely fly but hop and flap up into trees to roost. They search on the ground for insects and larvae, scratching around with their large, strong legs and feet.

Prior to mating, the male makes several earth mounds and displays near them before the female, spreading his shimmering tail right over himself and dancing. The nest is a large, well-camouflaged dome, made of grass and plant fiber and lined with rootlets. It is built on the ground near rocks or logs or sometimes in a tree. The female incubates her 1 egg for about 6 weeks and cares for the nestling.

## ATRICHORNITHIDAE:
### Scrub Bird Family

There are 2 species of scrub bird, both found in Australia; they are the closest relatives of lyrebirds. They have small wings, long, broad tails and strong legs. Male and female differ slightly in coloration and females are smaller.

NAME: **Noisy Scrub Bird**, *Atrichornis clamosus*
RANGE: **S.W. Australia: Two People's Bay**
HABITAT: **coastal scrub, vegetated gullies**
SIZE: **23 cm (9 in)** Ⓔ

Now an extremely rare bird, the noisy scrub bird was thought to be extinct for more than 70 years until it was rediscovered, in 1961, at Two People's Bay. It is now protected by law.

Noisy scrub birds live among dense vegetation on or near the ground and feed on insects and seeds. They usually live alone and rarely move far afield. The female bird builds a domed nest of dried rushes, in which she lays 1 egg. She incubates the egg for 36 to 38 days.

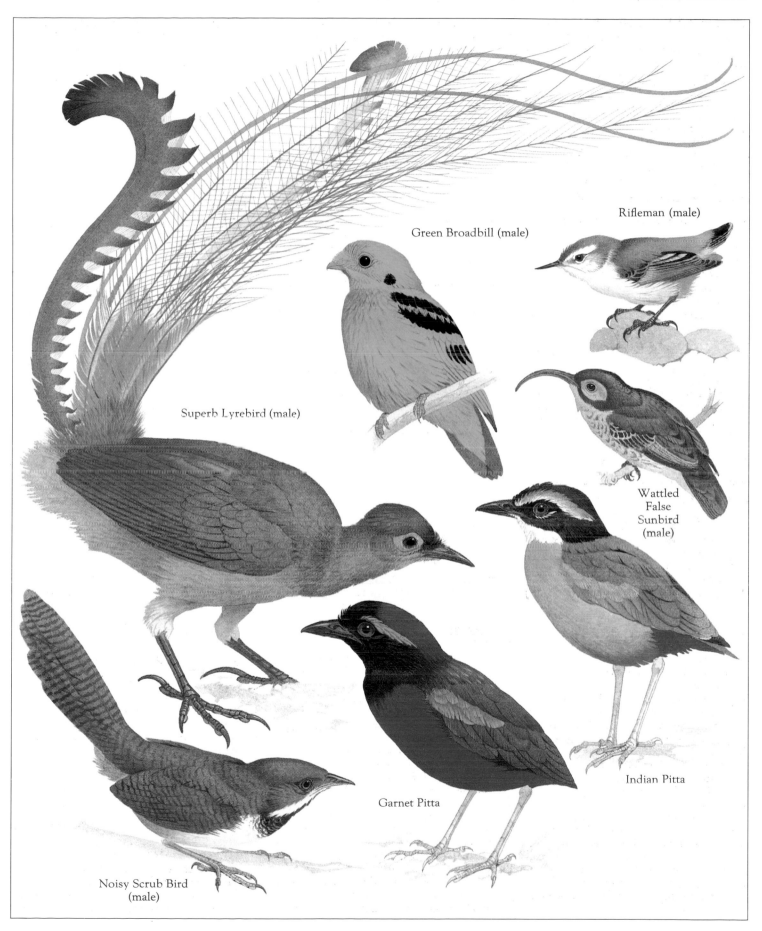

Green Broadbill (male)

Rifleman (male)

Superb Lyrebird (male)

Wattled
False
Sunbird
(male)

Indian Pitta

Garnet Pitta

Noisy Scrub Bird
(male)

# Larks

NAME: **Desert Lark, *Ammomanes deserti*.**
RANGE: **Africa: Sahara; Middle East, through Iran to Afghanistan**
HABITAT: **stony, hilly desert, dry wooded slopes**
SIZE: **15 cm (6 in)**

The plumage of the desert lark perfectly matches the color of the desert soil — the best example of soil camouflage in birds. The very dark subspecies, *A. d. annae*, blends with the black larval sand of central Arabia, while the pale race, *A. d. isabellina*, does not stray from areas of white sand.

The nest is usually built up against a rock or tuft of grass and is reinforced on the windward side by small decorative pebbles. In the harsh desert interior, 3 eggs are laid, while 4 or 5 may be produced at the desert edge.

NAME: **Singing Bushlark, *Mirafra javanica***
RANGE: **central and E. Africa, Middle East, S.E. Asia, New Guinea, Australia**
HABITAT: **open bush or scrub, rice fields**
SIZE: **15 cm (6 in)**

The vibrant songs of the singing bushlark can often be heard issuing from bushes or the air, even on bright moonlit nights. Darker and more evenly colored than other larks, this plump, gregarious bird has a heavy, finchlike bill, which it uses to pick up grass seeds and insects. With its shape, its strong, rapid gait and weak flight, the singing bushlark is well suited to life on the ground.

The igloo-shaped grass nest is built in the shelter of a rock or tuft of grass and has a side entrance and soft, grass lining. The female lays 3 to 5 eggs.

NAME: **Thick-billed/Clotbey Lark, *Ramphocoris clotbey***
RANGE: **N. Africa to Syria**
HABITAT: **stony desert**
SIZE: **17 cm (6¾ in)**

True to its name, this lark is distinguished by its large, powerful bill. The bird uses it to crush tough seed cases and hard-shelled desert insects and carries its head very straight or thrown backward, to counteract the weight of the bill. The male is sandy colored, with black spots on the underparts; the female has a redder tinge and fewer spots.

Although this species is normally sedentary, some birds move away from the heat of the desert outside the breeding season. The nest is sited up against a stone or grass tussock and starts out as a small hollow, filled with soft plant material. As it begins to overflow, the nesting material is supported by a collection of small pebbles. The female lays 2 to 5 eggs.

---

## ALAUDIDAE: Lark Family

The larks, about 75 species in all, are concentrated in the Old World except for the horned lark and the introduced skylark, found also in North America. Typically, the wings are fairly long and pointed and the beak rather long and slightly down-curved. Males and females look more or less alike, but the female is often smaller.

Most species favor an open habitat with low vegetation, such as tundra, meadowland or desert, where they are commonly seen walking or running along the ground. The diet consists of seeds, buds, insects and small underground invertebrates, obtained by bill-probing or digging.

---

NAME: **Short-toed/Red-capped Lark, *Calandrella cinerea***
RANGE: **Mediterranean area, Africa, Asia to Mongolia; occasional visitor to N. Europe and Britain**
HABITAT: **open sandy or stony plains**
SIZE: **14 cm (5½ in)**

The tiny short-toed lark is a widespread species with about 14 races. It varies in color throughout its range, from sandy to reddish — the South African race, for example, has a rufous cap on its head and reddish patches on the sides of its breast. In spite of its name, the ground-dwelling short-toed lark is a speedy runner. When alarmed, however, it escapes by flying low, then lands abruptly and sprints away. Short-toed larks feed on the ground on seeds and insects but perform prolonged, undulating song flights at a height of about 15 m (50 ft).

Northern populations migrate to their breeding grounds, south of the Sahara and in central India, in autumn. All races gather in large flocks out of the breeding season but disperse to mate, when they are seen singly or in pairs. The nest, deep and cup-shaped, holds two clutches of 3 to 5 eggs each in a year. Incubation lasts for 11 to 13 days.

NAME: **Horned Lark, *Eremophila alpestris***
RANGE: **N. America, Europe, N. Africa, Asia**
HABITAT: **varied: rocky alpine meadows up to 5,275 m (17,300 ft), stony steppe, tundra and desert, open grassland**
SIZE: **16 cm (6¼ in)**

One of only two larks found in the Americas, the horned lark comprises 40 widespread races. The male has a distinctive black and yellow head with short black tufts, or horns, of feathers; the female and juveniles are less black. In winter, northern groups migrate to southern breeding grounds, and most

---

populations winter in lowland fields, where they sometimes form flocks with buntings. In summer, they feed on seeds, buds, insects and their larvae, supplementing these with small crustaceans and mollusks in winter.

The nest is a simple structure of plant stems, lined with soft plant material; it is built on the ground and surrounded with sheep droppings, plant debris and pebbles. The female usually lays two broods of 4 eggs each, which she incubates for 10 to 14 days.

NAME: **Skylark, *Alauda arvensis***
RANGE: **Europe, Asia, N. Africa; introduced in Australasia and Canada**
HABITAT: **moorland, marshes, sand dunes, arable and pasture land**
SIZE: **18 cm (7 in)**

The skylark has dark wings and a long tail, both with a white fringe, a boldly streaked breast and a short, but prominent, crest. It is a terrestrial bird and roosts on the ground; it walks rather than hops and crouches when uneasy, emitting a liquid chirrup when flushed. Skylarks enjoy dust baths and prefer to perch on low walls, fences or telephone wires. They usually sing early in the morning and have a characteristic song flight, fluttering high in the sky and sustaining their song for long periods. Their diet consists of seeds and ground-living invertebrates.

The female builds a well-concealed grass nest in which she lays 3 to 5 eggs; she then incubates them for 11 days. Two or three broods are raised each year. Northern races migrate south of their range for the winter.

NAME: **Greater Hoopoe Lark/Bifasciated Lark, *Alaemon alaudipes***
RANGE: **Cape Verde Archipelago, across the Sahara to Middle East, W. India**
HABITAT: **open sandy desert**
SIZE: **20.5 cm (8 in)**

One of the larger species, the greater hoopoe lark is long legged, long billed and distinguished by its white eyebrow tufts. It uses its sturdy, down-curved bill to dig up to 5 cm (2 in) into the desert soil in search of grubs, locust pupae and seeds. This bold bird is not easily upset by human observers and defends its territory against competitors. It has a long, melodious call, but its song is a series of pipes and whistles, and it normally only flies during its extremely high, rising and falling song flight.

Like most larks, it nests on the ground, although in the hottest areas, the nest, which may be scanty or quite substantial, is placed a few inches off the ground in the shady lower branches of a bush. The female usually lays 2 eggs.

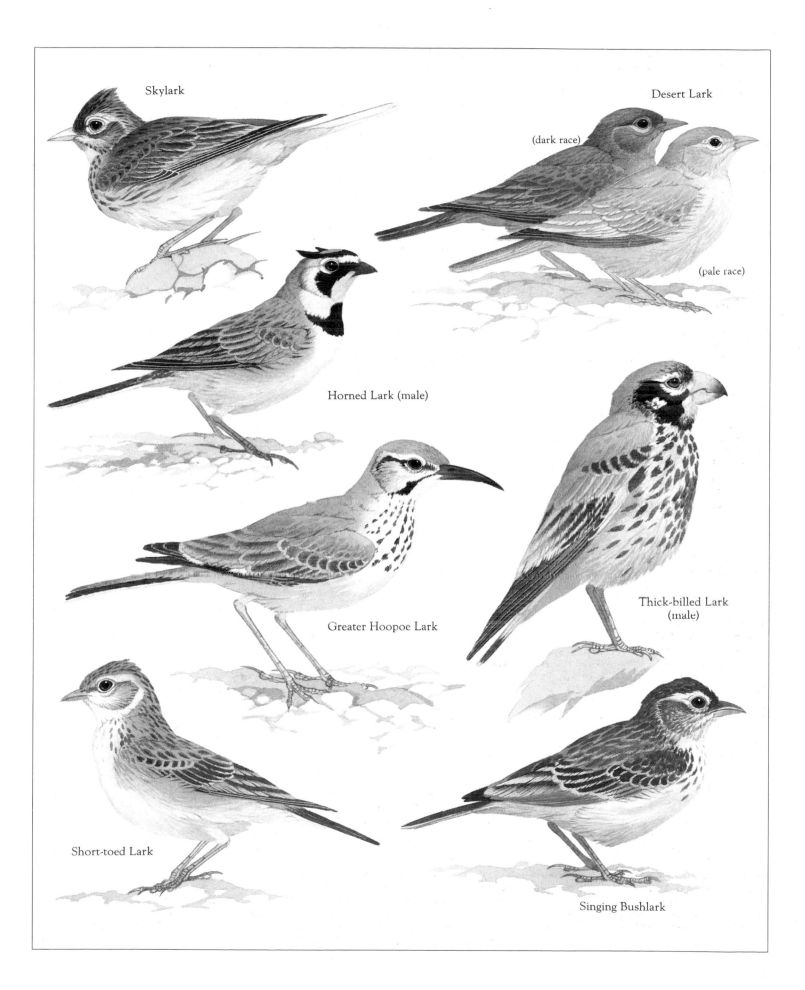

Skylark

Desert Lark

(dark race)

(pale race)

Horned Lark (male)

Thick-billed Lark
(male)

Greater Hoopoe Lark

Short-toed Lark

Singing Bushlark

# Swallows

NAME: **Barn Swallow**, *Hirundo rustica*
RANGE: **almost worldwide; breeds between 30°N and 70°N; winters in southern hemisphere**
HABITAT: **open cultivated country with buildings, near water**
SIZE: **19.5 cm (7¾ in)**

The barn swallow is absent only from very high latitudes and some oceanic islands. The male is metallic blue, with a deeply forked tail covered in white spots and a white breast. Females and young birds have shorter tails and less vibrant plumage. They feed on insects, caught on the wing or plucked from the surface of water.

In summer, barn swallows are seen in pairs and small groups, but in autumn they form huge flocks and roost in reed-beds before migrating south. The Old World races winter in Africa, south of the Sahara, the Indian subcontinent and northern Australia; the North American birds fly down to Panama, central Chile and northern Argentina.

Both sexes help to build the open nest, using mud and straw and lining it with feathers. They now seem to prefer ledges on buildings to the original cave or cliff sites. The female lays 4 or 5 eggs and incubates them for about 15 days, with some help from the male. Both parents feed the nestlings, which can fly at about 3 weeks old. There are two, sometimes three, broods a year.

NAME: **Bank Swallow**, *Riparia riparia*
RANGE: **temperate regions of Eurasia, N. America**
HABITAT: **steep sand or gravel banks, near water**
SIZE: **12–14 cm (4¾–5½ in)**

The tiny bank swallow is the smallest swallow in North America, with a wing-span of only 25.5 to 28 cm (10 to 11 in). This energetic little bird darts, twists and zigzags in flight, snapping up a variety of winged insects, including termites, leafhoppers and mosquitoes.

Bank swallows live in burrows, which they dig straight into sand or gravel banks, often by water or alongside roads and railway tracks. The birds start the burrow with their bills, and both male and female take turns to kick out the soil until the burrow is about 1 m (3¼ ft) long. Each spring, the bank swallows flock north, often returning to the previous year's hole, and fights over ownership are not unusual. The nest is built at the end of the burrow from soft grass, feathers, hair and rootlets. The female lays up to 8 eggs, usually 4 or 5, which are incubated alternately by both parents for 16 days. The young fly at 3 weeks old.

## HIRUNDINIDAE: Swallow Family

The 78 species of swallow and martin are all swift-flying birds, which display great agility in the air. They are found almost worldwide, and many make regular migrations between breeding and wintering areas, sometimes traveling as much as 13,000 km (8,000 mi). There is little consistent difference between the swallows and martins. All forms have smallish bodies, short necks and long, pointed wings. They are fast, agile fliers and catch their prey on the wing in their wide, gaping beaks. Swallows and martins are the passerine equivalents of swifts. The two families have become alike by adapting to a similar way of life in the air; swifts, however, do have longer wings and tend to fly higher than swallows.

On the ground, their short legs and weak feet are ill suited to locomotion, but the birds do perch. They frequently nest close to or in human dwellings or use natural hollows in trees, caves or cliffs in which to construct a burrow. Clutches of 3 to 7 eggs are laid, which both parents incubate.

Swallows and martins are generally gregarious birds and feed, nest and migrate in large flocks. Males and females look more or less alike, but in some species there may be minor differences, such as the male having longer tail feathers.

NAME: **White-eyed River Martin**, *Pseudochelidon sirintarae*
RANGE: **winters central Thailand**
HABITAT: **reedbeds in marshes**
SIZE: **24 cm (9½ in) including tail streamers of 9 cm (3½ in)**  ①

The white-eyed river martin is identified by its distinctive white spectacles and rump and by the long streamers flowing from its rounded tail. It also has a large, swollen, yellow bill, unusual for a swallow. The juvenile has a darker head and only very short streamers.

This rare species was discovered only in 1968 and is believed to be a migrant from the north. Its nearest relative, and the only other member of its subfamily, is *P. eurystomina*, which lives in Africa, in Zambia. The white-eyed river martin winters in central Thailand, at Bung Boraphet, where it roosts at night in large lakeside reedbeds in flocks with other species of swallows. By day, it perches on trees and wires and catches insects in flight.

Its summer migration and breeding habits remain a mystery, although it may breed in holes in riverbanks in Thailand or China.

NAME: **Purple Martin**, *Progne subis*
RANGE: **breeds Canada to Mexico; winters south to West Indies, Venezuela, Brazil**
HABITAT: **suburban gardens and farmland**
SIZE: **18 cm (7 in)**

The purple martin is one of the tamest birds of the family. The male's metallic blue plumage gradually fades out to brown on the wings and tail; the female is mainly brown, and the juvenile is a grayish-brown. This species supplements its diet of insects, taken on the wing, with snails, probably as a source of calcium.

These birds build their nests in trees or cliff holes, using grass, feathers and often green leaves, which may help to keep the nest cool and moist. The 3 to 5 eggs are incubated for 13 days, mainly by the female, and the young leave the nest within a month of hatching.

There are 2 races of purple martin. *P. s. subis* breeds in southern Canada, down the west coast of the USA to central Mexico and east to the Gulf Coast and Florida; it winters in Venezuela and southeast Brazil. *P. s. hesperia* breeds in the lowlands of Arizona, Baja California and the Mexican coast, but it is not known where it winters.

NAME: **Blue Rough-winged Swallow**, *Psalidoprocne pristoptera*
RANGE: **Africa: Ethiopia**
HABITAT: **high plateaus**
SIZE: **18 cm (7 in)**

The blue rough-winged swallow has glossy blue-black plumage above, with an oily green look to its wings and tail. The broad tail is not as deeply forked in the female as in the male. The juvenile is a dull, dark brown and blue. These birds are often seen in pairs, swooping over streams in search of insects, which they take on the wing.

The nesting hole is at the end of a tunnel, chiseled into a riverbank or cliff face, and is padded with layers of soft grass. The female lays 3 eggs, which are glossy white and thin shelled.

NAME: **Golden Swallow**, *Kalochelidon euchrysea*
RANGE: **Jamaica, Hispaniola**
HABITAT: **dry, wooded, limestone hills**
SIZE: **12.5 cm (5 in)**

This delicate, graceful bird earns its name from the bright golden gloss over its olive-green plumage. The juvenile keeps its duller colors and gray chest band until maturity. The Jamaican race is now believed to be rare, although there is insufficient information available at present to classify it as such.

Golden swallows feed entirely on the wing and nest in tree holes or under the eaves of houses. The female lays 3 eggs.

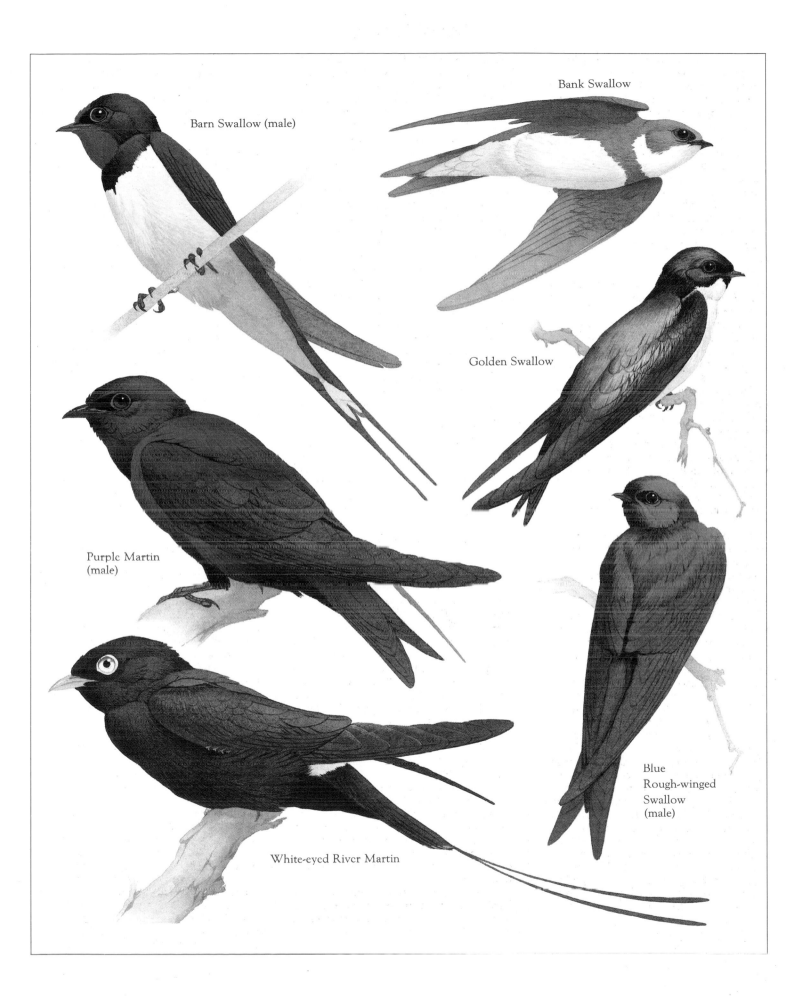

Barn Swallow (male)

Bank Swallow

Golden Swallow

Purple Martin
(male)

Blue
Rough-winged
Swallow
(male)

White-eyed River Martin

# Pipits

NAME: **Yellow-throated Longclaw,**
*Macronyx croceus*
RANGE: **Africa, south of the Sahara**
HABITAT: **wet grassland, open woodland,
swamps, cultivated land**
SIZE: **20.5 cm (8 in)**

The hind claw of this widespread species is nearly 5 cm (2 in) long. Male and female look alike, but the juvenile lacks the black chest marking of the adults and has only black spots. These birds live in pairs and are often seen perching in trees or on farmland. In flight they flap, rather like the larks, and occasionally dive into the grass to rummage for insects.

The male's courtship flight is leisurely, and he fans out his tail and sings at the same time. The loosely constructed nest, made of grass and roots, is usually hidden among long grass or under a tussock. The female lays 3 or 4 eggs.

NAME: **Golden Pipit,** *Tmetothylacus
tenellus*
RANGE: **Africa: Ethiopia, Somalia, Sudan
to Tanzania**
HABITAT: **dry scrub**
SIZE: **15 cm (6 in)**

The shy golden pipit is bright yellow, but the darker bars and mottling help it to blend with its arid scrub habitat. The female and juvenile are browner and paler than the male. All have a long hind claw. These birds are usually seen alone or in small family groups, wagging their tails as they perch above the ground, watching for the insects that form their food.

In his courtship display, the male flies down from a tree, with wings raised in a V-shape over his back, whistling as he goes. The female makes a grass nest, lined with rootlets, just off the ground in a clump of grass, and lays 2 to 4 eggs.

NAME: **Forest Wagtail,** *Dendronanthus
indicus*
RANGE: **E. Asia: breeds Siberia to N.
China; winters south to India and Java**
HABITAT: **glades and clearings in
montane forest, near water**
SIZE: **20.5 cm (8 in)**

The forest wagtail can be identified by the loud chirruping sound it makes as it flies, perches or runs about looking for the snails, slugs, worms and insects on which it feeds. When standing, by rotating its body, it wags its tail from side to side, rather than up and down as other wagtails do.

Bundles of plant material are bound together with spider's webs to form a compact nest, which is usually built on a horizontal branch overhanging water. The female lays 4 eggs.

## MOTACILLIDAE: Pipit Family

The family of longclaws, pipits and wagtails is absent only from the extreme north and small oceanic islands. Most of the 54 species are characterized by a long tail, which they wag up and down, and some by a long hind claw. All forms are essentially ground-living birds, with strong feet, and have narrow, pointed beaks and slender bodies, which, among the wagtails, have an elongated appearance. Males and females look alike in some species, unalike in others.

NAME: **Meadow Pipit,** *Anthus pratensis*
RANGE: **Europe, Asia; winters in
N. Africa, Middle East**
HABITAT: **tundra, grassland, heaths**
SIZE: **15 cm (6 in)**

The meadow pipit has the normal pipit plumage pattern, with white outer tail feathers, although its body coloration is very variable. In their southern, winter home, meadow pipits gather in small, loose groups; in the summer, individuals can be seen either perching high — on telephone wires for instance — or on the ground in open grassland or alpine meadows. The diet is varied and generally includes flies, mosquitoes, spiders, worms and some seeds.

To attract a female, the male displays by flying up from the ground and then, with wings stretched out and tail lifted, gliding down while he sings a simple song. The nest is made and lined with soft grasses and is often tucked into a tussock of heather or grass to hide it. The female lays two clutches of 4 or 5 eggs and incubates them for 2 weeks. The male helps to feed the young.

NAME: **Water Pipit,** *Anthus spinoletta*
RANGE: **widespread in N. America,
Europe, N. Asia**
HABITAT: **summers in marshy areas of
tundra, mountain and coast; winters in
plains and lowlands**
SIZE: **15–18 cm (6–7 in)**

The water pipit has a slender body and thin, pointed bill. Male and female look alike, both with grayish-brown plumage and creamy-white underparts. When walking, they nod their heads up and down and swing their tails from side to side. Water pipits feed on aquatic worms and insects, which they obtain by wading in shallow pools and from mud flats and mats of drifting seaweed. They also take seeds and insects such as weevils, aphids, grasshoppers and ants. In spring, flocks of up to 500 birds can be seen feeding together before they fly off to their breeding grounds.

The female alone builds the nest of dried grass and twigs in the shelter of a rock, mossy bank or tussock of grass; sometimes it may be only a scraped hollow on the ground. She also incubates the 4 or 5 eggs for about 2 weeks, and the young fly 2 weeks after hatching.

In America, northern populations migrate to Mexico in vast numbers for the winter.

NAME: **Yellow Wagtail,** *Motacilla flava*
RANGE: **Europe, Asia to W. Alaska;
winters in tropical Africa and Asia**
HABITAT: **marshy grassland, heaths,
moors, steppe, tundra**
SIZE: **16.5 cm (6½ in)**

The yellow wagtail is the most pipitlike of the wagtails. All forms are greenish and black, with yellow underparts, but the males display a variety of head colors such as black, green and gray. The female has a pale patch above the eye, and the juvenile has dark throat spots. Several races flock together to migrate to the tropics, where the birds settle by rivers and lakes for the winter. They feed on insects on the ground or in the air, particularly those flushed out by grazing animals.

During his courtship display flight, the male puffs up his feathers, fans out his tail, which he holds bowed, and vibrates his wings until they seem to shiver. The nest is made of plant fibers, softly lined with hair and wool, and is well hidden on the ground. The female lays 5 or 6 eggs, which she incubates for 13 days.

NAME: **Pied/White Wagtail,** *Motacilla
alba*
RANGE: **Europe, Asia, N. Africa; winters
south to S. Africa, S. Asia**
HABITAT: **riverbanks, steppe, tundra,
alpine meadows, cultivated land,
gardens, near water**
SIZE: **18 cm (7 in)**

This wagtail has two distinct races, both of which have similar black and white markings and develop a white throat in winter. The mantle and rump of the white wagtail, *M. a. alba*, of continental Europe, however, are gray, while those of the pied wagtail, *M. a. yarrellii*, of the British Isles, are black, or dark gray in the female. These wagtails often roost in hundreds in trees and reedbeds and occasionally wade in shallow water. They take off from a fast, tail-bobbing run into undulating flight and snap up insects in the air with dexterity.

The cup-shaped, grassy nest, lined with wool, hair and feathers, is usually made in a hollow in a steep bank, on a building or on flat ground. It houses two, or sometimes three, broods of 5 or 6 eggs, which the female incubates for 2 weeks.

Pied Wagtail

Forest Wagtail

Yellow Wagtail

races of
Yellow
Wagtail

Golden Pipit

Meadow Pipit

Yellow-throated
Longclaw

Water Pipit

# Cuckoo-shrikes and Minivets

**NAME:** Ground Cuckoo-shrike, *Pteropodocys maxima*
**RANGE:** Australia
**HABITAT:** dry, open country
**SIZE:** 33 cm (13 in)

The ground cuckoo-shrike is far more terrestrial than other cuckoo-shrikes, which only occasionally forage on the ground. A stout-legged bird, it walks and runs well as it searches for insects to eat. It usually lives in family groups.

The nest, usually placed in the fork of a tree, is made of grass, stems and rootlets, and spider's webs may be used to bind the plant material together. It may sometimes be built on top of the old nest of another bird species. The female usually lays 2 or 3 eggs; more than one female may lay eggs in the same nest.

**NAME:** Cicadabird, *Coracina tenuirostris*
**RANGE:** Sulawesi to Solomon Islands, New Guinea, Australia
**HABITAT:** forest edge, grassland, mangrove swamps
**SIZE:** 25.5 cm (10 in)

Known as the cicadabird because of its high, shrill song, this bird is rather shy and is more often heard than seen; it is usually silent, however, outside the breeding season. Insects, such as beetles, caterpillars and cicadas, are its main foods, and most are caught up in the trees.

The nest of the cicadabird is only about 7.5 cm (3 in) across and is made of twigs and spider's webs, camouflaged with lichen; it is usually placed on a horizontal, forked branch. The female lays only 1 egg, and the male defends the nest and his territory against any intruders. He feeds his mate while she incubates the egg.

**NAME:** Large/Black-faced Cuckoo-shrike, *Coracina novaehollandiae*
**RANGE:** India to S.E. Asia and Australia
**HABITAT:** light forest, gardens, suburbs, plantations
**SIZE:** 33 cm (13 in)

The large cuckoo-shrike is a heavily built, mostly gray bird. The male has some black, shrikelike markings on his head; the female looks similar in most respects, but her head markings are dark gray. Small groups of cuckoo-shrikes forage high in the treetops for food, mainly fruit such as figs, insects and insect larvae. They sometimes take insects in the air or dive to pick up food from the ground.

Large cuckoo-shrikes tend to return to the same breeding site, even the same branch, year after year. The nest is saucer shaped and made of twigs and spider's webs, usually in the fork of a branch. The female lays 2 or 3 eggs.

## CAMPEPHAGIDAE:
### Cuckoo-shrike and Minivet Family

Cuckoo-shrikes are not cuckoos, nor are they shrikes and, in fact, they are not even related to these two families, even though in plumage coloration and body form there are a number of similarities. Together, cuckoo-shrikes and minivets make up a family of about 70 species, found for the most part in the tropics of the Old World, including Australia.

Cuckoo-shrikes are rather drab, dull-colored birds, with strong, notched beaks, long pointed wings and strong bristles around the base of the bill. Most are arboreal. Minivets have brightly colored plumage, often red and black in males and yellow or orange and gray in females. Like cuckoo-shrikes, they are mainly forest and woodland birds.

Many of the birds in this family have densely packed erectile feathers on the back and rump. These have stiff, sharp-pointed shafts and are easily shed, possibly as a defensive measure against predators. The nest is usually cup shaped and built in a tree, and there are 2 to 5 eggs, which may be incubated by both parents or by the female alone. Male and female look alike in some species, unalike in others.

**NAME:** Pied/Bar-winged Flycatcher-shrike, *Hemipus picatus*
**RANGE:** India, Sri Lanka, S.E. Asia, Sumatra, Borneo
**HABITAT:** woodland, forest, forest edge
**SIZE:** 12.5 cm (5 in)

The pied flycatcher-shrike is a small cuckoo-shrike, which pursues insects in the air as skillfully as a true flycatcher. It also finds food by hopping around the branches, gleaning insects from leaves, and may sometimes feed on the ground, although it is primarily a tree-living bird. Small groups of about 6 birds usually live together out of the breeding season and may also join in mixed flocks. Male and female look similar, but the black plumage of the male is replaced by dark brown in the female in some races.

The shallow, saucer-shaped nest is built on a branch of a tree and is made of grass and rootlets, bound together with spider's webs. Lichen is used to camouflage the outside, and the sitting bird appears to be on a clump of lichen rather than a nest. The female lays 2 or 3 eggs. Once hatched, the young birds sit still, with their eyes closed and their heads raised together, and can easily be mistaken by the casual observer for a spur of dead wood.

**NAME:** Red-shouldered/Black Cuckoo-shrike, *Campephaga phoenicea*
**RANGE:** Africa, south of the Sahara
**HABITAT:** forest, woodland
**SIZE:** 20.5 cm (8 in)

Some races of this species have the distinctive red markings they are named for, but others have small yellow shoulder patches or none at all. Males have glossy black plumage, while females are mainly olive-brown or gray, with yellow-edged wings and tail. Restless, active birds, they are always on the move in pairs or in parties of several species. They feed on caterpillars and insects, gleaned from foliage or found on the ground.

A cup-shaped nest, made of moss and lichen bound together with spider's webs, is built in the fork of a tree, and the female lays 2 or 3 eggs. She incubates the eggs for about 20 days, and both parents then feed the newly hatched nestlings.

**NAME:** White-winged Triller, *Lalage sueurii*
**RANGE:** Java, Lesser Sunda Islands, Sulawesi, Australia, New Guinea
**HABITAT:** open forest, woodland
**SIZE:** 18 cm (7 cm)

The white-winged triller makes its melodious calls as it flies from tree to tree, taking insects from leaves and branches. Male and female differ in plumage, the female being largely brown, while the male is glossy black, gray and white.

Both partners of a breeding pair help to build a nest of plant material, usually in the fork of a branch. They both incubate the 1 to 3 eggs for about 14 days and feed the young.

**NAME:** Scarlet Minivet, *Pericrocotus flammeus*
**RANGE:** India, Sri Lanka, S. China, S.E. Asia to Philippines, Bali and Lombok
**HABITAT:** forest, woodland
**SIZE:** 23 cm (9 in)

One of the 10 species of minivet, the scarlet minivet, with its bright plumage, is typical of the group. The male is red and black, while the female has dark-gray and yellow plumage, distributed in the same manner. Both can be identified by the oval patch on each wing that is red in males and yellow in females. Strictly arboreal, scarlet minivets search among the treetops for large, soft-bodied insects to eat, often catching them in flight.

The shallow, cup-shaped nest is made on the branch of a tree from twigs, roots and grass stems, bound together with spider's webs. A covering of lichen and fragments of bark camouflages the nest. The female lays 2 or 3 eggs and incubates them alone. Both parents feed the young.

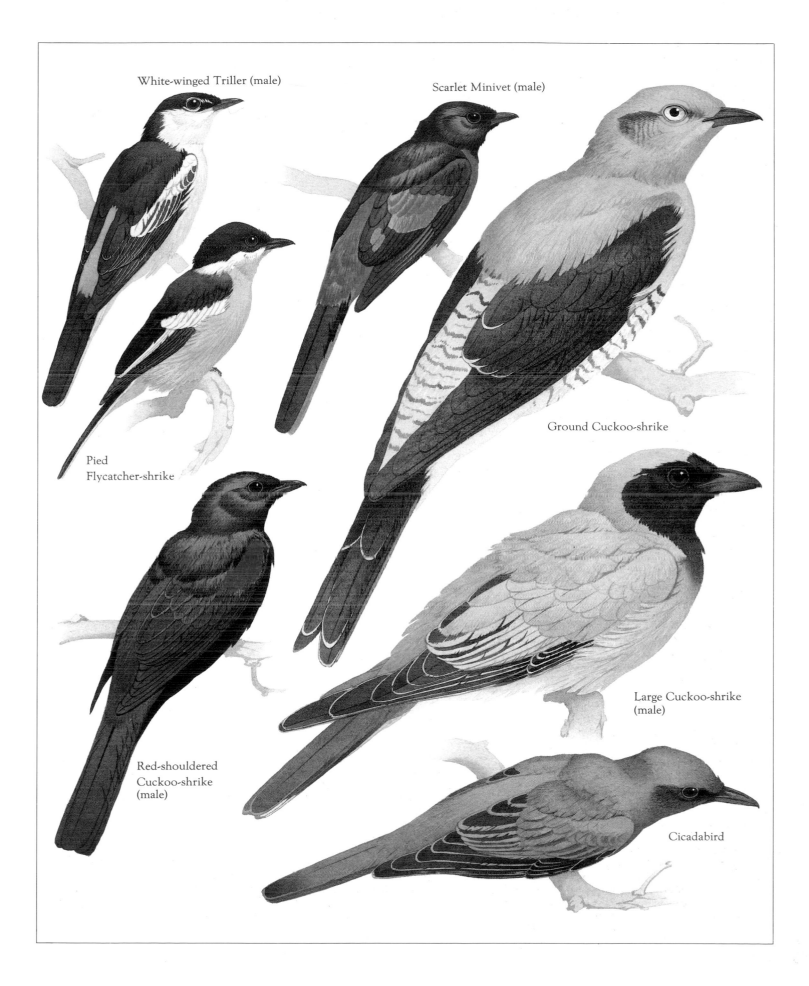

White-winged Triller (male)

Scarlet Minivet (male)

Pied
Flycatcher-shrike

Ground Cuckoo-shrike

Large Cuckoo-shrike
(male)

Red-shouldered
Cuckoo-shrike
(male)

Cicadabird

# Bulbuls

NAME: **Yellow-bellied/Yellow-breasted Greenbul,** *Chlorocichla flaviventris*
RANGE: **Africa: Tanzania to Namibia**
HABITAT: **forest, woodland with heavy undergrowth, coastal scrub**
SIZE: **22 cm (8½ in)**

Unexpectedly shy and skulking birds for their family, the greenbuls are found only in pairs or small parties, although they are widespread throughout their range. Male and female look alike, with yellowish underparts and olive-green plumage on the back, wings and head; in juveniles, the head and mantle are the same color. These birds creep through undergrowth and dense vegetation in search of seeds and berries to eat and will also cling to the trunks of trees like woodpeckers, looking for insects under the bark.

The flimsy nest is neatly made from tendrils, grass and some stems and is well hidden in dense cover. The female lays 2 eggs.

NAME: **Leaflove,** *Phyllastrephus scandens*
RANGE: **Africa: Senegal to Sudan, Uganda, Tanzania**
HABITAT: **forest**
SIZE: **22 cm (8½ in)**

The charmingly named leaflove is a mostly dusky, gray-green bird, with creamy-white and yellow underparts. Male and female look alike; the juvenile is duller and paler. These birds are completely arboreal, frequenting thickets, often near streams, and climbing among the foliage, looking for insects to eat. They move about in small parties, chattering incessantly; when disturbed they become extremely noisy.

The cup-shaped nest is made from fine grass and leaves and is often slung between the stems of a vine or creeper. There are normally 2 eggs.

NAME: **Black-eyed/White-vented Bulbul,** *Pycnonotus barbatus*
RANGE: **Africa**
HABITAT: **gardens, woodland, coastal scrub, open forest**
SIZE: **18 cm (7 in)**

Both male and female black-eyed bulbuls have grayish-white plumage on breast and belly and white undertail coverts. In fact, albinism is not uncommon in this species. The head appears slightly crested when the feathers are raised on the nape. These are tame, lively birds and have a habit of warbling briefly and slightly raising their wings when they land. They seem to eat equal quantities of fruit and insects.

The nest is neatly cup shaped, lightly made from grass and a few dead leaves, and is often suspended in the fork between two twigs. The female normally lays a clutch of 2 or 3 eggs.

## PYCNONOTIDAE: Bulbul Family

The bulbuls are a family of about 120 species, found in forest, orchards and cultivated land in tropical regions of Africa in particular but also in Madagascar, southern Asia and Southeast Asia. With a few exceptions, they are noisy, gregarious birds of medium size, with shortish wings and comparatively long tails. Beaks are long and notched, with stiff bristles at the base. Some forms possess a crest. Males and females look alike, although occasionally the male is larger.

Their food consists mainly of fruit, berries, buds, flower nectar and insects removed from vegetation.

NAME: **Red-whiskered Bulbul,** *Pycnonotus jocosus*
RANGE: **India, S.E. Asia, S. China, Andaman Islands; introduced in USA, Australia, Nicobar Islands, Mauritius**
HABITAT: **low scrub, cultivated land near villages, gardens, orchards**
SIZE: **20.5 cm (8 in)**

This widespread bird is locally abundant throughout its range. It is named for the tufts of deep-red feathers that sprout, like a mustache, on each side of the head; it also has red undertail feathers. Male and female look alike, but the tufts are white in the juvenile. It is a sprightly, cheerful bird, with a musical call, and in the summer, dozens can be seen feasting together in fruit trees. They do a great deal of damage to the crop, since they eat both green and ripe fruit; they also eat the insects they come across when feeding.

The cup-shaped nest is made from grass, roots and stalks, lined with fine grass, and, characteristically, some dry leaves and pieces of fern are woven into the bottom of it. The female lays 2 to 4 eggs.

NAME: **Crested Finchbill,** *Spizixos canifrons*
RANGE: **Assam to S.W. China, Burma, Laos, Tonkin**
HABITAT: **deciduous and evergreen forest**
SIZE: **20.5 cm (8 in)**

This handsome bird has a black crest, which, when erected, hangs forward, and a thick, finchlike beak; these characteristics give it its common name. Male and female look alike. Also known as the crested finch-billed bulbul, this bird is a typical bulbul in its habits, traveling in flocks of up to 100 through the trees and undergrowth and calling constantly with a typically chattering note. It feeds on seeds and fruit and on insects, which it often takes in the air, flycatcher-fashion. It is one of the few birds to profit by the slash-and-burn agricultural methods of the seminomadic tribes in its habitat, for it flourishes where scattered low trees grow through dense undergrowth.

The distinctive cup-shaped nest is always made from corkscrew tendrils of a vine, sometimes with a few twigs added, and is placed low in a tangle of bushes and brambles. There are 2 or 3, rarely 4, eggs.

NAME: **Black Bulbul,** *Hypsipetes madagascariensis*
RANGE: **Madagascar, Seychelles, S. and S.E. Asia to Taiwan, S. China**
HABITAT: **mountain forest up to 3,000 m (10,000 ft)**
SIZE: **25.5 cm (10 in)**

The bold, noisy black bulbul lives entirely in the trees, scarcely coming down even to the undergrowth. Its flight is swift and agile, but its legs and feet are weak, so it does not hop about in the branches but flies everywhere. It feeds on berries and may catch flies or other insects, which it snaps up when they visit flowers for their nectar.

The nest is cup shaped and made of coarse grass, dry leaves and moss, bound outside with spider's webs and lined with fine grass, moss roots and pine needles. Male and female birds appear to be very attached to each other, and while the female is sitting on her 2 to 4 eggs, the male remains close to her.

NAME: **White-throated Bulbul,** *Criniger flaveolus*
RANGE: **Himalayas in India, China: Yunnan Province, Burma**
HABITAT: **humid forest with thick undergrowth**
SIZE: **23 cm (9 in)**

These large, crested bulbuls are usually found in rowdy parties of 6 to 15 birds. They behave rather like laughing-thrushes, chattering to each other as they climb about in the trees and bushes or fly in a stream from one dense patch of jungle undergrowth to another. They are seldom found more than about 3 m (10 ft) from the ground, where they forage for berries, wild figs and insects, which they sometimes take on the wing. Their flight is strong and direct, and when they perch, they fan out their tails.

Both male and female help to build a substantial nest from fine roots, bamboo leaves and dead leaves; the nest is well concealed in the cover of vines or brambles about 1 m (3¼ ft) from the ground. The female lays 3 or 4 eggs, which both parents incubate for 13 days.

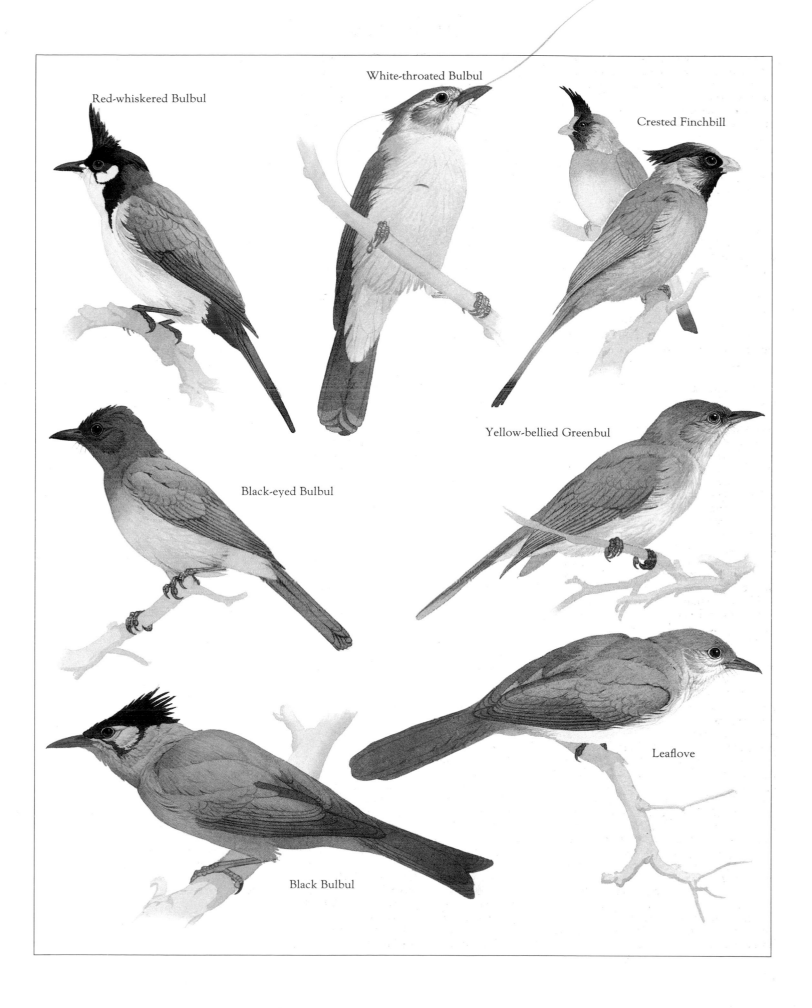

Red-whiskered Bulbul

White-throated Bulbul

Crested Finchbill

Yellow-bellied Greenbul

Black-eyed Bulbul

Leaflove

Black Bulbul

# Bulbuls, Leafbirds

NAME: **Bristlebill,** *Bleda syndactyla*
RANGE: **Africa: S. Sudan, Kenya, Uganda, Zaire**
HABITAT: **dense forest**
SIZE: **21.5 cm (8½ in)**

The bristlebill is a large, heavily built bird, with olive-brown plumage on the upperparts and a yellow throat and belly. Like all bulbuls, it has tufts of bristles near the bill base. Male and female look alike; the juvenile is duller and more rusty colored. The bill of the male is larger and more hooked than that of the female. These uncommon birds are shy and alert and difficult to observe as they move around in small trees and forest undergrowth; consequently little is known of their habits.

They are known to build a shallow, cup-shaped nest from leaves, sticks and plant fibers and to lay 2 eggs.

NAME: **Nicator,** *Nicator chloris*
RANGE: **Africa, south of the Sahara**
HABITAT: **tropical forest, thick woodland, scrub**
SIZE: **21.5 cm (8½ in)**

This shy forest bird is inconspicuous, often revealing itself only by a burst of clear, chattering song or by grunting, almost squirrel-like calls. It lives among the lower branches of trees or in dense undergrowth, feeding on plant matter and insects. Male and female look alike, but the juvenile has paler plumage on the upperparts and narrower, more pointed tail feathers.

Normally 2 eggs are laid in a nest that is either a shallow grass cup or a flat platform of stalks and tendrils, sited in the cover of thick vegetation.

NAME: **Hook-billed Bulbul,** *Setornis criniger*
RANGE: **Borneo, Sumatra, Bankga Island**
HABITAT: **primary lowland forest**
SIZE: **19 cm (7½ in)**

This bold and busy bird shows itself clearly as it moves about among the branches, searching for beetles, dragonfly nymphs, and small, stoneless berries. Usually seen alone, sometimes in pairs, hook-billed bulbuls are silent, only occasionally calling with loud, harsh cries. Males, females and juveniles look alike, the plumage of the young birds merely being duller.

No information is available on the birds' mating and nesting behavior.

## IRENIDAE: Leafbird Family

This family consists of 14 species, divided into 3 relatively distinct groups of songbirds: ioras, leafbirds and fairy bluebirds. All occur in southern and Southeast Asia, generally in forest, but in inhabited areas they are also found in gardens and orchards.

The family is probably closely related to the bulbuls. All forms have short legs, a moderately long bill and long, dense, somewhat fluffy plumage. The 4 species of iora are the smallest members of the family, some no bigger than 12.5 cm (5 in) long; they are mostly insect eaters and tend to be solitary birds. The leafbirds are larger and, as their name suggests, bright green in color. The 8 species consume fruit and berries, as well as insects, pollen and nectar. They are gregarious birds, moving in flocks through the forest canopy. The remaining group, the fairy bluebirds, consists of only 2 species of 25.5-cm (10-in) long, brilliant blue birds. They are highly arboreal and gregarious in their habits and gather in small flocks; they feed on fruit. In all species in the family, male and female look unalike, females usually being duller than males.

NAME: **Common Iora,** *Aegithina tiphia*
RANGE: **India to S.E. Asia, Java, Sumatra, Borneo**
HABITAT: **open country and gardens up to 1,700 m (5,600 ft)**
SIZE: **12.5 cm (5 in)**

There are considerable variations in coloration in this species, according to both sex and season. The male, in winter, tends to lose almost all his black feathers, and the yellow ones become paler; the female is green above and yellow below throughout the year, merely becoming paler in winter. Both sexes have noticeably soft and abundant feathers on their rumps. Ioras are frequently found in gardens, hopping inconspicuously about among the branches of trees and shrubs. They feed on insects, such as caterpillars, ants and beetles, and also on seeds.

In the breeding season, the male displays by flying up, fluffing out his feathers — particularly those on the rump — until he looks like a ball, then spiraling down to a perch. At the same time, he makes a strange croaking noise, rather like a frog. The nest is a neat structure, finely made from soft grass, covered in spider's webs, in which 2 to 4 eggs are laid.

NAME: **Gold-fronted Leafbird,** *Chloropsis aurifrons*
RANGE: **India, Sri Lanka, S.E. Asia, Sumatra**
HABITAT: **forest fringe, open country, gardens, damp hill country to 900 m (3,000 ft)**
SIZE: **18 cm (7 in)**

Despite their bright coloration, these arboreal birds are seldom seen, except when they fly briefly from clump to clump of trees or attract attention by calling or imitating other birds. The male is brilliant green, with a blue throat patch and a bright orange crown. With this primarily green plumage, leafbirds blend well with foliage. They are extremely agile and acrobatic in the trees, even swinging from the branches as if on a trapeze. They live in pairs or small groups, feeding among the leaves on insects, particularly caterpillars, spiders, berries and the nectar of the flowers of the coral tree (*Erythrina*), loranthus and the silk cotton tree. As they search for nectar, they may incidentally pollinate plants.

The small, cup-shaped nest is built among thickly growing foliage at the outer end of a branch, high up in a tree, and consequently is rarely found. The female lays 2 or 3 eggs and is thought to incubate them alone.

NAME: **Fairy Bluebird,** *Irena puella*
RANGE: **India to S.E. Asia, Greater Sunda and Andaman Islands, Philippines: Palawan**
HABITAT: **hill forest to 1,700 m (5,600 ft)**
SIZE: **25.5 cm (10 in)**

Fairy bluebirds are almost totally arboreal, preferring to spend their time high up in the branches of evergreen trees near running water. Males, particularly, are shy birds, not often clearly seen except when they come down to drink or bathe, when their striking coloration — bright ultramarine upperparts, with velvety black below — and red eyes make them conspicuous. Females are duller, with peacock-green and blackish-brown plumage. These birds feed mainly on the nectar of the flowers of the coral tree (*Erythrina*), and on fruit, especially ripe figs, often in the company of hornbills and pigeons.

The nest is built 3 to 6.5 m (10 to 21 ft) up in a small tree, in the darkest part of the forest, and is made of roots and twigs, covered with moss. Usually 2 eggs are laid.

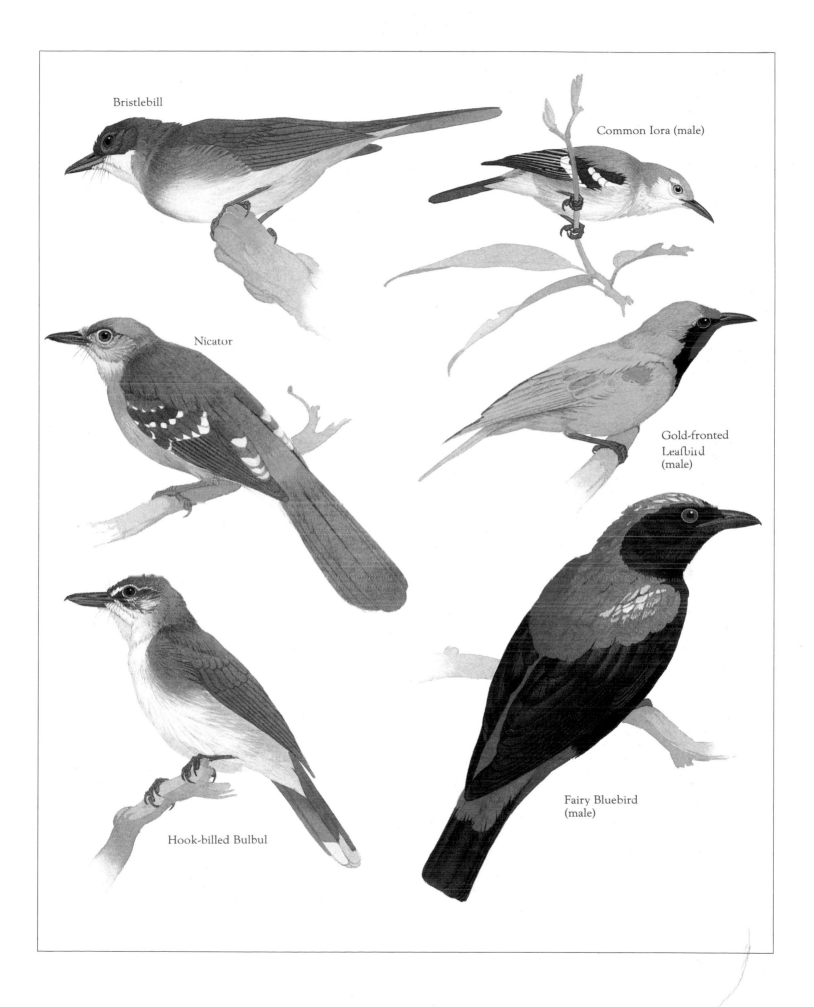

Bristlebill

Common Iora (male)

Nicator

Gold-fronted
Leafbird
(male)

Hook-billed Bulbul

Fairy Bluebird
(male)

# Shrikes

**NAME: Bornean Bristlehead,** *Pityriasis gymnocephala*
**RANGE:** Borneo
**HABITAT:** lowland forest to 1,200 m (4,000 ft), peat swamp, forest
**SIZE:** 25.5 cm (10 in)

This rare shrike has a large, extremely heavy, hooked bill and relatively short tail feathers, which gives it a top-heavy look. In keeping with their massive appearance, these birds are ponderous fliers, which keep to the middle layers of the forest. They feed on insects and their larvae, mainly beetles, grasshoppers and cockroaches, and also some spiders, noisily snapping them up with their large bills.

**NAME: Black-backed Puffback,** *Dryoscopus cubla*
**RANGE:** Africa: Kenya, west and south to Angola and South Africa
**HABITAT:** open woodland, gardens, scrub
**SIZE:** 15 cm (6 in)

There are 4 races of black-backed puffback; the race illustrated here is found in South Africa, and the other 3 occur throughout the rest of the range. The female is duller and paler than the male, with pale yellow eyes. When excited, this bird puffs up the feathers on its back and rump until it looks like a ball. These sociable little birds are usually found in pairs or in small parties with other bird species, hunting among the leaves of shrubs and trees for insect larvae. They often take insects in flight and, in the breeding season, eat the eggs and young of small birds.

The cup-shaped nest is made from bark fiber and rootlets, well hidden and bound to the fork of a tree with spider's webs. There are 2 or 3 eggs.

**NAME: Gray-headed Bush-shrike,** *Malaconotus blanchoti*
**RANGE:** Africa, south of the Sahara (not extreme south)
**HABITAT:** woodland, acacia trees, often near water (East Africa)
**SIZE:** 25.5 cm (10 in)

Despite their size and quite bright coloration, these birds are not easily seen in the thick foliage of the trees and bushes they frequent. Most often they can be located by their calls — either a brisk, chattering sound or a two- or three-note whistle. They have big, hooked bills and, in South Africa, are known to take prey as large as mice and lizards, which they find among leaf litter on the ground. Male and female look alike.

The conspicuous nest is built close to the ground. It is either a rough heap of grass and leaves or a platform of twigs with an inner cup, in which 2 or 3, rarely 4, eggs are laid.

## LANIIDAE: Shrike Family

This family of 65 species of songbird is divided into 4 subfamilies: the bushshrikes and helmet shrikes of Africa, the aberrant bristlehead of Borneo and the true shrikes of North America, Europe, Africa and Asia.

Shrikes are aggressive, insectivorous or carnivorous birds. They have strong, hooked beaks, with which they kill large insects and small reptiles, birds and mammals. Many species impale prey on thorns or hang it in the forks of branches, to be eaten later, hence one of their common names — butcherbird. They have strong legs and feet with sharp claws, which are used for manipulating prey during dismemberment. The tail is long and often rounded. Male and female look alike in some species, unalike in others.

Most shrikes inhabit areas with a mixture of tall vegetation and open spaces. Typically they keep watch from a high vantage point, swooping down to the ground to take prey or else catching it flycatcher fashion, on the wing, then returning to the perch.

**NAME: Northern Shrike,** *Lanius excubitor*
**RANGE:** widespread in N. America, Asia, Europe, N. Africa; winters south of breeding range
**HABITAT:** varied: woodland, open country, marsh, tundra, savanna, desert
**SIZE:** 24 cm (9½ in)

Northern shrikes perch in a prominent position and from there fly out to capture their prey: mainly insects, although small birds, mammals, reptiles and frogs are also taken. Normally they return to the perch to eat, but will sometimes store food and eat it later. They defend their territory strongly against all intruders, even hawks, and like hawks, they hover when hunting. The female looks like the male but is duller, with crescent-shaped markings on the underparts; the juvenile is even more heavily marked.

The bulky nest is built by both birds from twigs, moss and grass and is usually placed about 12 m (40 ft) from the ground. In the north, the female lays 5 to 7 eggs, which she incubates for 14 to 16 days. Fewer eggs are laid at a time in the south, but there may be two clutches in a year. This shrike is one of only 2 species found in North America; the other is the loggerhead shrike, *L. ludovicianus*, which is fairly similar to the northern shrike both in its appearance and its habits.

**NAME: White/Straight-crested Helmet Shrike,** *Prionops plumata*
**RANGE:** Africa: S. Ethiopia to Angola, Namibia, northern South Africa
**HABITAT:** open bush country, woodland
**SIZE:** 20.5 cm (8 in)

The tame and gregarious white helmet shrikes live in small flocks of 8 to 12 birds. They always move close together through the lower branches of trees and bushes, where they forage for insects, often in company with birds of other species. Male and female look alike.

Even when breeding, white helmet shrikes are sociable, and a number of birds will share the brooding and feeding at a single nest. Normally 3 or 4 eggs are laid.

**NAME: Crimson-breasted Shrike,** *Laniarius atrococcineus*
**RANGE:** Africa: southern E. Africa to Angola, South Africa
**HABITAT:** thorn veld, acacia bush
**SIZE:** 20.5 cm (8 in)

Surprisingly, these strikingly marked birds are not easy to see in the dense cover of the thornbushes they prefer, but they are not timid and, as soon as they come out into the open, they are conspicuous. Male and female look alike, the juvenile is duller, with crimson feathers only under the tail. Crimson-breasted shrikes usually travel in pairs, keeping in touch by calling, the male with a clear, deep whistle that the female answers with a throaty, growling sound. They feed mainly on insects.

The nest is a shallow cup, made from grass, plant fibers and dry bark, and is sited in the forked branch of a thorn tree. The female lays 2 or 3 eggs.

**NAME: Long-tailed Shrike,** *Corvinella melanoleuca*
**RANGE:** Africa: Kenya, Tanzania, Mozambique across to S. Angola
**HABITAT:** open country with scattered trees and bush
**SIZE:** 35.5–38 cm (14–15 in)

The black and white plumage of this large bird resembles that of a magpie, and it is also known as the magpie shrike. Male and female look alike; the juvenile is duller. Despite its striking coloration and its habit of sitting conspicuously on the tops of trees, this shrike is a rather shy bird. It usually moves in pairs or small parties, often with other bird species, and feeds on insects, which it catches on the ground by dropping down on them from a high perch. Long-tailed shrikes often skewer their prey on a thorn before eating it.

The nest is a bulky, untidy structure, sited among thorny branches, and is usually made of thorny twigs. There are normally 3 or 4 eggs.

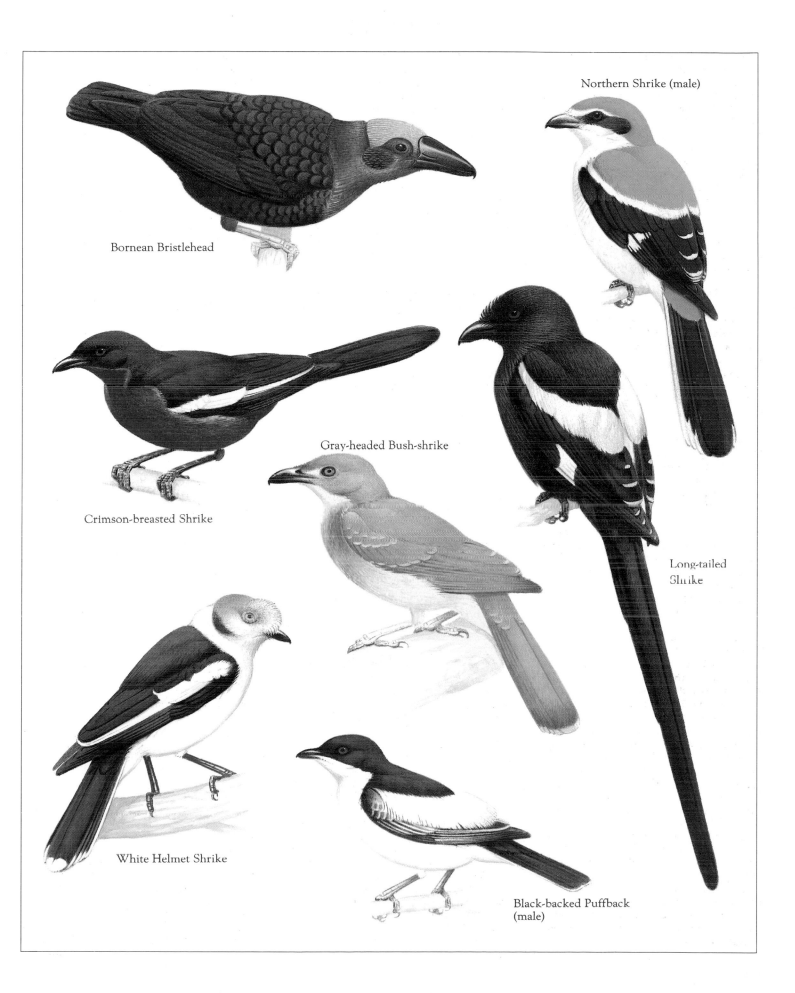

Bornean Bristlehead

Northern Shrike (male)

Crimson-breasted Shrike

Gray-headed Bush-shrike

Long-tailed
Shrike

White Helmet Shrike

Black-backed Puffback
(male)

# Vangas, Waxwings, Palm Chat

## VANGIDAE: Vanga Family

There are about 12 species of vanga, which are restricted to the island of Madagascar. They seem to have evolved from a shrikelike ancestor and are predators in the shrike fashion. Male and female do not look alike.

NAME: **Coral-billed Nuthatch**, *Hypositta corallirostris*
RANGE: **E. Madagascar**
HABITAT: **humid forest**
SIZE: **13 cm (5 in)**

The coral-billed nuthatch has been a taxonomical problem for ornithologists. It feeds like a treecreeper and looks somewhat like a nuthatch, but, more recently, it has been regarded as a close, but highly aberrant relative of the vangas. A brightly colored little bird, it clings with its feet to the bark on the upper part of tree trunks while it searches diligently in cracks and crevices for insects to eat. The female and young are blue above, with gray underparts.

NAME: **Hook-billed Vanga**, *Falculea palliata*
RANGE: **Madagascar**
HABITAT: **forest and secondary brush to 1,800 m (6,000 ft), mangrove swamps**
SIZE: **25 cm (9¾ in)**

These birds are usually seen alone or in pairs among the larger branches of trees, where they move about slowly and deliberately, searching for their prey. Their strong beaks, with sharply hooked tips, and the fact that they respond to squeaks and cheeping sounds suggest that they may eat small mammals and young birds, in addition to the chameleons, lizards, frogs and insects that are known to be part of their diet.

NAME: **Sicklebill**, *Vanga curvirostris*
RANGE: **Madagascar**
HABITAT: **woodland, dense savanna, forest edge, mangrove swamps**
SIZE: **32 cm (12½ in) including bill**

This vanga is more like the woodhoopoe, *Phoeniculus*, in appearance and habits than it is like the vangas, shrikes or sturnids, with which it has been classed. A party of up to 25 birds will suddenly appear in a patch of woodland, where, like woodhoopoes, they run about on the tree trunks and branches. They even hang upside down by their claws while they poke their long, curved beaks into crevices in the bark in search of large insects to eat.

The female builds a well-hidden nest from twigs some 12 m (40 ft) up in a tall, isolated tree. It is not known how many eggs are laid, since none has yet been found.

## BOMBYCILLIDAE: Waxwing Family

This complex family of songbirds is sometimes divided into 3 separate families, although it is here considered as a single rather heterogeneous assemblage. The waxwings proper, with 3 species, are found in high latitudes of the northern hemisphere, but they occasionally migrate south to Europe, central China, Japan and even Central America in the winter. Male and female look almost alike, with soft, silky plumage and crested heads. They feed on fruit and berries.

The silky flycatchers of the New World are a group of 7 species which also have prominent crests and eat berries. The gray hypocolius from southwest Asia is the only member of its group. It feeds on fruit and berries, and some insects are also taken.

NAME: **Gray Silky Flycatcher**, *Ptilogonys cinereus*
RANGE: **N. Mexico to Guatemala**
HABITAT: **oak and pine forest at 1,200–3,000 m (4,000 to 10,000 ft)**
SIZE: **21 cm (8¼ in)**

With their soft, silky plumage, these flycatchers resemble the waxwings, but their long, narrow tails are like those of the flycatchers, and it is this that gives them their common name. In fact, they live largely on fruit and berries, especially mistletoe berries, although they do also capture flying insects in the air. Silky flycatchers are usually found in small flocks outside the breeding season.

The female builds the nest high in a tree, using twigs and fibers bound together with spider's webs. She lays 2 or 3 eggs.

NAME: **Bohemian Waxwing**, *Bombycilla garrulus*
RANGE: **circumpolar regions of N. America, Europe and Asia**
HABITAT: **tall coniferous forest of the taiga**
SIZE: **18 cm (7 in)**

The name "waxwing" is derived from the drop-shaped and waxlike tips of the secondary wing feathers that are, in fact, elongations of the feathers' shafts. The sexes look much alike, except that the female's plumage is duller. Waxwings normally live on fruit and berries, although they will catch insects on the wing during the breeding season. In winter they sometimes migrate south of their range.

During his courtship display, the male presents the female with a berry or ant pupa, which the birds then pass back and forth from beak to beak but never swallow. The bulky nest is made from twigs, moss and plant fibers, mainly by the female, who lays 3 to 7 eggs, which she alone incubates.

NAME: **Gray Hypocolius**, *Hypocolius ampelinus*
RANGE: **N. Africa to Iran and India**
HABITAT: **semidesert**
SIZE: **23 cm (9 in)**

The unique gray hypocolius is generally a sociable bird, and outside the breeding season small parties of them are found eating fruit and berries, such as nightshade, mulberries, figs and, particularly, dates. They also take some insects. The female looks very much like the male, lacking only the black feathers on the head that can be erected into a small crest; juveniles are a buffy-brown, with no black on the tail. These are shy, slow-moving birds, like the waxwings, but their flight is strong and straight.

Both male and female hypocolius help to build the large, cup-shaped nest, which is usually well hidden among the leaves of a palm tree. It is roughly constructed from twigs and lined with soft plant matter and hair; the female lays 4 or 5 eggs. If the birds are disturbed, they will desert the nest and are reputed to return and destroy it, only to build a new one a week or so later.

## DULIDAE: Palm Chat Family

Previously considered as a member of the waxwing group, the palm chat from the West Indies is now regarded as constituting a family of its own.

NAME: **Palm Chat**, *Dulus dominicus*
RANGE: **West Indies: Hispaniola, Île de la Gonâve**
HABITAT: **open country with Royal Palms (*Roystonea*)**
SIZE: **17.5 cm (6¾ in)**

The plumage of the palm chat is thick and rough, quite different from that of the waxwings. Male and female look alike, but the juvenile has a dark throat and neck and a buff-colored rump. Palm chats are sociable birds which live in pairs or in groups of 2 to 5 pairs in a large communal nest about 1 m (3¼ ft) in diameter. The nest is loosely made from dry twigs, woven around the trunk and the base of the fronds of a royal palm tree. Within this structure, each pair of birds has a separate area, divided off from the others and with its own entrance. Here they roost and, in an inner chamber, raise their 2 to 4 young.

Palm chats feed on berries from the palms and other plants and also eat flowers.

Coral-billed Nuthatch (male)

Sicklebill (male)

Hook-billed Vanga

Bohemian Waxwing

Gray Hypocolius (male)

Gray Silky Flycatcher (male)

Palm Chat

# Wrens

TROGLODYTIDAE: Wren Family

**NAME: Winter Wren,** *Troglodytes troglodytes*
**RANGE: Iceland, Europe, N.W. Africa, Middle East, east to E. China, Japan; S. Canada, E. USA and Pacific coast**
**HABITAT: undergrowth in coniferous forest, gardens, heaths and parks**
**SIZE: 9.5–11.5 cm (3¾–4½ in)**

The only wren to occur in the Old World, this species is a plump bird with a short tail, which is almost always held cocked up, and a loud, vibrant song. An extremely active little bird, the winter wren forages in dense undergrowth for insects, mainly larvae, as well as for spiders and a few berries.

The breeding season begins in April in most of the range. These wrens are polygamous in some areas, and the male makes several nests, in which he may install mates. The nest is a bulky, domed structure, made of twigs, moss, grass and rootlets and situated in a protected cavity in a bank or among tree roots or in a hollow stump. The male may also make "dummy" nests, which are not actually used but may help to divert potential predators. Having lined her chosen nest with hair and feathers, the female bird lays 4 to 16 eggs (usually 5 or 6), which she incubates for 14 to 16 days. The young are fed by the female and fly at 16 or 17 days. Some populations migrate south of the breeding range in winter.

**NAME: House Wren,** *Troglodytes aedon*
**RANGE: S. Canada through USA and Central and South America; Trinidad and Tobago**
**HABITAT: woodland, gardens, parks**
**SIZE: 11–14 cm (4¼–5½ in)**

The common, widespread house wren is one of the plainest wrens, with gray-brown plumage and a faint stripe above each eye. It feeds on a wide variety of insects, such as crickets, beetles, ants, flies and caterpillars, as well as on some spiders and snails. House wrens winter to the south of their breeding range and migrate north again in spring.

Males arrive at breeding areas before females and build nests of twigs, leaves and other plant material. Nests are usually sited in cavities in trees or rocks but may be built almost anywhere that there is some degree of shelter and protection. When the females arrive, each selects a nest, which she lines with feathers, wool and hair. The female lays up to 9 eggs, usually 6 to 8, which she incubates for 13 to 15 days. The young leave the nest 12 to 18 days after hatching.

There are many subspecies of house wren; two Caribbean races are endangered and thought to be near extinction.

**TROGLODYTIDAE: Wren Family**

There are about 60 species of wren in the world, all except one confined to the Americas. The exceptional species is the bird known as the wren in Europe and the winter wren in North America.

The wren family is closely related to the dipper and mockingbird families. Most wrens are between 10 and 23 cm (4 and 9 in) long and are generally brown in color, with barred patterning. Wings are short and bodies plump, and a number of forms have stumpy tails, which can be cocked upward. Male and female look alike or nearly so.

Wrens occur in a wide range of habitats, including rain forest, cooler wooded areas, marshes, deserts, moorland and mountains. Where possible, they frequent dense, low vegetation, where they hunt for insects and other invertebrate prey with great agility and speed. They are excellent and varied songsters, often with loud vocal repertoires for birds of their size. In many species both sexes sing (not just the males), and some tropical wrens are known to perform "duets." Wrens generally produce two or more broods a season. The eggs are incubated by the female in most species, but both parents care for the young until they are able to fly, 2 or 3 weeks after hatching.

**NAME: Cactus Wren,** *Campylorhynchus brunneicapillus*
**RANGE: S.W. USA to central Mexico**
**HABITAT: desert, arid scrubland**
**SIZE: 18–22 cm (7–8½ in)**

The largest North American wren, the cactus wren has a distinctive white stripe over each eye and a longer-than-usual tail, which it does not normally cock up. Cactus wrens frequent areas with thorny shrubs, cacti and trees and forage mostly on the ground around vegetation for insects, such as beetles, ants, wasps and grasshoppers, and occasionally lizards or small frogs. Some cactus fruit and berries and seeds are also eaten. The wrens can run swiftly but usually fly if traveling any distance. Nests are made for roosting in at night and for shelter in bad weather.

The breeding season begins in March or April, and there may be two or three broods. The nest is a bulky, domed structure, made of plant fibers, twigs and dead leaves, with a tubelike side entrance that can be up to 15 cm (6 in) long; it is lined with fur or feathers. The nest is situated on a prickly cholla cactus or amid the sharp leaves of a yucca or other thorny bush. From 3 to 7 eggs, usually 4 or 5, are laid and then incubated by the female for about 16 days.

**NAME: Long-billed Marsh Wren,** *Cistothorus palustris*
**RANGE: S. Canada, USA, Mexico**
**HABITAT: marshes**
**SIZE: 10–14 cm (4–5½ in)**

The distinctive little marsh wren has a dark head, stripy markings on its back and a white streak above each eye. It lives among dense vegetation in marshland and feeds on aquatic insects.

The male builds several "dummy" nests before the female arrives in the breeding area. She, however, does most of the building of the nest that is actually used — a large coconut-shaped structure, which is lashed to bulrushes or other upright vegetation and which is made of water-soaked sedges and grasses, woven with rootlets and stems. There is a tubelike side opening, and the interior cavity is lined with feathers and shredded plant material. The 3 to 10, usually 5 or 6, eggs are incubated by the female for 13 to 16 days.

**NAME: Bewick's Wren,** *Thryomanes bewickii*
**RANGE: S.W. and central Canada, USA, Mexico**
**HABITAT: open woodland, thickets, gardens, pastures**
**SIZE: 14 cm (5½ in)**

Bewick's wren has a long, slim bill, which it uses to forage on the ground and on vegetation for insects, such as beetles, ants and caterpillars, as well as for spiders. It will also delve into crevices in buildings for food.

The nest is made by both partners of a breeding pair in almost any available cavity in a tree, rock or building, or in any hollow object, natural or man-made. It is cup shaped and constructed with sticks, bark, leaves, moss and other plant material and lined with feathers. The female lays 4 to 11, usually 5 to 7, eggs, which she incubates for 14 days.

**NAME: Rock Wren,** *Salpinctes obsoletus*
**RANGE: S.W. Canada, W. USA, south to Costa Rica**
**HABITAT: dry rocky valleys, cliffs**
**SIZE: 13–15 cm (5–6 in)**

A pale-plumaged bird, the rock wren blends well with its habitat. It frequents arid, bare country, where it clambers with great agility among rocks, searching for insects and spiders.

The nest is built by both members of a pair in a crevice in a rock, a pile of stones or a burrow and is made of grass, rootlets and stems, lined with fur and feathers. Although the nest is carefully concealed, there may be a path of small pebbles leading up to it, and the entrance to the nest cavity itself may be lined with stones, bones and other debris. The female usually lays 5 or 6 eggs, which she incubates.

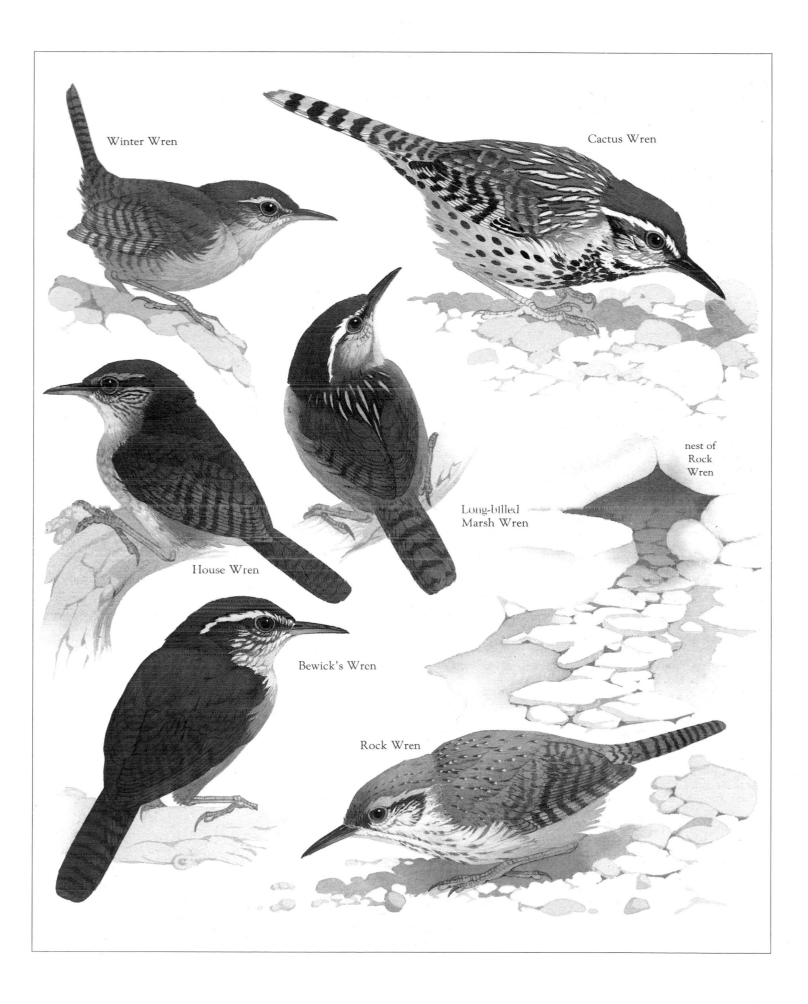

Winter Wren

Cactus Wren

House Wren

Long-billed
Marsh Wren

nest of
Rock
Wren

Bewick's Wren

Rock Wren

# Mockingbirds, Dippers, Accentors

## MIMIDAE: Mockingbird Family
Only about half of the 31 or so members of this family are called mockingbirds, the others are known as catbirds, tremblers and thrashers. All live in the Americas, from Canada to Argentina, usually in wooded country and scrub, and feed on or near ground level on insects and other invertebrates, as well as on fruit and seeds. Typically, they are slim-bodied birds, with long legs and tails, and are well known for their ability to mimic the songs of other birds and sounds such as piano notes, barking dogs and sirens. Male and female look alike or nearly so.

NAME: **Galápagos Mockingbird,** *Nesomimus trifasciatus*
RANGE: **Galápagos Islands**
HABITAT: **varied**
SIZE: **25.5 cm (10 in)**

There are 9 subspecies of Galápagos mockingbird, one of which is now rare and found only on Champion and Gardner islets. Some ornithologists group these subspecies into 4 separate species. The birds appear to use all available habitats on the islands and to feed on anything they can find, mainly insects, fruit and berries, but also carrion and seabird's eggs.

The twig nest is built in a cactus or low tree and 2 to 5 eggs are laid.

NAME: **Mockingbird (Northern Mockingbird),** *Mimus polyglottos*
RANGE: **USA, south to Mexico; West Indies; introduced in Hawaii**
HABITAT: **open woodland, gardens, orchards**
SIZE: **23–28 cm (9–11 in)**

One of the best-known American songbirds and the state bird of five US states, the male mockingbird sings night and day, often mimicking other birds and other sounds. Mockingbirds are aggressive and hold territories, which they defend vigorously against all enemies; in winter, female birds hold their own separate territories. They feed on insects, particularly grasshoppers and beetles, and also on spiders, snails and small reptiles. Fruit, too, is an important part of the diet.

At the onset of the summer breeding season, males court mates, flashing the white markings on the wings as they make display flights. Both partners help to build the nest, from twigs, leaves and bits of debris such as paper and wool; the nest is placed in a low tree or bush. The female incubates the 3 to 6 eggs for 12 days, and both parents help to feed the young. There may be two or three broods a year.

NAME: **California Thrasher,** *Toxostoma redivivum*
RANGE: **USA: California; Mexico: Baja California**
HABITAT: **chaparral, mountain foothills, parks, gardens**
SIZE: **28–33 cm (11–13 in)**

This large thrasher has a distinctive, downward-curving, sickle-shaped bill, which it uses to rake through leaves and dig in the soil for insects and berries. Its wings are rather short, and it is an awkward bird in flight, so it lives mainly on the ground, where it runs with its long tail raised. The male bird sings for prolonged periods from a perch on a bush and is an excellent mimic; females also sing.

Both parents help to build a large, cup-shaped nest of plant material a meter or so off the ground, in a low tree or bush. They incubate the 2 to 4 eggs for about 14 days. The young leave the nest 12 to 14 days after hatching, but the male continues to feed them for a little longer, even while the second brood is being incubated by the female.

NAME: **Gray Catbird,** *Dumetella carolinensis*
RANGE: **S. Canada, USA (not S.W.); winters Central America and West Indies**
HABITAT: **woodland, forest edge, thickets, gardens**
SIZE: **20.5–24 cm (8–9½ in)**

Named for its mewing, catlike call, the gray catbird usually lives in dense vegetation, where it forages for insects and berries, mainly on the ground. At the end of the winter, catbirds migrate north to breeding grounds in huge flocks, often at night.

The males arrive at breeding areas and sing to attract females. They display to, and chase, their mates. Both partners of a pair help to build a ragged nest of plant material in a low tree or bush. The 2 to 6 eggs, usually 4, are incubated for 12 to 15 days, mostly by the female, but the male helps to feed the newly hatched young. There are usually two broods a season.

NAME: **Trembler,** *Cinclocerthia ruficauda*
RANGE: **West Indies**
HABITAT: **rain forest, woodland**
SIZE: **23–25.5 cm (9–10 in)**

Tremblers vary from dark brown to olive-gray, the Saint Lucia birds being the palest and grayest. They are identified by, and named for, their characteristic habit of violently shaking the wings and body. Their main foods are insects and invertebrates, most of which are found on the forest floor.

A nest is made in a cavity in a tree or tree fern, and the female lays 2 or 3 eggs.

## CINCLIDAE: Dipper Family
The 5 species of dipper live in Europe, Asia and North and South America, usually in upland country near swift mountain streams. They are the only passeriform birds to have adopted a truly aquatic way of life, yet they have no webs on their feet and few obvious special adaptations other than movable flaps to close off the nostrils when underwater. Propelling themselves with their wings, they swim and dive underwater, and they also appear to be able to walk on the bottoms of streams. Male and female look alike.

NAME: **Dipper,** *Cinclus mexicanus*
RANGE: **Alaska, through N.W. America to Panama**
HABITAT: **mountain streams**
SIZE: **18–22 cm (7–8½ in)**

A wren-shaped bird, the dipper has a compact body, long, stout legs and a short, square-tipped tail. Its bill is hooked and is notched at the tip. Like all dippers, it frequents mountain streams and walks or dives into the water, swims underwater and even walks on the bottom, to obtain insect and invertebrate prey, especially caddis fly larvae.

A bulky, domed nest, made of moss and grass, is built by the female on a rock in a stream or beside a stream among tree roots or rocks; it has a side entrance. The female lays 3 to 6 eggs, which she incubates for 15 to 17 days.

## PRUNELLIDAE: Accentor Family
Accentors are small, sparrowlike birds, with inconspicuous plumage, found in Europe and Asia. There are 12 species, all in the genus *Prunella*. Male and female birds look similar.

NAME: **Dunnock/Hedge Sparrow,** *Prunella modularis*
RANGE: **Europe, Asia, east to Urals, south to Lebanon**
HABITAT: **woodland, scrub, gardens**
SIZE: **15 cm (6 in)**

The little brown dunnock is distinguished by its slender bill and gray underparts. Mainly a ground-living species, it forages among fallen leaves and other debris for insects, larvae and, particularly in winter, seeds.

The neat, cup-shaped nest is made of twigs, grass and roots and is situated in a bush. The female lays from 3 to 6 eggs, which she incubates for 12 to 14 days; the male helps to feed the young. There may be two broods a season.

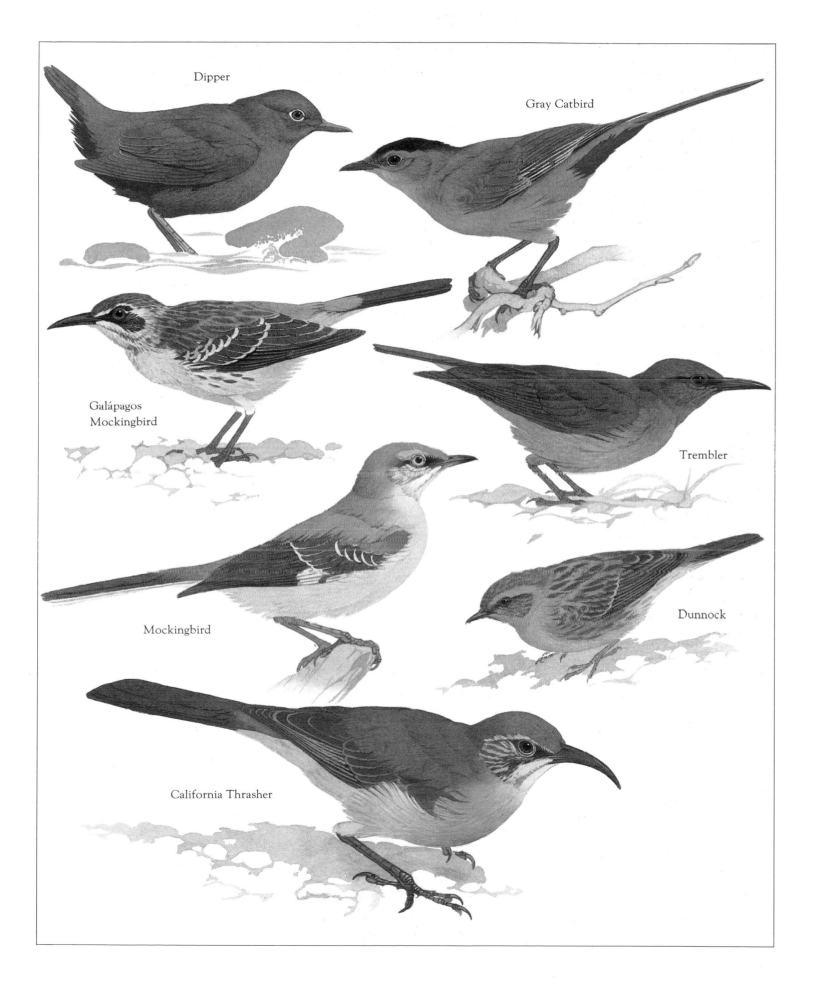

Dipper

Gray Catbird

Galápagos
Mockingbird

Trembler

Mockingbird

Dunnock

California Thrasher

# Thrushes

NAME: **White-browed/Blue Shortwing,**
*Brachypteryx montana*
RANGE: E. Nepal to W. and S. China,
south to S.E. Asia and Indonesia
HABITAT: forest undergrowth
SIZE: **15 cm (6 in)**

The male of this species is a distinctive
little bird with dark-blue plumage and
conspicuous, long white eyebrows;
females have brownish plumage, with
rusty-red markings on the forehead and
indistinct eyebrows. In some areas,
males are colored like females but with
white eyebrows. Shy, retiring birds,
they skulk around in the densest undergrowth, searching for insects, especially
beetles, and usually staying on or close
to the ground.

The globular nest is made on a tree
trunk or rock face, and the female lays
3 eggs.

NAME: **Karroo Scrub-robin,**
*Erythropygia coryphaeus*
RANGE: Africa: Namibia to South Africa:
Cape Province
HABITAT: arid, sandy regions
SIZE: **16 cm (6¼ in)**

An abundant, lively bird, the karroo
scrub-robin spends much of its time on
the ground, where it searches for insects,
as well as for seeds and berries when
available. It runs swiftly and darts for
cover if alarmed, after dancing around
and flicking its tail for a moment or two.

A cup-shaped nest, made of grass, is
built in a hollow in the ground, in a bush
or under vegetation. The female lays 2
or 3 eggs, which are incubated for 14 or
15 days.

NAME: **Nightingale,** *Erithacus*
(= *Luscinia*) *megarhynchos*
RANGE: Europe: S.E. England to
Mediterranean and N. Africa; east to
S.W. Siberia, Afghanistan; winters in
tropical Africa
HABITAT: woodland, thickets, hedgerows
SIZE: **16 cm (6¼ in)**

The nightingale sings from dawn to
dusk or even to midnight, and its
melodious song is its most characteristic
feature. Male and female look alike,
with brownish and creamy plumage. A
sturdy, solitary bird, the nightingale
skulks among dense vegetation, foraging for food, such as worms, insects and
larvae and berries on the ground. It
moves around with long hops, rarely
flying for other than short distances.

The breeding season begins in May,
and the female builds a nest of leaves on
or close to the ground, amid vegetation.
She lines the nest with grass or hair and
lays 4 or 5 eggs, which she incubates for
13 or 14 days. Both parents feed the
young, which are able to fly at about 11
or 12 days.

## MUSCICAPIDAE

This huge family of songbirds contains
over 1,000 species, formerly organized
in separate families. These are now
regarded as 13 closely related subfamilies of the Muscicapidae.

### TURDINAE: Thrush Subfamily

There are over 300 species in this subfamily, found almost all over the world
except on the polar ice caps and some
Pacific islands; formerly absent from
New Zealand, they have now been
introduced there. The group contains
not only the thrushes proper, in the
genus *Turdus*, but also robins, redstarts,
chats, wheatears, nightingales and
solitaires, among others. Male and
female look alike in some species but
differ in others.

Most members of the subfamily are
small to medium-sized songbirds — 10
to 33 cm (4 to 13 in) long — with slender
beaks. They are strong fliers, many
forms making regular, long migrations.
Insects and other invertebrates, such as
slugs, snails, worms and crustaceans,
make up the bulk of the diet for most
thrushes, but berries and other plant
foods are also eaten.

NAME: **Eurasian Robin,** *Erithacus*
*rubecula*
RANGE: Europe, Mediterranean islands,
N. Africa, east across Asia to Mongolia
HABITAT: forest, woodland, gardens
SIZE: **14 cm (5½ in)**

The familiar robin is easily identified by
its orange-red breast and face, separated
from the olive-brown upperparts by a
gray-blue border. Male and female look
alike. Although a shy forest bird over
much of its range, the robin has learned
to make use of humans and their gardens
in Britain and parts of western Europe
and has become a bold, easily tamed
species. Aggressive little birds, robins
live alone in winter, each defending its
territory against any intruders by presenting the red breast, with feathers erected, and emphasizing the warning color
by swaying from side to side. Robins
usually feed on the ground on small insects, larvae, spiders, worms and snails,
and on berries and small fruit in season.

In the breeding season, robins form
pairs, and males court before mating,
using a less aggressive form of the threat
display. The female then builds the cup-
shaped nest on an ivy-covered bank, in
a bush or hedge, in a hole in a tree or
stump or on a building or ledge. She lays
5 to 7 eggs, which she incubates for 12
to 14 days, and both parents feed the
young. There may be two or even three
broods a year.

NAME: **Red-flanked Bluetail,** *Erithacus*
(= *Tarsiger*) *cyanurus*
RANGE: Lapland, across N. Asia; winters
in S. Asia; separate population in
Himalayas and W. China
HABITAT: swampy coniferous forest,
open woodland
SIZE: **14 cm (5½ in)**

An attractive little bird, the red-flanked
bluetail has characteristic reddish-
orange patches on its sides. The male
has largely blue plumage, and this is
replaced in the female, except on the
tail, by olive-brown. It forages for food,
mainly insects, on the ground and in low
vegetation, quivering its tail as it moves;
it may also catch insects in the air.

The nest is made of moss and situated
in a hollow in the ground among moss
or tree roots. The female lays 3 to 7 eggs,
which she alone incubates.

NAME: **Robin Chat/Cape Robin,**
*Cossypha caffra*
RANGE: E. and S. Africa: S. Sudan to
Cape of Good Hope
HABITAT: forest, bush, cultivated areas,
town shrubberies
SIZE: **18 cm (7 in)**

Rather like the Eurasian robin, the
robin chat is usually a shy, retiring bird
but has become tame and accustomed to
man in inhabited areas. Male and female
look alike, and both have distinctive
white eye stripes. They feed mainly on
the ground on insects, spiders, worms,
small frogs and lizards and berries, but
dart for cover at any sign of danger.

The nest is made of moss and rootlets
and is situated in an overgrown tree
stump or on a well-vegetated bank. The
female lays 2 or 3 eggs, which she incubates for 13 to 19 days. Both parents
feed the nestlings for 14 to 18 days.

NAME: **Fire-crested Alethe,** *Alethe*
*diademata*
RANGE: Africa: Nigeria to Zaire and
Uganda
HABITAT: lowland forest
SIZE: **18 cm (7 in)**

One of 7 or so species of alethe living in
Africa, the fire-crested alethe is a bird of
dense forest and shady undergrowth.
Although it does not actually feed on
ants, it frequently watches army ants as
they march through the forest, in order
to catch the other insects that flee from
their path. Male and female birds look
alike, both with dark-brown plumage
and an orange streak of feathers along
the crown. When the bird is excited, it
erects this crest, while spreading its tail.

The cup-shaped nest is made of moss
and roots, lined with soft rootlets, and
is situated in a tree stump or among
heaps of debris on the forest floor. The
female lays 2 or 3 eggs.

White-browed Shortwing (male)

Red-flanked Bluetail (male)

Karroo Scrub-robin

Robin Chat

Eurasian Robin

Fire-crested Alethe

Nightingale

# Thrushes

NAME: **Black Redstart,** *Phoenicurus ochruros*
RANGE: **Europe, N. Africa, Asia, east to China and just into N. India**
HABITAT: **open rocky areas, near human habitation**
SIZE: **14 cm (5½ in)**

An adaptable bird, the black redstart has learned to live alongside humans in some areas. Both sexes have rusty-red tails, although the male's is brighter, and the male has dull black upperparts, while the female is brownish. The black redstart spends much of its time on the ground and also perches on rocks and buildings. Insects, caught on the ground and in flight, are its main food, but it also eats some berries. Holes in rocks and buildings are used as nighttime roosts.

The breeding season starts in early to late April, depending on the area. The female constructs a loose, cup-shaped nest from dry grass, moss and fibers, lined with hair, wool and feathers; it is situated on a cliff, rock or building or in a hollow tree. The female lays 4 to 6 eggs, which she incubates for 12 to 16 days. Both parents feed the young until they leave the nest 12 to 19 days after hatching. There are usually two broods, sometimes three.

NAME: **Eastern Bluebird,** *Sialia sialis*
RANGE: **N. America: S. Canada, east of the Rockies to Gulf Coast, USA; Mexico, Central America**
HABITAT: **open country, farmland, gardens, parks**
SIZE: **16.5–19 cm (6½–7½ in)**

A beautiful bird, the male eastern bluebird has distinctive, bright blue plumage on its upperparts; the female looks similar but has paler, duller plumage. The bluebird is beloved not only for its attractive appearance but also for its melodious song. It often perches in a hunched posture on wires and fences but takes most of its insect prey on the ground. Berries are also an important item of diet.

The male bluebird performs flight displays to court his mate and then both birds build a nest of grass, twigs and other plant material, lined with hair, fine grass and feathers. The nest is situated in a natural hole in a tree or stump, in an abandoned woodpecker hole or even in a bird box. The female lays 3 to 7 eggs, usually 4 or 5, which she incubates for 13 to 15 days, sometimes with assistance from her mate. The young are fed by both parents and leave the nest 15 to 20 days after hatching. There are usually two broods. Some northern populations migrate south for the winter.

NAME: **Magpie Robin,** *Copsychus saularis*
RANGE: **India, S. China, S.E. Asia, much of Indonesia, east to the Philippines**
HABITAT: **brush, gardens, cultivated land**
SIZE: **21.5 cm (8½ in)**

The male magpie robin has distinctive black and white plumage; the female looks similar but has dark-gray instead of black plumage. This widespread, common bird often lives near human habitation and feeds in the open, usually near or on the ground. A good mimic, the magpie robin imitates other birds but also has a loud, melodious song of its own, which it uses to announce its presence. Insects, such as crickets, beetles and ants, are its main foods.

The large, cup-shaped nest is made of fine roots and is situated among tree roots or branches or in any protected hole. The female lays 3 to 6 eggs, usually 5, which both parents incubate for 12 or 13 days.

NAME: **White-crowned Forktail,** *Enicurus leschenaulti*
RANGE: **Sikkim to S. China and Hainan, S.E. Asia to Bali**
HABITAT: **rocky streams in forest**
SIZE: **20.5–28 cm (8–11 in)**

Both male and female white-crowned forktails have similar, sharply contrasting plumage and long tails. These long-legged birds frequent streams and feed on aquatic insects, which they take from the water surface or the streambed. They wade from stone to stone, searching for food and occasionally dipping under the water in pursuit of prey.

The cup-shaped nest is always built in a damp area, often near a stream, and is generally sited on a rock, in a crevice or among stones or tree roots. The female lays 2 eggs.

NAME: **Andean Solitaire,** *Myadestes ralloides*
RANGE: **Central and South America: Costa Rica to N. Bolivia, Venezuela**
HABITAT: **mountain forest**
SIZE: **18 cm (7 in)**

The shy, secretive Andean solitaire usually lives between altitudes of 900 and 4,500 m (3,000 and 15,000 ft). It is an excellent songster and sings more or less throughout the year in a pure, clear voice. True to its name, the solitaire tends to live alone for much of the time, but birds are also found in pairs. Its bill is rather short and wide, and it feeds on fruit and insects.

A nest is made on the ground or in a tree, and about 3 eggs are laid and incubated for 12 or 13 days.

NAME: **Stonechat,** *Saxicola torquata*
RANGE: **Europe, Africa, W. and central Asia**
HABITAT: **moors, fields, hill scrub, agricultural land**
SIZE: **13 cm (5 in)**

The plump little stonechat is a lively, restless bird. It seldom moves on the ground but flies fast and perches in exposed spots, such as on a post or on top of a bush, to watch for insect prey; it also eats plant matter and grain. The female has paler, browner plumage than the male and her white markings are less distinct.

The breeding season begins between late March and early June, depending on area. The male displays to the female, spreading his wings and tail to show off his markings. The nest is usually made by the female from coarse grass, moss and plant stems, lined with hair, fine grass or feathers. It is sited in an open area on the ground, under cover of a bush or actually in a bush. The female lays 5 or 6 eggs, which she incubates for about 14 days, sometimes assisted by the male. The young remain in the nest for 12 or 13 days, being fed on insects by both parents. Some northern populations may migrate south in winter.

NAME: **Wheatear,** *Oenanthe oenanthe*
RANGE: **Europe, N.W. Africa, W. and central Asia, arctic N. America; winters mainly in Africa**
HABITAT: **open country, moors, tundra, heaths**
SIZE: **14 cm (5½ in)**

A widely distributed species, this is the only wheatear to have become established in the New World. In summer breeding plumage, the male has a grayish crown, black marks on the cheeks and a white stripe above each eye. Both sexes have distinctive white rumps, but the female is brownish and buff; in winter the male resembles the female. Primarily a ground-dweller, the wheatear finds much of its food, such as insects, spiders, centipedes and small mollusks, on the ground. It flits from one perch to another and may sometimes fly up to catch an insect on the wing.

In display, the male reveals his white rump to the female and dances with spread wings. The nest is made in open country in a hole on the ground, in a rock or wall, or in debris such as a can or drainpipe. The female lays 5 or 6 eggs, occasionally up to 8, which are incubated for about 14 days. She does most of the incubation, although the male may assist. Both parents feed the young, which remain in the nest for about 15 days.

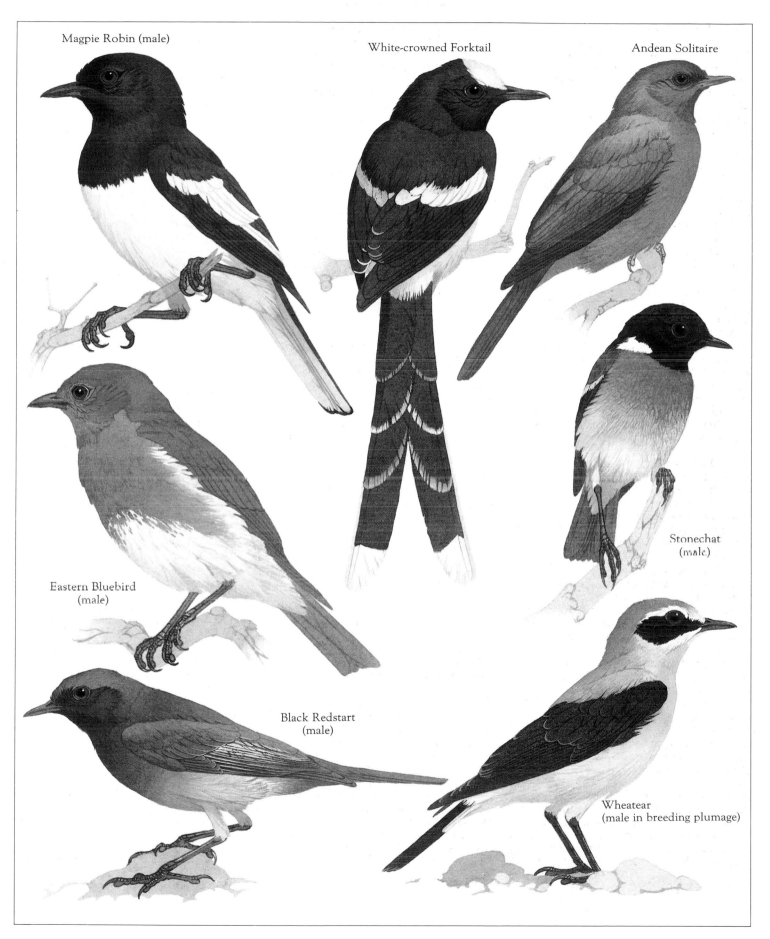

Magpie Robin (male)

White-crowned Forktail

Andean Solitaire

Eastern Bluebird
(male)

Stonechat
(male)

Black Redstart
(male)

Wheatear
(male in breeding plumage)

# Thrushes

NAME: **Cape Rock-thrush,** *Monticola rupestris*
RANGE: **South Africa: Transvaal to Cape Province**
HABITAT: **scrub, rocky country**
SIZE: **22 cm (8½ in)**

The male Cape rock-thrush is recognized by his blue-gray head, neck and throat, while the female's head is mottled brown and black. They are fairly common birds, seen in pairs or small groups, often perching on rocks, boulders or the tops of bushes. Insects and small mollusks are their main foods, mostly found on the ground.

The shallow, cup-shaped nest is made of grass, small twigs and plant fibers, lined with rootlets; it is usually situated in a rock crevice or even under a roof. The female lays 3 to 5 eggs.

NAME: **White's Thrush,** *Zoothera dauma*
RANGE: **USSR (stragglers as far west as Britain), India, China, Taiwan, Philippines, Sumatra and Java, south to Australia, N. Melanesia**
HABITAT: **forest, woodland**
SIZE: **11 cm (4¼ in)**

White's thrush is characterized by the crescent-shaped, scalelike markings on its back and underparts. Juveniles have barred, rather than scaly, markings. A shy, retiring bird, white's thrush spends much of its life on the ground, feeding on insects and berries. Some birds migrate in winter, and vagrants may even stray into Europe.

The nest is rather different from that of most thrushes. Situated up to 4 m (13 ft) above ground in a tree, it is large and flat and made mostly from pine needles, with a base of mud and moss to fix it to the branch. The female lays 3 to 5 eggs.

NAME: **Veery,** *Catharus fuscescens*
RANGE: **S. Canada; USA: Oregon to New Mexico, Great Lakes area and New England, south to Georgia; winters in South America**
HABITAT: **moist woodland**
SIZE: **16–18 cm (6¼–7 in)**

More often heard than seen, the veery is an inconspicuous little bird with a beautiful, musical song. It feeds on insects, spiders and earthworms, as well as on fruit and berries, which it finds by foraging in the trees and by searching under leaves on the woodland floor.

The bulky, cup-shaped nest is made of weed stems, grass, pieces of bark and twig, lined with dry leaves and rootlets, and is situated on or near the ground in a bush or clump of plants. The female lays 3 to 6 eggs, usually 4, which she incubates for 11 or 12 days. Both birds care for the young, which leave the nest 10 to 12 days after hatching.

NAME: **American Robin,** *Turdus migratorius*
RANGE: **N. America, Mexico, Guatemala**
HABITAT: **open woodland, forest edge, gardens, city parks**
SIZE: **23–28 cm (9–11 in)**

The adaptable American robin has learned to live alongside man in urban areas, and city birds have become bolder than the shy, forest robins. The coloration is variable, but in the breeding season, the male is generally gray above, with a black head and tail and reddish breast. The female is duller and paler, with a gray head and tail. Robins feed in open areas and in vegetation on insects, earthworms, fruit and berries.

Although some robins winter in the northern states, generally they are migratory birds, breeding north of the Gulf Coast. Males arrive first in small flocks and begin singing and courting when the females arrive. Nests are made in a variety of sites: in a tree or bush, on a post, a ledge on a building or cliff, or even on the ground. The inner part of the nest is a deep cup of mud, which is surrounded by twigs, weeds and stems and lined with grass. The female lays 3 to 6 eggs, usually 4, which she incubates for 12 to 14 days.

NAME: **Blackbird,** *Turdus merula*
RANGE: **Europe, N. Africa, Asia (except N.E. and S.); introduced in New Zealand**
HABITAT: **forest, woodland, scrub, gardens, parks**
SIZE: **25.5 cm (10 in)**

One of the most familiar European birds, the blackbird has adapted well to man's environments, finding the short grass of lawns, parks and recreation areas ideal for foraging for insects and worms. It also feeds on many kinds of fruit and berries. Much of its time is spent on the ground, but the blackbird finds a prominent, often exposed perch from which to sing. While the male is black, with a yellowish-orange bill and eye-ring, the female has dark-brown plumage with paler underparts.

A variety of nest sites is used, such as branches of low trees and bushes, ledges on or in buildings, and crevices in rocks or walls. The female builds the nest, which has an outer layer of plant stems, twigs and leaves covering the inner cup of mud and plant material and is lined with fine grass or dead leaves. The female lays up to 9 eggs, usually 3 to 5, at daily intervals. She incubates the clutch for 12 to 15 days. Both parents care for the young during their 12 to 15 days in the nest and continue to feed them for a further 3 weeks.

NAME: **Cape/Olive Thrush,** *Turdus olivaceus*
RANGE: **Africa, south of the Sahara**
HABITAT: **forest, cultivated land**
SIZE: **24 cm (9½ in)**

Several races of Cape thrush, which vary in coloration, occur over its range. Male and female look alike, but juveniles have streaked upperparts and dusky spots on underparts. It is an adaptable bird and has taken well to life in urban gardens, where it tends to dominate other birds. Much of its food is found by scratching around on the ground to uncover insects and invertebrates such as snails and earthworms. It also feeds on fruit.

The courting male puffs himself up, spreads his tail, then shuffles around the female with his wings trailing. The nest is made of grass, on a foundation of twigs, roots and earth, and is situated on a branch, tree stump or bush. The female lays 2 or 3 eggs, which are incubated for about 14 days.

NAME: **Austral Thrush,** *Turdus falcklandii*
RANGE: **South America: S. Argentina, S. Chile; Falkland and Juan Fernandez Islands**
HABITAT: **open country with shrubs**
SIZE: **28–29 cm (11–11½ in)**

The southern counterpart of the robin of North America, the austral thrush is common on both sides of the Andes up to about 2,000 m (6,600 ft). It is similar to the robin in its habits, digging for earthworms and other invertebrates on grassland and in damp places. It also feeds on fruit.

The cup-shaped nest is made of twigs, bound with grass and mud, and is usually well concealed in dense vegetation. The female produces two, sometimes three, clutches a season, each containing 2 or 3 eggs.

NAME: **Island Thrush,** *Turdus poliocephalus*
RANGE: **islands from Christmas Island through Indonesia, New Guinea to New Caledonia, Fiji and Samoa**
HABITAT: **forest edge**
SIZE: **23–25.5 cm (9–10 in)**

There may be 50 or more forms of island thrush, all varying slightly in appearance, some found on only one island or on a small group of islands. Most males have largely black plumage, and females look similar, but usually duller, in color. Generally a shy, solitary bird, the island thrush takes refuge in trees but feeds on the ground in the open, on plant matter, such as seeds and fruit, and on a few insects.

The female normally lays 1 egg in a nest on a bush or rocky ledge.

American Robin (male)

Austral Thrush

Blackbird (male)

Cape Thrush

Island Thrush (male)

Cape Rock-thrush (male)

Veery

White's Thrush

# Babblers

NAME: **White-necked/White-eared Babbler**, *Stachyris leucotis*
RANGE: **Malaysian Peninsula, Sumatra, Borneo**
HABITAT: **forest**
SIZE: **15 cm (6 in)**

The white-necked babbler is identified by its white eyebrow streaks, linked to the row of white spots on the sides of its neck. Male and female look similar. It is mainly a ground-living bird, found in the undergrowth of forest, and does not fly well. It feeds on insects such as black beetles and flies.

The neat, cup-shaped nest is made of grass, roots and plant fibers, in a tree or dense undergrowth. The female is thought to lay 3 eggs, but few nests have been observed.

NAME: **Large Wren-babbler**, *Napothera macrodactyla*
RANGE: **Malaysian Peninsula, Sumatra, Java**
HABITAT: **lowland forest**
SIZE: **19 cm (7½ in)**

A big, plump, short-tailed babbler, the large wren-babbler has white patches between the beak and eyes, a white throat and characteristic scalelike markings on breast and upperparts. The bill is stout and the feet large and strong. An uncommon bird, this babbler lives in undergrowth and feeds near or on the ground on insects. It perches on bushes to sing.

Little is known of its nesting habits, but it is thought to lay 2 eggs.

NAME: **Scaly-breasted Illadopsis**, *Trichastoma albipectus*
RANGE: **Africa: S. Sudan, Zaire, east to Kenya**
HABITAT: **forest, dense high bush**
SIZE: **14 cm (5½ in)**

The scaly-breasted illadopsis lives on the floor or in the undergrowth of thick forest, often side by side with the pale-breasted illadopsis, *T. rufipennis*, which it closely resembles. A rather quieter bird than most babblers, it moves in small groups, close to or on the ground, searching for ants, beetles and other insects. Male and female look alike, both with pale chest feathers edged with gray, which creates a scaly appearance.

The cup-shaped nest is made of dead leaves and hidden among leaves or on an overgrown tree stump. The female lays 2 eggs.

---

## TIMALIINAE: Babbler Subfamily

This large, diverse subfamily of the family Muscicapidae includes about 250 species of babbler, all found in the warmer parts of the Old World, with the greatest diversity in Africa and South Asia. A notoriously confusing group to classify, the babbler subfamily includes several species that are probably not closely related. As their name suggests, most are extremely vocal, noisy birds, and some are fine songsters.

Babblers tend to have short, rounded wings and are poor fliers, spending much of their time on the ground or clambering around in the low levels of trees and bushes. Their feathers are soft, and the plumage varies from dull browns to bright colors, often with bold markings on the head and neck. Most have thickset bodies and fairly long tails when compared to thrushes. Their legs and feet are strong, enabling them to probe and dig in thick vegetation and ground litter for invertebrate prey and small berries and fruit. Feeding activity is generally accompanied by the loud, varied "babbling" calls that give the group its common name. Much of this calling behavior may be linked to keeping the small feeding flocks together in dense vegetation.

Males and females look alike in some species but differ in others. The nest is generally cup shaped or domed, and the female lays up to 7 eggs. In some species both parents incubate the clutch, but in others only the female incubates. Both parents care for the young.

---

NAME: **Rufous-crowned Babbler**, *Malacopteron magnum*
RANGE: **Malaysian Peninsula, Sumatra, Borneo**
HABITAT: **forest**
SIZE: **18 cm (7 in)**

The rufous-crowned babbler is identified by its reddish-brown crown and the black plumage at the back of the neck. Its wings and tail are longer than those of many babblers. An arboreal bird, it rarely descends to the ground but frequents the lower branches of tall trees and the forest undergrowth, where it forages for insects such as black beetles and grasshoppers. It also feeds on seeds.

The cup-shaped nest, made of twigs and rootlets and lined with fungal threads, is built in a small tree. The female lays 2 eggs.

---

NAME: **Coral-billed Scimitar-babbler**, *Pomatorhinus ferruginosus*
RANGE: **Himalayas, northern S.E. Asia to Thailand**
HABITAT: **forest undergrowth**
SIZE: **24 cm (9½ in)**

This large babbler has a distinctive stout red bill and characteristic black face markings on either side of the white eyebrow streaks. In noisy flocks, it searches for insects and larvae on the forest floor or in the undergrowth. It hops from perch to perch and rarely flies unless forced to do so.

The domed nest is made on the ground or in a low bush and is built from bamboo leaves, grass and plant fibers, bound together with plant stems or vines and lined with fine grass and fibers. The female lays 3 to 5 eggs.

NAME: **Chestnut-capped Babbler**, *Timalia pileata*
RANGE: **Nepal, S.E. Asia (not Malaysian Peninsula), Java**
HABITAT: **bamboo thickets, forest, scrub**
SIZE: **18 cm (7 in)**

Small parties of chestnut-capped babblers forage for insects in dense undergrowth, remaining well within cover. They tend to stay just above ground. If alarmed, the birds scatter and dive for shelter, regrouping once the danger is past. This babbler is identified by its reddish-brown crown, black bill and white feathers on forehead, throat and breast.

The female lays 3 or 4 eggs in a ball-shaped nest, made of bamboo leaves or grass and lined with fine grass or hair. The nest is often situated at the base of a bamboo clump.

NAME: **Yellow-eyed Babbler**, *Chrysomma sinense*
RANGE: **E. Pakistan, India through S.E. Asia (not Malaysian Peninsula) to S. China**
HABITAT: **bamboo thickets, scrub, cultivated land**
SIZE: **18 cm (7 in)**

True to its name, the yellow-eyed babbler has yellowish eyes and orange markings ringing the eyes. Pairs or small parties of these babblers forage together in the undergrowth, searching for insects and larvae among the foliage. Much of their time is spent in cover, but they will emerge into the open to sun themselves for a moment and perhaps to sing.

A compact nest is made from grass and strips of bark and covered with spider's webs; it may be lined with finer grass and stems. It is usually built above ground in a bush or tree, or it may be attached to thick grass stems. The female lays 5 eggs.

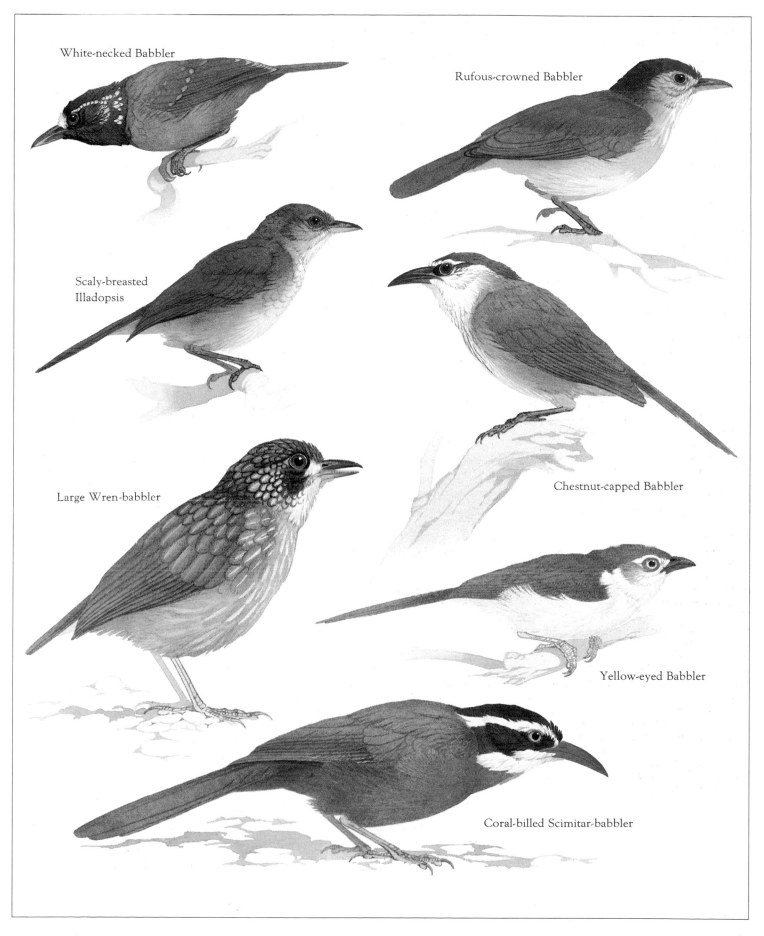

White-necked Babbler

Rufous-crowned Babbler

Scaly-breasted
Illadopsis

Large Wren-babbler

Chestnut-capped Babbler

Yellow-eyed Babbler

Coral-billed Scimitar-babbler

# Babblers

NAME: **Brown-cheeked Fulvetta,** *Alcippe poioicephala*
RANGE: **India to S.W. China, S.E. Asia**
HABITAT: **forest, scrub, bamboo scrub**
SIZE: **15 cm (6 in)**

The brown-cheeked fulvetta is a rather plain little bird, with mainly buffy-brown plumage. Both male and female have gray plumage on the top of the head. In small groups of 4 to 20, these babblers forage in the forest undergrowth for insects. They rarely, if ever, descend to the ground but may climb farther up trees into the canopy layers. The birds keep in touch by calling to one another and are extremely wary of any danger.

The nest is made on a branch of a tree or bush a few meters above ground or is suspended from a few twigs. It is cup shaped and built of moss and dead leaves, lined with fine moss and ferns. The female usually lays 2 eggs, which are incubated by both parents.

NAME: **Stripe-throated Yuhina,** *Yuhina gularis*
RANGE: **Himalayas to northern S.E. Asia and W. China**
HABITAT: **forest**
SIZE: **15 cm (6 in)**

A distinctive little babbler, the stripe-throated yuhina has a prominent crest, dark streaks on its throat and an orange-rufous streak on the wings. Male and female look alike. Small parties of these active little birds forage in the trees for insects, such as beetles and wasps, and sometimes join in mixed flocks with other species of babbler. They also feed on seeds and nectar, and their crests become coated with pollen as they fly from flower to flower.

Little is known of the breeding habits of these birds, but nests made of roots and of moss have been described. The female is thought to lay 4 eggs.

NAME: **Brown Babbler,** *Turdoides plebejus*
RANGE: **Africa: Senegal, east to Sudan, Ethiopia and W. Kenya**
HABITAT: **bush, savanna**
SIZE: **23 cm (9 in)**

Both male and female brown babblers have mainly grayish-brown plumage, with some white markings and light underparts. Typical babblers, they form noisy flocks, flying from one bush to another while making chattering, babbling calls. They feed on insects and some fruit, which they find in the low levels of bushes or by scratching about on the ground.

The cup-shaped nest is made of rootlets, lined with fine plant material, and is situated in a dense bush. The female lays 2 to 4 eggs.

NAME: **White-crested Laughingthrush,** *Garrulax leucolophus*
RANGE: **Himalayas, S.W. China, S.E. Asia, W. Sumatra**
HABITAT: **forest**
SIZE: **30.5 cm (12 in)**

One of the larger babblers, the white-crested laughingthrush has an erectile crest on its white head, a white throat and breast and characteristic black masklike markings on its head. There are several races within the range, which may differ slightly in the shade of the darker areas of plumage. Like most laughingthrushes, they are sociable birds, which move in small flocks, foraging in the undergrowth and on the ground. Insects, berries and seeds are their main foods, but they take nectar and small reptiles as well. Large items of prey are held down with the foot while being torn to pieces with the bill. The laughingthrushes seem to prefer densely vegetated areas, and birds in the flock communicate by chattering calls, often followed by wild, cackling sounds, which resemble laughter and are the origin of the common name.

The nest is well hidden in a low tree or bush. It is cup shaped and made of grass, bamboo leaves, roots and moss, all bound together with tendrils of vine and lined with rootlets. The female lays 3 to 6 eggs, usually 4, and both parents incubate the clutch for about 14 days. The chestnut-winged cuckoo, *Clamator coromandus*, is known to lay its eggs in the nest of the white-crested laughingthrush, making it an unwitting foster parent.

NAME: **Red-billed Leiothrix/Peking Robin,** *Leiothrix lutea*
RANGE: **Himalayas, mountain areas of northern S.E. Asia and S. China; introduced in Hawaii**
HABITAT: **forest undergrowth, scrub, grass**
SIZE: **15 cm (6 in)**

The male red-billed leiothrix is an attractive bird, with an orange-red bill and bright yellow and orange plumage on the throat, breast and wing feathers; his bill has a blackish base in winter. The female has duller plumage, with a paler throat and breast, and she lacks the bright wing feathers. These birds live in many different types of forest where they forage in the undergrowth for insects. They are lively, gregarious birds, usually seen in small groups, except in the breeding season when they form pairs.

The courting male perches on top of a bush and delivers what has been described as "a delightful song," while fluffing out his feathers to attract his mate. The cup-shaped nest is made of

leaves, moss and lichen, of moss only or of bamboo leaves, depending on what plant material is available, and it is lined with fine threads of fungal material. Usually rather conspicuous, the nest is placed on a horizontally forked branch or in an upright fork, or is bound to several twigs or stems. The female lays 3 eggs and there is usually more than one brood. This leiothrix is a familiar cage bird, under the name of the Peking robin.

NAME: **Fire-tailed Myzornis,** *Myzornis pyrrhoura*
RANGE: **Himalayas from Nepal to Burma; S.W. China**
HABITAT: **bush, forest**
SIZE: **12.5 cm (5 in)**

An exquisite little bird, the fire-tailed myzornis has touches of black, white and red on its mainly green plumage. The female looks similar to the male, but her red plumage is duller, and the throat and belly tend toward buff-brown. Generally found in forest above 1,800 m (6,000 ft), the myzornis lives alone or in small groups of 3 or 4, which may sometimes join with mixed flocks of other babblers and warblers. It is a most adaptable bird in its feeding techniques: it forages on foliage and flowers for insects and spiders, like other babblers, but can also run up mossy tree trunks to find prey or hover like a sunbird in front of flowers. Using its bristly tongue, it will probe the flowers of shrubs, such as rhododendrons, for nectar and also feeds on sap, which it obtains from trees.

Little is known of the breeding habits of this bird, the only representative of its genus. The one nest that has been found was in dense, mossy forest, and both parents appeared to be feeding the young.

NAME: **Bush Blackcap,** *Lioptilus nigricapillus*
RANGE: **South Africa: E. Cape Province, Natal, N.E. Transvaal**
HABITAT: **damp forest**
SIZE: **16.5–18 cm (6½–7 in)**

A rare, little-known babbler, the bush blackcap is a quieter, less conspicuous bird than many of its relatives. Alone or in pairs, it forages for berries and other fruit, much of which it finds on or near the ground in dense undergrowth. Both male and female birds have characteristic black markings on the head, and the rest of the plumage is brownish and gray.

The neat, cup-shaped nest is made of twigs and moss, lined with rootlets, and is usually situated just above the ground in a bush. The female lays 2 eggs.

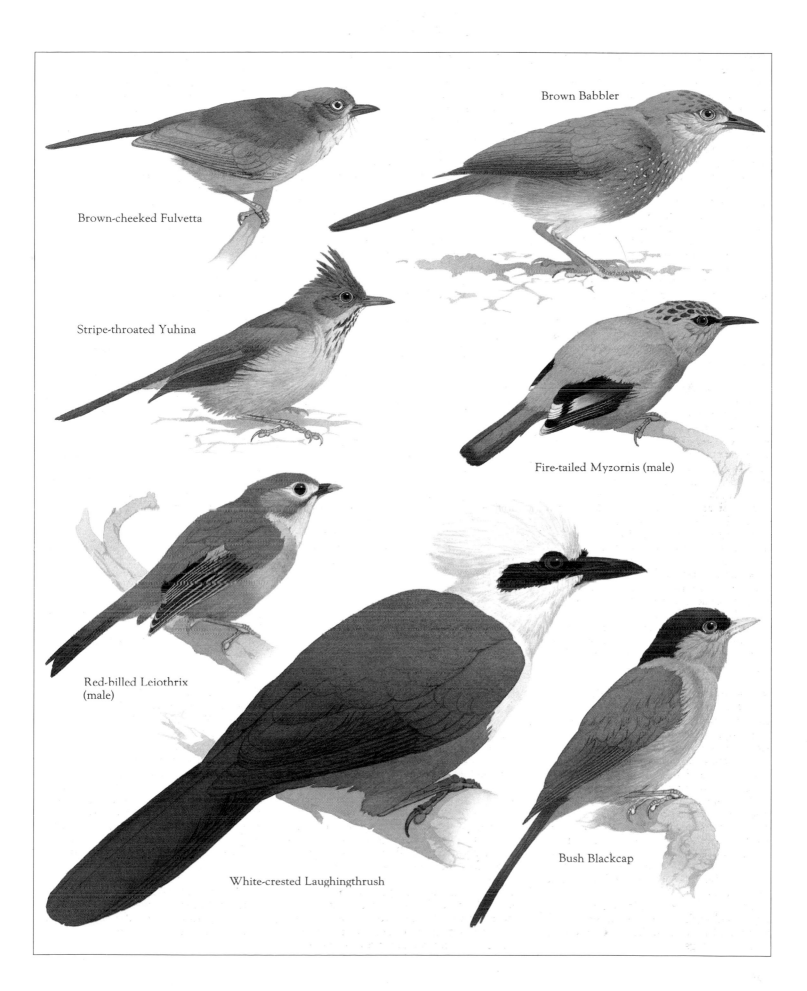

Brown-cheeked Fulvetta

Brown Babbler

Stripe-throated Yuhina

Fire-tailed Myzornis (male)

Red-billed Leiothrix
(male)

White-crested Laughingthrush

Bush Blackcap

# Babblers, Parrotbills and relatives

NAME: **Wrentit**, *Chamaea fasciata*
RANGE: **USA: Pacific coast, Oregon to California; Mexico: coast of Baja California**
HABITAT: **scrub, chaparral**
SIZE: **15–17 cm (6–6¾ in)**

The single species of wrentit is included in the main babbler subfamily, the Timaliinae, or, sometimes, placed in its own subfamily. Believed to be closely related to babblers and to parrotbills, the Panurinae, its relationships and classification have been the subject of much dispute.

An elusive, inconspicuous little bird, the wrentit spends all its life within its selected territory, which it defends throughout the year, seldom flying across any distance of open country. Pairs mate for life and forage and roost together. Insects, spiders and berries are their main foods.

Together the paired wrentits build a neat, cup-shaped nest from bark, plant fiber and grass, bound together with spider's webs. The nest is usually above ground in a bush or small tree. The female lays 3 to 5 eggs, generally 4, which she incubates for 15 or 16 days although the male may take a turn.

## PANURINAE: Parrotbill Subfamily

The 19 species of parrotbill are closely related to the babblers, which are sometimes included in the same subfamily, but they have short, heavy, usually yellowish bills, resembling those of parrots. They feed on insects, seeds and berries. All the species occur in Asia, and 1, the bearded tit, also lives in Europe. Male and female look alike in some species but differ in others.

NAME: **Spot-breasted/White-throated Parrotbill**, *Paradoxornis guttaticollis*
RANGE: **N.E. India (Assam), S.W. China, northern S.E. Asia**
HABITAT: **scrub, grass, bamboo clumps**
SIZE: **20.5 cm (8 in)**

The spot-breasted parrotbill can be identified by its yellow, parrotlike bill, the reddish-brown plumage on its head and the dark, arrowhead markings on its throat and breast. Male and female look alike. In noisy flocks, parrotbills forage in dense vegetation for insects, seeds and berries.

The cup-shaped nest is made above ground, from bamboo leaves and grass, bound with spider's webs. The female lays 2 to 4 eggs.

NAME: **Bearded Tit/Reedling**, *Panurus biarmicus*
RANGE: **scattered locations in S. and central Europe, east across USSR and S. central Asia to Manchuria**
HABITAT: **reedbeds, swamps, near lakes and streams**
SIZE: **16 cm (6¼ in)**

The only babblerlike bird to occur in Europe, the bearded tit has a long tail for its size and a smaller, weaker bill than other parrotbills. The male has a distinctive gray head, with black mustache markings, while the female has a brown head and no black markings. An active little bird, it moves with agility through reed stems, often straddling two stalks as it picks off insects. It may also come to the ground to scratch for insects and in winter feeds on seeds. Though their flight seems labored, bearded tits do often wander great distances, and northern populations may migrate in winter.

The male displays to court his mate, raising his head feathers, puffing out his "mustaches" and spreading his tail. The pair builds a nest of reed and grass stalks, lined with flowering reed heads, which is concealed among reeds or aquatic vegetation. The female lays 5 to 7 eggs, which are incubated for 12 or 13 days by both parents. The nestlings are fed by their parents for 9 to 12 days. There may be two or more broods a season.

## PICATHARTINAE: Bare-headed Rockfowl Subfamily

The 2 species of bare-headed rockfowl, also called picathartes or bald crows, are thought by most authorities to be close relatives of the babblers, being similar in many respects to laughingthrushes. Both species are large, long-tailed birds, found in the forests of West Africa, and they are similar in their biology and habits. The common name comes from the characteristic bare patch on the head.

NAME: **Guinea Bare-headed Rockfowl**, *Picathartes gymnocephalus*
RANGE: **W. Africa: Guinea and Sierra Leone to Togo**
HABITAT: **forest**
SIZE: **38–41 cm (15–16 in)** Ⓥ

Recognizable by the bare, yellow head, with two black patches at the back, both male and female rockfowls have gray and white plumage and powerful legs and feet. Rockfowls spend much of their life on the ground, where they move with graceful hops, searching for insects, snails, crustaceans and small frogs. The species is becoming rare,

partly because of forest clearance and partly from trapping to fulfill the demands of zoos and private collectors. It is protected by law in Ghana.

Rockfowls nest colonially in caves, in nests made of mud and fibrous plant materials and attached to the walls of the caves. Unfortunately, this habit of colonial nesting in often easily identified sites makes the birds easy prey for collectors. Both parents incubate the 2 eggs for about 21 days and then feed their young with insects.

## ORTHONYCHINAE: Quail Thrush Subfamily

In this diverse group are 17 species of whipbird, logrunner and quail thrush, all but 1 found in Australia and New Guinea; the exception occurs farther north, in Malaysia. They are babblerlike birds, often included with the babbler group.

NAME: **Eastern Whipbird**, *Psophodes olivaceus*
RANGE: **Australia: Queensland to Victoria**
HABITAT: **thickets in or near forest**
SIZE: **25–28 cm (9¾–11 in)**

The eastern whipbird has mainly dark plumage, with some touches of white, and a long, broad tail; male and female look alike. It lives on or near the ground but usually stays in dense undergrowth, searching for insects, larvae and spiders among the leaf litter. It hops and runs swiftly and can climb up into bushes but flies rarely and only for short distances.

The nest of twigs and rootlets is made near the ground in dense undergrowth. The female lays 2 eggs.

NAME: **Cinnamon Quail Thrush**, *Cinclosoma cinnamomeum*
RANGE: **Australia: drier areas, Western Australia to Queensland and Victoria**
HABITAT: **semidesert, scrub**
SIZE: **20 cm (7¾ in)**

Alone or in small family groups, the cinnamon quail thrush skulks among bushes or hides in holes and burrows to escape predators and the heat of the day. It usually feeds in the cool of dawn and dusk, on seeds and insects. It may also hunt for insects over open country, flying low with noisy, whirring wings. Male and female differ in plumage, the female lacking the male's characteristic black markings.

The nest is sited in a shallow dip in the ground or under a bush or fallen branch and is made of grass and twigs, lined with bark and leaves. The female lays 2 or 3 eggs.

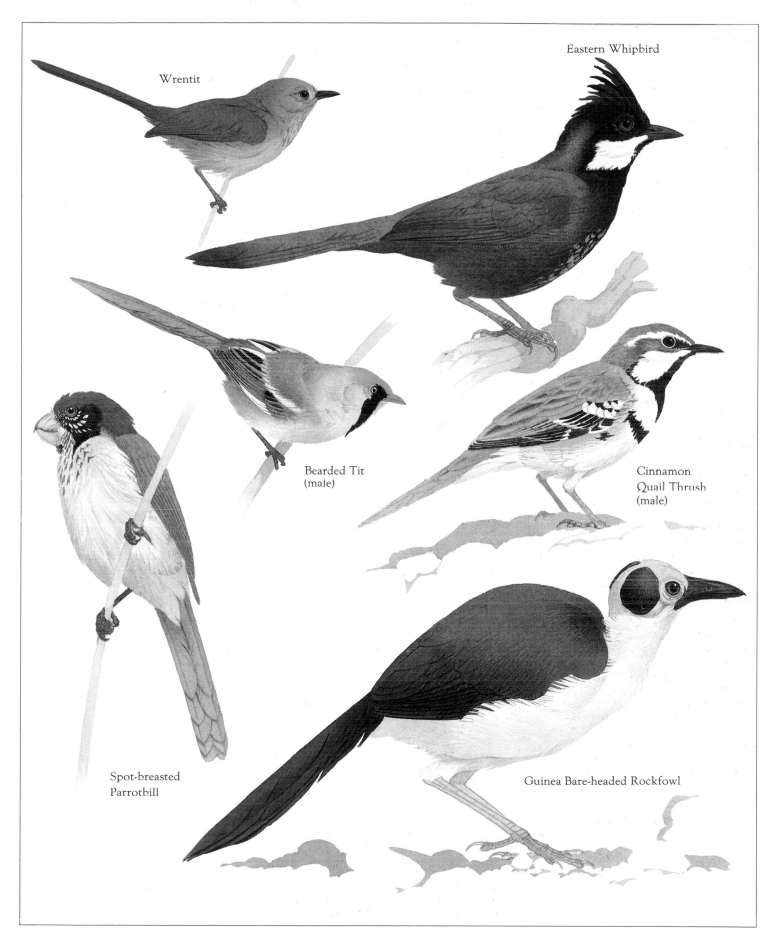

Wrentit

Eastern Whipbird

Bearded Tit
(male)

Cinnamon
Quail Thrush
(male)

Spot-breasted
Parrotbill

Guinea Bare-headed Rockfowl

# Gnatcatchers, Old World Warblers

## POLIOPTILINAE:
### Gnatcatcher Subfamily

There are 12 species in this subfamily of the family Muscicapidae, found in North, Central and South America. They are small, dainty birds, related to and resembling Old World warblers but with bluish-gray and white plumage. Male and female may differ slightly in appearance.

NAME: **Blue-gray Gnatcatcher**, *Polioptila caerulea*
RANGE: **USA, Mexico, Cuba and Bahamas**
HABITAT: **forest, woodland, swamps, inhabited areas**
SIZE: **10–13 cm (4–5 in)**

The blue-gray gnatcatcher is a slender, lively, little bird with a long tail, often held cocked like a wren's. Male and female look similar, but the female tends to be less blue in color and lacks the black head markings developed by the breeding male. They search for insects, larvae and spiders in the trees, sometimes launching themselves into the air to catch prey.

The cup-shaped nest is usually sited on a horizontal branch and is made from plant fibers lined with fine bark, grass and feathers. The parents incubate the 3 to 6 eggs in shifts for about 14 days and care for the young.

## SYLVIINAE:
### Old World Warbler Subfamily

Small, often dull-colored birds, many of the 350 or so species of Old World warbler are noted for their marvelous songs. Most of the species occur in Europe, Asia and Africa, but there are 3 species in North America and about 20 in Australia.

Almost without exception, warblers are active, quick-moving birds, found in woodland, moorland, marshes and reedbeds feeding on insects and fruit. Male and female generally look alike.

NAME: **Long-tailed/Common Tailorbird,** *Orthotomus sutorius*
RANGE: **India, S. China, S.E. Asia to Java**
HABITAT: **scrub, bamboo thickets, gardens**
SIZE: **12 cm (4¾ in)**

Distinguished by their rufous caps, both male and female have similar plumage, but in the breeding season, the male's two central tail feathers grow much longer than the others, adding about 4 cm (1½ in) to his length. The tailorbird is a common, widespread species, which spends much of its time hopping about in bushes and low trees, searching for insects, larvae and small spiders; it will also feed on nectar.

Pairs mate for life and nest on a bush or low branch. The nest is made in a cradle, formed by sewing together the edges of a large leaf or two smaller leaves of the tree. The tailorbird makes a series of small holes in the edges of the leaf with its beak and then pulls through strands of wool, spider's web or cocoon silk, to draw them together. Each stitch is separate. The 2 or 3 eggs are laid inside this cradle, on a nest of soft fibers. Both parents incubate the eggs and tend the young.

NAME: **Blackcap,** *Sylvia atricapilla*
RANGE: **breeds in Europe, Britain and Scandinavia to Mediterranean countries, east to Iran and Siberia; winters south of range and in Africa**
HABITAT: **woodland, gardens, orchards**
SIZE: **14 cm (5½ in)**

The male blackcap is distinguished from other *Sylvia* warblers by his black crown and gray neck; females and juveniles have rusty-brown caps and are otherwise similar to males but browner. An active, lively bird, it forages in trees and bushes for insects and eats more fruit than most other warblers.

The male courts his mate by raising his head and back feathers and drooping and flapping his wings. The nest is made in a low bush or other low cover and is constructed from dry stems, spider's webs and wool. Both parents incubate the 3 to 6 eggs for 10 to 15 days and feed their young.

NAME: **Fan-tailed Warbler/Zitting Cisticola,** *Cisticola juncidis*
RANGE: **Africa, south of the Sahara; S. Europe; India, China, Japan; S.E. Asia to N. Australia**
HABITAT: **grassland, scrub, rice fields, cultivated land**
SIZE: **10 cm (4 in)**

A ground-living bird, the fan-tailed warbler skulks in grass, feeding on insects, and flies only when disturbed or in courtship. Males and females look similar, but breeding males have more strongly defined streaks on the head.

In the breeding season, males perform various courtship displays, including a jerky, dipping flight, accompanied by a particular song. The unique nest is built amid grass taller than itself, for camouflage. It is pear shaped, with the entrance at the top, and is made of soft grass stems, bound together with spider's webs and lined with plant down. Some blades of the surrounding grass are woven into the nest for support. The 3 to 6 eggs are incubated by both parents for about 10 days.

NAME: **Graceful/Striped-backed Prinia,** *Prinia gracilis*
RANGE: **E. Africa: Egypt to Somalia; east across S. Asia to N. India**
HABITAT: **scrub, bushy areas**
SIZE: **10 cm (4 in)**

As much as half the length of this little warbler is accounted for by its tail of graduated feathers, the outer ones of which are tipped with white. The graceful prinia tends to frequent sandy ground near rivers, where there is some grass and bushy cover. It forages for insects in the vegetation and comes into the open only to fly clumsily from one patch of cover to the next.

The courting male sings a somewhat monotonous song from a perch on a tall grass stem. The tiny, domed nest is made of fine grass and is woven into a thick clump of grass stems, a meter or so above ground; there is an entrance at one side. Both parents incubate the 3 or 4 eggs for about 12 days. There are usually two broods a year.

NAME: **Yellow-breasted/Black-breasted Apalis,** *Apalis flavida*
RANGE: **Africa, south of the Sahara to South Africa: Transvaal**
HABITAT: **forest, bush**
SIZE: **11 cm (4¼ in)**

The yellow-breasted apalis occurs in a variety of well-vegetated areas. It usually moves in pairs or small family groups, carefully searching through the foliage for insects.

The domed, pear-shaped nest is made of moss, lichen and spider's webs and is bound to a twig of a low bush with spider's webs; there is a side opening. Alternatively, this apalis may take over an old domed nest abandoned by another bird species. The female lays 2 or 3 eggs.

NAME: **Long-billed Warbler,** *Acrocephalus (= Conopoderas) caffra*
RANGE: **Society and Marquesas Islands**
HABITAT: **woodland bordering rivers, hillside forest**
SIZE: **22 cm (8½ in)**

One of the largest warblers, the long-billed warbler has a distinctive beak that can be 4 cm (1½ in) long. Subspecies on the different islands vary in coloration, and on Tahiti alone, there are some birds with olive upperparts and yellow underparts and other birds that are blackish-brown all over.

Long-billed warblers forage in trees and bushes for insects; they do not feed on the ground. They have a musical, varied song, performed from a high perch. The nest is usually made in a bamboo thicket, 9 m (30 ft) or more above ground.

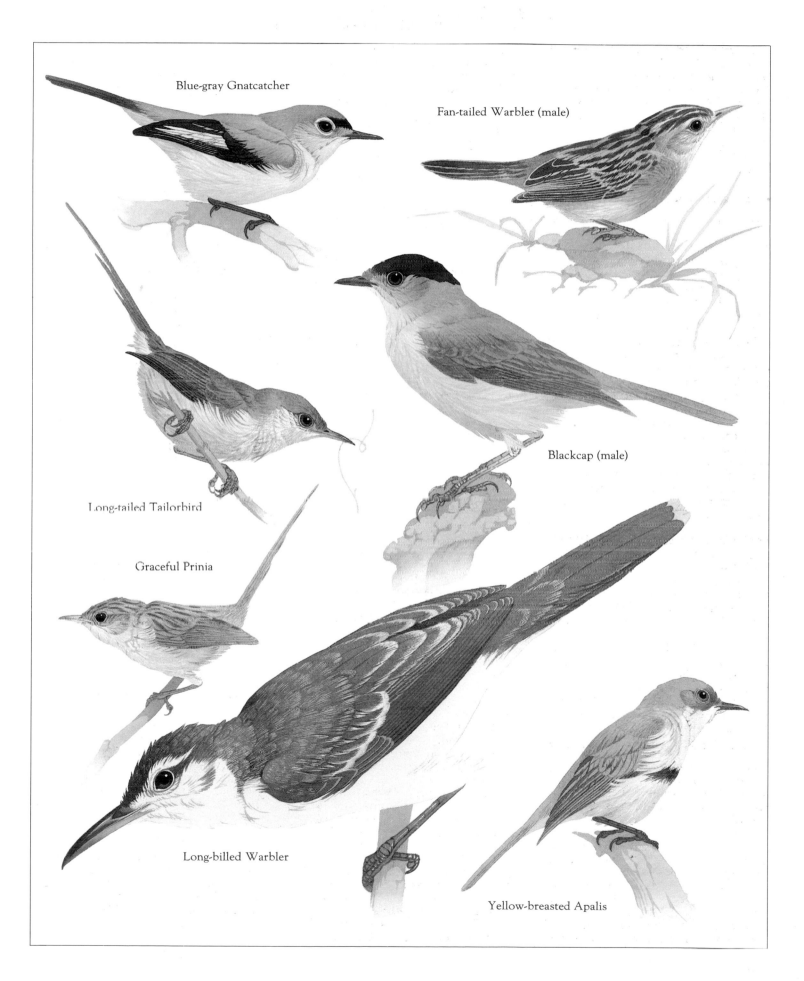

Blue-gray Gnatcatcher

Fan-tailed Warbler (male)

Long-tailed Tailorbird

Blackcap (male)

Graceful Prinia

Long-billed Warbler

Yellow-breasted Apalis

# Old World Warblers

**NAME:** Chestnut-headed Warbler, *Seicercus castaneiceps*
**RANGE:** Himalayas, S. China, S.E. Asia, Sumatra
**HABITAT:** forest
**SIZE:** 10 cm (4 in)

An attractive little bird, the chestnut-headed warbler has a reddish-brown crown, with dark bands at the sides of the head, and yellow underparts. Male and female look alike. They live in dense forest and, outside the breeding season, move in mixed flocks, searching for insects in the middle to canopy layers of the forest. In the Himalayas, the birds breed at between 1,800 and 2,400 m (6,000 and 7,900 ft), moving down the mountains in winter.

The compact, oval nest is situated on the ground, well hidden by moss or creepers in a hollow at the base of a tree or bush or in a bank or hillside. Both partners help to build the nest, which is made of densely woven moss, and incubate the 4 or 5 eggs. The emerald cuckoo, *Chalcites maculatus*, often lays its eggs in the nests of this warbler.

**NAME:** Willow Warbler, *Phylloscopus trochilus*
**RANGE:** N. Europe and Asia: Britain and Scandinavia, south to central France, east to USSR; winters in Africa and S. Asia
**HABITAT:** open woodland, cultivated land with scattered trees and bushes
**SIZE:** 11 cm (4¼ in)

Typical of the many species in the genus *Phylloscopus* in appearance, the willow warbler is extremely hard to distinguish from the chiffchaff, *P. collybita*, except by its song. It is said to look "cleaner" than the chiffchaff, and its eyebrow streak is more marked. Male and female birds look similar, but juveniles have much more yellow on their underparts. Willow warblers search in the vegetation for insects and also sometimes catch prey in the air. In autumn, they feed on berries, before migrating south for the winter. Some northern birds travel as far as 12,000 km (7,500 mi) to winter in African forest and savanna.

Willow warblers nest on the ground, in vegetation under a bush, tree or hedge, or sometimes a little above ground in a bush or on a creeper-covered wall. The female builds the domed nest from grass, moss, stems and roots, lined with finer stems and feathers. She lays 6 or 7 eggs, which she incubates for 13 days. Both parents tend the young, which spend 13 to 16 days in the nest. Birds in the south of the range may produce two broods.

**NAME:** Grasshopper Warbler, *Locustella naevia*
**RANGE:** Europe: Britain and S. Sweden, south to N. Spain and Italy, east to central Siberia; winters in Africa and Asia
**HABITAT:** marsh edge, open woodland
**SIZE:** 13 cm (5 in)

The grasshopper warbler is a retiring, secretive species, which quickly disappears into thick cover when disturbed. It feeds on insects and larvae. Male and female birds have similar streaked plumage.

The male warbler performs courtship displays, spreading his tail and flapping his wings. The nest, built by both birds, is placed in thick cover on the ground or just above it in grasses or rushes and is made of plant stems and grass on a base of dead leaves. The female lays 4 to 7 eggs, usually 6, which both parents incubate for 13 to 15 days. The young spend 10 to 12 days in the nest, tended and fed by both parents. Birds in the south of the range have two broods, and those in the north usually only one. In autumn, the birds migrate south for the winter.

**NAME:** Strong-footed/Brownish-flanked Bush Warbler, *Cettia fortipes*
**RANGE:** Himalayas, S. China, S.E. Asia, Indonesia
**HABITAT:** open forest, swamp-jungle, gardens
**SIZE:** 10 cm (4 in)

A small, skulking warbler, the strong-footed warbler has a distinctive whistling call, culminating in a loud, explosive phrase, but is rarely seen. It is a solitary bird and forages for insects in the dense undergrowth found in its habitat. It may hop up into bushes but rarely climbs trees. Mountain birds make seasonal movements, descending to lower altitudes in winter and breeding between 2,000 and 3,000 m (6,600 and 10,000 ft).

The untidy nest is built in a bush, usually less than a meter or so above ground. It may be a cup-shaped or, sometimes, a domed structure, with an entrance near the top. Both parents incubate the 3 to 5, usually 4, eggs.

**NAME:** Ceylon Bush Warbler, *Bradypterus palliseri*
**RANGE:** Sri Lanka
**HABITAT:** montane forest undergrowth, dwarf bamboo thickets
**SIZE:** 16 cm (6¼ in)

Ceylon bush warblers live at altitudes of over 900 m (3,000 ft). In pairs, they skulk in dense undergrowth, searching under leaves and among stems for insects and worms, and rarely climb more than 2 m (6½ ft) above ground.

The male performs a sketchy courtship, climbing a little farther than usual up a stem to sing a brief song and then flying from one patch of vegetation to another. The nest is relatively large for the size of the birds and is made of moss, grass and bamboo leaves, lined with fine fibers. It is situated in a bush, close to the ground. The female lays 2 eggs.

**NAME:** Golden-crowned Kinglet, *Regulus satrapa*
**RANGE:** Alaska, S. Canada, USA; winters Mexico and Central America
**HABITAT:** forest, usually coniferous
**SIZE:** 8–10 cm (3–4 in)

This tiny bird is one of the 3 members of the Old World warbler subfamily to occur in North America. The plumage is restrained for the most part, but there is a conspicuous black-bordered crown, which is orange in the male and yellow in the female, hence the common name; juveniles develop the crown patch as they mature. Kinglets join mixed flocks to forage in the trees and bushes for insects and larvae.

The birds nest high in a conifer, usually a spruce. The female builds a globular nest of moss, lichen, pine needles and grass, bound together with spider's webs and lined with fine rootlets, fibers and feathers. This structure has an opening at the top and is suspended from twigs, to which it is bound with spider's webs. The female alone is thought to incubate the 8 to 10 eggs for 14 to 17 days, but both parents tend the young.

**NAME:** Little Grassbird, *Megalurus gramineus*
**RANGE:** Australia (except N.); Tasmania
**HABITAT:** swamps
**SIZE:** 14 cm (5½ in)

The little grassbird lives amid the vegetation of coastal and inland swamps. A furtive bird, it stays in cover as it creeps about, foraging for insects and small aquatic animals. It seldom flies in its everyday life, but since it occurs in temporary swamps, it must occasionally make quite long flights to find a new home, when its existing one dries out. Birds occupying permanent swamps are sedentary. Male and female look alike, with streaked brownish plumage and broad white eye stripes. The long tail accounts for almost half of the bird's length.

The nest is made in thick vegetation, sometimes over the swamp water. It is cup shaped and made of grass, lined with feathers. The female lays a clutch of 3 or 4 eggs.

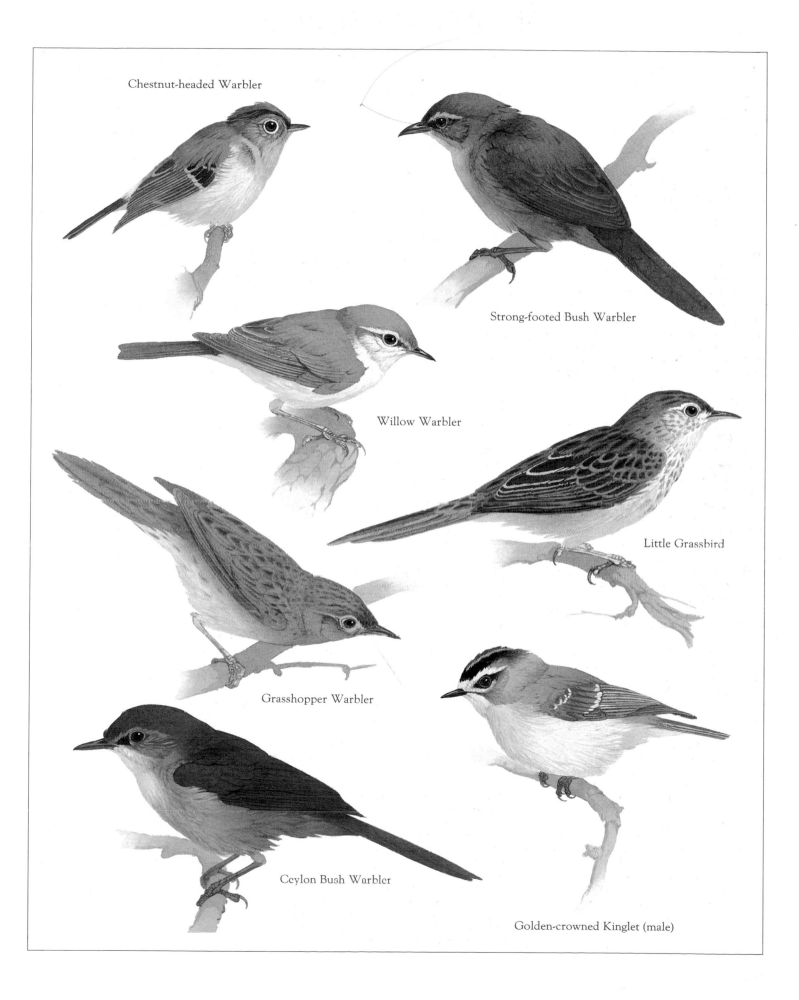

Chestnut-headed Warbler

Strong-footed Bush Warbler

Willow Warbler

Little Grassbird

Grasshopper Warbler

Ceylon Bush Warbler

Golden-crowned Kinglet (male)

# Australian Warblers

NAME: **Superb Blue Wren**, *Malurus cyaneus*
RANGE: **Australia: Victoria to Queensland; Tasmania**
HABITAT: **woodland, savanna, parks**
SIZE: **13 cm (5 in)**

Only in the male breeding plumage is this little bird superb. The breeding male has attractive, shiny blue plumage around the head and neck, contrasting with some bold black markings; older, dominant males tend to keep this plumage all year. Nonbreeding males and females are mainly brownish and dull white. The birds live in groups, ruled by a dominant pair, and together defend a territory from intruders. Hopping about with tails cocked, they forage for insects on the ground and among the vegetation.

All members of the group combine to build the dome-shaped nest, which is situated near the ground in a bush or on a tussock and is made of grass, rootlets and bark, bound with spider's webs. The dominant female lays 3 or 4 eggs, and again, all the group members assist with the 14-day incubation and the rearing of the young.

NAME: **Eyrean Grass Wren**, *Amytornis goyderi*
RANGE: **South Australia: Lake Eyre area**
HABITAT: **cane grass on sandhills, spinifex grassland**
SIZE: **14 cm (5½ in)** Ⓘ

The Eyrean grass wren is apparently a rare bird, but the exact state of the population is not known. In 1976, it was recorded in some numbers in the sandhills of Simpson Desert, in South Australia, but by the following year, the habitat had deteriorated, and the birds had largely gone. Prior to 1976, it had been recorded only at its discovery in 1874, in 1931 and in 1961.

A furtive little bird, the Eyrean grass wren stays well hidden as it forages among the tussocks of vegetation. Little is known of its breeding habits, but the observed nests have been partly domed, made of interwoven grass and stems.

NAME: **White-browed Scrubwren**, *Sericornis frontalis*
RANGE: **E. and S.E. Australia, islands in Bass Strait**
HABITAT: **bushy coastal vegetation**
SIZE: **11 cm (4¼ in)**

The white-browed scrubwren lives on or near the ground, keeping hidden in the thick undergrowth while it hops about in search of insects and other small invertebrates.

The domed nest is built in the undergrowth on or near the ground. It is made of leaves and fibers and has a side entrance. The female lays 3 eggs.

## MALURINAE:
### Australian Warbler Subfamily

Within this somewhat uncertain assemblage are 3 main tribes of birds: the Australian warblers (Acanthizini), the Australian wrens (Malurini) and the Australian chats (Epthianurini).

In the Australian warbler tribe are about 67 species of bird, with diverse common names such as gerygone, thornbill, bristlebird and scrubwren. Most are small birds, with sober plumage, which live in forest undergrowth.

Of the 30 species of Australian wren, one or two are also found in New Guinea. Male birds are brightly or boldly plumaged, with long, slender tails. Some have strange social and reproductive habits, which may be their way of dealing with the often harsh conditions of their habitat. Groups of birds hold a territory together, which they defend from other birds, and each group builds a single, spherical nest, in which one dominant female lays her eggs. All other adult members of the group then assist in the incubation and care of the young. Sometimes pairs nest alone, but they tend to have a high failure rate.

The 5 species of Australian chat are boldly marked little birds, which make erratic, nomadic migrations, according to the unpredictable rains in their arid range.

The position of the silktail within the huge family Muscicapidae is uncertain, and it has even been placed among the birds of paradise.

NAME: **Yellow-rumped Thornbill**, *Acanthiza chrysorrhoa*
RANGE: **Australia, south of Tropic of Capricorn**
HABITAT: **open woodland, savanna**
SIZE: **10 cm (4 in)**

The male and female of this species both have somewhat sober plumage but with deep-yellow rump feathers, the origin of their common name. They feed on insects and plant matter, such as seeds, which they find on the ground and by foraging in bushes and trees.

The large, untidy nest is made of grass and plant fibers and has a hooded brood chamber with a low, overhung entrance. It is usually situated in a low bush or other foliage. The female lays 3 eggs, which she incubates for 18 to 20 days; both parents then tend the young. The birds produce up to four broods a season, and young from earlier broods assist in the care of subsequent nestlings. This unusual habit is common to many members of this subfamily.

NAME: **White-throated Warbler**, *Gerygone olivacea*
RANGE: **S.E. New Guinea, coastal N. and E. Australia**
HABITAT: **open forest, woodland**
SIZE: **11 cm (4¼ in)**

An arboreal bird, the white-throated warbler forages for insects on bark and foliage and occasionally pursues prey on the wing. It usually occurs alone or in scattered, loosely knit groups. Male and female look alike, both with grayish-brown upperparts and yellow underparts.

The long, oval-shaped nest is suspended from twigs up to 15 m (50 ft) above ground. It is made of plant fiber and strips of bark, interwoven with spider's webs and lined with feathers or plant down; it has a hooded entrance near the top. The female lays 2 or 3 eggs.

NAME: **Crimson Chat**, *Epthianura tricolor*
RANGE: **Australia**
HABITAT: **grassy plains with some bush cover**
SIZE: **10–11 cm (4–4¼ in)**

The male crimson chat is a vividly plumaged little bird, with his red, white and brownish-black markings. The female bird is plainer, with more brown plumage, but she does have a crimson rump. The birds forage on or near the ground in grass or low trees and bushes and may poke their bills into flowers to find insects. If a large insect is caught, the chat wedges it in a forked twig and then tears it apart as it devours it.

Breeding takes place after heavy rainfall, when food supplies are assured; the birds usually breed in loose colonies. Courting males perform display flights, with crimson crown feathers erect. The cup-shaped nest, made of grass and twigs, is situated in a bush or on a tussock, and the female lays 3 or 4 eggs. Both parents incubate the eggs and tend the young.

NAME: **Silktail**, *Lamprolia victoriae*
RANGE: **Fiji**
HABITAT: **mature mountain forest**
SIZE: **12 cm (4¾ in)**

The silktail is a striking bird, with dark, velvety plumage, scattered with metallic blue spangles, and a white rump. It forages for its insect prey on the foliage of the forest understory and also goes down to the ground to find food. Swift and agile in flight, it darts between the trees and may also pursue slow-flying insects.

The nest is made in a tree, of fibers, rootlets, vines and slivers of bark and is lined with feathers. The female lays a single egg.

Silktail

Superb Blue Wren (male)

White-browed Scrubwren

Eyrean Grass Wren

Yellow-rumped Thornbill

White-throated Warbler

Crimson Chat (male)

# Old World Flycatchers

NAME: **Flame Robin,** *Petroica phoenicea*
RANGE: **Tasmania and adjacent Australian mainland**
HABITAT: **dry forest, woodland, open country**
SIZE: **13–14 cm (5–5½ in)**

The flame robin is so called because of the bright red throat and belly of the male bird, reminiscent of those of the European robin. The female has pale buff underparts, with sometimes a touch of orange-red on the belly. The birds feed on insects, taken on the ground and in trees, and continually flit from perch to perch. Normally solitary, they may form flocks, sometimes of one sex, outside the breeding season.

The nest is made of grass and bark strips, bound together with spider's webs. It may be in a tree fork or hollow, on a bank or among tree roots. The female lays 3 eggs.

NAME: **Spotted Flycatcher,** *Muscicapa striata*
RANGE: **Europe: Scandinavia, south to Mediterranean countries; N. Africa to central Asia; winters tropical Africa and S.W. Asia**
HABITAT: **forest edge, woodland, scrub, gardens, parks**
SIZE: **14 cm (5½ in)**

The spotted flycatcher feeds in the manner typical of its group, perching in exposed spots and making swift aerial sallies after insects. While perched, it constantly flicks its wings and tail. Male and female look alike, both with mainly grayish-brown plumage.

The female does most of the work of nest-building, making a neat structure of moss, bark and fibers, lined with rootlets and feathers. The nest may be in a variety of sites such as on a ledge, in a cavity or tree fork or on a wall or rock. Both parents incubate the 4 to 6 eggs for 12 to 14 days and tend the young. They often produce two broods.

NAME: **Rufous-tailed Jungle Flycatcher,** *Rhinomyias ruficauda*
RANGE: **Philippines, Borneo**
HABITAT: **forest**
SIZE: **14 cm (5½ in)**

A rather rare bird, the rufous-tailed jungle flycatcher frequents dense undergrowth, where it feeds on insects and spiders. Much of its food is gleaned from foliage, but it makes swift flights into the air to catch winged insects. The subspecies of this bird vary slightly in coloration, but all have the distinctive chestnut tail. The female looks similar to the male in most respects.

The breeding habits of this species are not known.

## MUSCICAPINAE: Old World Flycatcher Subfamily

This large subfamily of the family Muscicapidae includes nearly 150 species of insect-eating songbirds. All occur in the Old World, with the greatest diversity in Africa, Asia and Australasia. Some are brightly plumaged, others are dull, and flycatchers have diversified into a wide range of body forms and habits to fit different niches. Males and females look alike in some species and differ in others.

The "typical" flycatchers, which include some examples that occur in Europe, have a flat, wide beak, the base of which is surrounded by prominent bristles. Their method of insect capture is extremely characteristic: the feeding bird sits on a perch in a good vantage position for observing prey; if an insect passes, the bird launches itself into the air for a brief, agile, hunting flight and deftly captures the prey in its bill; it takes the prey back to its perch to eat. Some birds, of course, do use other methods of catching prey and feed on the ground or on foliage.

NAME: **Blue-throated Flycatcher,** *Niltava rubeculoides*
RANGE: **Himalayas through northern S.E. Asia to China; winters south of range**
HABITAT: **forest, gardens**
SIZE: **14 cm (5½ in)**

The blue-throated flycatcher lives in well-wooded areas with plenty of undergrowth. It does make aerial dashes after insect prey but hardly ever returns to the same perch, or even the same tree, to consume the catch. It may also drop down to the ground to find food and may flush out a concealed cricket or grasshopper with its open wings. Male and female differ in plumage, the female having mainly olive-brown and buff feathers instead of the distinctive blue of the male.

The nest is made in a hollow in a mossy bank, in a rock crevice or in a hole in a tree or bamboo stem. The female lays 3 to 5 eggs, usually 4, which both birds incubate for 11 or 12 days.

NAME: **Citrine Canary Flycatcher,** *Culicicapa helianthea*
RANGE: **Philippines, Sulawesi**
HABITAT: **forest, woodland**
SIZE: **about 10 cm (4 in)**

Also called the sunflower flycatcher, this bird has mostly yellow plumage of various shades; the upperparts of juvenile birds tend to be darker and more green than those of adults. It perches on the outer branches of trees and makes short aerial dashes after passing insects in true flycatcher fashion; it also sometimes feeds in mixed flocks.

NAME: **Maroon-breasted Flycatcher,** *Philentoma velata*
RANGE: **Malaysia, Sumatra, Java, Borneo**
HABITAT: **forest**
SIZE: **20.5 cm (8 in)**

A noisy, active bird, the maroon-breasted flycatcher frequents the lower to middle layers of the forest, often perching on low branches, vines and creepers. It catches all its prey on the wing and does not forage on foliage. It normally lives in pairs, and both sexes have loud, harsh calls. Male and female differ slightly in plumage: the female is a darker blue than the male and lacks his maroon chest patch. Nearly always found near water, these flycatchers love to bathe.

The nest is made on a forked branch of a tree.

NAME: **Pale/Mouse-coloured Flycatcher,** *Bradornis pallidus*
RANGE: **Africa, south of the Sahara**
HABITAT: **woodland, coastal scrub, gardens, cornfields**
SIZE: **15–18 cm (6–7 in)**

The pale flycatcher has largely grayish-brown plumage and is less conspicuous than many flycatchers; juvenile birds have some streaked and spotted plumage. In pairs or small, loosely knit groups, they forage on the ground for much of their food, such as spiders and termites, but also catch flies and moths in the air. They are quiet birds, making only an occasional twittering call.

Breeding begins at the start of, or just before, the rainy season. The small, neat, cup-shaped nest is made of rootlets and sited on a forked branch of a tree or bush. The female lays 2 or 3 eggs. Families remain together for a prolonged period, and there is some evidence that birds other than the parents help to rear broods.

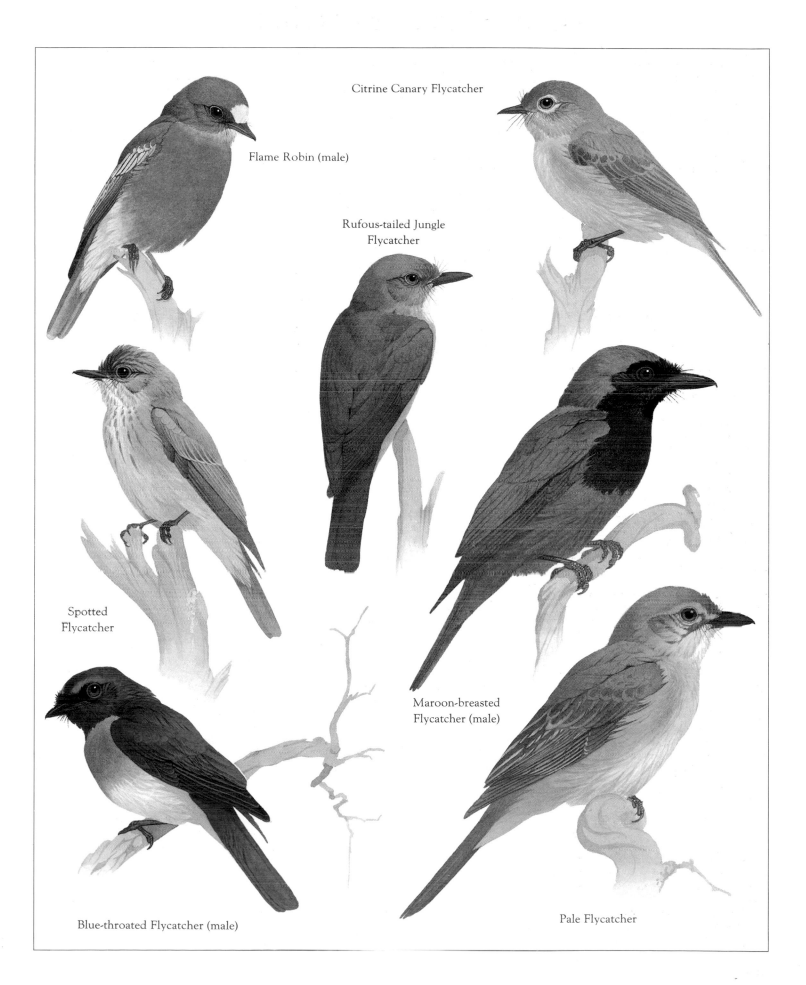

Citrine Canary Flycatcher

Flame Robin (male)

Rufous-tailed Jungle
Flycatcher

Spotted
Flycatcher

Maroon-breasted
Flycatcher (male)

Blue-throated Flycatcher (male)

Pale Flycatcher

# Monarch Flycatchers

## MONARCHINAE:
### Monarch Flycatcher Subfamily

Monarchs and paradise flycatchers are boldly plumaged birds of forest areas. Some dart out from perches to catch prey, while others search the foliage of the trees.

**NAME: Black-naped (Blue) Monarch,** *Hypothymis azurea*
**RANGE: India, S. China, S.E. Asia to Lesser Sunda Islands and Philippines**
**HABITAT: forest, scrub, bamboo thickets, cultivated land**
**SIZE: 16.5 cm (6½ in)**

The male black-naped monarch has bright blue plumage, with a little patch of black feathers on the nape of the neck that can be erected when the bird is excited. There is also a narrow black band across his chest. The female looks similar to the male but has grayish-brown plumage on the upperparts and lacks the black nape and chest markings.

This flycatcher tends to perch in higher trees than other species and makes agile looping flights after insect prey such as butterflies and moths; it also forages in undergrowth and on the ground. When a large insect is caught, the bird will hold it down with its foot and tear it apart before eating it. Usually seen alone or in pairs, the black-naped monarch is an extremely active, lively bird, constantly on the move as it flits from perch to perch.

The neat, cup-shaped nest is built on a forked branch, to which it is bound with spider's webs, or in a bush, sapling or bamboo clump. The female bird does most of the work, using grass and bark for the cup and covering the outside with moss, spider's webs and egg cases; the male attends her closely throughout the nest-building. She lays 3 or 4 eggs, which she incubates for 15 or 16 days. Both parents tend the young.

**NAME: White-tailed Crested Flycatcher,** *Trochocercus albonotatus*
**RANGE: Africa: Uganda, W. Kenya to Malawi, Zambia, Zimbabwe**
**HABITAT: highland forest**
**SIZE: 10 cm (4 in)**

The white-tailed crested flycatcher is an attractive little bird, with black, gray and white plumage; male and female look alike. It feeds on insects, making short, jerky flights after prey or foraging rapidly over foliage.

The male bird displays to his mate, hopping around her with his tail raised and his wings trailing. The neat little nest is made of woven moss, bound with cobwebs, and is built around a fork of a low tree. The female lays 2 eggs.

**NAME: Asian Paradise Flycatcher,** *Terpsiphone paradisi*
**RANGE: Turkestan to N.E. China; S.E. Asia, Indonesia**
**HABITAT: open forest, mangrove swamps, gardens, cultivated land**
**SIZE: 22.5 cm (8¾ in)**

The male Asian paradise flycatcher is a beautiful bird, with extremely long central tail feathers, which add 25.5 cm (10 in) or more to his length. Males occur in two color phases: white and rufous. The white male has white body and tail plumage, with a black head, crest and throat; the rufous male is more variable, according to race, but has rufous tail, back and wings. The female is similar to the rufous male but lacks the crest and long tail feathers.

Alone, or sometimes in pairs or mixed hunting parties, the paradise flycatcher frequents the higher branches of trees, flitting from perch to perch. Its flight is swift and it makes brief sallies from a perch to catch insect prey, returning to the same tree or to another to consume the item. It may also flush out insects on the ground. Flies, dragonflies, beetles, moths and butterflies are its main prey.

The courting male displays to his mate by arching his tail streamers gracefully, while singing and beating his wings. Both sexes help to build the nest, which is a deep, inverted cone, made in a horizontal forked branch of a tree, often near or overhanging water. The 3 or 4 eggs are incubated mostly by the female for 15 or 16 days; unusually for such a decorative bird, the male may sometimes assist and sits with his long tail hanging out behind him. The male bird also helps tend the nestlings.

**NAME: Boat-billed Flycatcher,** *Machaerirhynchus flaviventer*
**RANGE: Australia: N.E. Queensland; New Guinea and adjacent islands**
**HABITAT: rain forest**
**SIZE: 12 cm (4¾ in)**

The broad, flat bill is the distinctive feature of this flycatcher and the reason for its common name. Male and female differ slightly in appearance, the female having yellowish-olive upperparts, with areas of brownish-black, and fewer yellow and more white markings than the male has. A tree-living bird, it gleans insects from the foliage, moving busily from branch to branch, and also makes short flights to catch prey on the wing.

The shallow, cup-shaped nest is made of strips of bark, bound together with spider's webs and decorated with lichen; the interior is lined with vine tendrils. It is usually built fairly high up on a slender, forked branch. The female lays 2 eggs.

**NAME: Spectacled Monarch,** *Monarcha trivirgata*
**RANGE: E. Australia, New Guinea, the Moluccas, Timor, Flores**
**HABITAT: wet forest, mangrove swamps, woodland**
**SIZE: 15 cm (6 in)**

Both male and female spectacled monarchs have the black, masklike markings on the face that are the origin of their common name. A solitary, arboreal species, this monarch frequents low, dense vegetation, where it moves swiftly, yet quietly, hunting for insect prey. It may sometimes feed on the ground.

The cup-shaped nest is made of bark strips, lined with spider's webs, and is usually situated low in a bush or sapling. The female lays 2 eggs.

## PLATYSTEIRINAE: African Monarch Flycatcher Subfamily

These are chunky, boldly patterned flycatchers with short tails and strong bills. Many species have brightly colored wattles on the face.

**NAME: Black-headed Puffback,** *Batis minor*
**RANGE: Africa: Sudan to Somalia, south to Cameroon and Angola**
**HABITAT: open woodland, bush**
**SIZE: 10 cm (4 in)**

A small, rather stumpy flycatcher, the puffback can erect the plumage on its back, making itself appear rotund and fluffy — hence the common name. Male and female look alike in most respects, but the female lacks the male's black head plumage and has a dark chestnut, instead of black, band on the chest. They are restless little birds and move in pairs, searching the foliage for insect prey or making brief hunting flights in true flycatcher fashion.

The nest is made of fibers and lichen, bound with spider's webs, and is usually placed in a forked branch of a tree. The female lays 2 or 3 eggs.

**NAME: (Common) Wattle-eye,** *Platysteira cyanea*
**RANGE: W., central and N.E. Africa**
**HABITAT: forest, woodland, crop fields**
**SIZE: 13 cm (5 in)**

Distinctive red wattles over the eyes make the common wattle-eye easily recognizable. Wattle-eyes behave more like warblers than flycatchers, foraging in pairs over foliage and twigs for insect prey. In noisy, chattering flocks they make some seasonal migrations.

The cup-shaped nest is made of fine grass, plant fibers and lichen and is bound to a forked branch with spider's webs. The female lays 2 eggs.

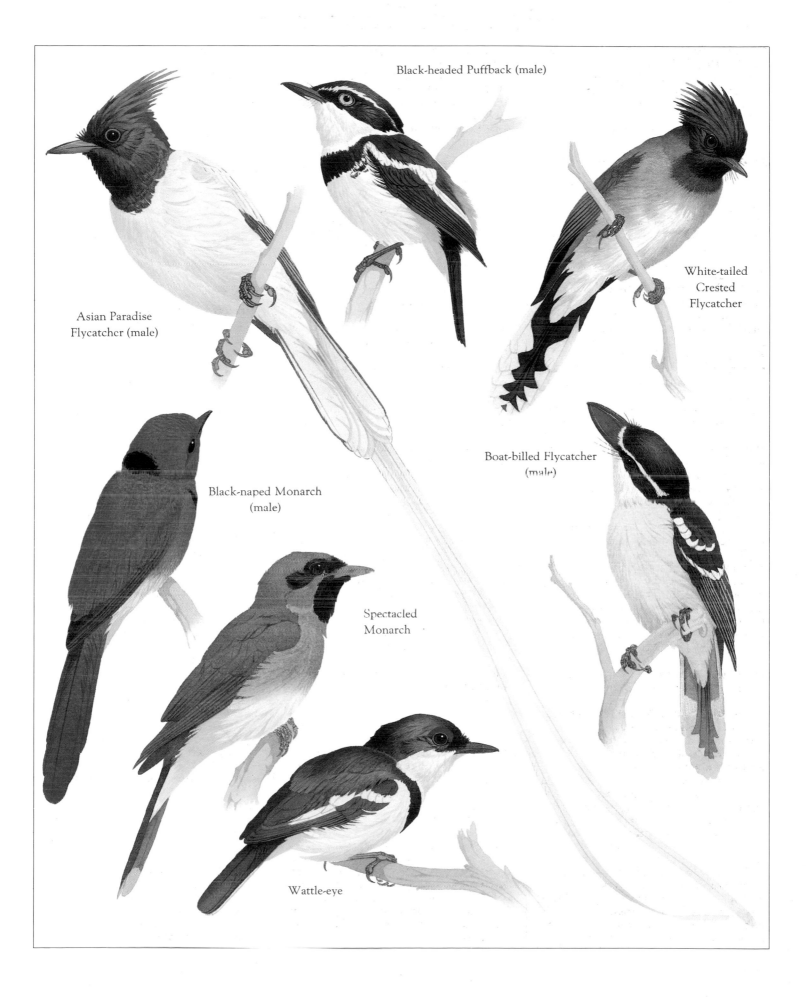

Black-headed Puffback (male)

Asian Paradise
Flycatcher (male)

White-tailed
Crested
Flycatcher

Black-naped Monarch
(male)

Boat-billed Flycatcher
(male)

Spectacled
Monarch

Wattle-eye

# Fantail Flycatchers, Whistlers

## RHIPIDURINAE:
### Fantail Flycatcher Subfamily

Most fantails occur in Australasia, with a few species in Asia. Their common name comes from their habit of continually spreading and wagging their tails as they move through low vegetation.

NAME: **Yellow-bellied Fantail, *Chelidorhynx hypoxantha***
RANGE: **Himalayas to S.W. China; northern S.E. Asia: Burma, Thailand, Laos**
HABITAT: **forest**
SIZE: **13 cm (5 in)**

The yellow-bellied fantail has bright yellow underparts and distinctive white tips to some of the tail feathers. Male and female birds look similar, but the male has black, masklike markings on the face, which are dark olive-brown in the female.

A lively, restless little bird, this fantail frequents the undergrowth up to the lower levels of the forest canopy, where it prances around with its tail fanned out, foraging for insects. It also feeds on tiny insects, which it takes in the air during brief, aerobatic flights, and it may flush insects out of vegetation with its spread wings.

The nest is made the same width as the horizontal branch on which it is sited, which provides a measure of camouflage. It is built from moss, covered with lichen and spider's webs and lined with hair and feathers. The female lays 3 eggs.

NAME: **Willie Wagtail, *Rhipidura leucophrys***
RANGE: **Australia, New Guinea, Solomon Islands, the Moluccas, Lesser Sunda Islands**
HABITAT: **forest edge to desert edge, parks, gardens, cultivated land**
SIZE: **20 cm (7¾ in)**

A common, adaptable bird, the willie wagtail has learned to take advantage of man-made environments. Male and female birds look alike, and their black and white plumage gives them a resemblance to the European pied wagtail, hence the common name. The willie wagtail generally lives alone, outside the breeding season, and finds food on the ground as well as in flight. It also sometimes sits on the backs of cattle and feeds on the insects disturbed by their hoofs.

The nest is made of grass, bark strips or plant fiber, bound tightly with spider's webs. It is usually built on a horizontal branch but may be made almost anywhere above ground. The female lays 4 eggs.

NAME: **Rufous Fantail, *Rhipidura rufifrons***
RANGE: **Lesser Sunda and W. Papuan Islands, N. and E. Australia, coastal areas of New Guinea, Louisiade Archipelago, Solomon and Santa Cruz Islands, Micronesia**
HABITAT: **forest, mangrove swamps**
SIZE: **16.5 cm (6½ in)**

With its tail fanned out, this flycatcher flies with speed and dexterity through the undergrowth, catching insects in flight and picking them off the foliage. Although a tree-living bird, it also feeds on the ground.

A pear-shaped nest, made of coarse plant material bound together with spider's webs, is built on a thin, forked branch as much as 9 m (30 ft) from the ground. Both parents incubate the 2 eggs for about 15 days and feed the young. The young fantails are able to fly about 15 days after hatching. Breeding birds may produce two to five broods a year, depending on food supplies.

## PACHYCEPHALINAE:
### Whistler Subfamily

The whistlers occur in Australia, New Guinea and Southeast Asia and have a variety of common names. Most of these flycatchers have attractive songs, and many pairs perform duets.

NAME: **Golden Whistler, *Pachycephala pectoralis***
RANGE: **Indonesia: Java to the Moluccas; Bismarck Archipelago to Fiji and Tonga; E., S. and S.W. Australia, Tasmania**
HABITAT: **forest, woodland, mallee (eucalyptus) scrub**
SIZE: **18 cm (7 in)**

Divided into perhaps 70 or 80 races, distributed among the many islands in its range, the golden whistler may have more subspecies than any other bird, some of which are as distinct as species. There is enormous variation between the races, particularly of head plumage, but the male bird is generally olive-green, yellow and black or gray. Females usually have olive-brown to olive-gray upperparts, with grayish throat and breast and whitish belly plumage.

A tree-dwelling bird, the golden whistler feeds in the trees on insects and sometimes on berries. It perches for long periods and is rather inactive compared to most flycatchers.

Both partners of a breeding pair help to build the nest, which is usually in a fork of a small tree or bush. It is made of grass, bark and leaves, lined with fine grass. Both birds incubate the 2 or 3 eggs and tend the young.

NAME: **Rusty Pitohui, *Pitohui ferrugineus***
RANGE: **New Guinea area, Aru Islands**
HABITAT: **lowland forest**
SIZE: **25.5–28 cm (10–11 in)**

One of the largest flycatchers, the rusty pitohui is a gregarious bird which lives in pairs or small parties. It moves slowly through the low levels of the forest, feeding on insects and fruit and often uttering soft calls. Male and female birds look alike, with mainly brown and rufous plumage.

The deep, cup-shaped nest is built on a multiple-forked branch, several meters up in a tree. It is made of twigs, pieces of vine and fiber and is lined with dead leaves, with a further lining of fine plant material. The female lays 1 egg.

NAME: **Gray Shrike-thrush, *Colluricincla harmonica***
RANGE: **Australia, Tasmania, islands in Bass Strait, S.E. New Guinea**
HABITAT: **forest, woodland, grassland, suburban parks**
SIZE: **23 cm (9 in)**

The gray shrike-thrush is a widespread species, common in Australia but found only in a restricted area in New Guinea. A solitary bird, it feeds in undergrowth and among lower branches of trees, as well as on the ground. Unusually for a flycatcher, it eats other small invertebrates, as well as insects. It sings beautifully, with clear, musical notes. The female differs slightly from the male in plumage, having a touch of brown on the upperparts, less distinct white facial markings and streaks on the breast.

The bowl-shaped nest is built on the ground, in a tree or bush or on a rock ledge and is made of bark strips and grass. Alternatively, the birds may take over an old nest of another species. The female lays 2 or 3 eggs, and there may be more than one brood.

NAME: **Crested Shriketit, *Falcunculus frontatus***
RANGE: **Australia (patchy distribution)**
HABITAT: **dry forest, woodland**
SIZE: **17–19 cm (6¾–7½ in)**

The crested shriketit has a rather unusual bill for a flycatcher: it is deep, laterally compressed and slightly hooked. The bird often clings to tree trunks and uses its bill to strip off bark in its search for insects and larvae. It also forages among foliage for insects and is beneficial to mankind in that it eats many larvae of the codlin moths that attack orchards.

The deep, cup-shaped nest is built in a fork of a tree, such as a eucalyptus sapling, and the male often clears the area around it by breaking twigs above the nest. The female lays 2 or 3 eggs.

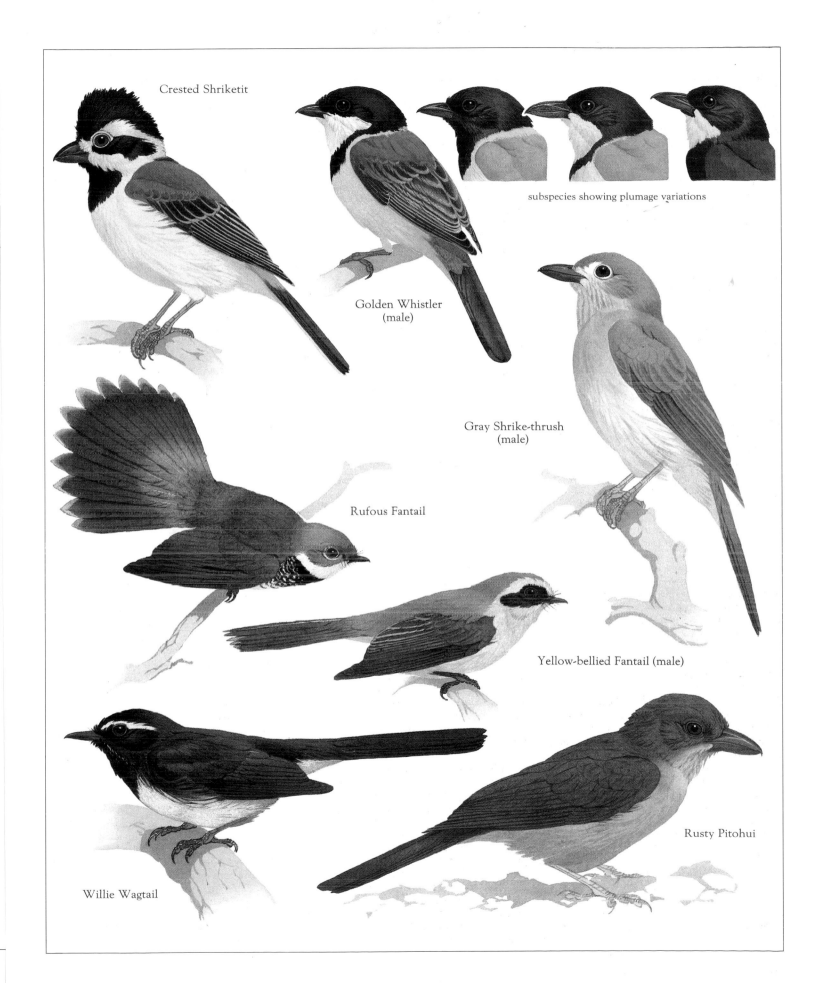

Crested Shriketit

subspecies showing plumage variations

Golden Whistler
(male)

Gray Shrike-thrush
(male)

Rufous Fantail

Yellow-bellied Fantail (male)

Willie Wagtail

Rusty Pitohui

# Treecreepers, Philippine Creepers, Nuthatches

## CERTHIIDAE: Treecreeper Family

The 6 species of treecreeper occur throughout the northern hemisphere in North and Central America, Europe, North Africa and Asia; and 1 species, the spotted creeper, lives in Africa, south of the Sahara. This bird is sometimes placed in its own separate family. Treecreepers are arboreal birds which clamber up tree trunks searching for insects to eat. They have sharp claws, enabling them to cling to bark, and long, thin bills, used for probing insect holes. All but the spotted creeper have stiff tails, which help to support them as they climb. Male and female look alike or nearly so.

NAME: **Brown Creeper**, *Certhia familiaris*
RANGE: **Canada, USA, Mexico, Central America; Europe and Asia, from Britain to Japan, south to the Himalayas**
HABITAT: **forest, parks**
SIZE: **13–15 cm (5–6 in)**

Using its stiff tail feathers as a prop, the brown creeper slowly makes its way up a tree trunk in a spiral path, searching every crevice in the bark for insects. When it reaches the top of one tree, it flies off to another and begins again at the base of that trunk. It also feeds on nuts and seeds. Male and female look alike, and both have long claws and slender, curved bills.

The nest is usually made behind a piece of loose bark and lined with moss and feathers. The female incubates the 5 or 6 eggs for 14 or 15 days, sometimes assisted by the male.

NAME: **Spotted Creeper**, *Salpornis spilonotus*
RANGE: **Africa: irregular distribution south of the Sahara to Angola and Zimbabwe; N. India**
HABITAT: **forest, savanna, woodland**
SIZE: **15 cm (6 in)**

The spotted creeper differs from other treecreepers in its soft tail, which it holds away from the tree trunk as it clambers up, searching for insects. With its long, curved bill, it probes every crevice in the bark for insects.

The cup-shaped nest is made in a vertically forked branch. Both parents incubate the 2 or 3 eggs.

## RHABDORNITHIDAE:
### Philippine Creeper Family

Both species in this small family live in the Philippines. Male and female look unalike.

NAME: **Stripe-headed Creeper**, *Rhabdornis mysticalis*
RANGE: **Philippines**
HABITAT: **forest**
SIZE: **15 cm (6 in)**

The stripe-headed creeper has strong legs and feet, well suited to climbing tree trunks, and a long, slightly curved bill with which it probes the bark for insects. It feeds in the same manner as the treecreepers, gradually working its way up a tree. It also licks up nectar from flowers with its brush-tipped tongue and feeds on fruit. The female has lighter plumage than the male and is brown where he is black.

Little is known of the breeding habits of this bird other than that it makes its nest in a hole in a tree.

## CLIMACTERIDAE:
### Australian Treecreeper Family

The 6 species of Australian treecreeper resemble the treecreepers of the family Certhiidae in their appearance and habits. With the aid of their long, curved bills, they feed primarily on bark-dwelling insects, but some species also feed on the ground. They occur in New Guinea as well as Australia. Male and female differ slightly in plumage.

NAME: **Brown Treecreeper**, *Climacteris picumnus*
RANGE: **Australia: Queensland to Victoria**
HABITAT: **forest, woodland**
SIZE: **15 cm (6 in)**

The brown treecreeper feeds largely on insects, which it picks from crevices in the bark of a tree trunk as it climbs upward in a spiral path. It makes short, fluttering flights from tree to tree and occasionally feeds on the ground. Male and female look more or less alike, but the female has a chestnut, not black, patch on the throat.

A cup-shaped nest is built in a hole, low down on a tree or in a rotting stump or post, and the female lays 3 or 4 eggs.

## SITTIDAE: Nuthatch Family

There are about 25 species in this family, which includes the nuthatches and the wallcreeper, found in North America, Europe and Asia, and the 3 species of sitella, all of which occur in Australasia. They are all robust little birds, with strong legs and feet and sharp claws to help them climb. Their strong, pointed bills are ideal for probing crevices in bark or rocks for insects. Male and female look alike in many species but differ slightly in others.

NAME: **Red-breasted Nuthatch**, *Sitta canadensis*
RANGE: **Alaska, Canada, USA**
HABITAT: **coniferous or mixed woodland**
SIZE: **11–12 cm (4¼–4¾ in)**

The male red-breasted nuthatch is identified by his white-edged black cap, black eye stripe and rusty-colored breast. The female has a dark-gray cap. The birds move rapidly over tree trunks and branches, searching for seeds and insects, and deftly investigate pinecones with their bills and extract any food items. Very large insects may even be wedged into bark crevices so that the nuthatches can bite off pieces. They also pursue insects in the air and collect seeds on the ground.

The breeding season begins in April or May. The nest is made in a tree hole, or a cavity is excavated in the stump or branch of a dead tree. Resin from coniferous trees is smeared around the entrance. Both parents incubate the 4 to 7 eggs for about 12 days.

NAME: **Varied Sitella**, *Neositta chrysoptera*
RANGE: **Australia**
HABITAT: **open forest, woodland**
SIZE: **10–12 cm (4–4¾ in)**

An agile little bird, the varied sitella runs up or down tree trunks with equal ease. Most of its life is spent in the trees, and it flits from place to place, probing crevices in the bark for insects. It is a gregarious bird and usually moves in small groups. There are many forms, all now included in this one species, which differ greatly in coloration.

The cup-shaped nest is made on a forked branch and camouflaged with pieces of bark. Both parents incubate the 3 or 4 eggs and feed the young.

NAME: **Wallcreeper**, *Tichodroma muraria*
RANGE: **central and S. Europe, across Asia to Mongolia and W. China**
HABITAT: **mountain cliffs**
SIZE: **16.5 cm (6½ in)**

An unusual bird with similiarities to both nuthatches and treecreepers, the wallcreeper is sometimes placed in its own monotypic family. It has a long, curved bill and broad, rounded wings with distinctive red patches. In its search for insects to feed on, it climbs up cliff faces, investigating every crevice, and then flits down to the bottom and starts again on another section of rock. It also forages on the ground under stones but is rarely seen on trees.

The male courts the female with display flights, which show off his wing colors. He helps the female build a nest of moss, grass and rootlets in a rock crevice. The female incubates the 3 to 5 eggs, and both parents feed the young.

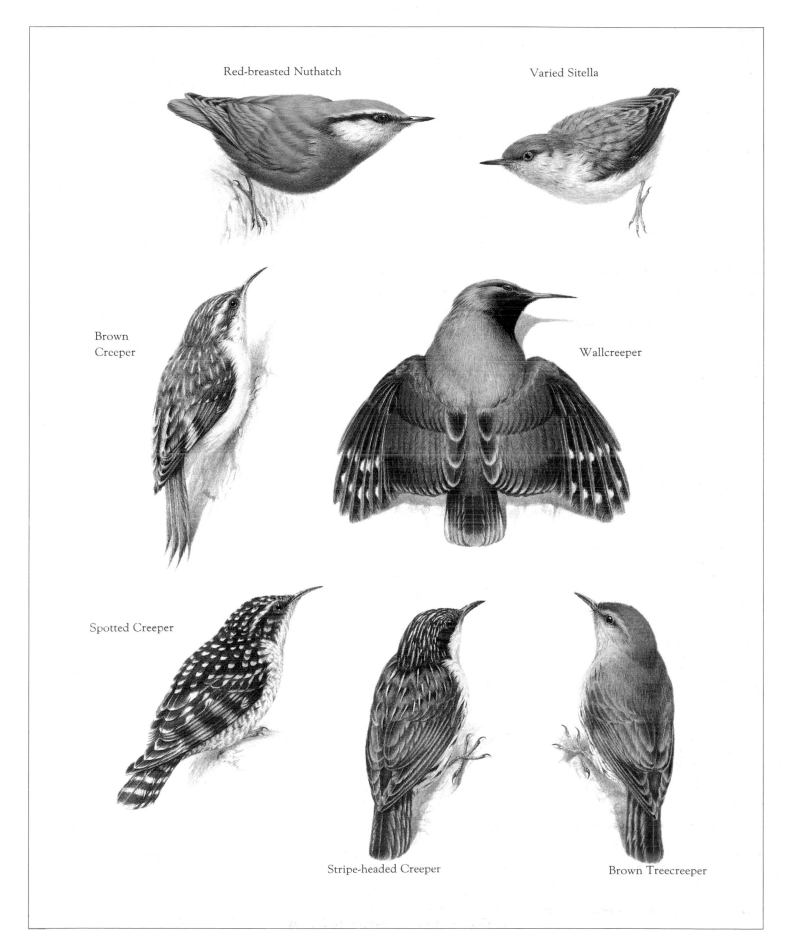

Red-breasted Nuthatch

Varied Sitella

Brown
Creeper

Wallcreeper

Spotted Creeper

Stripe-headed Creeper

Brown Treecreeper

# Flowerpeckers, White-eyes

## DICAEIDAE: Flowerpecker Family

The 58 species of flowerpecker live in Asia, from India to China, and south to Australasia. The greatest diversity of species occurs in the New Guinea area and the Philippines. Flowerpeckers are small birds with short legs and tails. Their bills vary in shape but are partially serrated, which perhaps helps them deal with sticky fruit. The tongue is forked, with the edges rolled into almost complete tubes, an adaptation probably linked to nectar-feeding. Fruit and berries are the flowerpeckers' most important foods, but the birds are often seen on flowers and do take some nectar as well as insects.

Some flowerpeckers have rather drab plumage, and in these species the sexes are similar. In others, however, the males are brightly colored. The 7 species of pardalote, which may not actually belong to this family, have bold, spotted plumage.

NAME: **Crimson-breasted Flowerpecker,** *Prionochilus percussus*
RANGE: **Burma, Malaysia, Borneo, Java, Sumatra and adjacent small islands**
HABITAT: **forest, secondary growth**
SIZE: **10 cm (4 in)**

A red patch on the breast and one on the crown are characteristics of the male of this species, which also has a bright yellow belly and blue upperparts. The female is mainly olive-green, with some grayish plumage and an indistinct orange patch on the crown. An active little bird, the crimson-breasted flowerpecker flies with quick, darting movements and feeds high in the trees, mostly on berries.

The purse-shaped nest is suspended from a branch of a tree and is made of pieces of tree fern. Little is known of the laying habits of this species, but it is thought to produce 1 egg.

NAME: **Black Berrypecker,** *Melanocharis nigra*
RANGE: **New Guinea, Japen and other associated islands, including Aru Islands**
HABITAT: **lowland forest**
SIZE: **11.5 cm (4½ in)**

An agile, quick-moving bird, the black berrypecker usually feeds in the lower levels of the forest, eating mainly berries and fruits but also spiders and insects; it will occasionally drink nectar. It may fly to an isolated tree outside the forest to feed. Although usually solitary, black berrypeckers do sometimes congregate at feeding trees. Male and female differ in appearance: the male is all black or black and green, while the female is dull green and gray.

NAME: **Mistletoe Bird,** *Dicaeum hirundinaceum*
RANGE: **Australia, Aru Islands**
HABITAT: **forest, scrub**
SIZE: **10 cm (4 in)**

The handsome male mistletoe bird has shiny, blue-black, red and white plumage, while the female is a duller brownish-gray. A tree-dwelling species, the mistletoe bird forages high in the trees for berries, particularly those of the mistletoe; the young also feed on insects. The soft part of the berry passes to the stomach, while the hard seeds bypass the specialized digestive system and are quickly expelled. Thus the bird is of great aid to the plant in dispersing its seeds. A solitary bird, this flowerpecker wanders wherever it can find mistletoe in fruit.

The female makes a nest in the shape of an inverted cone, which hangs from a branch of a tree. She lays 3 eggs and incubates them for about 12 days. Both parents feed the young.

NAME: **Spotted Pardalote,** *Pardalotus punctatus*
RANGE: **Australia, Tasmania**
HABITAT: **forest, woodland**
SIZE: **9 cm (3½ in)**

The colorful spotted pardalote has characteristic spots on its plumage that are mostly white in the male and yellow in the female. It feeds on insects, which it finds on the ground and in trees; an agile climber, it clings to twigs in almost any position as it makes a thorough search of the foliage. Outside the breeding season, these pardalotes live alone or in small flocks, sometimes including other species.

A breeding pair excavates a tunnel in a bank or slope and makes a globular nest of bark and grass in a chamber at the end of it. There are usually 4 eggs, incubated by both parents for 14 to 16 days.

## ZOSTEROPIDAE: White-eye Family

The 80 or so species of white-eye are a remarkably uniform group of birds. Most are small, with rounded wings and short legs, and have a greenish back, yellow underparts and characteristic rings of white feathers around the eyes. There are some exceptions which are larger in size and duller in plumage. The center of their distribution is Indonesia, but white-eyes also extend into Africa, New Zealand, Japan and the islands of the Pacific. They tend to live in wooded country and gardens, rather than forest, and they feed on insects, fruit and nectar. Male and female look alike.

NAME: **Japanese White-eye,** *Zosterops japonica*
RANGE: **Japan, E. and S. China, Taiwan, Hainan, Philippines; S.E. Asia; Burma, Thailand, Laos**
HABITAT: **woodland, scrub**
SIZE: **11.5 cm (4½ in)**

The Japanese white-eye has some gray plumage on the lower part of its belly; its beak is slender and pointed. A small, active bird, it forages in flocks over trees and bushes, searching for insects, particularly ants, and their eggs and larvae; it also feeds on buds, seeds and fruit. It flits from tree to tree, constantly making its faint, plaintive call, and never comes to the ground.

A cup-shaped nest is made of grass stems and fiber, lined with moss, and is placed in the fork of a thin branch. The female lays 3 or 4 eggs.

NAME: **Gray-breasted White-eye (Silver-eye),** *Zosterops lateralis*
RANGE: **E. and S.E. Australia, Tasmania, New Zealand, Vanuatu, Fiji**
HABITAT: **varied, with trees**
SIZE: **12 cm (4¾ in)**

An adaptable bird, the gray-breasted white-eye tolerates almost any habitat at any altitude, particularly on the islands in its range. It forages at any level of trees, on agricultural land or in gardens, feeding on fruit, insects and nectar from flowers. It occasionally comes to the ground to feed and even into open country. Male and female look alike, both with sharply pointed and slightly curved bills.

The nest is made of plant fiber and grasses, bound together with cobwebs, and is attached to twigs of a tree or bush by its rim. The female lays 2 to 4 eggs, which are incubated by both parents for about 11 days.

NAME: **Príncipe Island Speirops,** *Speirops leucophoea*
RANGE: **Príncipe Island (Gulf of Guinea)**
HABITAT: **forest**
SIZE: **13.5 cm (5¼ in)**

One of the few African species of white-eye, this speirops has largely buff-gray plumage, with some white on throat and belly. In small parties, these restless, active little birds feed in the trees, searching the foliage for insects and also consuming seeds. Their movements are quick and agile, with much flicking of the wings.

The nest is made of grass and bound to a branch with cobwebs or fine plant fiber. The female lays 2 eggs.

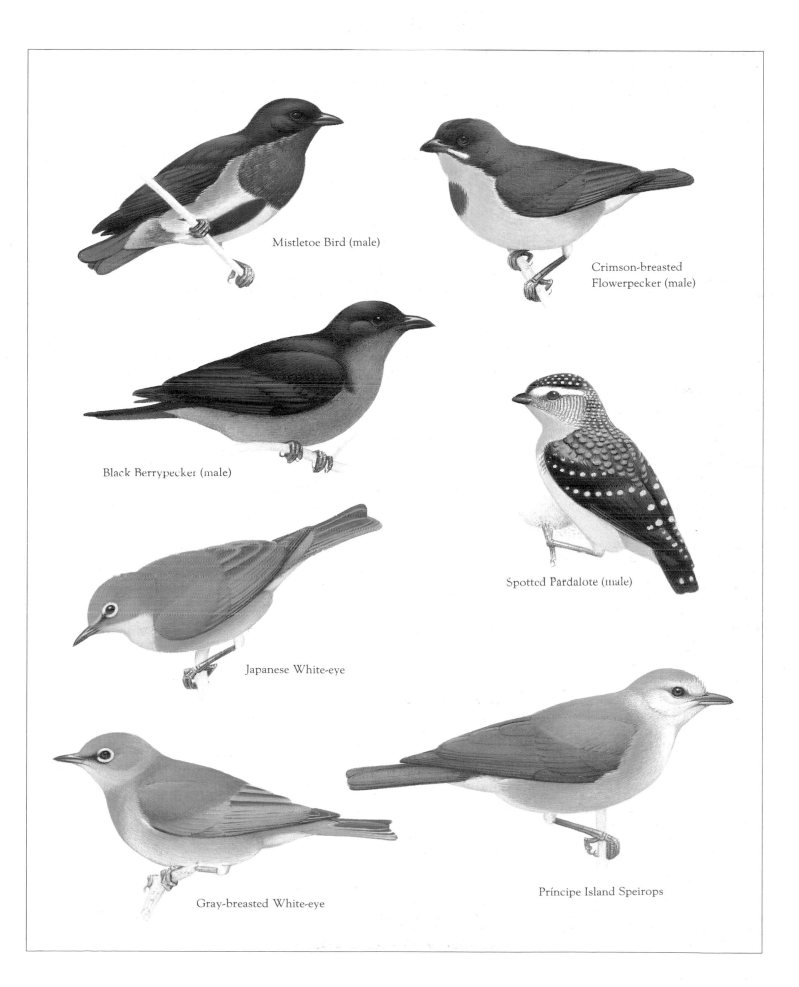

Mistletoe Bird (male)

Crimson-breasted
Flowerpecker (male)

Black Berrypecker (male)

Spotted Pardalote (male)

Japanese White-eye

Gray-breasted White-eye

Príncipe Island Speirops

# Sunbirds

NAME: **Crimson/Yellow-backed Sunbird**,
*Aethopyga siparaja*
RANGE: India, S.E. Asia, Sumatra, Java,
Borneo, Sulawesi, Philippines
HABITAT: forest, cultivated land
SIZE: 11 cm ($4\frac{1}{4}$ in)

The elongate central feathers of the male's metallic green tail add another few centimeters to his length. The female lacks his bright crimson plumage and is olive-green, with yellowish underparts. These sunbirds forage among flowers of trees, shrubs and garden plants, clinging to the stems and twigs while they suck nectar from the blooms. A few insects and spiders are also eaten.

A pear-shaped nest, made of plant down, rootlets, moss and grass, is suspended from a branch or twig. The female lays 2 or 3 eggs.

NAME: **Ruby-cheeked Sunbird**,
*Anthreptes singalensis*
RANGE: E. Himalayas to Burma,
Thailand, Malaysia, Sumatra, Java,
Borneo and adjacent islands
HABITAT: open forest, scrub
SIZE: 11.5 cm ($4\frac{1}{2}$ in)

Both male and female ruby-cheeked sunbirds have pale orange throats and yellow bellies, but the female is otherwise less brilliantly colored than the male, with largely olive-green plumage. These sunbirds flit quickly around the foliage, searching for insects and probing blossoms for nectar.

The pear-shaped nest is suspended in a bush from twigs not far from the ground. It is made of fine plant fiber and stalks and has a side entrance, sheltered by an overhanging porch. The female lays 2 eggs.

NAME: **Long-billed Spiderhunter**,
*Arachnothera robusta*
RANGE: Thailand, Malaysia, Sumatra,
Java, Borneo
HABITAT: forest
SIZE: 19–21.5 cm ($7\frac{1}{2}$–$8\frac{1}{2}$ in)

The long-billed spiderhunter is a large sunbird, with an extremely long, thick bill. Like all spiderhunters, it has duller plumage than other sunbirds; male and female look similar, but the male has small orange-yellow tufts at each side of his breast. This spiderhunter usually forages at the tops of tall trees, darting from one to another in search of insects and spiders or perching on high branches. Its flight is strong and direct.

The nest is made under a large leaf, such as a banana leaf, which forms the top of the nest. This structure of coarse plant fiber is attached to the leaf by threads of fiber, passed through the leaf and twisted into knots on its upper surface. An entrance is left near the tip of the leaf. The female lays 2 eggs.

## NECTARINIIDAE: Sunbird Family

With their brilliantly colorful, glossy, iridescent feathers, fluttering, rapid flight and sharp, metallic calls, the sunbirds are distinctive and conspicuous. In ecological terms, sunbirds are the Old World counterparts of the hummingbirds of the Americas, but they are less skillful in flight and far more uniform in their appearance.

There are 116 species of sunbird. More than half of these live in Africa, south of the Sahara, but others occur in southern Asia and Australasia. In all species (except for the group known as spiderhunters, which are all soberly colored) males have much more showy plumage than their mates, although some females, too, have patches of iridescence. The female bird generally incubates the eggs for a period of 13 or 14 days and cares for the young; in some species the male may help to find food. The typical sunbird has short, rounded wings, strong legs and feet and a long, downward-curving bill. Using their specialized bills, almost all forms feed on nectar and also on insects. The beak is inserted into the flower, and the sugary liquid is sucked out through the tubular, split-tipped tongue. If it cannot reach the nectar, the sunbird will pierce the flower base to obtain it. Unlike the hummingbirds, sunbirds can hover only briefly, so they use their sturdy legs and feet to perch while they feed.

NAME: **Olive-backed Sunbird**, *Nectarinia jugularis*
RANGE: Hainan, S.E. Asia, Indonesia,
New Guinea, Bismarck Archipelago,
Solomon Islands; Australia:
N.E. Queensland
HABITAT: forest, scrub, mangrove
swamps, gardens
SIZE: 12 cm ($4\frac{3}{4}$ in)

The only sunbird found in Australia, this species is common throughout its range. Darting from tree to tree, it searches flowers for insects and nectar, sometimes also catching insects in the air. It will hover briefly before a flower but normally clings to the foliage. Male and female differ in appearance, the female having a bright yellow throat and underparts but the same olive back as the male. Nonbreeding males sometimes look similar to females but have a blue-black band down the center of the throat and an orange tinge to the throat and upper breast.

The nest is made of plant fibers and bark, bound with cobwebs and suspended from a twig of a bush or low tree. The female lays 2 or 3 eggs.

NAME: **Purple-throated Sunbird**,
*Nectarinia sperata*
RANGE: Assam, Bangladesh, Burma,
Thailand, Laos, Malaysia, Sumatra,
Java, Borneo, Sulawesi, Philippines
HABITAT: scrub, second growth forest,
mangrove swamps, gardens
SIZE: 10 cm (4 in)

The colorful male purple-throated sunbird is distinguished by his glittering amethyst throat. The female has olive upperparts and a yellow belly. This sunbird does eat small insects, but its main food is nectar, which it extracts from flowers with its slender, curved bill. It hops and climbs with ease around trees and bushes, but its flight is weak.

An oval nest, made of plant fiber and rootlets bound with spider's webs, is suspended from a branch or palm frond up to 6 m (20 ft) above ground. The female lays 2 eggs.

NAME: **Scarlet-tufted Malachite Sunbird**,
*Nectarinia johnstoni*
RANGE: Africa: mountain ranges in
E. Zaire, W. Uganda, Kenya,
Tanzania, Malawi, Zambia
HABITAT: alpine zone of mountains up to
the limits of plant growth
SIZE: male: 25.5–30.5 cm (10–12 in)
female: 14–15 cm ($5\frac{1}{2}$–6 in)

The elongate central tail feathers of the male of this species account for much of the difference in length between the sexes. In nonbreeding plumage the male's gleaming, metallic feathers are dark brown, but the long tail feathers are retained. The female is dark brown but, like the male, has red tufts at each side of the breast. This sunbird is attracted to the flowers of the protea bushes and giant lobelias found in its alpine habitat. Its main food, however, is insects, particularly flies, which it often catches on the wing.

Its oval nest is made in a low shrub from plant down, dried stems and rootlets. The female lays 1 or 2 eggs.

NAME: **Superb Sunbird**, *Nectarinia superba*
RANGE: Africa: Sierra Leone to Angola,
Uganda
HABITAT: forest edge, clearings
SIZE: 14 cm ($5\frac{1}{2}$ in)

The superb sunbird forages in the forest canopy for insects and also sucks nectar from flowers. It is partial to the flowers of erythrina trees, which occur near forest, and also to the flowers of forest creepers. The male bird has multicolored plumage, some of it with a metallic sheen, while the female is olive-green with greenish-yellow underparts.

An untidy nest is made of grass, leaves and lichen and suspended from a branch. The female lays 1 or 2 eggs.

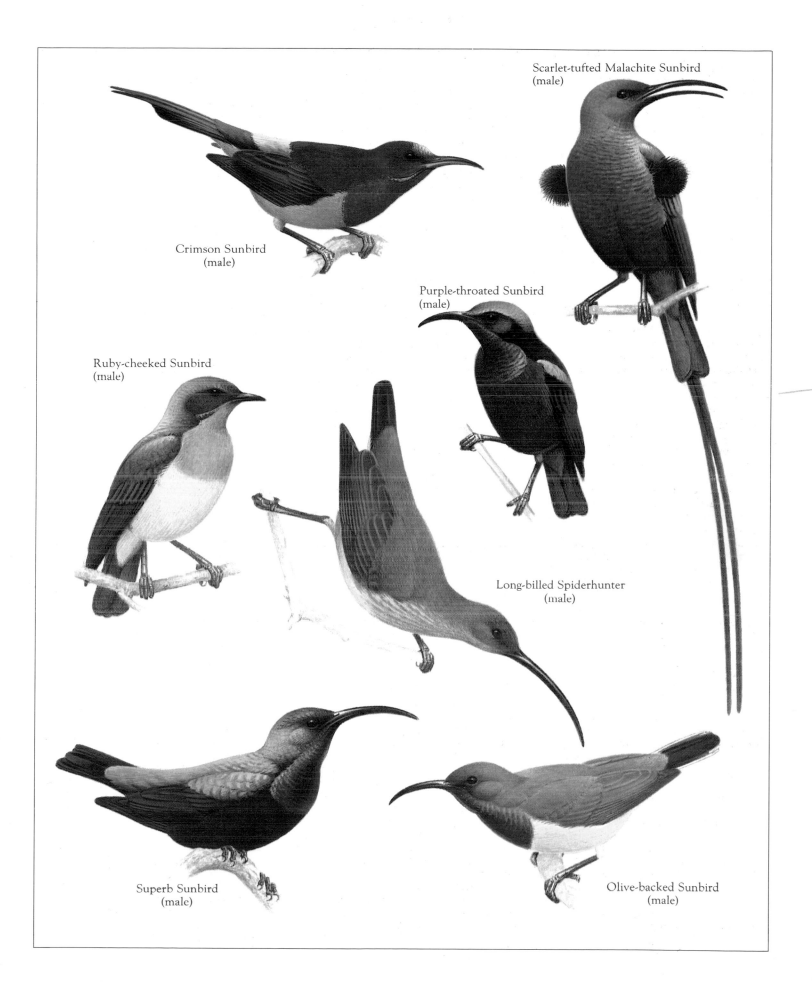

Scarlet-tufted Malachite Sunbird
(male)

Crimson Sunbird
(male)

Purple-throated Sunbird
(male)

Ruby-cheeked Sunbird
(male)

Long-billed Spiderhunter
(male)

Superb Sunbird
(male)

Olive-backed Sunbird
(male)

# Honey Eaters

NAME: Kauai O-o, *Moho braccatus*
RANGE: Hawaiian Islands: Kauai
HABITAT: montane rain forest
SIZE: 19–21.5 cm (7½–8½ in)                    Ⓔ

Thought to be extinct, like the other 3 species of Hawaiian o-o, the Kauai species was rediscovered in 1960 in the Alakai Swamp. Its relatives were taken in large numbers for their colorful yellow feathers and eventually wiped out, but the more sober coloration of this species saved it from exploitation. It has, however, suffered from the introduction of avian competitors and predators and seems to be intolerant of any alteration in its rain forest habitat. Thus changes, such as the introduction of herbivores and exotic plants, pose a serious threat to the bird's survival. The present population is protected but very small, perhaps only a few birds.

The Kauai o-o feeds on nectar, berries, spiders, insects and snails. It makes its nest in a cavity in an ohia tree and lays 2 eggs on a bed of dead plant material. Both parents feed the young.

NAME: **Brown Honey Eater,** *Lichmera indistincta*
RANGE: **Australia, New Guinea, Aru Islands, Lesser Sunda Islands to Bali**
HABITAT: **forest, woodland, mangrove swamps, cultivated land, gardens**
SIZE: 12–15 cm (4¾–6 in)

A restless, active bird, the brown honey eater feeds among flowering trees and bushes on nectar and insects; it also catches insects on the wing. It lives alone, in small groups or in larger flocks and is always found near water. It has one of the most beautiful voices of all Australian songbirds.

The nest is cup shaped and made of tightly packed bark shreds and grass, bound with cobwebs. It is suspended from a twig or placed among the foliage of a bush or tree. The female lays 2 eggs.

NAME: **Strong-billed Honey Eater,** *Melithreptus validirostris*
RANGE: **Tasmania, islands in Bass Strait**
HABITAT: **open forest, woodland**
SIZE: 14 cm (5½ in)

Popularly known as the bark-bird, this honey eater has the unusual habit of hopping about on tree trunks, stripping off the bark in its eager search for insects. It is often seen on eucalyptus trees, some of which have loose bark. Nectar, so important to most of the honey eaters, forms only a small part of this bird's diet, and it is rarely seen among tree blossoms. Male and female look alike.

The nest is suspended from a drooping branch and is made of bark strips and grass. The female lays 2, or sometimes 3, eggs.

## MELIPHAGIDAE:
## Honey Eater Family

With a few exceptions, the 167 species of honey eater occur in the Australian and southwest Pacific regions; 1 species, *Lichmera indistincta*, occurs in Bali. There are, however, 2 species of sugarbird which occur in Africa; both are in the genus *Promerops*. These birds are included with the honey eaters or sometimes classified in their own family. There is some argument as to whether they are a related, but separate group of birds or a part of the main honey eater stock that became isolated millions of years ago.

As their name indirectly suggests, the honey eaters consume nectar from flowers in a manner similar to sunbirds. They are usually larger than sunbirds, however, and most have duller, green or brownish plumage; they are also much more diverse, having adapted to a variety of habitats. Honey eaters have remarkable specializations for nectar-feeding. Despite the variation in body size and beak shape among honey eaters, all have a highly modified, long, protrusible tongue. At its base, this tongue can be curled up to form two long, nectar-transporting grooves; and at its tip, it splits into four parts, each of which is frilled, making the entire end of the tongue an absorbent brush for nectar collection. Honey eaters also eat insects, for protein, and fruit.

Generally tree-dwelling, honey eaters are gregarious birds, aggressive to other species. Male and female look alike in some species, unalike in others.

NAME: **Cardinal Honey Eater,** *Myzomela cardinalis*
RANGE: **Loyalty Islands, Vanuatu, Samoa, Torres and Santa Cruz Islands, Palau Islands, Mariana and Caroline Islands, Solomon Islands (marginally)**
HABITAT: **forest, open woodland, cultivated land**
SIZE: 9 cm (3½ in)

The cardinal honey eater is one of the smallest honey eaters, and with its bright coloration, does resemble a sunbird. It forages for small insects and nectar and will often form large groups at favored feeding sites. Its flight is fast and direct. Male and female differ in appearance; the male has vivid red and black plumage, while the female is mainly olive-gray, with some red on her rump and lower back.

A small, cup-shaped nest, made of grass stems, is built on a forked branch. The female lays 1 or 2 eggs.

NAME: Fuscous Honey Eater, *Meliphaga fusca*
RANGE: S.E. New Guinea, E. and N. Australia
HABITAT: open forest
SIZE: 15 cm (6 in)

The fuscous honey eater forages busily among the foliage at various heights, searching for nectar and insects. It also makes aerial dashes to catch insects on the wing. It is a fairly common bird and generally lives alone or in small parties. Male and female look alike, with olive-brown plumage enlivened by touches of yellow and dark markings on the cheeks.

The female lays 2 or 3 eggs in a cup-shaped nest, made of plant fiber and grass and suspended in a tree.

NAME: **Little Friarbird,** *Philemon citreogularis*
RANGE: **E. and N. Australia, S. New Guinea, islands in Banda Sea**
HABITAT: **open forest, woodland**
SIZE: 25–28 cm (9¾–11 in)

Like all friarbirds, the little friarbird has an area of bare skin on its head, the origin of its common name. Male and female look similar and, despite the name "little," are not much smaller than any other friarbirds. The little friarbird forages in all kinds of trees and bushes for fruit, insects and nectar. It makes a variety of harsh cries, particularly when feeding in a squabbling flock, but also has a more attractive musical song. In the south of Australia, these birds are thought to make regular seasonal movements.

The cup-shaped nest is made of bark strips and plant fiber and is built on a forked branch or suspended from a branch, often overhanging water. The female lays 2 to 4 eggs.

NAME: **Long-bearded Honey Eater,** *Melidectes princeps*
RANGE: **New Guinea**
HABITAT: **mountain forest, alpine grassland**
SIZE: 26.5 cm (10½ in)

Distinguished by the white "whiskers" on its throat, the long-bearded honey eater has largely black plumage, with some light-colored bare skin around the eyes. Less arboreal than other honey eaters, this bird spends much of its time on the ground, probing the leaf litter with its long, curved bill to find insects and sedge seeds. It also flies jerkily from tree to tree and will climb trees occasionally to feed on berries and fruit.

A bulky nest, made of moss and fungal threads, is built in a bush or tree a meter or so off the ground. The female lays 1 egg.

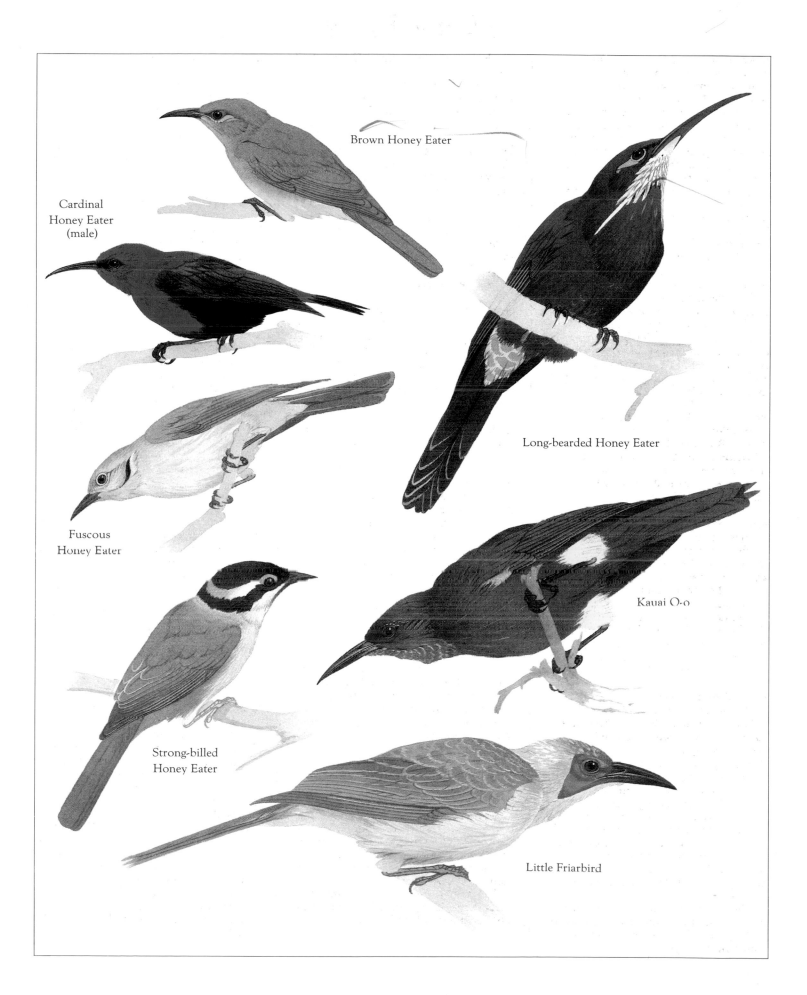

Brown Honey Eater

Cardinal
Honey Eater
(male)

Fuscous
Honey Eater

Long-bearded Honey Eater

Kauai O-o

Strong-billed
Honey Eater

Little Friarbird

# Honey Eaters

**NAME:** Common Melipotes, *Melipotes fumigatus*
**RANGE:** mountains of central New Guinea
**HABITAT:** forest at 1,300–2,700 m (4,300–9,000 ft)
**SIZE:** 21.5 cm (8½ in)

A quiet, slow-moving bird, the common melipotes moves about the trees in search of insects, particularly the sedentary, rather than the active varieties. It may, however, chase any flying insects that it disturbs. The common melipotes also feeds on fruit but is rarely seen on a flowering tree; its tongue has no brush-tip for nectar feeding. It lives alone or in pairs or sometimes gathers in flocks. Male and female look alike, with short bills and some bare, orange-yellow skin on the face.

The nest is a deep cup, made of mosses and plant fibers and lined with dead leaves and ferns. It is attached by its rim to the end of a branch. Like many mountain-dwelling honey eaters with sparse food supplies, this species lays only 1 egg. The young bird is fed with berries.

**NAME:** Tui, *Prosthemadera novaeseelandiae*
**RANGE:** New Zealand and coastal islands; Kermadec, Chatham and Auckland Islands
**HABITAT:** forest, suburban areas
**SIZE:** 29–32 cm (11½–12½ in)

Also aptly known as the parson bird, the tui has a bib of white tufts at the throat and a ring of fine, lacy feathers which form a collar. The female tui has smaller throat tufts than the male and a paler belly. Juveniles develop throat tufts within a month of hatching and have full adult plumage by about 3 months.

Tuis are noisy, vigorous birds; they fly around in the trees at high speed, sometimes plummeting down from considerable heights. They feed on insects, fruit and, using their brushlike tongues, on nectar. Tuis are aggressive, defending their food and nests against intruders

In the breeding season, male tuis make spectacular aerial dives, rolling and looping as they descend. The nest is usually made in the fork of a tree and is built with sticks and twigs and lined with fine plant material. The female incubates the 2 to 4 eggs for about 14 days. Throughout the incubation period, the male seems to sing almost continuously from a nearby tree but helps the female to feed the young once they hatch. There are often two broods a season.

**NAME:** Red Wattlebird, *Anthochaera carunculata*
**RANGE:** Australia: New South Wales to Western Australia
**HABITAT:** open forest, woodland, suburban parks and gardens
**SIZE:** 32–35 cm (12½–13¾ in) including tail of 16 cm (6¼ in)

The aggressive, noisy red wattlebird is the largest honey eater in mainland Australia. It is very active in the trees, preferring banksia and eucalyptus, and feeds on nectar, fruit and insects. It lives alone or wanders in small parties; in the west of its range it makes regular north-south movements. Male and female look alike, both with fleshy red wattles behind the eyes.

The nest is made of sticks and twigs on a horizontal branch of a bush or tree; it is sometimes lined with grass. The female lays 2 or 3 eggs.

**NAME:** Pygmy Honey Eater, *Oedistoma pygmaeum*
**RANGE:** New Guinea and adjacent islands
**HABITAT:** forest
**SIZE:** 7.5 cm (3 in)

One of the smallest of New Guinea birds, the pygmy honey eater bears little resemblance to other members of its family. The male has olive plumage with lighter underparts and an off-white throat; the female is slightly smaller and has duller plumage. Both sexes have short tails and curved bills. The pygmy honey eater frequents the lower levels of the forest but also forages in the tallest flowering trees. It feeds on nectar, insects and spiders.

**NAME:** Noisy Miner, *Manorina melanocephala*
**RANGE:** Australia: Queensland to Victoria; Tasmania, islands in Bass Strait
**HABITAT:** woodland, suburban parks
**SIZE:** 26–28 cm (10¼–11 in)

The noisy miner spends much of its life in trees and bushes but will also forage on the ground; it feeds on insects, fruit and nectar. An active, inquisitive bird, it often harasses other birds and, in groups, will attack an owl or hawk. Noisy miners nearly always live in colonies, which forage, feed and roost together.

A cup-shaped nest, made of grass, twigs and pieces of bark, is built on a forked branch of a tree or sapling and lined with soft plant material, on which the female lays 2 to 4 eggs.

**NAME:** Eastern Spinebill, *Acanthorhynchus tenuirostris*
**RANGE:** Australia: Queensland to Victoria; Tasmania, islands in Bass Strait
**HABITAT:** rain forest, scrub, cultivated land and gardens
**SIZE:** 12–15 cm (4¾–6 in)

The eastern spinebill is a restless, swift-flying bird which flits from tree to tree, searching for insects and nectar. It will often hover beside a flower while it probes the bloom with its spinelike bill and takes nectar. Primarily an arboreal bird, the eastern spinebill lives alone or in groups and seems to make regular seasonal movements. The female has duller plumage than the striking male.

The cup-shaped nest is built by the female, using grass, bark and moss. The nest is suspended from a thin forked twig in a bush or small tree. The female incubates the 2 or 3 eggs while the male guards the territory. Both parents feed the young, and they may produce two broods a season.

**NAME:** Cape Sugarbird, *Promerops cafer*
**RANGE:** South Africa: Cape Province
**HABITAT:** mountain slopes where protea bushes grow
**SIZE:** male: 43 cm (17 in); female: 23–28 cm (9–11 in)

The male Cape sugarbird's extremely long tail feathers account for the difference in size between the sexes. Male and female otherwise look similar in plumage. Cape sugarbirds are generally associated with protea bushes, where they forage for insects and take nectar from the flowers. They do, however, visit many other trees and bushes and take some insects in the air. Their flight is swift and direct, the tail held straight out behind. Outside the breeding season, sugarbirds are gregarious and live in small groups.

Breeding takes place in the winter months, particularly April to June. The male bird establishes a territory and perches on top of a protea bush to sing and warn off other males. He performs a courtship display for the female over the nesting site, twisting and turning the tail feathers, which are held curved over his back, and clapping his wings. The female bird builds a cup-shaped nest of twigs, grass and stems, lined with fine plant material and the down from protea leaves. The nest is positioned in the fork of a bush, usually protea. She incubates the 2 eggs for about 17 days and does most of the work of feeding the young on insects, spiders and nectar. The young are able to fly about 20 days after hatching but are tended by their parents for another 2 weeks. There are usually 2 broods a season.

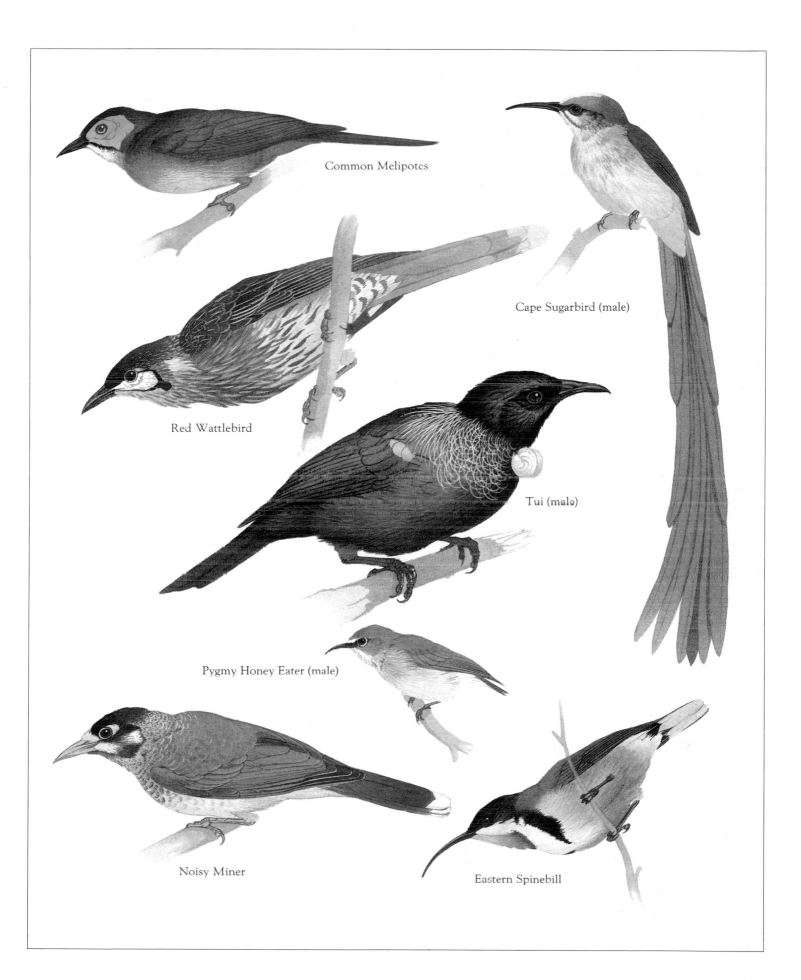

Common Melipotes

Cape Sugarbird (male)

Red Wattlebird

Tui (male)

Pygmy Honey Eater (male)

Noisy Miner

Eastern Spinebill

# Buntings

NAME: **Reed Bunting,** *Emberiza schoeniclus*
RANGE: **Europe, N. Africa, central and N. Asia**
HABITAT: **reedbeds, swamps; in winter, farmland and open country**
SIZE: **15 cm (6 in)**

The male reed bunting is identified by his black head and throat and white collar, while the female has a brown and buff head, with prominent black and white mustache streaks. The reed bunting forages on low vegetation and reed stems and hops briskly on the ground while it searches for food such as the seeds of marsh plants, grasses and grain. In spring and summer, it also feeds on insects and larvae.

The female makes a nest on the ground or in low vegetation and lays 4 or 5 eggs. She does most of the 13- or 14-day incubation, but the male helps to feed the young.

NAME: **Yellowhammer,** *Emberiza citrinella*
RANGE: **Europe, W. Asia to Urals**
HABITAT: **grassland, farmland, open country with bush and scrub**
SIZE: **16 cm (6¼ in)**

The yellowhammer feeds for the most part on the ground on seeds, grains, berries, leaves and some insects and invertebrates. The male bird is distinguished by his mainly yellow head and chestnut rump, while the female is duller, with less yellow plumage.

After a courtship chase and display, a nest is made on or near the ground, often in a hedge or under a bush. The female lays 3 or 4 eggs, which she incubates, mostly on her own, for 12 to 14 days. There may be two or three broods.

NAME: **Song Sparrow,** *Zonotrichia melodia*
RANGE: **N. America: Aleutian Islands, east to Newfoundland, south through Canada and USA to Mexico**
HABITAT: **forest edge, scrub with nearby water, cultivated and suburban areas**
SIZE: **13–18 cm (5–7 in)**

An extremely widespread and familiar North American bird, the song sparrow occurs in more than 30 subspecies, which vary in appearance from the small sandy-colored scrub and desert birds to the larger, dark-plumaged northern varieties. The song sparrow feeds on insects, particularly in summer, but also eats wild fruit and berries and forages on the ground for seeds.

The male bird establishes a territory, and his mate builds a neat nest, concealed among vegetation on the ground or in a bush. She incubates her 3 to 6 eggs for 12 or 13 days. There may be two or three broods a season.

## EMBERIZIDAE: Bunting Family

The taxonomic and evolutionary relationships between the buntings and their allies on the one hand and the finches (Fringillidae) on the other are complex and disputed by authorities on these birds. Here, the Emberizidae is taken to include the buntings, the plush-capped finch, cardinals and grosbeaks, the swallow-tanager and tanagers, all described as subfamilies.

## EMBERIZINAE: Bunting Subfamily

Common names for the approximately 290 species of songbird in this subfamily are confusing. Species occur in both the Old and New Worlds, and while most of those in the Old World are called buntings, many of the North American forms are termed sparrows or finches, the name "bunting" being reserved for a number of species in the subfamily Cardinalinae.

There is little doubt that this group of birds originated in the Americas and has subsequently colonized many parts of the Old World. They are small to medium-sized songbirds, usually about 15 cm (6 in) in length, with somber brown or black plumage, occasionally enlivened with patches of yellow and orange-brown. Their beaks are short and conical, well suited for handling their seed-dominated diet. Males and females usually look unalike.

Included in the Emberizinae are the Darwin's finches, sometimes considered to be a separate subfamily.

NAME: **Snow Bunting,** *Plectrophenax nivalis*
RANGE: **breeds in Iceland, Scandinavia, N. Scotland, Arctic and subarctic Asia, N. America; winters south of breeding range**
HABITAT: **open stony country, tundra, mountains; winters also on coasts and open country**
SIZE: **16 cm (6¼ in)**

In breeding plumage, the male snow bunting is almost pure white, except for his black back, central tail and primary wing feathers. In winter, his white plumage becomes mottled with rusty brown. The female has a gray-brown head and back in summer and is simply paler and duller in winter. The snow bunting spends much of its time feeding on seeds and insects on the ground, where it can run quickly and hop.

The nest is made from dead grass, moss and lichen and is concealed among stones. The female lays 4 to 6 eggs, which she incubates for 10 to 15 days. The male bird feeds his mate during the incubation period and helps to feed the young.

NAME: **Dark-eyed Junco,** *Junco hyemalis*
RANGE: **N. America: Alaska, east to Newfoundland, south through Canada and USA to Mexico**
HABITAT: **clearings, woodland edge, roadsides, parks, gardens**
SIZE: **13–16 cm (5–6¼ in)**

There are 4 subspecies of this junco, with considerable variations in color; the subspecies illustrated here is *J. h. insularis*. Females of all races are less colorful than males. A lively little bird, this junco feeds largely on the ground, eating mainly seeds in the winter and seeds, berries, insects and spiders in summer.

The male establishes a breeding territory, and his mate builds a nest on the ground, near vegetation or tree roots or in the shelter of a bank or ledge. She lays 3 to 6 eggs and incubates them for 11 or 12 days. There are usually two broods. Northernmost populations migrate to southern USA in winter.

NAME: **Savannah Sparrow,** *Ammodramus sandwichensis*
RANGE: **Alaska, Canada, much of USA (does not breed in S.E.), Mexico, Guatemala**
HABITAT: **tundra, open grassland, marshes**
SIZE: **11–15 cm (4¼–6 in)**

There are many subspecies of savannah sparrow, each differing slightly in coloration and song. Primarily a ground-feeder, the savannah sparrow hops about, while scratching and foraging, or runs, mouselike, through the grass; its main foods are seeds and insects such as beetles, grasshoppers and ants.

The female makes a grassy nest on the ground, usually in a natural hollow, and lays 4 or 5 eggs. Both parents take turns to incubate the eggs for about 12 days. Northern populations migrate south to winter in southern USA and Central America.

NAME: **Chipping Sparrow,** *Spizella passerina*
RANGE: **Canada, USA, Mexico, Central America to Nicaragua**
HABITAT: **open woodland, clearings in forest, gardens, parks**
SIZE: **13–15 cm (5–6 in)**

Both sexes of chipping sparrow have distinctive chestnut caps, edged by white eyebrow stripes. They are inconspicuous little birds and often live in suburban and inhabited areas. Grass seeds are their main food, but they also eat weed seeds, insects and spiders.

The female bird makes a nest in a vine or on a branch of a bush or tree. She lays 3 to 5 eggs, and her mate feeds her while she incubates the eggs for 11 to 14 days. There may be two broods in a season.

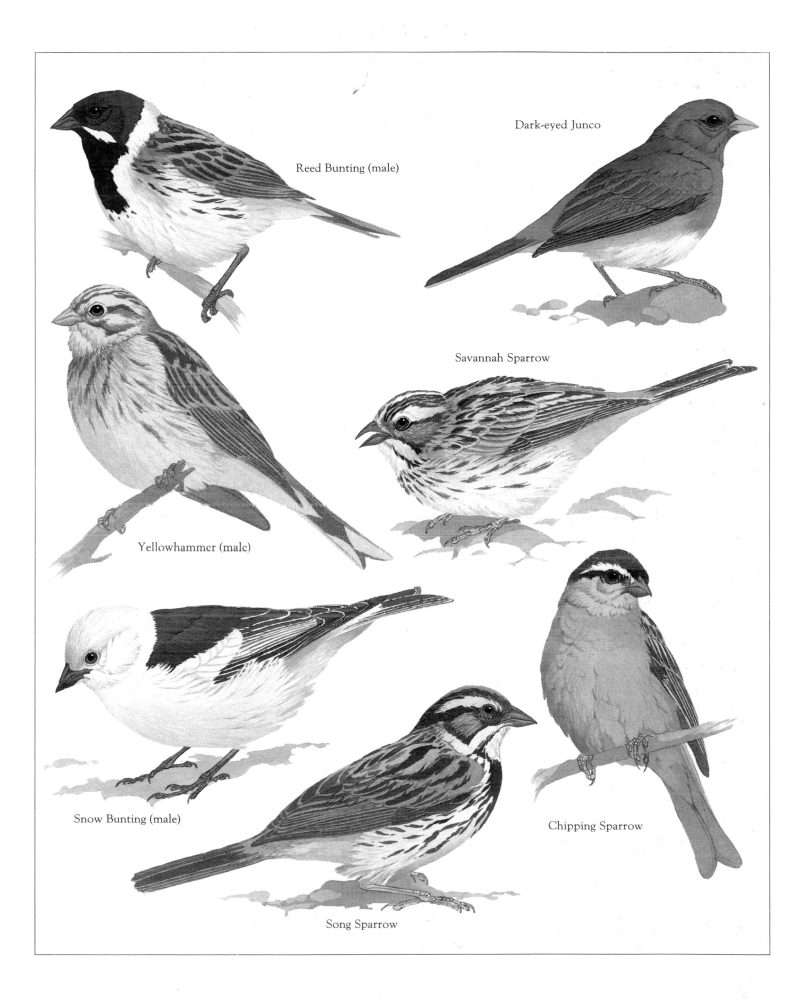

Reed Bunting (male)

Dark-eyed Junco

Savannah Sparrow

Yellowhammer (male)

Snow Bunting (male)

Song Sparrow

Chipping Sparrow

# Buntings

NAME: **Patagonian Sierra-finch,**
   *Phrygilus patagonicus*
RANGE: **South America: Chile, central**
   **Argentina to Tierra del Fuego**
HABITAT: **heavily vegetated ravines**
SIZE: **15–16 cm (6–6¼ in)**
This highly specialized bunting prefers areas with plenty of seed-bearing bushes, and rocky outcrops smothered with vines. It feeds mainly on seeds, but also on some insects. The female differs slightly from the male in plumage, having mainly dark-olive upperparts and yellowish-green underparts.

The nest is concealed among tangled roots and detritus and is made of grass, lined with soft plant material. The female lays 2 to 4 eggs.

NAME: **Variable Seedeater,** *Sporophila*
   *americana*
RANGE: **Central and South America:**
   **Mexico to Peru and Brazil**
HABITAT: **forest, grassland, parks,**
   **gardens**
SIZE: **11.5 cm (4½ in)**
Small flocks of variable seedeaters often associate with other seedeater species as they hop about on grass stems and weeds or perch on bushes or small trees. With fast-beating wings, they also make short flights in the open. These birds feed on grass seeds and insects and also share the thick, fruiting catkins of *Cecropia* trees with many other birds. Males may vary in plumage but are generally black and white, while females are olive-brown, with some buffy-white on the lower belly.

The female makes a nest of rootlets and fibers, placed in a tree or bush and fastened to a branch with cobwebs. She usually lays 2 eggs, which she incubates for about 12 or 13 days. The male may occasionally feed her during this period, and both parents feed the young with regurgitated seeds. There are at least two broods a year.

NAME: **White-naped Brush Finch,**
   *Atlapetes albinucha*
RANGE: **Mexico, through Central**
   **America to Colombia**
HABITAT: **forest edge, scrub**
SIZE: **18 cm (7 in)**
Male and female of this species look alike, both with distinctive black and white heads. Basically terrestrial birds, they flutter and hop about on the ground and up on to stems and low branches. They forage in the litter of the forest floor by flicking leaves aside with sweeps of the bill as they search for grass seeds and some insects.

A grassy nest is built by the female in a low bush. She usually lays 2 eggs.

NAME: **Rufous-sided Towhee,** *Pipilo*
   *erythrophthalmus*
RANGE: **S. Canada, USA, Mexico,**
   **Guatemala**
HABITAT: **forest edge, woodland, parks,**
   **gardens**
SIZE: **18–22 cm (7–8½ in)**
The male rufous-sided towhee is recognized by his mainly black and white plumage and the distinctive rufous patches on each side of the belly. The female has a similar plumage pattern but is brown where the male is black. Both sexes have red eyes. The birds scratch around on the ground and under vegetation for a wide variety of food, including insects, such as caterpillars, beetles and ants, snails, small lizards, snakes and salamanders, spiders, millipedes, seeds and berries.

The courting male chases the female and fans his tail to expose the white markings; he sings to her from a perch in a bush or tree. The female builds the nest on or close to the ground, using grass, rootlets, leaves, bark shreds and twigs. She lays 3 to 4 eggs, which she incubates for 12 or 13 days. The young leave the nest some 10 to 12 days after hatching, and there may be a second brood. Birds from the north of the range and mountainous areas migrate south in winter.

NAME: **Grassland Yellow-finch,** *Sicalis*
   *luteola*
RANGE: **S. Mexico, through Central and**
   **South America to Argentina east of**
   **Andes**
HABITAT: **grassland, open pasture, cliffs**
SIZE: **11.5–14 cm (4½–5½ in)**
Primarily a ground-dweller, the grassland yellow-finch hops about, rather than runs. Sometimes it perches on low branches of shrubs and trees, and it will also fly in the open. It feeds on the seeds of a variety of plants. In Chile and Argentina, it is the most numerous small bird, and in winter and spring, large flocks will gather and sing. The female has duller plumage than the male; her upperparts are tinged with brown, and her underparts are pale gray, washed with yellow.

The male courts the female with a display flight and song. She lays 3 to 5 eggs in a cup-shaped nest, concealed among grass or small plants. There are two, sometimes three, broods. Birds in the south of the range migrate north in winter.

NAME: **Large Ground Finch,** *Geospiza*
   *magnirostris*
RANGE: **Galápagos Islands**
HABITAT: **arid zones**
SIZE: **16.5 cm (6½ in)**
The large ground finch is one of the 14 species known as Darwin's finches, found only on the remote Galápagos and Cocos islands; they were a key factor in the formation of Darwin's theories. It is almost certain that all species are derived from a single finch-like form that colonized the islands less than a million years ago. As there are few passerine species in the Galápagos, there were plenty of vacant ecological niches for the birds to adapt to, hence the gradual separation into different species. Although most species are similar in plumage, they differ in their ways of life and feeding habits, and this is reflected in their varying bill shapes. Some have huge bills for cracking hard seeds; others have parrotlike bills, used for tearing soft plants; another, a slender bill for seizing insects.

The massive, powerful bill of the large ground finch is ideally suited to coping with its diet of hard seeds; this bird only rarely eats insects. Male and female differ in appearance, the male being largely black and the female gray.

The breeding habits of the large ground finch are similar to those of all Darwin's finches. The male establishes a territory and builds several dome-shaped nests. He displays to the female, and she selects a nest or helps to build another one. The male feeds the female during the period before she lays her 2 to 5 eggs and for about 12 days while she incubates them. Both parents feed the young birds until they leave the nest 13 or 14 days after hatching. There may be several broods, depending on food supplies.

NAME: **Warbler Finch,** *Certhidea olivacea*
RANGE: **Galápagos Islands**
HABITAT: **humid to dry zones**
SIZE: **10 cm (4 in)**
The most agile and lively in flight of all the Darwin's finches, the warbler finch maneuvers well as it flits through the vegetation, searching for insects and spiders. Its bill is thin and pointed like that of a warbler, and its manner of picking its food from the foliage is distinctly warblerlike. Some males have orange throat patches, but otherwise males and females look alike.

The male bird selects a territory and builds several nests in bushes or low trees for the female to choose from. She lays 2 to 5 eggs, which she incubates for about 12 days.

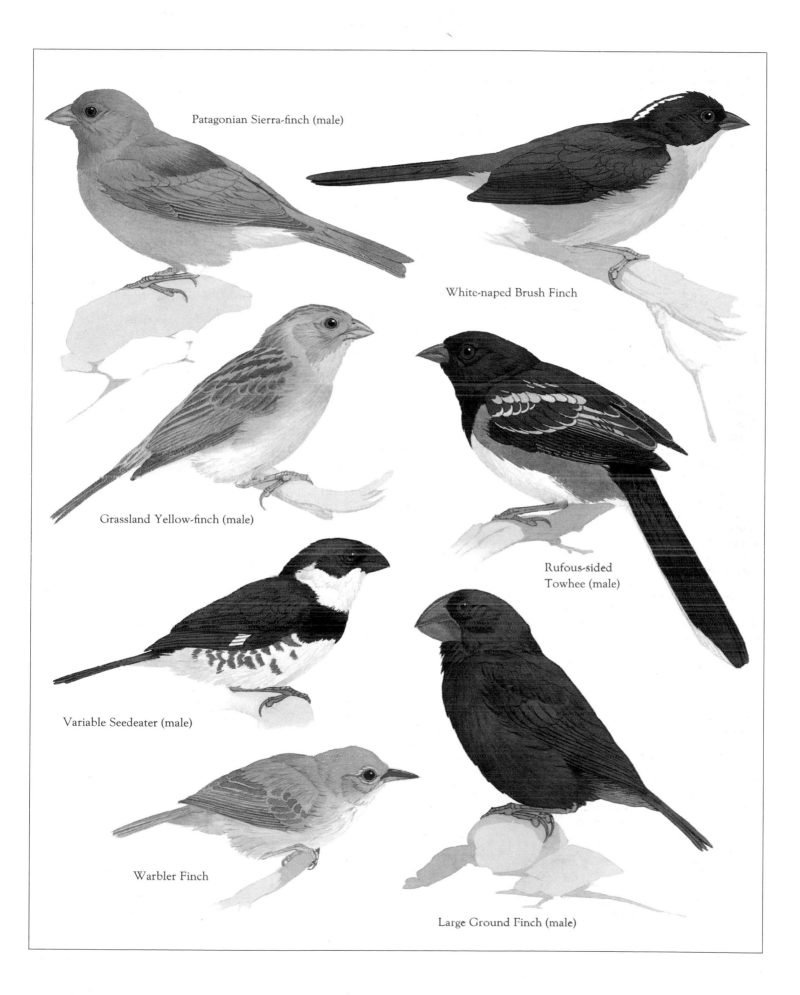

Patagonian Sierra-finch (male)

White-naped Brush Finch

Grassland Yellow-finch (male)

Rufous-sided
Towhee (male)

Variable Seedeater (male)

Warbler Finch

Large Ground Finch (male)

# Plush-capped Finch, Cardinals and Grosbeaks, Swallow-tanager

## CATAMBLYRHYNCHINAE: Plush-capped Finch Subfamily

The single species of South American songbird in this family represents a puzzle for taxonomists. It is finchlike, but its relationships with other bird groups are obscure. Here it is treated as a distinct subfamily of the Emberizidae but in the opinion of some ornithologists, it should have its own family.

NAME: **Plush-capped Finch,** *Catamblyrhynchus diadema*
RANGE: **Andes, from Venezuela to N.W. Argentina**
HABITAT: **cloud forest, forest edge, clearings**
SIZE: **14 cm (5½ in)**

A golden-yellow crest of short, erect feathers is the distinguishing feature of this bird. Male and female have similar plumage. Little is known of the plush-capped finch, which occurs in inaccessible mountain forest, but it appears to live alone or in pairs, foraging in low vegetation and on the ground for its insect food.

## CARDINALINAE: Cardinal and Grosbeak Subfamily

The 39 species of cardinal and grosbeak occur in the New World, from Canada in the north to Argentina in the south. All are stocky birds with short, strong bills, which enable them to feed on very hard seeds. Males have brightly colored plumage, ranging from the fiery red of the cardinal to the bright blue of the blue grosbeak. Females have duller, plainer plumage.

NAME: **Rose-breasted Grosbeak,** *Pheucticus ludovicianus*
RANGE: **S. Canada, central and E. USA, south to N. Georgia; winters from Mexico to northern South America**
HABITAT: **woodland, borders of swamps and streams, cultivated land**
SIZE: **20.5 cm (8 in)**

The male rose-breasted grosbeak is a handsome bird, easily identified by his black and white plumage and his red breast patch; the female has streaked brown and white plumage. This grosbeak forages in trees, searching for seeds, buds, blossoms and insects. It is particularly fond of beetles and is a popular bird with farmers because of its habit of feeding on the harmful potato beetles and their larvae.

The nest is made on a low branch of a small tree or bush, usually by the female. She lays 3 or 4 eggs, which are incubated by both parents for 12 or 13 days.

NAME: **(Northern) Cardinal,** *Cardinalis cardinalis*
RANGE: **Canada: S. Ontario; E. USA: Great Lakes and New England, south to Gulf Coast, S. Texas and Arizona; Mexico, Guatemala**
HABITAT: **woodland edge, thickets, parks, gardens**
SIZE: **20–23 cm (7¾–9 in)**

The male cardinal is an unmistakable, brilliant red bird, while the female is buffy-brown, with a reddish tinge on wings and crest and a red bill. Cardinals are strongly territorial and aggressive birds and have a rich and varied repertoire of songs; both sexes are heard singing at all times of year. They feed on the ground and in trees on seeds and berries and, in the breeding season, also take insects.

The female builds the nest on a branch of a small tree or bush, usually among tangled foliage and vines. She incubates the 3 or 4 eggs for 12 or 13 days. Two or more broods may follow.

NAME: **Buff-throated Saltator,** *Saltator maximus*
RANGE: **Mexico; Central and South America: Panama to Brazil**
HABITAT: **forest edge, tangled secondary growth, plantations**
SIZE: **20.5 cm (8 in)**

A long-tailed, thick-billed bird, the buff-throated saltator is identified by the black-bordered buff patch on its throat. Male and female look alike. They forage in pairs or small flocks in the treetops, feeding on berries and fruit such as the fruiting catkins of *Cecropia* trees.

The female builds a bulky nest in a tree or bush close to the ground. The male stays near her, singing and feeding her from time to time. She incubates the 2 eggs for 13 or 14 days, and both parents feed the young. There may be two or more broods.

NAME: **Painted Bunting,** *Passerina ciris*
RANGE: **S. USA, Mexico; winters from Gulf states to Central America**
HABITAT: **woodland edge, thickets beside streams, gardens, roads**
SIZE: **13–14 cm (5–5½ in)**

An extremely colorful bird, the male painted bunting would look quite at home in a tropical forest; the female is bright yellowish-green. Painted buntings feed on a variety of grass seeds, and also on spiders and insects such as grasshoppers, caterpillars and flies. The male is strongly territorial and will battle fiercely with intruders.

The cup-shaped nest, made of grasses, stalks and leaves, is built in a bush, low tree or vine a meter or so above ground. The female incubates her 3 or 4 eggs for 11 or 12 days.

NAME: **Dickcissel,** *Spiza americana*
RANGE: **USA: Great Lakes, south through Midwest to Gulf states; winters from Mexico to northern South America**
HABITAT: **grassland, grain and alfalfa fields**
SIZE: **15–18 cm (6–7 in)**

The common name of this little bird is derived from its constantly repeated call, which sounds like "dick-dick-cissel." The male is characterized by his heavy bill, yellow breast and black bib and chestnut wing patches. The female is sparrowlike, with streaky plumage, but has a yellowish breast and small chestnut wing patches. Dickcissels feed mainly on the ground on weed seeds, grain, spiders and insects such as crickets and grasshoppers.

The male establishes the nesting territory by calling from a conspicuous perch. The cup-shaped nest, made of weed stems, grasses and leaves, is built on the ground, often in the shelter of alfalfa or grain crops, or in a tree or bush. The female usually lays 4 eggs, which she incubates for 12 or 13 days. There are generally two broods a year.

## TERSININAE: Swallow-tanager Subfamily

Like the plush-capped finch, the swallow-tanager is an enigmatic member of the assemblage of buntinglike birds. Found in South America, it is similar to the true tanagers, with which it is sometimes grouped, but differs from them in a number of respects. Male and female are unalike in plumage.

NAME: **Swallow-tanager,** *Tersina viridis*
RANGE: **E. Panama to Bolivia, Paraguay, N.E. Argentina, S.E. Brazil**
HABITAT: **open forest, clearings, parks**
SIZE: **14 cm (5½ in)**

The swallow-tanager is a gregarious bird out of the breeding season and moves in pairs or small groups. It forages at all levels, from the ground to the highest branches of trees, feeding on fruit and catching insects on the wing. Both male and female are eye-catching birds, the male having mainly turquoise and black plumage, and the female bright green, with a brownish face and throat and touches of yellow on flanks and belly.

The male bird establishes and defends the breeding territory, and the female makes a cup-shaped nest in a hole in a wall or at the end of a burrow, which she digs in a bank. She lays 3 eggs, which she incubates for 14 to 17 days. In some parts of their range, swallow-tanagers breed in highland regions, descending to lowlands for the rest of the year.

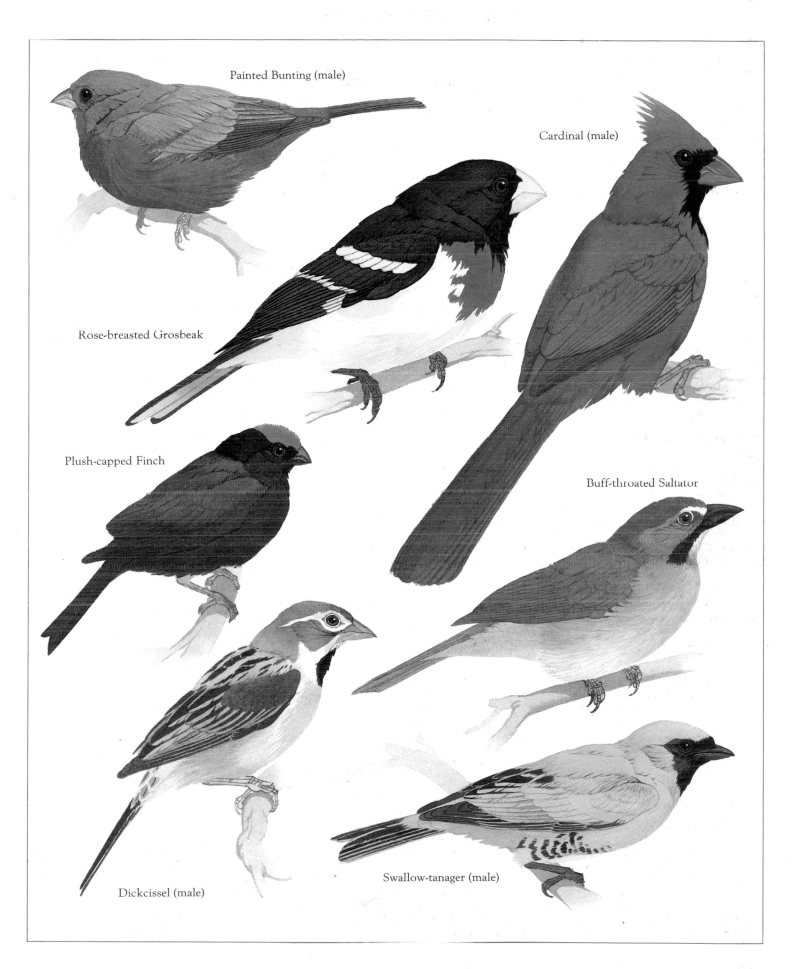

Painted Bunting (male)

Cardinal (male)

Rose-breasted Grosbeak

Plush-capped Finch

Buff-throated Saltator

Dickcissel (male)

Swallow-tanager (male)

# Tanagers

**NAME: Scarlet Tanager,** *Piranga olivacea*
**RANGE: extreme S.E. Canada, E. central states of USA; winters in E. South America**
**HABITAT: woodland, parks and gardens**
**SIZE: 19 cm (7½ in)**

In his summer breeding plumage, the male scarlet tanager is unmistakable, with his gleaming red head and body and black wings and tail; in winter, he is similar to the female, with mainly olive-green plumage, but retains his black wings and tail. Despite his brilliance, the scarlet tanager is hard to see when he moves slowly or perches high in the trees, feeding on berries and fruit. The scarlet tanager also feeds on insects, slugs, snails and spiders, many of which it catches on the ground.

Male birds return from the wintering grounds a few days before females, and each establishes a territory in the trees. When the female birds arrive, they are courted by the singing males. The female builds a nest in a large tree, using twigs, rootlets, weed stems and grass. She lays 3 to 5 eggs, which she incubates for 13 or 14 days.

**NAME: Magpie Tanager,** *Cissopis leveriana*
**RANGE: northern South America, south to Brazil and N.E. Argentina**
**HABITAT: rain forest, scrub, cultivated land, clearings**
**SIZE: 28 cm (11 in)**

As its common name suggests, this large tanager resembles a magpie and is certainly different from all other tanagers. It is a black and white bird, with long, graduated tail feathers, tipped with white. Male and female look alike, and both have black eyes. Little is known of this tanager, which inhabits areas up to 2,000 m (6,600 ft) in some parts of its range. In pairs or small groups of 4 or 5 birds, it frequents the middle layers of the forest, flying from tree to tree, feeding on insects and berries.

There is no information available about the breeding habits of this tanager.

**NAME: Black-capped Hemispingus,** *Hemispingus atropileus*
**RANGE: Andes, from N.W. Venezuela to Bolivia**
**HABITAT: forest at 2,300–3,000 m (7,500–10,000 ft)**
**SIZE: 16.5 cm (6½ in)**

The black-capped hemispingus inhabits the high-altitude cloud forests and the sparse, stunted woods above this zone. Alone or in small groups, it forages among the trees for fruit and insects. Male and female look similar, both with black crowns and largely olive plumage. The cup-shaped nest is made in a tree.

## THRAUPINAE: Tanager Subfamily

The approximately 238 species of tanager occur in the New World, mostly in the tropics, and are among the most vividly colored and conspicuous of all the thousands of bird species found in the tropical zone of the Americas. Although a few species are soberly plumaged, most are brilliant, often with a combination of many contrasting plumage colors. In many species, male and female birds share the same spectacular appearance, but in the 4 species that have penetrated the temperate zones of North America, male and female differ.

Tanagers are finch- or bunting-shaped songbirds which frequent the upper layers of forests and woods and also the clearings and fringes of such vegetation. Their feet and legs are well developed for their essentially tree-dwelling life. The diet of a typical tanager consists of both fruit and insects. Tanagers capture the latter by plucking them from foliage or catching them in the air, or by following army ant columns to seize the insects they disturb. Tanagers are not noted as songsters; only a few species, such as the rose-breasted thrush tanager, *Rhodinocichla rosea*, are known to have well-developed singing abilities.

Most tanagers make open, cup-shaped nests in trees and bushes. Clutches contain 1 to 5 eggs and are incubated by the female bird. The male brings his mate food while she incubates, and he helps with the feeding of the nestlings.

Honeycreepers are similar to tanagers but feed on nectar, as well as on fruit and insects. Most male honeycreepers are brightly colored, but females are duller in plumage. Some honeycreepers are included with the tanagers, and others with the American wood warblers, Parulidae; they are sometimes all placed in a subfamily of their own.

**NAME: White-shouldered Tanager,** *Tachyphonus luctuosus*
**RANGE: Honduras to Panama, south to N. Bolivia, Amazonian Brazil**
**HABITAT: rain forest, open woodland, plantations, clearings**
**SIZE: 13 cm (5 in)**

The white-shouldered tanager varies slightly in coloration over its range — for example, males in western Panama have yellow or tawny crowns — but in most instances, males are bluish-black, with the white shoulders of their common name, while females are gray, olive and yellow. These active, noisy birds live in pairs or small groups or may join in mixed flocks. They forage for fruit and insects from the treetops down to the undergrowth, calling to each other with harsh, loud calls.

The open, cup-shaped nest is made of leaves and grasses and is built in a tree, not far from the ground. The female incubates the 2 eggs, and both parents feed the young.

**NAME: Blue-gray Tanager,** *Thraupis episcopus*
**RANGE: S.E. Mexico, Central and South America to Brazil and Bolivia; Trinidad and Tobago**
**HABITAT: open and cleared woodland, cultivated land, parks, gardens**
**SIZE: 16.5 cm (6½ in)**

An adaptable, widespread bird, the blue-gray tanager is equally at home in humid and dry areas, in coastal lowlands and at altitudes up to 2,200 m (7,200 ft). Birds remain paired throughout the year, and together or in small flocks, they forage in the trees for berries, fruit such as wild figs and bananas, and insects, which they take from foliage or catch on the wing.

The cup-shaped nest may be made in a variety of sites: high in a tree, in a low bush, even in an open shed or the abandoned nest of another bird species. It is made of rootlets, plant fibers, moss and grass, matted together and bound with cobwebs. The blue-gray tanager may even take over the nest of another tanager and incubate the eggs with its own. Normally the female lays 2 or 3 eggs, which she incubates for 13 or 14 days. Both parents feed the young until they leave the nest about 17 to 20 days after hatching. There are at least two broods in a year.

**NAME: Common Bush-tanager,** *Chlorospingus ophthalmicus*
**RANGE: Mexico, Central and South America to N. Argentina**
**HABITAT: rain and cloud forest, woodland**
**SIZE: 14.5 cm (5¾ in)**

The common bush-tanager is a noisy, active bird, common in many areas. In small groups, these birds roam the forest, foraging for insects and fruit, mainly in low vegetation but also in the treetops. They may join mixed flocks of birds. Males and females are similar in appearance.

The female may build her nest in a tree or on the ground. The top of the nest is usually concealed by the vegetation among which it is built. The female lays 2 eggs, which she incubates for 14 days, and both parents feed the young.

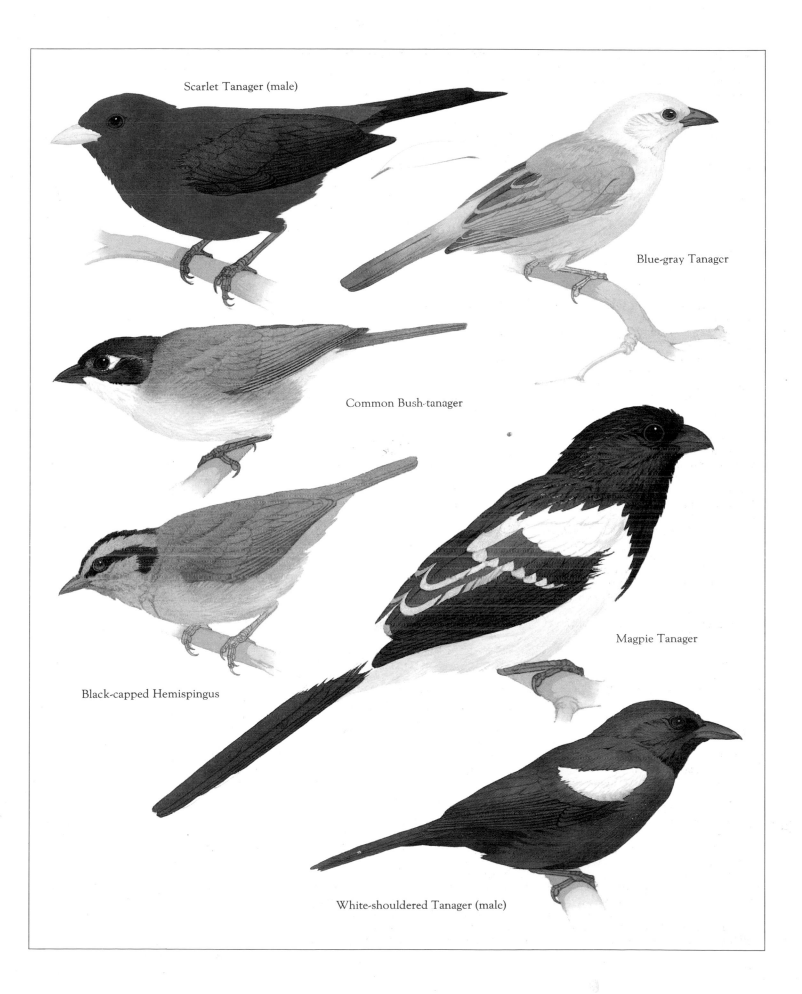

Scarlet Tanager (male)

Blue-gray Tanager

Common Bush-tanager

Black-capped Hemispingus

Magpie Tanager

White-shouldered Tanager (male)

# Tanagers

**NAME: Blue-crowned/Turquoise-naped Chlorophonia, *Chlorophonia occipitalis***
**RANGE: S.E. Mexico to W. Panama**
**HABITAT: forest, usually over 1,500 m (5,000 ft)**
**SIZE: 14 cm (5½ in)**

The male blue-crowned chlorophonia is a beautiful little bird, with bright green and blue plumage set off by touches of yellow. The female is largely green, with less blue and yellow, and young males resemble females until they acquire full adult plumage at about a year old. Arboreal birds, these chlorophonias frequent the treetops, where they feed on fruit; when fruit is scarce in their high-altitude habitat, they may sometimes descend to lower levels. For a few months after the end of the breeding season in July, the birds move in flocks of up to 12, but for the rest of the year, they live in pairs.

The breeding season begins in March. Both partners of a pair help to build a neat, domed nest high in a tree, usually among camouflaging moss and epiphytic plants — profuse in these high forests. The nest is made of moss, roots of epiphytes and spider's webs. There are believed to be 3 or more eggs in a typical clutch, and these are incubated by the female alone. Whenever she leaves the nest to feed, she drops almost to the ground before flying off, in order to confuse predators. Once hatched, the young are fed by both parents on regurgitated food, and they remain in the nest for 24 to 25 days. A second brood may follow.

**NAME: Blue Dacnis, *Dacnis cayana***
**RANGE: E. Nicaragua to Panama, tropical South America to N. Argentina**
**HABITAT: open forest, secondary growth, orange groves**
**SIZE: 11.5 cm (4½ in)**

The blue dacnis is one of the honeycreeper group of tanagers but differs from them in having a short, conical bill. The male bird is bright blue and black, while the female is bright green, with some blue, gray and black plumage. These active little birds forage in the treetops, alone or in small groups, sometimes joining mixed flocks of tanagers and other honeycreepers. They feed on fruit, nectar and insects, some of which they catch in the air, and are particularly partial to the large flower heads of mango trees and wild figs.

The female makes an open, cupshaped nest in a tree, using fine plant material. She incubates the 2 or 3 eggs and does most of the work of feeding the young, although the male does help with this. The young leave the nest about 12 days after hatching.

**NAME: White-vented Euphonia, *Euphonia minuta***
**RANGE: Mexico, Central and northern South America to Amazonian Brazil**
**HABITAT: rain forest, secondary growth, scrub, clearings**
**SIZE: 9 cm (3½ in)**

The white-vented euphonia lives in pairs or small groups and forages high in the trees, feeding primarily on mistletoe berries but also on insects and spiders. The birds may have to travel considerable distances to find the berries. The hard seeds of the mistletoe are excreted in due course, usually up in the trees, where they stick to the branches and germinate. All the euphonia species feed on mistletoe berries, and they are the birds most responsible for the spread of this parasitic plant. The male bird is a colorful mixture of yellow, white, black and gray-blue, while the female is green, gray and yellowish. Both have short bills and tails.

Like the chlorophonias, the whitevented euphonia builds a rounded nest with a side entrance. The nest is made of moss or dry plant material and is placed in a cleft in bark or rock or in a hole in a tree trunk. The female incubates her 2 to 5 eggs for 14 to 18 days, and both parents feed the young with regurgitated food.

**NAME: Silver-beaked Tanager, *Ramphocelus carbo***
**RANGE: northern South America east of Andes, south to Bolivia, Paraguay, Brazil**
**HABITAT: woodland, secondary growth, cultivated land**
**SIZE: 18 cm (7 in)**

The distinguishing feature of this tanager is the conspicuous silvery-white base to the lower mandible of its black beak. The plumage of male birds varies slightly from area to area, being either black or dark maroon on the upperparts, with a red throat and breast. Females seem always to be a dark maroon. Often found near water, silverbeaked tanagers tend to live on or near the edge of wooded areas, rather than inside them. Alone or in small groups, they forage actively for insects and fruit, from the lowest branches to the middle story of trees.

The female bird builds a large nest in a bush or thicket. Her mate brings food to her while she incubates the 2 eggs for about 12 days. The young birds are able to leave the nest about 11 to 13 days after hatching.

**NAME: Paradise Tanager, *Tangara chilensis***
**RANGE: northern South America east of the Andes, south to Bolivia and Amazonian Brazil**
**HABITAT: rain forest**
**SIZE: 14 cm (5½ in)**

An extremely beautiful bird, the paradise tanager has gleaming, multicolored plumage; males and females look alike. In groups that often include other species, paradise tanagers forage for berries, spiders and insects in the middle and upper layers of the forest.

The breeding habits of this species are probably similar to those of other tanagers.

**NAME: Purple Honeycreeper, *Cyanerpes caeruleus***
**RANGE: Trinidad; northern South America to Bolivia, Paraguay, Brazil**
**HABITAT: rain forest, forest edge, mangrove swamps, plantations**
**SIZE: 10 cm (4 in)**

Groups of purple honeycreepers frequent flowering trees in many different types of wooded areas. Fruit, especially bananas, and insects are important foods, but these birds also perch by flowers and suck nectar from them with their long, curved bills. Male and female differ in plumage, but both are attractive birds; the male is largely bluishpurple and black, with yellow legs, while the female is rich green, with buff and blue patches on the head and breast.

The female builds a cup-shaped nest in the fork of a tree or bush and lays 2 eggs, which she incubates for 12 to 14 days. The young leave the nest about 14 days after hatching.

**NAME: Giant Conebill, *Oreomanes fraseri***
**RANGE: South America: Andes in S. Colombia to Bolivia**
**HABITAT: forested and scrub slopes**
**SIZE: 17–18.5 cm (6¾–7¼ in)**

Although not really a giant, this conebill is distinctly larger than other conebills. It has fairly sober, mainly gray and chestnut plumage and a straight, sharp bill about 1.25 cm (½ in) long. Little is known about this bird, which inhabits the *Polylepis* woods at high altitudes in the Andes — between 3,000 and 4,000 m (10,000 and 13,000 ft). These woods are cold and impoverished, with only the *Polylepis* trees and little vegetation other than mosses and ferns. The giant conebill explores the trunks and branches of the trees for insects, its plumage providing good camouflage against the bark of the trees. It is usually found in chattering groups, sometimes with mixed flocks of flycatchers and finches.

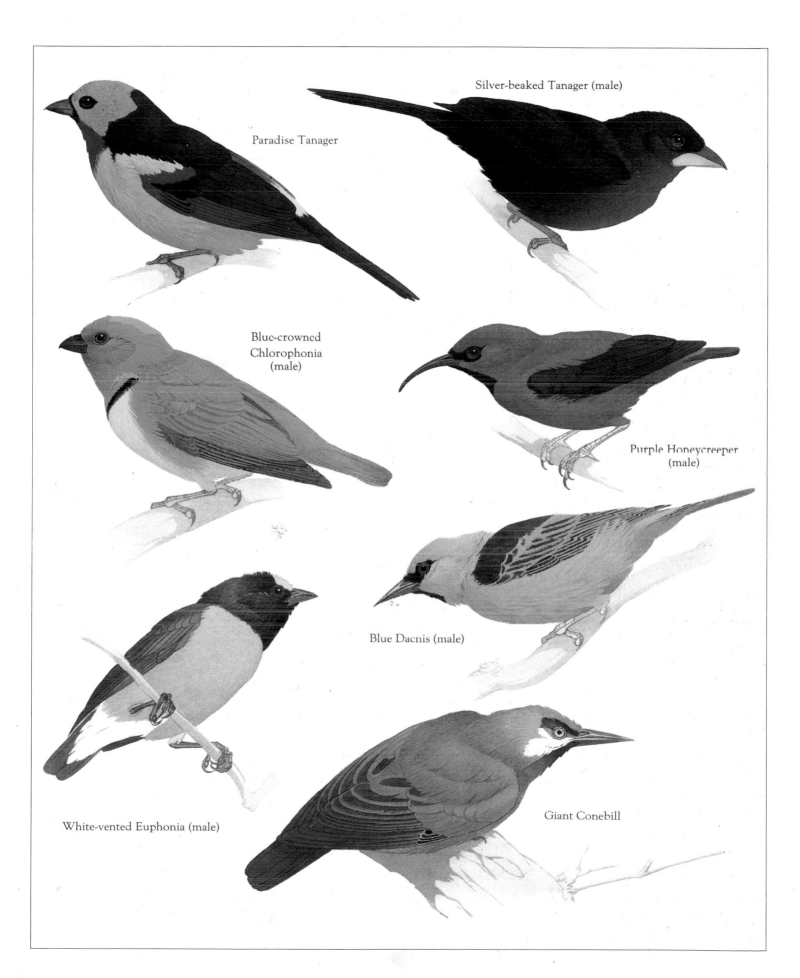

Paradise Tanager

Silver-beaked Tanager (male)

Blue-crowned
Chlorophonia
(male)

Purple Honeycreeper
(male)

Blue Dacnis (male)

White-vented Euphonia (male)

Giant Conebill

# American Wood Warblers

**NAME:** Bananaquit, *Coereba flaveola*
**RANGE:** Mexico, Central and South America to N. Argentina; West Indies
**HABITAT:** forest, mangrove swamps, gardens, parks, plantations
**SIZE:** 9.5 cm (3¾ in)

An extremely adaptable, widespread bird, the bananaquit is equally at home in dense rain forest or dry coastal areas but must have some cover. It lives alone or in pairs and never forms flocks. Bananaquits feed mainly on insects and fruit but also on nectar, probing blossoms with their curved bills or piercing large blooms at the base to obtain the nectar.

A globular nest is built, usually suspended from a branch or vine. The female incubates the 2 or 3 eggs for 12 or 13 days, and both parents feed the nestlings with nectar or insects. There are at least two broods a year.

**NAME:** Black-and-White Warbler, *Mniotilta varia*
**RANGE:** breeds S. Canada, USA, east of Rockies; winters S. USA to N.W. South America
**HABITAT:** deciduous and mixed forest, parks, gardens
**SIZE:** 11.5–14 cm (4½–5½ in)

Both male and female of this species are boldly striped with black and white, but the male has a black throat while the female's is white. Insects are their main food, and these warblers creep over branches and tree trunks, searching for caterpillars, ants, flies and beetles and also spiders.

The cup-shaped nest is made on the ground at the foot of a tree or by a rock, and the female incubates the clutch of 4 or 5 eggs for 10 to 12 days. The young are tended by both parents until they leave the nest 8 to 12 days after hatching.

**NAME:** Golden-winged Warbler, *Vermivora chrysoptera*
**RANGE:** breeds N.E. USA; winters south to Central America and Venezuela
**HABITAT:** woodland, thickets
**SIZE:** 11–14 cm (4¼–5½ in)

Identified by their bright yellow wing patches and crowns, male and female golden-winged warblers look similar, but the female has a lighter throat and eye patch. They forage at all levels of trees and bushes, searching the foliage for insects and spiders.

The nest is made on the ground or just above it in vegetation, and the female incubates the 4 or 5 eggs, sometimes 6 or 7, for about 10 days. Both parents feed the young, which leave the nest about 10 days after hatching. This warbler often interbreeds with the blue-winged warbler, *V. pinus*, where their ranges overlap.

## PARULIDAE:
### American Wood Warbler Family

There are approximately 125 species of American wood warbler, found from Alaska and northern Canada to the south of South America. Some of these birds, such as the conebills and the bananaquit, are of uncertain affinity, and there are arguments for placing them in other families.

Despite their name, wood warblers have no close connection with the Old World warblers and, indeed, do not have particularly tuneful songs. Small, slender birds, most are brightly colored, particularly in breeding plumage. Those species that breed in the more tropical zones tend to be sedentary in their habits, but species breeding in the north of the range are highly migratory and form a spectacular part of the north-south bird migrations of the New World. Male and female look alike in some species and differ in others.

**NAME:** Northern Parula, *Parula americana*
**RANGE:** breeds S.E. Canada, eastern USA; winters S. Florida, West Indies, Mexico to Nicaragua
**HABITAT:** coniferous forest, swamps, mixed woodland in winter
**SIZE:** 11 cm (4¼ in)

A sedate little warbler, the northern parula forages for insects, especially caterpillars, in the trees, creeping over the branches and hopping from perch to perch; it also feeds on spiders. Male and female look similar, but the female is slightly duller.

The nest is usually built in hanging tree lichen or Spanish moss. The female incubates the 4 or 5 eggs for 12 to 14 days. Both parents tend the young.

**NAME:** Yellow Warbler, *Dendroica petechia*
**RANGE:** Alaska, much of Canada, USA; Mexico, Central and South America to Peru; West Indies
**HABITAT:** damp thickets, swamps
**SIZE:** 11–13 cm (4¼–5 in)

An extremely widespread species, the yellow warbler varies considerably over its range, but the male breeding plumage is, typically, bright yellow with chestnut or orange streaks; males are duller outside the breeding season, and females are generally more greenish in color. Yellow warblers forage in the foliage of trees and shrubs for insects, feeding largely on caterpillars but also on bark beetles and moths, as well as spiders.

The female builds a cup-shaped nest in a tree or bush and incubates the 4 or 5 eggs for about 11 days.

**NAME:** Ovenbird, *Seiurus aurocapillus*
**RANGE:** breeds central and E. Canada and USA to N. Gulf states; winters Gulf of Mexico to northern South America
**HABITAT:** forest
**SIZE:** 14–15 cm (5½–6 in)

The ovenbird is distinguished by its brownish-orange crown, edged with black, and its white eye rings. It finds most of its food on the forest floor by searching under fallen leaves and other debris for insects, spiders, slugs, snails and other small creatures; it also eats seeds and berries.

The female builds a domed, oven-shaped nest on the ground; it has a side entrance. She lays 4 or 5 eggs, which she incubates for 11 to 14 days.

**NAME:** Mourning Warbler, *Geothlypis philadelphia*
**RANGE:** breeds central and E. Canada, N.E. USA; winters from Nicaragua to Ecuador and Venezuela
**HABITAT:** thickets, wet woodland
**SIZE:** 12.5–14.5 cm (5–5¾ in)

Male and female mourning warblers both have gray hoods, and the male has a black patch on the throat. An elusive, skulking warbler, it forages among low vegetation for insects and spiders.

The bulky nest is made on the ground or in a low bush, and the female incubates the 3 to 5 eggs for 12 to 13 days.

**NAME:** Painted Redstart, *Myioborus pictus*
**RANGE:** S.W. USA, Mexico to Nicaragua
**HABITAT:** woodland, mountain canyons
**SIZE:** 12.5–14.5 cm (5–5¾ in)

Lively little birds, both male and female painted redstarts have bright red breasts and white bellies. They feed entirely on insects, most of which they catch in the air by darting out from a perch.

The nest is made in a small hollow in the ground near a boulder or clump of grass. The female incubates the 3 or 4 eggs for 13 or 14 days.

**NAME:** Golden-crowned Warbler, *Basileuterus culicivorus*
**RANGE:** Mexico, through Central and South America to N. Argentina; Trinidad
**HABITAT:** rain forest, plantations, scrub
**SIZE:** 12.5 cm (5 in)

A yellow or rufous-orange patch on the crown, bordered with black, is the distinguishing feature of this warbler. Alone or in pairs, it forages in the lower levels of dense vegetation and rarely flies into the open. Insects are its main food — caught among the foliage or on the wing.

The female builds a domed, oven-shaped nest on the ground and incubates her clutch of 3 eggs for 14 to 17 days.

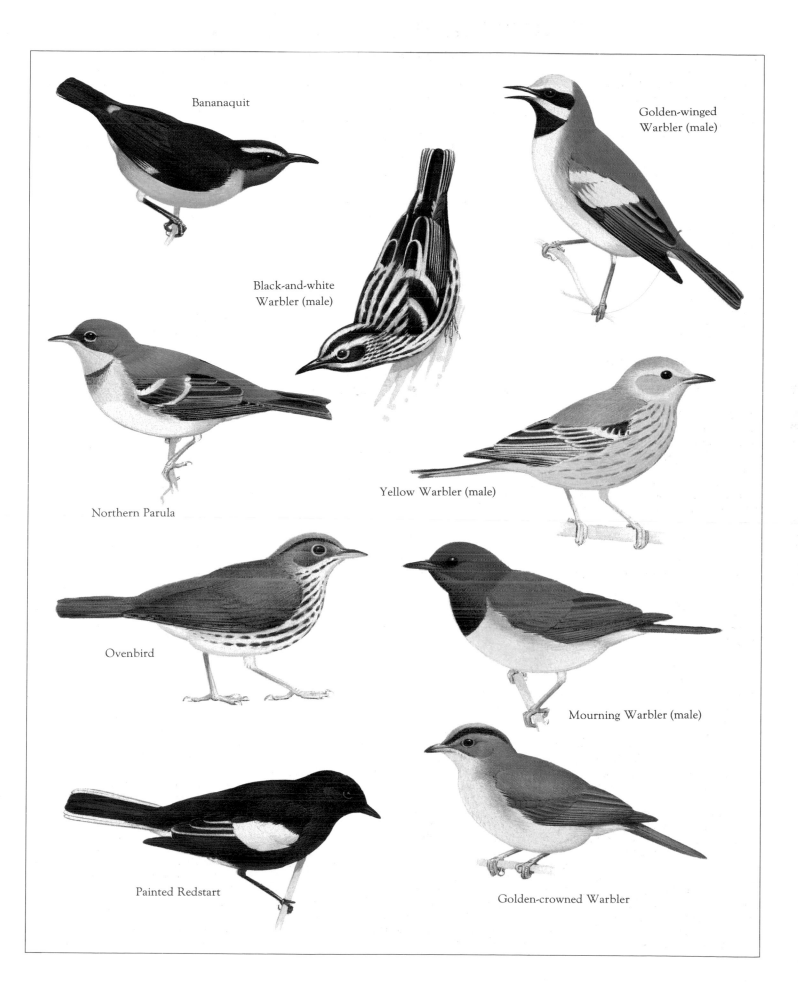

Bananaquit

Golden-winged
Warbler (male)

Black-and-white
Warbler (male)

Northern Parula

Yellow Warbler (male)

Ovenbird

Mourning Warbler (male)

Painted Redstart

Golden-crowned Warbler

## DREPANIDIDAE:
### Hawaiian Honeycreeper Family

Even Darwin's finches on the Galápagos Islands do not surpass the Hawaiian honeycreepers as an object lesson in the ability of a single bird type to differentiate into a range of species when released from competition and provided with a wide diversity of habitats. It seems highly likely that the 15 or so existing Hawaiian honeycreepers, as well as forms now extinct, are all derived from a single colonization of the island cluster by a single type of migratory American wood warbler (Parulidae).

The existing forms divide into two distinct groups: first, the nectar-feeders, which also consume insects and have reddish and black plumage; and second, a group of finchlike birds, which feed mostly on seeds and have yellowish-green plumage. Species differ most dramatically in bill shape, in accordance with their different feeding habits. Male and female differ in some species and look alike in others.

---

NAME: **Palila, *Psittirostra bailleui***
RANGE: **Hawaii: Mauna Kea**
HABITAT: **forest**
SIZE: **15 cm (6 in)**  (E)

Previously more widely distributed in Hawaii, the palila is now found only on the western slope of Mauna Kea. It is a seriously endangered bird, largely because of disturbance and the destruction of its forest habitat. It is dependent on the mamani tree of its native forest for its existence and feeds principally on the seeds and flowers of this tree. The bird nips off a seedpod and holds it down on a branch with its claw while it extracts the seeds.

The female builds a nest in a mamani tree and lays 2 eggs, which she incubates for 21 to 27 days. Both parents feed the young with regurgitated food, probably insects on which adults also feed in the breeding season.

NAME: **Akepa, *Loxops coccinea***
RANGE: **Hawaii, Maui, Kauai**
HABITAT: **forest**
SIZE: **10–12.5 cm (4–5 in)**  (E)

Abundant in some areas of the Hawaiian Islands up to the end of the nineteenth century, the akepa population is in serious decline, and the Oahu Island race is already extinct. An active, sprightly little bird with a short, conical bill, the akepa feeds largely on caterpillars and spiders, which it usually finds on leaves and small twigs. It also drinks nectar. The female lays 3 eggs in a cavity in a tree.

NAME: **Akiapolaau, *Hemignathus wilsoni***
RANGE: **Hawaii**
HABITAT: **forest**
SIZE: **14 cm (5½ in)**  (E)

Formerly widespread and common on Hawaii, this honeycreeper is now found only in small numbers in a few areas. Two major reasons for its decline are the deterioration of its forest home and the introduction of predators, particularly arboreal rats. The akiapolaau forages on large branches and tree trunks, creeping up and down with equal ease. It has a unique bill: the upper mandible is long and curved and the lower short, straight and wedge-shaped. Using this extraordinary bill, the bird opens up the burrows of wood-boring insects and then uses its thin, brushlike tongue to extract its prey.

---

## VIREONIDAE: Vireo Family

There are about 43 species in this family, all found in the New World. The true vireos dominate the group — there are about 38 species. They all feed on insects among the foliage in wooded areas. Similar to the American wood warblers, Parulidae, in appearance, vireos are more stoutly built, have heavier bills and tend to be more deliberate in their movements.

The remaining birds in the family are divided into two groups, sometimes classified as separate families: the 2 species of peppershrikes and the 3 of shrike-vireos. All are slightly larger birds than vireos and have heavy, hooked bills; they feed in the trees, mainly on insects and fruit.

In all species of this family, male and female look alike or nearly so.

---

NAME: **Red-eyed Vireo, *Vireo olivaceus***
RANGE: **Canada, much of USA (not S.W.), Central and South America to Argentina; West Indies**
HABITAT: **deciduous forest and woodland, gardens, parks, orchards**
SIZE: **14–17 cm (5½–6¾ in)**

This widespread vireo is distinguished by its ruby-red eyes; immature birds have brown eyes. It occurs almost anywhere that there are deciduous trees and moves slowly through the lower levels and undergrowth, foraging for insects and berries. A persistent singer, it sings more than any other bird on hot summer days.

The neat, cup-shaped nest is suspended between the twigs of a horizontal fork in a tree or bush. There are usually 4 eggs, which the female incubates for 11 to 14 days. The young leave the nest some 10 to 12 days after hatching.

NAME: **Tawny-crowned Greenlet, *Hylophilus ochraceiceps***
RANGE: **S. Mexico, Central and South America to Bolivia**
HABITAT: **rain forest, woodland**
SIZE: **11 cm (4¼ in)**

This little vireo has mainly yellowish and brown plumage, with a tawny forehead and crown. It forages among the leaves of bushes and saplings for insects and other small invertebrates. It usually moves in small groups, often with other forest birds.

The female lays 2 eggs in a strongly built, cup-shaped nest, attached by its rim to a forked twig. Both parents feed their young with insects and larvae until they leave the nest at about 14 days old.

NAME: **Rufous-browed Peppershrike, *Cyclarhis gujanensis***
RANGE: **N.E. Mexico, through Central and South America to N. Argentina; Trinidad**
HABITAT: **forest, woodland, cultivated land**
SIZE: **15 cm (6 in)**

A heavy-bodied bird with a large head and strong legs and feet, this peppershrike is a good climber and forages in trees, but it is weak in flight. It is slow and deliberate in its movements as it searches for insects and berries, particularly at the ends of branches and twigs. If a large insect is caught, the bird holds it down with its foot and tears it apart with its strong, hooked bill. A secretive bird, this peppershrike rarely comes into the open but is often heard singing loudly and persistently from a perch. It usually lives alone or in pairs.

The nest is woven from bark and grasses and suspended in the fork of a branch in a bush or tree. Both parents incubate the 2 or 3 eggs and feed the young.

NAME: **Chestnut-sided Shrike-vireo, *Vireolanius melitophrys***
RANGE: **Mexico to Guatemala**
HABITAT: **forest**
SIZE: **18 cm (7 in)**

All 3 species of shrike-vireo are more brightly plumaged than typical vireos, and the chestnut-sided shrike-vireo is particularly attractive, with its green back, chestnut flanks and boldly striped head. It has a stout, hooked bill and strong legs and feet. Seldom seen, this bird lives high up in the canopy and rarely flies in the open or perches in exposed spots. It feeds on insects, holding down large ones with its foot and tearing them apart with its bill, and it also eats some fruit.

The nest is suspended from a forked branch of a tree, but the breeding habits of this shrike-vireo are not known.

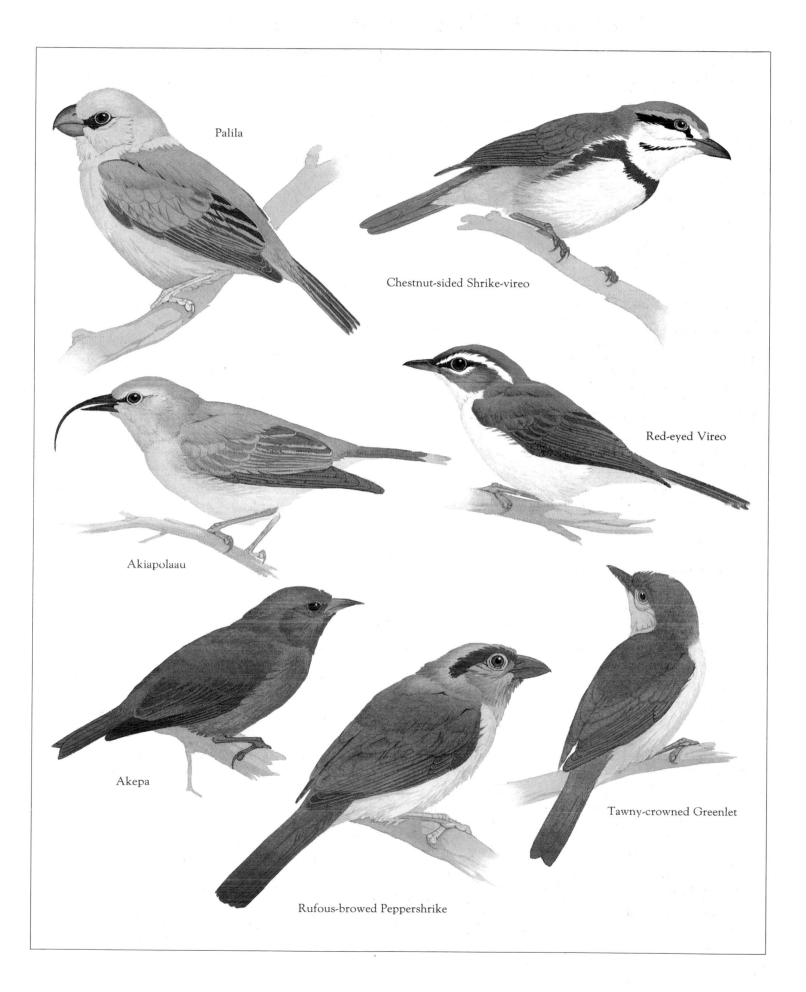

Palila

Chestnut-sided Shrike-vireo

Red-eyed Vireo

Akiapolaau

Akepa

Tawny-crowned Greenlet

Rufous-browed Peppershrike

# Icterids

**NAME: Wagler's Oropendola, *Psarocolius wagleri***
**RANGE: S. Mexico, through Central America to N.W. Ecuador**
**HABITAT: forest, clearings**
**SIZE: 28–35.5 cm (11–14 in)**

Wagler's oropendola has dark plumage, with a characteristic chestnut head and yellow tail feathers. The male is larger than the female and has a crest of a few hairlike feathers. A tree-dwelling bird, it hops and flutters in the middle and upper layers, searching for fruit, seeds and insects.

Colonies of these oropendolas nest together, 50 to 100 pairs making their nests in the same isolated or well-exposed tree or clump of trees. The female bird weaves a long, pouchlike nest, which hangs from an outer branch.

**NAME: Northern Oriole, *Icterus galbula***
**RANGE: S. Canada, much of USA except Gulf Coast and Florida, N. Mexico; winters from S. Mexico to Colombia**
**HABITAT: woodland, parks, gardens**
**SIZE: 18–21 cm (7–8¼ in)**

There are two forms included in this species: the Baltimore oriole, found in the east, and Bullock's oriole, found in the west. Previously they were thought to be separate species. The Baltimore oriole is the subspecies illustrated, and while the western race is similar in many respects, the male Bullock's has a largely orange head and a white wing patch. The two forms interbreed at the center of their range. Northern orioles forage in trees and bushes for caterpillars, beetles, ants and other insects, as well as for fruit and berries.

The female bird makes the nest, which is a deep pouch, woven from plant fiber and other long strands of material and hung from a forked twig. She lays 3 to 6 eggs, usually 4 or 5, which she incubates for about 14 days. Both parents tend the young.

**NAME: Yellow-rumped Cacique, *Cacicus cela***
**RANGE: Panama, south to N. Bolivia, E. Brazil; Trinidad**
**HABITAT: rain forest, secondary growth, open country with scattered trees**
**SIZE: 23–28 cm (9–11 in)**

The yellow-rumped cacique is a gregarious bird, which feeds, nests and roosts in groups. Much of its food, such as fruit and insects, is found in the trees, but it may also dart after flying termites and catch them in the air.

A colonial nester, the female cacique weaves a long, pouchlike nest, from grass and plant fibers, which is suspended from a branch, close to other nests of the colony. She lays 2 eggs, which she incubates for about 12 days.

## ICTERIDAE: Icterid Family

There are about 93 species of icterid, found throughout the Americas. An extremely successful and diverse family, it includes many different groups of birds such as oropendolas, caciques, grackles, American blackbirds and American orioles, cowbirds and meadowlarks. The majority of icterids live in woodland or forest, but others occur in all types of habitat, including marshes, desert and open country. Females are usually duller in plumage and smaller than males.

**NAME: Common Grackle, *Quiscalus quiscula***
**RANGE: S. Canada; USA, east of Rockies**
**HABITAT: open woodland, fields, parks, gardens, orchards**
**SIZE: 28–34 cm (11–13¼ in)**

The common grackle is a glossy black bird, with an iridescent sheen of purple or other colors, depending on the race. Females are smaller than males. Always gregarious birds, common grackles gather in large, noisy flocks and roost in groups. The diet of the common grackle is extremely varied. It forages in trees and bushes for nuts, fruit and the eggs and young of small birds. On the ground, it probes for worms and chases insects, mice and lizards, and it will even wade into ponds or streams to catch aquatic creatures such as frogs and crayfish.

A bulky nest of twigs, stalks and grass is made in a bush or tree or on a building. The birds usually nest in colonies. The female incubates the 5 or 6 eggs for 13 or 14 days, and both parents tend the young. Most populations winter just south of their breeding range, but some are resident.

**NAME: Bobolink, *Dolichonyx oryzivorus***
**RANGE: S. Canada; USA, south to Pennsylvania, Colorado, California; winters in South America**
**HABITAT: prairie, cultivated land**
**SIZE: 15–20 cm (6–7¾ in)**

In breeding plumage the male bobolink is largely black, with a white rump, a white streak on the back and a yellow nape. In winter, he looks like a larger version of the female, with yellow-brown plumage. Insects are the main diet of the bobolink in summer, but in winter, as it migrates south, it feeds on grain crops — in former times particularly on rice.

The bobolink performs the longest migration of any member of its family, traveling at least 8,000 km (5,000 mi) from Argentina to northern USA and Canada. Once at the breeding grounds,

males court females with display flights and bubbling songs; males may have many mates. The female makes a nest on the ground and lays 5 or 6 eggs, which she incubates for 13 days.

**NAME: Brown-headed Cowbird, *Molothrus ater***
**RANGE: S. Canada, USA; winters south of breeding range, from Maryland to Texas and California; Mexico**
**HABITAT: woodland, farmland, fields, open country**
**SIZE: 15–20 cm (6–7¾ in)**

As the common name suggests, the male of this species is distinguished by his shiny brown head; the female is uniformly gray. They are gregarious birds, forming large flocks in winter and gathering in small groups of up to 6 in the breeding season. They feed largely on plant matter, such as grain, seeds, berries and fruit, and on some insects, spiders and snails.

These cowbirds are brood parasites: the female lays her eggs in the nests of other birds. She lays up to 12 eggs a season, each in a different nest, which need to be incubated for 11 or 12 days. This cowbird has been known to use over 185 different species as hosts, most with smaller eggs than its own. The young cowbirds hatch more quickly and are bigger than the hosts' young, which usually perish.

**NAME: Eastern Meadowlark, *Sturnella magna***
**RANGE: S.E. Canada; USA: New England to Minnesota, south to Florida, Texas and New Mexico; Mexico, Central and South America to Brazil**
**HABITAT: open country: prairie, fields, grassland**
**SIZE: 21.5–28 cm (8½–11 in)**

The eastern meadowlark bears a close resemblance to the yellow-throated longclaw, *Macronyx croceus*, of the wagtail and pipit family. The two are not related but have adapted to a similar way of life in a similar habitat. The eastern meadowlark often perches in conspicuous spots on wires and posts but finds much of its food on the ground. It eats insects, such as grasshoppers, ants, beetles and caterpillars, grain and weed seeds. It will also consume the remains of birds killed by traffic.

After wintering just south of their breeding range, eastern meadowlarks return in the spring, the male birds arriving before females to establish territories. Each male may have more than one mate. The grass nest is made in a dip in open ground and is often dome-shaped. The female usually lays 5 eggs, which she incubates for 13 or 14 days. Both parents feed the young.

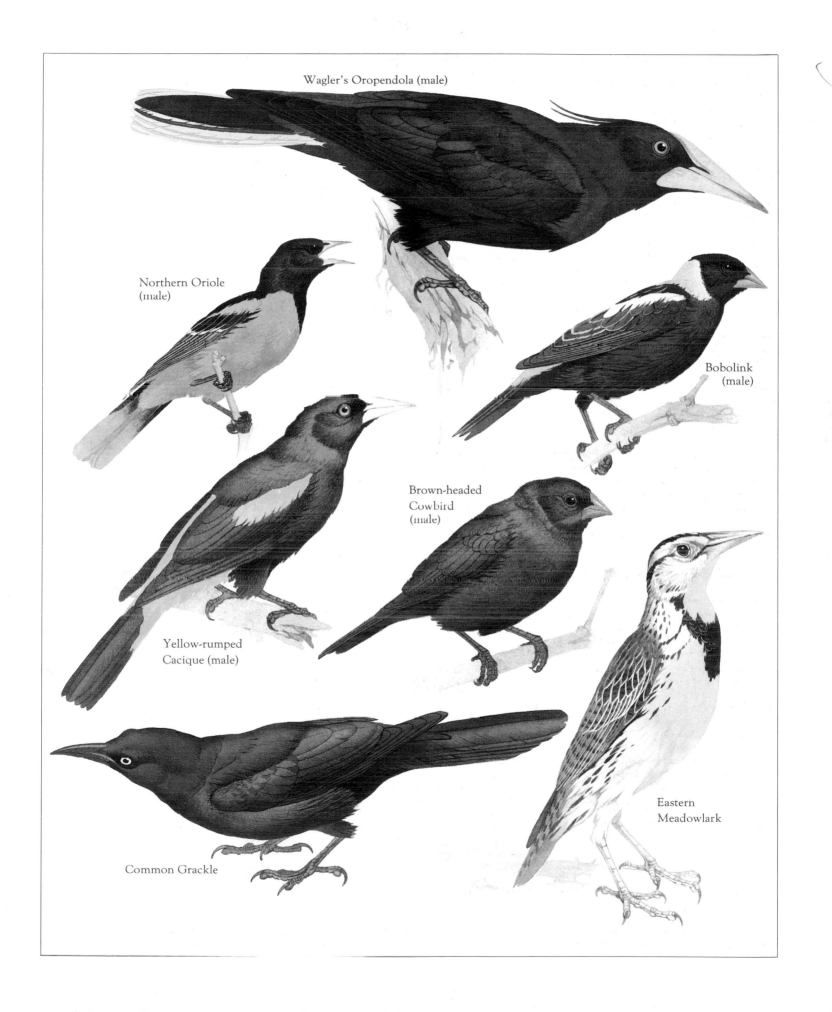

Wagler's Oropendola (male)

Northern Oriole
(male)

Bobolink
(male)

Brown-headed
Cowbird
(male)

Yellow-rumped
Cacique (male)

Eastern
Meadowlark

Common Grackle

# Finches

**NAME:** Chaffinch, *Fringilla coelebes*
**RANGE:** Europe, across Asia to Afghanistan, Mediterranean region, N. Africa, Canary Islands, Azores
**HABITAT:** forest, woodland, gardens
**SIZE:** 15 cm (6 in)

The abundant, widespread chaffinch varies in plumage coloration over its range, and its attractive song exists in many different dialects. The female has duller plumage than the male, being mostly grayish and olive-brown. The chaffinch searches for food in the trees and on the ground, where it hops or moves with short, quick steps; it flies in the undulating manner typical of the finches. Three-quarters of its food intake is plant material, mostly seeds, fruit and corn, but it also eats insects, spiders and earthworms.

A neat, well-constructed nest is made in a tree or bush, and the female lays 4 or 5 eggs, which she incubates for 11 to 13 days. Northern populations migrate south for the winter.

**NAME:** Purple Finch, *Carpodacus purpureus*
**RANGE:** N. America: British Columbia, south to Baja California, east to Newfoundland and N.E. USA; winters in W. and E. USA and Mexico
**HABITAT:** woodland, coniferous forest
**SIZE:** 14–16 cm (5½–6¼ in)

The male purple finch is distinguished by his rich, reddish coloration, while the female is mainly brown and gray. Outside the breeding season, these finches form large feeding flocks and search out seeds of weeds and trees. In spring and summer, they also feed on beetles and caterpillars.

In the breeding season, the male displays to the female, dancing around her and beating his wings while he sings his rich, warbling song. A nest is made of twigs and grasses, usually in a conifer, and the female lays 4 or 5 eggs, which she incubates for 13 days.

**NAME:** Canary, *Serinus canaria*
**RANGE:** Canary Islands, Madeira, Azores; introduced in Bermuda
**HABITAT:** wooded areas, gardens
**SIZE:** 12.5 cm (5 in)

All races of domestic canaries are descended from this species, which was first made popular as a cage bird by the Spanish conquerors of the Canary Islands. The female is generally brown and duller than the bright yellow and brown male. Canaries feed on seeds and usually remain hidden in the trees, but their attractive song is often heard.

A cup-shaped nest is made in a tree or bush, and the female lays 4 or 5 eggs, which she incubates for 13 or 14 days.

## FRINGILLIDAE: Finch Family

The finches are a successful and widely distributed group of small, seed-eating songbirds. They are most numerous in Europe and northern Asia, but some species occur in other parts of the Old World and in the Americas.

Finches generally live in trees and feed on seeds and nuts in the trees or under them. Their bodies are unspecialized, but, in keeping with their different diets, there is a great diversity of bill shapes within the family. These include the thin, pointed bill of the goldfinches, used for extracting tiny seeds from thistle and teasel heads; the stout, conical bill of generalist finches; and the heavy, "nutcracker" beak of hawfinches and grosbeaks, which enables them to crack cherry stones.

Male and female usually differ in appearance, and young resemble females.

**NAME:** Red/Common Crossbill, *Loxia curvirostra*
**RANGE:** Europe, Asia, south to Himalayas; N. America, south to Nicaragua
**HABITAT:** coniferous forest
**SIZE:** 13–16 cm (5–6¼ in)

This crossbill feeds almost entirely on conifer seeds, which it extracts from the cones by using its specialized crossed mandibles. The bird may hang upside down to feed at cones or tear off the cone and hold it in its foot. It rarely comes down to the ground, where it moves awkwardly. In summer, it also eats insects. Male and female differ in plumage, the female being greenish-gray.

After a pair-forming gathering, a cup-shaped nest is made in a conifer. The female lays 3 or 4 eggs, which she incubates for 13 to 16 days; both parents feed the young, which hatch with symmetrical bills.

**NAME:** European Goldfinch, *Carduelis carduelis*
**RANGE:** Europe, N. Africa, Azores, Canary Islands, Madeira; Asia, east to Lake Baikal, south to Himalayas
**HABITAT:** open woodland, gardens, orchards, cultivated land
**SIZE:** 12 cm (4¾ in)

Unmistakable birds, both male and female goldfinches have red faces and black and white heads. Their wings are long and pointed and their strong bills almost conical. Outside the breeding season, goldfinches often fly to open country to feed near the ground on thistles and other weed seeds, especially small seeds; they also eat some insects.

The female builds a nest on a branch of a tree and lays 5 or 6 eggs.

**NAME:** Pine Grosbeak, *Pinicola enucleator*
**RANGE:** N. Scandinavia, USSR, Asia; Alaska, Canada, N. USA
**HABITAT:** coniferous and mixed forest
**SIZE:** 20 cm (7¾ in)

A large, long-tailed finch, the pine grosbeak uses its stout, heavy bill to crush the stones of fruit such as cherries and plums; it also feeds on seeds, buds and insects in summer. It finds its food in trees and on the ground and is a strong flier. Male and female differ in plumage, the female being largely a bronzy color.

The nest is usually made in a conifer or a birch tree, and the female lays 4 eggs, which she incubates for 13 or 14 days. The male feeds her during this period and later on helps to feed the young by regurgitating food for them.

**NAME:** Common Redpoll, *Acanthis flammea*
**RANGE:** breeds in Iceland, Ireland, Britain, Scandinavia, central European mountains, N. Asia to Bering Sea, northern N. America; winters south of breeding range
**HABITAT:** woodland, forest, tundra
**SIZE:** 13–15 cm (5–6 in)

The redpoll is able to survive lower temperatures than any songbird other than its close relative the arctic, or hoary, redpoll, *A. hornemanni*. It feeds on seeds, particularly those of birch and alder, and will hang upside down to reach the catkins. It also scratches on the ground to find seeds and in summer feeds on insects.

At the start of the spring breeding season, males perform display flights. The female builds a nest on a forked branch, usually of an alder, willow or spruce, and lays 4 or 5 eggs. She incubates the eggs for 10 or 11 days.

**NAME:** Bullfinch, *Pyrrhula pyrrhula*
**RANGE:** Scandinavia, Britain, south to Mediterranean regions (not S. Spain); Asia to Japan
**HABITAT:** coniferous forest, woodland, parks, gardens, cultivated land
**SIZE:** 14–16 cm (5½–6¼ in)

The male bullfinch is identified by his black cap, rose-red underparts and black and white wings; the female looks similar but has pinkish-gray underparts. A shy bird, it usually perches in cover in a bush or tree and does not often come to the ground. In spring, it feeds largely on the buds of fruit trees and can cause considerable damage; buds of other trees are also eaten, as well as berries and seeds.

A nest of twigs and moss is built by the female in a bush or hedge. She lays 4 or 5 eggs, which she incubates for 12 to 14 days.

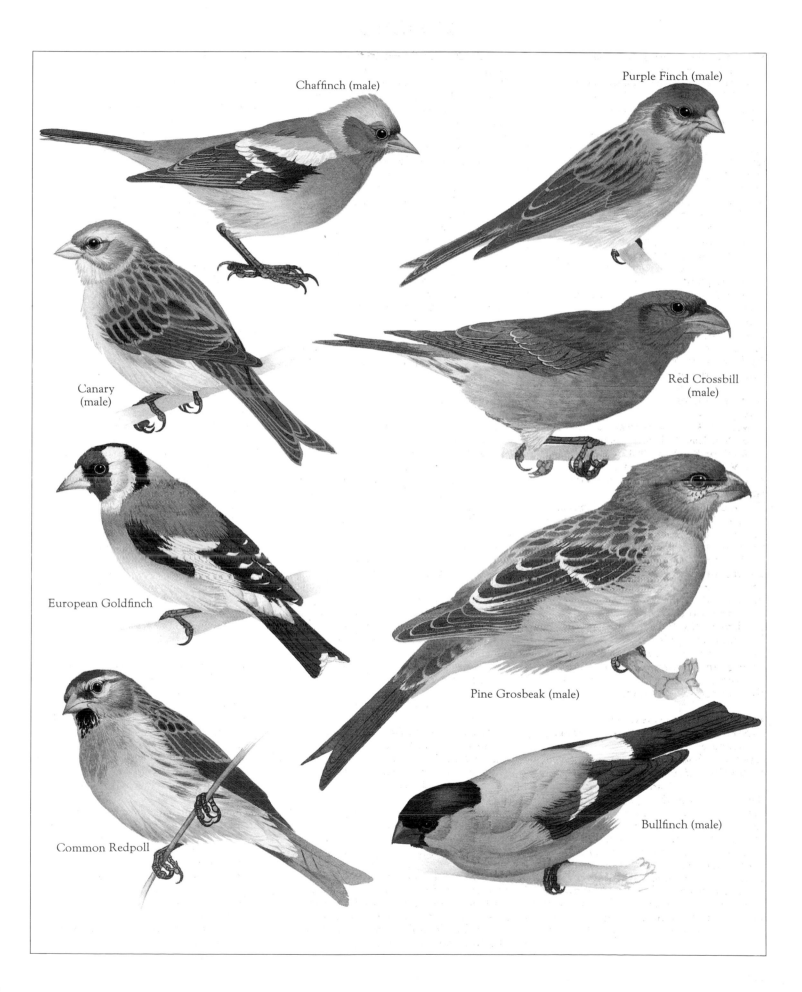

Chaffinch (male)

Purple Finch (male)

Canary (male)

Red Crossbill (male)

European Goldfinch

Pine Grosbeak (male)

Common Redpoll

Bullfinch (male)

# Waxbills

NAME: **Red-billed Fire-finch,**
*Lagonosticta senegala*
RANGE: **Africa, south of the Sahara (not extreme south)**
HABITAT: **scrub, thickets, cultivated land, near habitation**
SIZE: **9 cm (3½ in)**

One of the most widespread and common of African birds, the red-billed fire-finch often feeds on grass and other seeds on the ground in towns and villages. The female is much plainer than the male, having only a touch of red on the face and rump; her underparts are buff, with white spots on the breast. Outside the breeding season, these birds gather in small flocks.

The globular nest, usually made of dry grass, is built on a low wall or in a bush or thatched roof. The female lays 3 to 6 eggs, usually 4, which are incubated by both parents.

NAME: **Red-cheeked Cordon-bleu,**
*Uraeginthus bengalus*
RANGE: **Africa: Senegal to Ethiopia, south through E. Africa to Zambia**
HABITAT: **open country, cultivated land**
SIZE: **12.5 cm (5 in)**

The male red-cheeked cordon-bleu is easily recognized by his crimson cheek patches; females and juveniles are duller in plumage and lack the red markings. A widespread, common bird, it feeds on the ground on various kinds of grass seeds and often comes close to human habitation. Cordon-bleus live in pairs or small family groups.

The globular or oval-shaped nest is made of dry grass and has an entrance hole at the side. It is built in a bush, tree or thatched roof. The female lays 4 or 5 eggs.

NAME: **Red Avadavat,** *Amandava amandava*
RANGE: **India, Pakistan, S.W. China, Hainan, S.E. Asia (introduced in Malaysia), Java, Lesser Sunda Islands**
HABITAT: **scrub, grassland, reedbeds, cultivated land**
SIZE: **9–10 cm (3½–4 in)**

A distinctive bird in breeding plumage, the male red avadavat sports bright crimson plumage, dotted with many characteristic white spots; his dark wings, too, are spotted with white. Outside the breeding season, he resembles the female, with a grayish-buff throat and breast. Both sexes have red bills and a patch of red at the base of the tail. Often found in swampy land, the red avadavat feeds on grass seeds. It lives in pairs or groups of up to 30, often with other waxbill species.

The ball-shaped grass nest has an entrance at the side; it is built low in a bush or among rushes or grass. The female incubates the 6 to 10 eggs.

## ESTRILDIDAE: Waxbill Family

The range of types of specialist seed-eating songbirds in the Old World is confusing with respect to the inter-relationships of the various groups. Various taxonomical treatments have been proposed, but the one adopted here places the weavers, finches, buntings and warblers all in separate families. Common names, too, are confusing in these groups, for many species of estrildid are called sparrow, finch or weaver.

All members of the waxbill family are small, predominantly seed-eating birds. There are about 126 species, distributed throughout tropical regions of Africa, southern Asia, Australasia and the Pacific islands. The family includes several distinct groups: the waxbills themselves, the grassfinches and the mannikins (a totally separate group from the New World manakins). Most are very colorful birds with striking patches of bright plumage. The bill is typically short and stubby, suited to the diet of seeds. Generally gregarious, flocking birds, many species of waxbill nest socially. Nestlings have remarkable patterns inside their mouths, and the sight of their gapes, marked with black lines and spots, stimulates parents to feed the young. Male and female look alike in some species, different in others.

NAME: **Java Sparrow,** *Padda oryzivora*
RANGE: **Java, Bali; introduced in Sri Lanka, Burma, some Indonesian islands, Seychelles, Zanzibar, St. Helena, Hawaii**
HABITAT: **rice fields, scrub, mangrove swamps, urban areas**
SIZE: **16 cm (6¼ in)**

One of the mannikin group, the Java sparrow has become widely established outside its native range, in some places by deliberate introduction, in others by the escape from captivity of large numbers of caged birds. Male and female look alike, both with pinkish-red bills and boldly marked black and white heads. The Java sparrow feeds largely on rice and is thus considered a pest in many areas. It also feeds on fallen seeds of other plants and climbs with great agility on stalks and trees. A gregarious bird, it moves in flocks.

The domed nest is made of grass and built on a wall, under the roof of a building or in a tree. The female lays up to 7 or 8 white eggs, which are incubated for 13 or 14 days. The young are fed on insects until they are able to adopt the adult diet of rice and seeds, which is hard to digest.

NAME: **Gouldian Finch,** *Chloebia gouldiae*
RANGE: **tropical N. Australia**
HABITAT: **savanna**
SIZE: **14 cm (5½ in)**

A most beautifully plumaged bird, the gouldian finch occurs in 3 forms that vary in the color of the forehead and face, which may be black, scarlet or, rarely, yellow. Male and female look similar, but the females have duller plumage. The gouldian finch feeds primarily on seeds, which it takes directly from grass heads. It seldom flies down to the ground but clings to grass stems or to the low twigs of bushes and trees within reach of grass heads. It also eats insects in the breeding season. A gregarious bird, it lives in flocks when not breeding. It is seldom far from water and in a drought may become nomadic, wandering in search of water.

The gouldian finch lays its 4 to 8 eggs in a hole in a tree or in a termite mound, sometimes on a sketchy, globular nest.

NAME: **Blue-faced Parrot-finch,**
*Erythrura trichroa*
RANGE: **Sulawesi, the Moluccas, New Guinea, Bismarck Archipelago, Solomon Islands: Guadalcanal; N.E. Australia, Caroline Islands, Vanuatu, Loyalty Islands**
HABITAT: **rain forest, mangrove swamps**
SIZE: **12 cm (4¾ in)**

The blue-faced parrot-finch lives alone or in small groups, frequenting bushes, low trees and vegetation, where it feeds on seeds of various kinds. Male and female look alike, both with blue, green, scarlet and black plumage.

The domed or pear-shaped nest is made of moss and plant fiber and has a side entrance; it is built in a tree or bush. There are 3 to 6 eggs in a clutch.

NAME: **Zebra Finch,** *Poephila guttata*
RANGE: **Australia, Lesser Sunda Islands,**
HABITAT: **woodland, dry, open country with bushes and trees**
SIZE: **9 cm (3½ in)**

A common bird throughout Australia, the zebra finch is gregarious and sometimes occurs in large flocks. It feeds in the trees and on the ground on seeds and also on insects, particularly in the breeding season. Male and female differ in appearance: the female lacks the male's facial markings and chestnut flanks and has a grayish-brown throat, with no gray barring.

The timing and frequency of the breeding season depend on rainfall, and in times of drought, birds may wander in search of better conditions. A domed nest is made of grass and twigs low in a tree or bush. There are usually 4 to 6 eggs in a clutch.

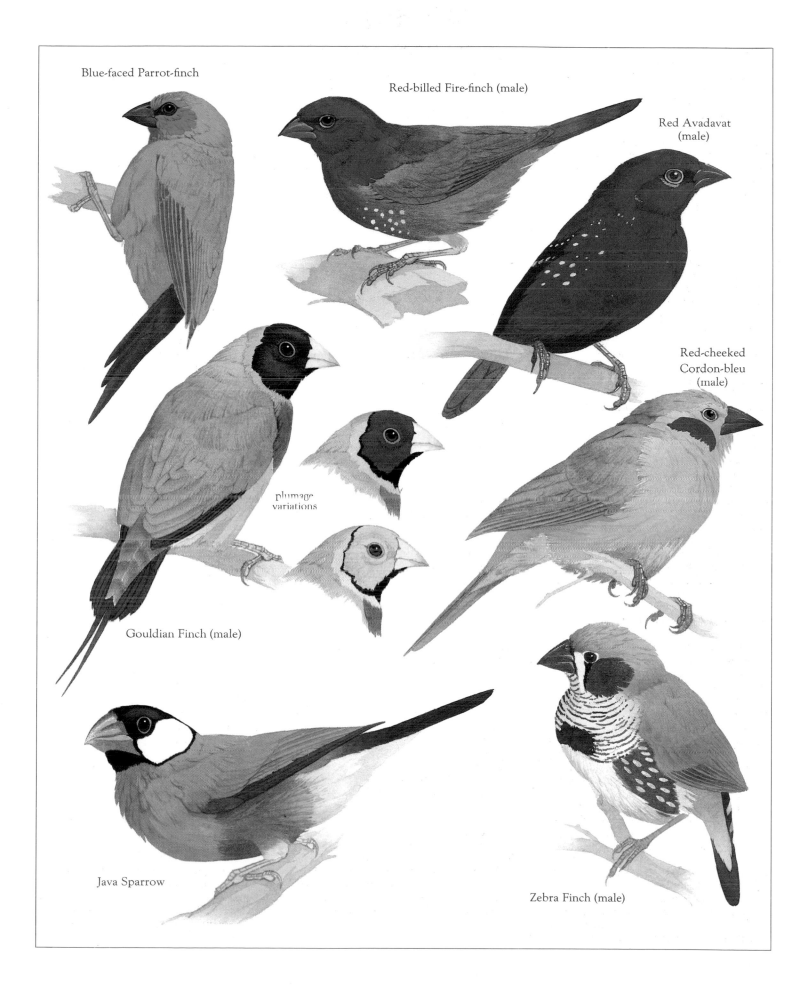

Blue-faced Parrot-finch

Red-billed Fire-finch (male)

Red Avadavat (male)

Gouldian Finch (male)

plumage variations

Red-cheeked Cordon-bleu (male)

Java Sparrow

Zebra Finch (male)

# Weavers

**NAME: Red-headed Weaver,** *Malimbus rubriceps*
**RANGE: Africa, south of the Sahara**
**HABITAT: open woodland, bush country, savanna, cultivated land**
**SIZE: 14 cm (5½ in)**

In the breeding season, the male of this species has bright red plumage on the head, neck and breast; the female looks similar but is yellow where the male is red. The nonbreeding male resembles the female. A rather shy, quiet bird compared to most weavers, the red-headed weaver lives in pairs or small groups and forages in the branches of trees for insects; it also eats seeds.

The polygamous male builds a pendulous woven nest for each of his mates. The nests hang from the ends of high branches and have long entrance tubes. Females lay 2 or 3 eggs.

**NAME: Grosbeak/Thick-billed Weaver,** *Amblyospiza albifrons*
**RANGE: Africa, south of the Sahara**
**HABITAT: bush country, marshes**
**SIZE: 19 cm (7½ in)**

Identified by its thick, heavy bill, the grosbeak weaver is a fairly common species which lives in small parties or pairs. It feeds mainly on seeds and on some berries when available. The male usually has a white forehead and white wing patches but is otherwise various shades of brown; the female is brown, with heavily streaked underparts.

The birds usually nest in small colonies of about 6 nests. Males may be polygamous. The male weaves a neat nest of fine grass, which is strung between two reed or grass stems. The 3 eggs are incubated by the female.

**NAME: Cuckoo/Parasitic Weaver,** *Anomalospiza imberbis*
**RANGE: Africa: Sierre Leone to Ethiopia, south to South Africa: Transvaal**
**HABITAT: grassland, bush, cultivated land**
**SIZE: 11.5 cm (4½ in)**

A gregarious bird, the cuckoo weaver congregates in large flocks outside the breeding season. It feeds mainly on grass seeds. Male and female differ in plumage, the female lacking the male's bright yellow markings and having buff and brown plumage. Juvenile birds are quite different in plumage from adults, being dull olive-green streaked with black, with dusky edges to the feathers.

Cuckoo weavers are brood parasites: they lay their eggs in the nests of other birds and leave the foster parents to incubate and rear their young. With plumage markedly different from that of their true parents, the young cuckoo weavers resemble the young of *Cisticola* warblers, birds often used as foster parents.

## PLOCEIDAE: Weaver Family

The weavers, buffalo weavers, sparrows and whydahs form a large and successful family of approximately 143 species of seed-eating birds. The group contains birds able to live in close association with humans, one of the most common of these being the house sparrow, which has probably thrived precisely because of this ability. Although originally a native of the Old World, like all of its family, the house sparrow, *Passer domesticus*, has become firmly established in the New World.

This family is so diverse that it is hard to generalize about its members, other than to state that they are seed-eaters, with stout, sharp bills, and that most are gregarious. Male and female look alike in some species but differ in others.

**NAME: Baya Weaver,** *Ploceus philippinus*
**RANGE: India, Sri Lanka to S.W. China, parts of S.E. Asia, Sumatra, Java**
**HABITAT: cultivated land, grassland, secondary scrub**
**SIZE: 15 cm (6 in)**

A common, gregarious bird, the baya weaver lives in flocks all year round and nests in colonies. It hops around on the ground, feeding on grass and weed seeds and also raids grain crops; this damage is compensated for by its huge consumption of insects, some of them pest species. In breeding plumage, the male has a yellow cap and blackish face mask, but in winter he resembles the female, which has a buff-brown crown.

The male builds a globular nest with a long entrance tube at the bottom, suspended from a branch. There may be up to 200 nests in a single tree. There are usually 3 eggs, which the female incubates for 14 or 15 days. Males are polygamous and may have several mates and nests.

**NAME: Village Weaver,** *Ploceus cucullatus*
**RANGE: Africa, south of the Sahara (not extreme south), Príncipe Island**
**HABITAT: forest, bush, cultivated and inhabited areas**
**SIZE: 18 cm (7 in)**

Noisy, conspicuous birds, the village weavers live in flocks and breed in colonies. They generally frequent the lower levels of trees in areas near water. Although they damage grain crops, these weavers compensate to some degree by feeding on vast quantities of weed seeds, as well as on some insects. The brightly plumaged male bird is largely yellow, with a black throat and mask and characteristic mottling on the back. The female is duller, with olive-brown on the upperparts and yellowish-white below.

Village weavers breed in colonies, with as many as 100 nests in the same tree. Males are polygamous and may mate several times. The nest is woven from long grass stems and hangs from an outer branch; it has an entrance low down. The female incubates the 1 to 3 eggs.

**NAME: Red-billed Quelea,** *Quelea quelea*
**RANGE: Africa, south of the Sahara**
**HABITAT: savanna, cultivated land, almost anywhere with trees**
**SIZE: 12.5 cm (5 in)**

An extremely abundant and gregarious species, the red-billed quelea flies in cloudlike flocks of thousands of birds, which descend to feed on grain crops and do incredible damage. They also feed on weed seeds. These birds were one of the main agricultural problems in Africa and have been destroyed on a huge scale, but their numbers have recently decreased, apparently due to natural causes, to the point where controls have been relaxed. In breeding plumage the male bird has a reddish tinge to his crown and chest; his face, chin and throat may be white, buff or black. Out of the breeding season, the male's bill is still red, but he otherwise resembles the female, which has streaky brown and buff plumage and a brownish crown.

Red-billed queleas form monogamous pairs and breed in dense colonies. The male builds the kidney-shaped nest, which hangs from a branch and has a side entrance. The 2 or 3 eggs are incubated by the female for 12 days, and both parents feed the young.

**NAME: Red Bishop,** *Euplectes orix*
**RANGE: Africa, south of the Sahara**
**HABITAT: open grassland, often near water**
**SIZE: 12.5 cm (5 in)**

Outside the breeding season, these abundant weavers form huge flocks, which are capable of doing enormous damage to grain crops. They also feed on grass seeds. In breeding plumage the male bird is largely red and black, while the female is streaked buff and brown; the nonbreeding male resembles the female but is darker.

Each male red bishop has 3 or 4 mates, which all nest within his defined territory. He weaves an oval grass nest among bulrushes or reeds or in sugarcane plantations or cornfields. The female lines the nest and lays 3 eggs, which she incubates for 11 to 14 days. She feeds her young with insects until they fly, 13 to 16 days after hatching.

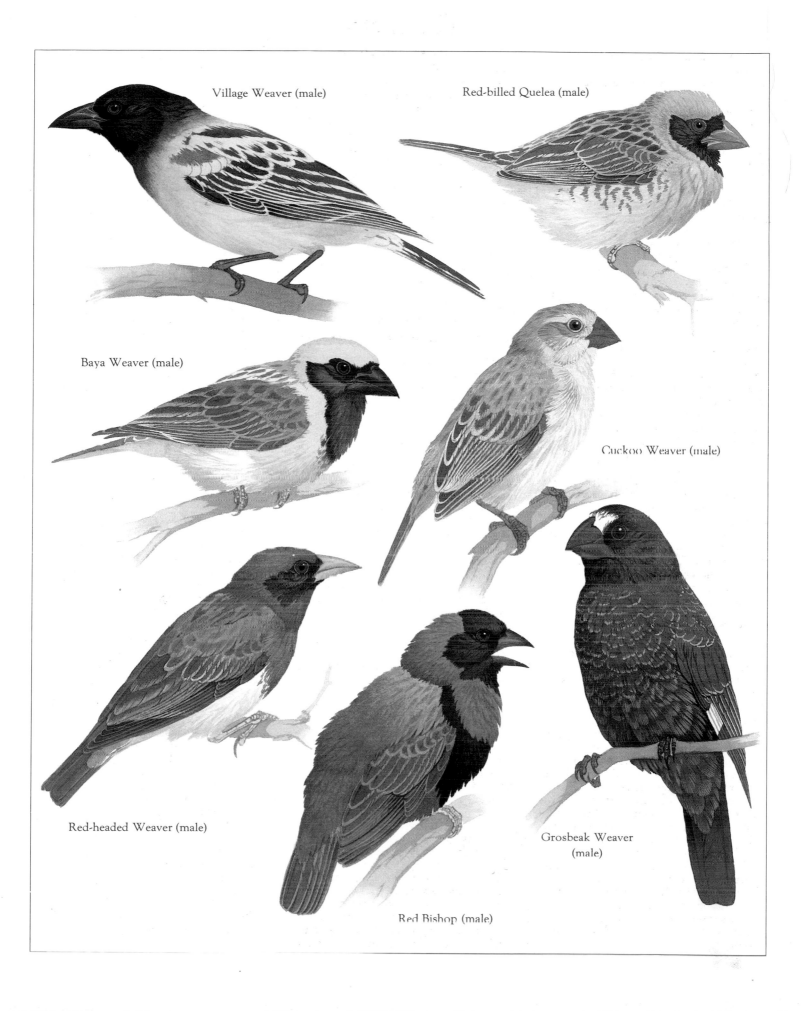

Village Weaver (male)

Red-billed Quelea (male)

Baya Weaver (male)

Cuckoo Weaver (male)

Red-headed Weaver (male)

Grosbeak Weaver
(male)

Red Bishop (male)

# Weavers

**NAME: Buffalo Weaver,** *Bubalornis albirostris*
**RANGE: Africa, south of the Sahara**
**HABITAT: savanna, scrub, cultivated land**
**SIZE: 24 cm (9½ in)**

Usually seen in small flocks, the buffalo weaver feeds mainly on the ground on a variety of grass seeds and insects. The plumage of the male is black, but with white bases to the feathers, and he has a black and white or reddish bill. The female has mottled brown plumage and a blackish or red bill.

Up to 8 pairs of buffalo weavers make a huge communal nest in a tree; it is kept in good order all year round and used for years. The framework of the nest is made of thorny sticks, and each individual nest within it is lined with fine grass and rootlets. Females usually lay 2 to 4 eggs and feed their young on insects.

**NAME: Gray-headed Sparrow,** *Passer griseus*
**RANGE: Africa, south of the Sahara**
**HABITAT: bush, cultivated land, near human habitation**
**SIZE: 15 cm (6 in)**

A bold little bird, the gray-headed sparrow is common in towns and villages and is similar to the house sparrow in its behavior. It feeds on almost any grain, plant matter and insects and does some damage to crops. The male is slightly larger than the female, but the two look alike, both with distinctive gray heads and mottled wings.

An untidy nest made of grass is built in a tree, in a thatched roof or at any other suitable site, or the birds may use an old nest of another species. There are usually 2 to 4 eggs in a clutch.

**NAME: House Sparrow,** *Passer domesticus*
**RANGE: temperate Europe and Asia, Africa, north of the Sahara; introduced worldwide**
**HABITAT: cultivated land, human habitation**
**SIZE: 14.5 cm (5¾ in)**

An extremely adaptable and successful bird, the house sparrow lives in close association with humans all over the world and is one of the most familiar of all birds. House sparrows were first introduced into the USA in 1850, when a few birds were released in Central Park, New York City. Since then, the species has spread all over North and South America, and the birds seem able to adapt remarkably quickly to new environments.

House sparrows often perch on trees and buildings but feed mainly on the ground. They eat almost anything: grain, weed seeds, insects, refuse and food scraps put out by humans.

Gregarious birds, they usually move in flocks and roost in closely packed groups. The male bird is identified by his gray crown, edged with chestnut, his black bib and brown and black-striped back and wings. The female is brownish-gray, with gray underparts.

Both members of a breeding pair help to build the nest, although the male does most of the work. Built in any hole or crevice in a building or wall, such as under eaves or in pipes, or sometimes in a tree or creeping plants, the nest is made of straw, plant stems, paper, cloth or any other available material. The 3 to 5 eggs are incubated, mostly by the female, for 11 to 14 days. Both parents feed the young, mainly on insects. There may be two or three broods a year.

**NAME: Rock Sparrow,** *Petronia petronia*
**RANGE: N. Africa, Madeira and Canary Islands; S.W. Europe, east through Balkans and central Asia to N. China**
**HABITAT: stony mountain slopes, ruined buildings, semidesert**
**SIZE: 14 cm (5½ in)**

Although not as bold with humans as the house sparrow, the rock sparrow often lives near villages and dwellings. It is a gregarious bird and moves in flocks, searching for seeds, insects and berries to eat. Male and female look alike.

The nest is made in a crevice in a rock, wall or building or sometimes in a tree or a rodent's burrow. The female lays 4 to 8 eggs, usually 5 or 6. Both parents tend and feed the young, and there may be a second brood.

**NAME: Sociable Weaver,** *Philetairus socius*
**RANGE: Africa: Namibia, South Africa**
**HABITAT: dry scrub**
**SIZE: 14 cm (5½ in)**

Sociable weavers move in flocks of anything up to a few hundred birds. They feed on insects and seeds, all of which they take on the ground. Male and female look alike and are identified by their grayish-brown crowns, black bibs and the cream-edged dark feathers on the back that give the plumage a scaly look.

The most remarkable feature about these birds is their enormous communal nest, usually made in a large acacia tree, which may be a home for up to a hundred pairs. The birds do not use the nest just for breeding but live and roost in it all year round. Nests are constantly repaired and rebuilt and may be used for years. Sociable weavers are monogamous birds, and within the communal nest, each pair has its own chamber and entrance. The average clutch contains 3 or 4 eggs.

**NAME: Snow Finch,** *Montifringilla nivalis*
**RANGE: S. Europe, across central Asia to the Himalayas**
**HABITAT: barren, stony ground on mountains at 1,800–2,100 m (6,000–7,000 ft)**
**SIZE: 18 cm (7 in)**

Although it seldom leaves its mountain habitat, the snow finch may descend to alpine valleys in bad winter weather. It perches on rocks and buildings and hops and walks quickly on the ground as it forages for insects and, in summer, the seeds of alpine plants. A bold little bird, it is often seen by skiers in alpine resorts and readily approaches to collect crumbs of food. The male is identified by his gray head, black throat and black and white wing and tail feathers. The female has a brownish head and less white on the wings and tail. Adults have black bills in the breeding season and orange-yellow bills in the autumn and winter.

The nest of feathers, dead grass and moss is made in a hole in a rock or building, where these exist, or in a mammal's burrow. The female lays 4 or 5 eggs on a warm lining of feathers and hair. Both parents incubate the eggs for 13 to 14 days and feed the young; a second brood may follow.

**NAME: Paradise Whydah,** *Vidua paradisaea*
**RANGE: E. and S. Africa: Sudan to Angola; South Africa: Natal**
**HABITAT: dry open country**
**SIZE: male: 38 cm (15 in) female: 15 cm (6 in)**

The elongated central tail feathers of the male account for the discrepancy in size between male and female paradise whydahs. The female bird has mottled brown and buff plumage similar to, but duller than, that of the male in non-breeding plumage. Often gathering in small flocks, paradise whydahs usually feed on the ground on seeds.

In his courtship display, the male bird flies with his long central tail feathers raised almost at a right angle and may also hover near the female, slowly beating his wings. Like all whydahs, this species is a brood parasite: it lays its eggs in the nests of other bird species, usually the melba finches of the waxbill family, Estrildidae. The young of the melba finch have complex patterns on the lining of their mouths which stimulate their parents to feed them, and the association between brood parasite and host has become so strong that the young whydahs have similar mouth patterns. They can also mimic the calls and postures of their foster siblings.

communal
nest

Sociable Weaver

Paradise
Whydah
(male)

Buffalo
Weaver
(male)

Rock Sparrow

House Sparrow
(male)

Gray-headed Sparrow

Snow Finch (male)

# Butcherbirds, Wood Swallows, Mudnest Builders

## CRACTICIDAE:
### Butcherbird Family

The 8 species in this Australasian family are strongly built birds, with heavy, hooked bills and, generally, black, gray and white plumage. Primarily tree-dwelling birds, they are noisy and gregarious. Males and females look alike in some species, unalike in others.

**NAME:** Black Butcherbird, *Cracticus quoyi*
**RANGE:** Australia: Queensland, coast of Northern Territory; New Guinea, Japen and Aru Islands
**HABITAT:** forest
**SIZE:** 32–36 cm (12½–14¼ in)

A bold, often aggressive bird, the black butcherbird feeds mostly on the ground, where it hops along on its short legs. Using its sharp, hooked bill, it tears up prey too large to be swallowed whole such as large insects, particularly grasshoppers, and small vertebrates. Male and female look alike and live alone or in small family groups.

A nest of twigs is made on a forked branch, and the female lays 3 or 4 eggs.

**NAME:** Australian Magpie, *Gymnorhina tibicen*
**RANGE:** S. New Guinea, Australia, Tasmania; introduced in New Zealand
**HABITAT:** open woodland, grassland, parks, gardens
**SIZE:** 36–40 cm (14¼–15¾ in)

Although it roosts and nests in trees, the Australian magpie does much of its feeding on the ground, searching for larvae, beetles and grasshoppers. Fruit and vegetation are also part of its diet. Australian magpies are gregarious birds and live in groups consisting of two pairs of adults or a larger number of birds, led by a dominant, polygamous male. Males and females look more or less alike.

The nest is made in a tree, and the female lays 3 eggs, which she incubates for 20 to 21 days. She also does most of the feeding of the young.

**NAME:** Pied Currawong, *Strepera graculina*
**RANGE:** Australia: Queensland to Victoria; Lord Howe Island
**HABITAT:** forest, clumps of trees in parks, suburban land
**SIZE:** 45 cm (17¾ in)

Primarily an arboreal bird, the pied currawong climbs in the trees in search of insects, larvae and fruit; it will also feed on the young and eggs of other bird species. It flies between feeding areas and sometimes feeds on the ground, turning over debris to find insects.

Noisy, gregarious birds, pied currawongs live in flocks. Their name is derived from the similar sounding call the birds make, often while in flight.

The nest is made in a tree, and the female lays 3 or 4 eggs.

## ARTAMIDAE:
### Wood Swallow Family

The 10 species of wood swallow are essentially Australasian birds, which have extended their range as far as India and southern China. They have stocky bodies and long, pointed wings and are skilled fliers. Launching themselves from frequently used perches, they chase and catch insect prey in the air. Male and female look alike or nearly so.

**NAME:** White-breasted Wood Swallow, *Artamus leucorhynchus*
**RANGE:** Australia and New Guinea, Philippines, Andaman, Palau and Fiji Islands
**HABITAT:** woodland, mangrove swamps
**SIZE:** 17 cm (6¾ in)

A gregarious bird, the white-breasted wood swallow lives in groups of 10 or more birds, which often sit huddled together on a branch, waiting for prey. Together they will attack passing birds, and individuals dart off in pursuit of insect prey. They return to the perch to consume the catch. If there is a shortage of flying insects, these wood swallows feed on ground insects and larvae.

Both members of a breeding pair help to build a cup-shaped nest in the fork of a tree, a hole in a trunk or branch or a disused magpie lark's nest. The female lays 3 or 4 eggs, which both parents incubate for about 19 days.

**NAME:** White-browed Wood Swallow, *Artamus superciliosus*
**RANGE:** Australia: breeds Victoria, New South Wales to S.E. Queensland; winters throughout continent
**HABITAT:** arid scrub, savanna
**SIZE:** 18–20 cm (7–7¾ in)

A highly nomadic bird, the white-browed wood swallow disperses over much of the continent out of the breeding season, often moving in mixed flocks with other species of wood swallow. Like them, white-browed wood swallows perch in groups on branches and fly out to catch insects in the air. The female is duller in plumage than the male, and her "eyebrow" streaks are less distinct.

The nest is built in a tree or on a tree stump and is made of sticks and dry grass. Both parents incubate the 2 or 3 eggs for about 16 days.

## GRALLINIDAE:
### Mudnest Builder Family

The mudnest builders are a small family of medium to large songbirds that live in Australia and New Guinea. There are only 4 species, divided into 2 subfamilies, which are linked merely by their method of building nests; all build large mud nests in trees. One subfamily contains the magpie lark and the torrent lark, both strikingly marked black and white birds; the other contains the apostlebird and the white-winged chough. Male and female magpie larks differ slightly in appearance, but in the other species the sexes look similar.

**NAME:** Magpie Lark, *Grallina cyanoleuca*
**RANGE:** Australia
**HABITAT:** open woodland, parks
**SIZE:** 25–28 cm (9¾–11 in)

A distinctive black and white bird, the magpie lark spends much of its time on the ground, feeding on insects. It is not shy and is common near human settlements and by roadsides. Many of the insects it consumes are considered pests; it also feeds on the freshwater snails that harbor the liver fluke, so often transmitted to cattle and sheep. The female differs from the male in having a white throat and forehead and has no patches of white plumage above or below her eyes.

Magpie larks pair for life and tend to nest in the same tree year after year, several pairs nesting near one another. The bowl-shaped nest is made from mud lined with grass and is situated on a branch. The female lays 3 to 5 eggs, which are incubated by both parents. The young are also fed by both parents and are independent at 4 weeks.

**NAME:** Apostlebird, *Struthidea cinerea*
**RANGE:** Australia: Victoria, New South Wales, Queensland
**HABITAT:** open woodland, scrub, cultivated land
**SIZE:** 33 cm (13 in)

The gregarious apostlebird usually lives in groups of about 12 birds — hence its common name — which keep together even in the breeding season. The group may be led by a dominant pair. The birds feed mostly on the ground on insects and seeds, but they will also jump from branch to branch in the trees and fly for short distances.

The bowl-shaped mud nest is lined with grass and made in a tree, usually near several other nests. The female lays 4 or 5 eggs, sometimes more than one female laying in the same nest; the eggs are incubated for 19 days. The young are fed by the group.

White-breasted
Wood Swallow

White-browed
Wood Swallow
(male)

Black Butcherbird

Australian Magpie

Pied Currawong

Magpie Lark
(male)

Apostlebird

# Bowerbirds, Birds of Paradise

## PTILONORHYNCHIDAE: Bowerbird Family

The 18 species of bowerbird all occur in New Guinea and Australia and are closely related to the birds of paradise, also from those regions. Bowerbirds have stout bills, straight or curved, and strong legs and feet. Much of their life is spent on the ground, but they feed and nest in trees. Females have much duller plumage than males, usually brownish and gray.

The family gets its common name from the "bower-building" activities of all but a few species: the males build ornate bowers on the ground, which they decorate with colorful objects to attract the attention of females.

NAME: **MacGregor's/Gardener Bowerbird,** *Amblyornis macgregoriae*
RANGE: **mountains of New Guinea (not N.W.)**
HABITAT: **forest**
SIZE: **25.5 cm (10 in)**

The male MacGregor's bowerbird is distinguished by his spectacular crest but otherwise has sober plumage. The female looks similar but lacks the crest. They are common, but shy birds and feed on fruit. The male's bower consists of a saucer-shaped platform of moss with a central column of twigs, both decorated with berries, flowers and bright objects such as shiny dead beetles. The bird attends his bower daily, repairing it and cleaning away any debris. Once he has attracted a mate, he displays and then chases her before mating.

The female builds a practical, cup-shaped nest in a tree and incubates her single egg herself.

NAME: **Satin Bowerbird,** *Ptilonorhynchus violaceus*
RANGE: **Australia: Queensland to Victoria**
HABITAT: **forest**
SIZE: **27–33 cm (10½–13 in)**

The male satin bowerbird has a violet sheen to his black plumage — hence the common name — while the female is mainly olive-green, tinged with yellow. Noisy, gregarious birds outside the breeding season, they feed on fruit and insects and often raid orchards. They make a variety of calls and also mimic other sounds. The male's display bower is an "avenue" of twigs, which sweeps upward at both ends and is liberally decorated with berries, flowers and any other bright objects. This bowerbird is particularly attracted to anything blue and will collect items such as bits of blue glass, paper or plastic. If a female shows interest, the male dances in his bower, alternately drooping and raising his wings and puffing up his feathers.

The female builds a nest of twigs and leaves in a tree and lays 2 eggs, which she alone incubates for 19 to 23 days.

## PARADISAEIDAE: Bird of Paradise Family

There are 42 known species of bird of paradise, and this aptly named group probably contains the most visually spectacular of all birds. They inhabit the rain forests of New Guinea, the Moluccas and northern Australia and feed on fruit, berries, insects, frogs and lizards.

The males are renowned for their extraordinarily varied and colorful plumage and often have long, decorative tail and head feathers. They use this ornate plumage in the complex courtship dances they perform to attract females. Female birds have dull, usually brown, plumage and look quite different from males.

NAME: **King of Saxony Bird of Paradise,** *Pteridophora alberti*
RANGE: **mountains of New Guinea**
HABITAT: **rain forest**
SIZE: **23 cm (9 in)**

The male King of Saxony bird of paradise has two unique head plumes, one extending from each side of its head. These plumes are two or three times the body length and consist of wirelike shafts bearing a series of horny plates. The bird chooses a display site on a high branch, holds his head plumes up, and bounces up and down while expanding and retracting his back feathers and hissing. The whole effect is quite spectacular. As the female approaches, the male sweeps the long head plumes in front of her and then follows her, and they mate.

The female bird is brownish-gray, with black-barred white underparts. The birds live in the middle and upper layers of the forest and feed on fruit.

NAME: **Crinkle-collared Manucode,** *Manucodia chalybatus*
RANGE: **New Guinea, Misoöl Island**
HABITAT: **rain forest**
SIZE: **37 cm (14½ in)**

The crinkle-collared manucode is a glossy purplish-black bird with curly green feathers adorning its head and neck. Male and female look alike and have none of the spectacular adornments associated with other birds of paradise. They live in the middle to upper stories of the forest and feed on fruit.

These manucodes form monogamous pairs and nest on forked branches. The female is thought to lay 1 egg.

NAME: **King Bird of Paradise,** *Cicinnurus regius*
RANGE: **New Guinea; Japen, Misoöl, Salawati and Aru Islands**
HABITAT: **lowland rain forest**
SIZE: **30.5 cm (12 in) including tail**

A spectacular crimson bird, the king bird of paradise has two wirelike, lyre-shaped tail feathers tipped with metallic green and a fanlike plume at each shoulder. The female lacks the male's long tail wires and has brown plumage edged with chestnut and olive. These birds feed mainly on fruit at all levels of the forest. The male chooses a horizontal branch as his display ground and spends much time there. He adopts various display postures to attract a mate, including raising his tail wires, hanging upside down, and vibrating his wings.

The female makes her nest in a hole in a tree — the only bird of paradise to do so. She lays 2 eggs, which she is thought to incubate for about 12 days.

NAME: **Ribbon-tailed Astrapia/Bird of Paradise,** *Astrapia mayeri*
RANGE: **mountains of central New Guinea**
HABITAT: **rain forest**
SIZE: **1.2 m (4 ft) including tail of up to 91.5 cm (36 in)**

Ribbonlike central tail feathers are the main identifying feature of the male of this species, which is mainly black with patches of green iridescence. The tail feathers play a central role in the male's courtship display, when they are twitched from side to side. The female bird has a much shorter tail and glossy black, green and brown plumage.

One of the last birds of paradise to be discovered, this species lives in a very restricted area of the central highlands. It frequents the branches of tall trees and feeds on fruit. The shallow, cup-shaped nest is made on a base of leaves from moss and vine tendrils.

NAME: **Blue Bird of Paradise,** *Paradisaea rudolphi*
RANGE: **mountains of S.E. New Guinea**
HABITAT: **rain forest**
SIZE: **28 cm (11 in) excluding tail**

The male blue bird of paradise has a velvety black breast and long, lacy flank plumes. His distinctive tail feathers, are narrow and straplike and play an important part in the display dance he performs to attract the much plainer female. The male hangs upside down from a branch, with the flank plumes spread out and the tail straps held in graceful curves. In this position, he swings to and fro, all the while making a strange, grating call.

A nest is made by the female in a low tree, and she is thought to lay 1 egg.

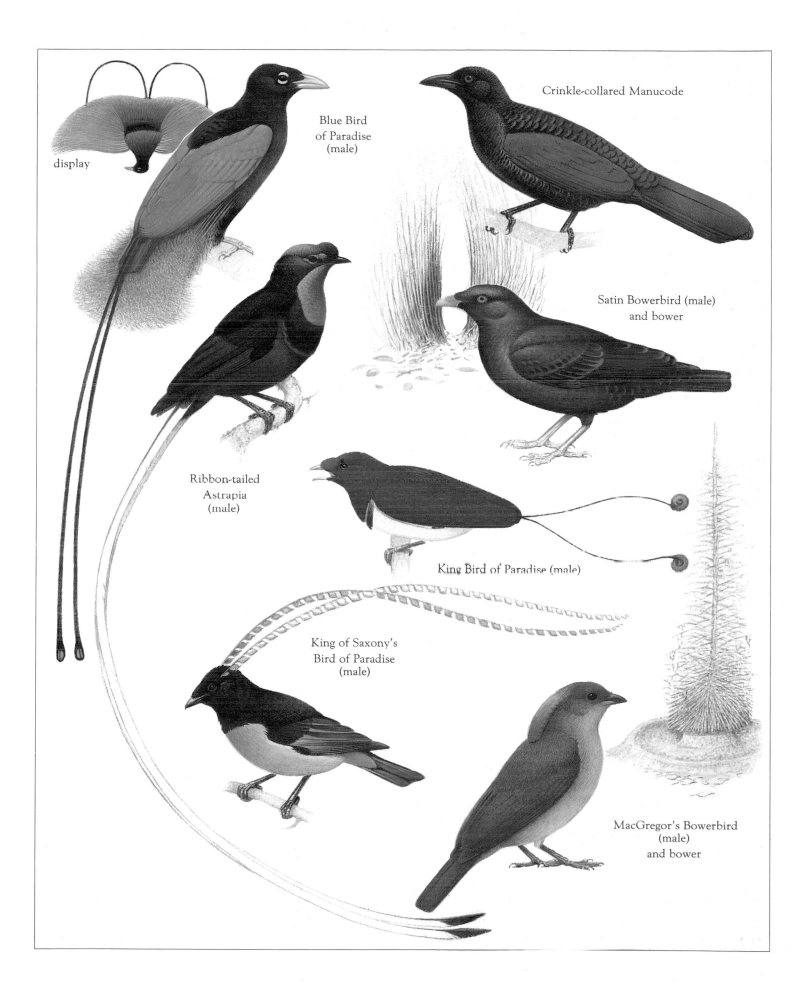

display

Blue Bird
of Paradise
(male)

Crinkle-collared Manucode

Satin Bowerbird (male)
and bower

Ribbon-tailed
Astrapia
(male)

King Bird of Paradise (male)

King of Saxony's
Bird of Paradise
(male)

MacGregor's Bowerbird
(male)
and bower

# Crows

**NAME:** Common Crow, *Corvus brachyrhynchos*
**RANGE:** S. Canada, USA
**HABITAT:** open country, farmland, open woodland, woodland edge, parks
**SIZE:** 43–53 cm (17–20¾ in)

This stocky, black-plumaged crow is extremely abundant and widespread and adapts well to most habitats. Almost omnivorous, it feeds largely on the ground, but also in trees, on insects, spiders, frogs, reptiles, small mammals, birds and their eggs and carrion. It also eats grain, fruit and nuts and scavenges on refuse. These crows usually forage in pairs, although lone males are seen in the breeding season; in winter, they gather in huge flocks to fly to communal roosts.

A nest of sticks and twigs is made in a tree, bush or, occasionally, on a telephone pole. The 3 to 6 eggs are incubated for about 18 days, probably by the female alone. Northern populations migrate south in winter.

**NAME:** Rook, *Corvus frugilegus*
**RANGE:** Europe, N. Asia, east to China
**HABITAT:** open country and farmland with clumps of trees, small woods
**SIZE:** 45 cm (17¾ in)

The glossy black rook is distinguished by the patch of bare skin on its face in front of the eyes and the shaggy, loose feathers on its thighs. It feeds largely on grain crops and earthworms, which it obtains by driving its bill into the earth (hence the bare forehead, which avoids soiled plumage) and then forcing it open to seize the worm. Insects and other invertebrates, small mammals, young birds, eggs, nuts and fruit are also included in its diet. Primarily a ground-feeder, the rook will fly up into trees to take nuts or other specific items. Rooks live in pairs but in autumn and winter gather in large communal roosts.

Colonies of rooks nest at the tops of tall trees, each pair making a nest of sticks and twigs. The male bird feeds the female while she incubates the 3 to 5 eggs for 16 to 18 days. Both parents tend and feed the young. Northern birds migrate south in winter.

**NAME:** Hume's Ground Jay, *Pseudopodoces humilis*
**RANGE:** China
**HABITAT:** open, sandy country
**SIZE:** 20 cm (7¾ in)

One of a distinct group of ground-living corvids, Hume's ground jay runs speedily on its long legs and has a heavy bill, with which it probes and digs in the ground for its insect food.

It digs its own nest in the earth, and the female lays 4 to 6 eggs.

## CORVIDAE: Crow Family

The 105 species of crow, jay and magpie constitute an advanced and highly successful family of tough, intelligent and adaptable songbirds. They occur worldwide except in New Zealand and some oceanic islands.

All members of the family are large for songbirds, with powerful, often hooked bills. Their legs are strong, and crows are able to move fast on the ground as well as in the air. The woodland-living jays are the most brightly colored of the family; the nutcrackers are spotted, while magpies and the crows themselves are predominantly black. Male and female generally look alike or nearly so.

**NAME:** (Black-billed) Magpie, *Pica pica*
**RANGE:** Europe to N. Africa; Asia to Himalayas and just into S.E. Asia; Alaska, W. Canada and USA to Utah
**HABITAT:** open country with trees, woodland edge, grassland
**SIZE:** 44–57 cm (17¼–22½ in)

This sprightly magpie has black and white plumage and a long tail; the many subspecies show slight variations in plumage, some having a pronounced green, purple or golden sheen. It feeds mainly on the ground on insects, snails, slugs and spiders, but also takes grain, small mammals and carrion and will fly up into a tree to take fruit, nuts and young birds. Some magpies remain in their breeding territory all year round, usually in pairs or small groups, while others gather in communal roosts out of the breeding season.

The large, domed nest is made in a tree or bush by both members of a pair. The male feeds the female while she incubates the 5 to 8 eggs for 17 or 18 days.

**NAME:** Blue Jay, *Cyanocitta cristata*
**RANGE:** S.E. Canada, E. USA to Gulf of Mexico
**HABITAT:** woodland, city parks, gardens
**SIZE:** 30 cm (11¾ in)

This colorful jay is mainly blue but has black and white plumage on the wings and tail and black markings on the face. It feeds on the ground and in trees on nuts, seeds, grain, fruit, berries, insects and invertebrates, and the eggs and young of other birds. Seen in family parties in summer, blue jays gather in larger groups in autumn. They are noisy birds, and groups have the habit of attacking predators or intruders.

The nest is made in a tree or bush, and the female incubates the 2 to 6 eggs for 16 to 18 days. The male feeds her and helps to tend the brood.

**NAME:** Green Jay, *Cyanocorax yncas*
**RANGE:** USA: S. Texas; through Mexico and Central and South America to Brazil and Bolivia
**HABITAT:** forest, woodland, thickets
**SIZE:** 30 cm (11¾ in)

The green tail feathers of this bright green, yellow and blue bird help to identify it in flight. The many subspecies found over the wide range show slight variations in plumage. Green jays usually live in pairs or small groups and feed largely on insects. They also eat acorns and seeds and sometimes the eggs and young of other birds.

The 3 to 5 eggs are laid in a nest in a tree or bush and are incubated by the female. Both parents tend the young.

**NAME:** Jay, *Garrulus glandarius*
**RANGE:** Europe to N. Africa; Asia, south to Burma, China and Taiwan
**HABITAT:** forest, woodland, orchards
**SIZE:** 34 cm (13¼ in)

An extremely variable species over its wide range, the European jay has a pinkish-brown body, with brilliant wing patterns of blue and black bars. Alone or in pairs, it feeds in trees and on the ground on insects and other small invertebrates, such as spiders, snails and slugs, and also on acorns, berries and grain.

The female lays 3 to 7 eggs in a nest made in a tree and incubates her clutch for 16 to 19 days. The male feeds his mate while she incubates and brings all the food for the brood until the female is able to leave the nest and assist him.

**NAME:** Ceylon Magpie, *Urocissa ornata*
**RANGE:** Sri Lanka
**HABITAT:** forest, gardens
**SIZE:** 46 cm (18 in)

A handsome bird with chestnut-red and blue plumage, the Ceylon magpie lives alone, in pairs or in small groups. It feeds in trees and on the ground on insects, invertebrates and fruit.

The nest is made in a small tree, and the female lays 3 to 5 eggs.

**NAME:** Piapiac, *Ptilostomus afer*
**RANGE:** Africa: Senegal to Nigeria, east to Ethiopia
**HABITAT:** open country, palm groves
**SIZE:** 46 cm (18 in)

A slender, long-tailed bird with a thick bill, the piapiac lives in flocks of 10 or more. It feeds mainly on the ground on insects and invertebrates, often following herds of large animals to pick up the insects they disturb; it also takes insects from the backs of large mammals and eats the fruit of the oil palm.

The nest is made in a palm or other tree, and the female lays 3 to 7 eggs.

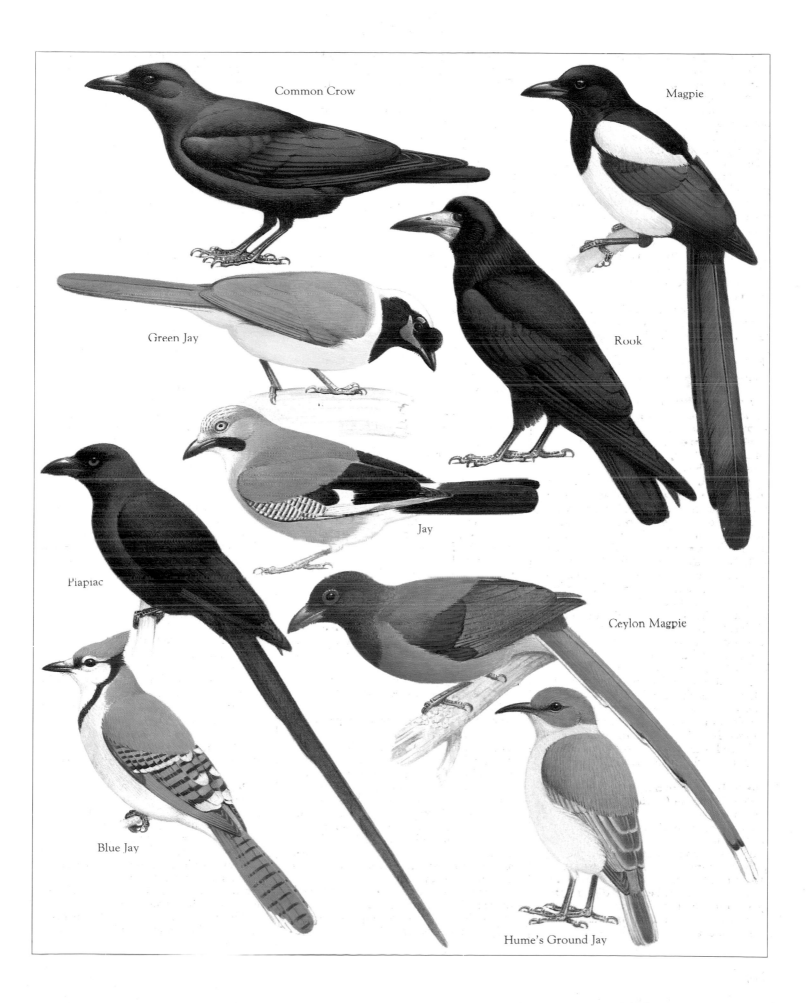

Common Crow

Magpie

Green Jay

Rook

Piapiac

Jay

Ceylon Magpie

Blue Jay

Hume's Ground Jay

# Classification

CLASS AVES: **Birds**

**Order Struthioniformes**
Family Struthionidae: Ostrich

**Order Rheiformes**
Family Rheidae: Rheas

**Order Casuariiformes**
Family Casuariidae Cassowaries
Family Dromaiidae: Emu

**Order Apterygiformes**
Family Apterygidae: Kiwis

**Order Tinamiformes**
Family Tinamidae: Tinamous

**Order Sphenisciformes**
Family Spheniscidae: Penguins

**Order Gaviiformes**
Family Gaviidae: Loons

**Order Podicipediformes**
Family Podicipedidae: Grebes

**Order Procellariiformes**
Family Diomedeidae: Albatrosses
Family Procellariidae: Petrels
Family Hydrobatidae: Storm-petrels
Family Pelecanoididae: Diving-petrels

**Order Pelecaniformes:**
Family Phaethontidae: Tropicbirds
Family Pelecanidae: Pelicans
Family Sulidae: Gannets, Boobies
Family Phalacrocoracidae: Cormorants
Family Anhingidae: Darters
Family Fregatidae: Frigatebirds

**Order Ciconiiformes**
Family Ardeidae: Herons, Bitterns
Family Balaenicipidae: Shoebill
Family Scopidae: Hammerkop
Family Ciconiidae: Storks
Family Threskiornithidae: Ibises and Spoonbills
Family Phoenicopteridae: Flamingos

**Order Anseriformes**
Family Anhimidae: Screamers
Family Anatidae: Ducks, Geese, Swans

**Order Falconiformes: Birds of Prey**
Family Cathartidae: New World Vultures
Family Pandionidae: Osprey
Family Sagittariidae: Secretary Bird
Family Accipitridae: Old World Vultures, Eagles, Hawks
Family Falconidae: Falcons

**Order Galliformes**
Family Megapodiidae: Megapodes
Family Cracidae: Curassows
Family Opisthocomidae: Hoatzin
Family Phasianidae:
　Subfamily Phasianinae: Pheasants
　Subfamily Tetraoninae: Grouse
　Subfamily Odontophorinae: American Quail
　Subfamily Meleagridinae: Turkeys
　Subfamily Numidinae: Guineafowl

**Order Gruiformes**
Family Mesitornithidae: Mesites
Family Turnicidae: Buttonquails
Family Pedionomidae: Plains-wanderer
Family Gruidae: Cranes
Family Aramidae: Limpkin
Family Psophiidae: Trumpeters
Family Rallidae: Rails
Family Heliornithidae: Finfoots
Family Rhynochetidae: Kagu
Family Eurypygidae: Sunbittern
Family Cariamidae: Seriemas
Family Otididae: Bustards

**Order Charadriiformes**
Family Jacanidae: Jacanas
Family Rostratulidae: Painted-snipes
Family Haematopodidae: Oystercatchers
Family Charadriidae: Plovers
Family Scolopacidae: Sandpipers
Family Recurvirostridae: Avocets
Family Ibidorhynchidae: Ibisbill
Family Dromadidae: Crab Plover
Family Burhinidae: Thick-knees
Family Glareolidae: Pratincoles
Family Thinocoridae: Seedsnipes
Family Chionididae: Sheathbills
Family Stercorariidae: Skuas
Family Laridae: Gulls, Terns
Family Rynchopidae: Skimmers
Family Alcidae: Auks

**Order Columbiformes**
Family Pteroclididae: Sandgrouse
Family Columbidae: Pigeons

**Order Psittaciformes: Parrots**
Family Loriidae: Lories
Family Cacatuidae: Cockatoos
Family Psittacidae: Parrots

**Order Cuculiformes**
Family Cuculidae: Cuckoos
Family Musophagidae: Turacos

**Order Strigiformes**
Family Tytonidae: Barn Owls
Family Strigidae: Owls

**Order Caprimulgiformes**
Family Steatornithidae: Oilbird
Family Podargidae: Frogmouths
Family Nyctibiidae: Potoos
Family Aegothelidae: Owlet-nightjars
Family Caprimulgidae: Nightjars

**Order Apodiformes**
Family Apodidae: Swifts
Family Hemiprocnidae: Crested Swifts
Family Trochilidae: Hummingbirds

**Order Coliiformes**
Family Coliidae: Mousebirds

**Order Trogoniformes**
Family Trogonidae: Trogons

**Order Coraciiformes**
Family Alcedinidae: Kingfishers
Family Todidae: Todies
Family Momotidae: Motmots
Family Meropidae: Bee-eaters
Family Coraciidae: Rollers
Family Brachypteraciidae: Ground Rollers
Family Leptosomatidae: Cuckoo-roller
Family Upupidae: Hoopoe
Family Phoeniculidae: Woodhoopoes
Family Bucerotidae: Hornbills

**Order Piciformes**
Family Galbulidae: Jacamars
Family Bucconidae: Puffbirds
Family Capitonidae: Barbets
Family Indicatoridae: Honey Guides
Family Ramphastidae: Toucans
Family Picidae: Woodpeckers

**Order Passeriformes: Perching Birds**
Sub-oscines: Primitive Passerines

Family Furnariidae: Ovenbirds
Family Formicariidae: Antbirds
Family Dendrocolaptidae: Woodcreepers
Family Conopophagidae: Gnateaters
Family Rhinocryptidae: Tapaculos
Family Pipridae: Manakins
Family Cotingidae: Cotingas
Family Oxyruncidae: Sharpbill
Family Phytotomidae: Plantcutters
Family Tyrannidae: Tyrant Flycatchers
Family Eurylaimidae: Broadbills
Family Pittidae: Pittas
Family Xenicidae: New Zealand Wrens
Family Philepittidae: Asities
Family Menuridae: Lyrebirds
Family Atrichornithidae: Scrub Birds

Oscines: Advanced Passerines

Family Alaudidae: Larks
Family Hirundinidae: Swallows, Martins
Family Motacillidae: Pipits
Family Campephagidae: Cuckoo-shrikes and Minivets
Family Pycnonotidae: Bulbuls
Family Irenidae: Leafbirds
Family Laniidae: Shrikes
Family Vangidae: Vangas
Family Bombycillidae: Waxwings
Family Dulidae: Palm Chat
Family Troglodytidae: Wrens
Family Cinclidae: Dippers
Family Mimidae: Mockingbirds
Family Prunellidae: Accentors
Family Muscicapidae:
  Subfamily Turdinae: Thrushes
  Subfamily Timaliinae: Babblers
  Subfamily Panurinae: Parrotbills
  Subfamily Picathartinae: Bare-headed Rockfowl
  Subfamily Orthonychinae: Quail Thrushes
  Subfamily Polioptilinae: Gnatcatchers
  Subfamily Sylviinae: Old World Warblers
  Subfamily Malurinae: Australian Warblers
  Subfamily Muscicapinae: Old World Flycatchers
  Subfamily Monarchinae: Monarch Flycatchers
  Subfamily Platysteirinae: African Monarch Flycatchers
  Subfamily Rhipidurinae: Fantail Flycatchers
  Subfamily Pachycephalinae: Whistlers
Family Aegithalidae: Long-tailed Titmice
Family Remizidae: Penduline Tits

Family Paridae: Titmice
Family Sittidae: Nuthatches
Family Certhiidae: Treecreepers
Family Rhabdornithidae: Philippine Creepers
Family Climacteridae: Australian Treecreepers
Family Dicaeidae: Flowerpeckers
Family Zosteropidae: White-eyes
Family Nectariniidae: Sunbirds
Family Meliphagidae: Honey Eaters
Family Emberizidae:
  Subfamily Emberizinae: Buntings
  Subfamily Catamblyrhynchinae: Plush-capped Finch
  Subfamily Cardinalinae: Cardinals and Grosbeaks
  Subfamily Tersininae: Swallow-tanager
  Subfamily Thraupinae: Tanagers
Family Parulidae: American Wood Warblers
Family Drepanididae: Hawaiian Honeycreepers
Family Vireonidae: Vireos
Family Icteridae: Icterids
Family Fringillidae: Finches
Family Estrildidae: Waxbills
Family Ploceidae: Weavers
Family Sturnidae: Starlings
Family Oriolidae: Orioles
Family Dicruridae: Drongos
Family Callaeidae: Wattlebirds
Family Grallinidae: Mudnest Builders
Family Artamidae: Wood Swallows
Family Cracticidae: Butcherbirds
Family Ptilonorhynchidae: Bowerbirds
Family Paradisaeidae: Birds of Paradise
Family Corvidae: Crows

221

# Acknowledgments

The Publishers received invaluable help during the preparation of the *Macmillan Illustrated Encyclopedia of Birds* from: Heather Angel, who lent us reference slides; Angus Bellairs, who gave advice; Dr H. G. Cogger, who lent us reference slides; Rosanne Hooper and Zilda Tandy, who assisted with research; the staff of the Ornithology Department of the British Museum (Natural History) outstation at Tring, particularly Pete Colston, who gave assistance with the specimen collection; the staff of the Science Reference Library, London; the IUCN Conservation Monitoring Centre, Cambridge, England, for data on threatened species.